SAGE was founded in 1965 by Sara Miller McCune to support the dissemination of usable knowledge by publishing innovative and high-quality research and teaching content. Today, we publish over 900 journals, including those of more than 400 learned societies, more than 800 new books per year, and a growing range of library products including archives, data, case studies, reports, and video. SAGE remains majority-owned by our founder, and after Sara's lifetime will become owned by a charitable trust that secures our continued independence.

Los Angeles | London | New Delhi | Singapore | Washington DC | Melbourne

Thank you for choosing a SAGE product!
If you have any comment, observation or feedback,
I would like to personally hear from you.
Please write to me at **contactceo@sagepub.in**

Vivek Mehra, Managing Director and CEO,
SAGE Publications India Pvt Ltd, New Delhi

Bulk Sales

SAGE India offers special discounts
for bulk institutional purchases.

For queries/orders/inspection copy requests
write to **textbooksales@sagepub.in**

Publishing

Would you like to publish a textbook with SAGE?
Please send your proposal to **publishtextbook@sagepub.in**

Get to know more about SAGE

Be invited to SAGE events, get on our mailing list.
Write today to **marketing@sagepub.in**

This book is also available as an e-book.

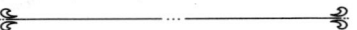

UNDERSTANDING WOMEN'S LAND RIGHTS

Land Reforms in India: Volume 13

LAND REFORMS IN INDIA

This is the thirteenth volume in a series of studies conducted under the aegis of the Lal Bahadur Shastri National Academy of Administration (LBSNAA), Mussoorie. These studies are an outcome of a research programme entrusted to the LBSNAA by the Ministry of Rural Development, Government of India. The primary aim of this series is to assess the current status of land reforms in India.

The collection of basic data was entrusted to successive batches of probationers of the Indian Administrative Service (IAS). The field of study component was divided into four major sections covering respectively the implementation of land ceiling laws, the status of tenant cultivators, the progress in allotment of government lands to the poor and landless and the position concerning tribal lands and forest rights and gender land rights. In the process the probationers collected village-level primary data by interviewing landowners, tenants, allottees of surplus lands and tribals, and supplemented the data by consulting land records and other official documents.

This material was processed by the LBSNAA's project core group of land reforms comprising scholars from diverse disciplines. The findings were analysed, refined and integrated into comprehensive all-India and state-level reports which form the bulk of the volumes in the series. In addition, the LBSNAA conducted state-level workshops bringing together administrators, academics, activists and legal experts to explore the various dimensions of land reforms in India.

The series will comprise about 14 volumes in all.

Board of Editors

General Editor
B.N. Yugandhar
Former Member, Planning Commission, Government of India

Editor's Introduction by
Prem Chowdhry

Members

Upma Chawdhry
Director
LBSNAA

Hukum Singh Meena
Joint Secretary
Department of Land Resources
Ministry of Rural Development
Govt. of India

Dr. Prem Singh
NITI AAYOG
(National Institution for Transforming India)
Delhi

C. Sridhar
Deputy Director (Senior) and
Centre Director
CRS, LBSNAA

Aswathy S.
Deputy Director and
Centre Director
National Gender Centre
LBSNAA

UNDERSTANDING WOMEN'S LAND RIGHTS

Gender Discrimination in Ownership

Land Reforms in India: Volume 13

Edited by

PREM CHOWDHRY

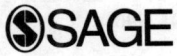

Los Angeles | London | New Delhi
Singapore | Washington DC | Melbourne

Copyright © Lal Bahadur Shastri National Academy of Administration, Mussoorie, 2017

All rights reserved. No part of this book may be reproduced or utilized in any form or by any means, electronic or mechanical, including photocopying, recording, or by any information storage or retrieval system, without permission in writing from the publisher.

First published in 2017 by

SAGE Publications India Pvt Ltd
B1/I-1 Mohan Cooperative Industrial Area
Mathura Road, New Delhi 110 044, India
www.sagepub.in

SAGE Publications Inc
2455 Teller Road
Thousand Oaks, California 91320, USA

SAGE Publications Ltd
1 Oliver's Yard, 55 City Road
London EC1Y 1SP, United Kingdom

SAGE Publications Asia-Pacific Pte Ltd
3 Church Street
#10-04 Samsung Hub
Singapore 049483

Published by Vivek Mehra for SAGE Publications India Pvt Ltd, typeset in 10/12 pt Times New Roman by Zaza Eunice, Hosur, Tamil Nadu, India and printed at Chaman Enterprises, New Delhi.

Library of Congress Cataloging-in-Publication Data

Name: Chowdhry, Prem, editor.
Title: Understanding women's land rights : gender discrimination in ownership/ [edited by] Prem Chowdhry.
Other titles: [Land reforms in India ; v. 13].
Description: Thousand Oaks, California : SAGE Publications Inc, 2017. |
  Series: [Land reforms in India ; v. 13] | Includes bibliographical references and index.
Identifiers: LCCN 2017012990| ISBN 9789386446312 (print hb) | ISBN 9789386446336 (e-pub) | ISBN 9789386446329 (e-book)
Subjects: LCSH: Land tenure—India. | Women landowners—India. | Sex discrimination against women—India. | Land tenure—Law and legislation—India.
Classification: LCC HD873 .U53 2017 | DDC 333.3/154082—dc23 LC record available at https://lccn.loc.gov/2017012990

ISBN: 978-93-864-4631-2 (HB)

SAGE Team: Rajesh Dey, Alekha Chandra Jena, Megha Dabral, and Ritu Chopra
Cover Image: From a painting by Prem Chowdhry

Contents

List of Tables	vii
List of Figures	xi
Foreword by Upma Chawdhry	xiii
A Note from the Centre Director by C. Sridhar	xv
Acknowledgements by Saroj Arora	xix

1. **Editor's Introduction**
   Persisting Gender Discrimination in Land Rights   1
   Prem Chowdhry

2. **Andhra Pradesh**
   Land Rights and Land Access to Women in
   Andhra Pradesh   25
   E. Revathi

3. **Arunachal Pradesh**
   Engendering Tribal Land Rights for Gendering the Land:
   A Case Study Among Apatani and Nyishi Communities   59
   Rimi Tadu

4. **Chhattisgarh**
   Gender Issues in Landownership in Chhattisgarh:
   Existing Land Laws, Policies, and Practices   88
   Ramesh Sharma

5. **Goa**
   Women and Land Rights in the Context of Legal Propertied
   Equality in Goa   106
   Ritu Dewan

6. **Gujarat**
   Women Empowerment Through Landownership Rights:
   Critical Assessment of Their Status in Gujarat   133
   Itishree Pattnaik

7. **Jammu and Kashmir**
   Gendering the Landownership Question in Jammu
   and Kashmir   154
   Abha Chauhan

8. **Jharkhand**
   Understanding Women and Land Rights in Jharkhand   182
   M. N. Karna

9. **Maharashtra**
   Land, Land Rights, and Women in Maharashtra   209
   Ritu Dewan

10. **Mizoram**
    Women's Access and Ownership of Land: A Case of
    Mizoram State in India   234
    Saroj Arora

11. **Nagaland**
    Gender and Land Relations in Nagaland: Emerging Issues   260
    C. Sridhar, Saroj Arora, and Khunenchu Magh

12. **Rajasthan**
    Persisting Inequalities: Gender and Land Rights
    in Rajasthan   296
    Kanchan Mathur

13. **Sikkim**
    Locating Gender in Land Rights Discourse of Sikkim   325
    Sohel Firdos

14. **Tamil Nadu**
    Women's Land Rights in the Context of Neo-liberal
    Tamil Nadu   344
    Ranjani K. Murthy

15. **Uttarakhand**
    Gender Justice and Law: A Gender-specific Study of
    Landownership in Uttarakhand   376
    Indu Pathak

About the Editor and Contributors   403
Index   405

List of Tables

2.1	Determinants of Women Accessing Land Under Different Situations	35
2.2	Determinants of Women's Access to Land from Natal Family Under Different Situations	37
2.3	Major Land Issues Identified and Resolved Under LAP	44
2.4	Number of Women Leased Land Under PoP Strategy in CMSA (2005–08)	46
3.1	Sex Ratio in Arunachal Pradesh	72
4.1	Field Area and Respondents	93
4.2	Operational Landholdings Status in Chhattisgarh	95
4.3	Operational Landholdings Amongst the STs in Chhattisgarh	96
4.4	Operational Landholdings Amongst the SCs in Chhattisgarh	96
5.1	Gendered Rural Labour Force Participation Rate for 2011–12	110
5.2	Gendered Rural Worker Population Ratio for 2012–13	110
5.3	Gendered Rural Workforce Participation Rate for 2011	110
5.4	Gendered Operational Holdings (Goa and India for 2000–01 and 2010–11; Actual and %)	111
5.5	Gendered Landholding Pattern for 2000–01 and 2010–11 (Actual Numbers and %)	113
5.6	Gendered Land Area Pattern for 2000–01 and 2010–11 (Actual Area and %)	114
6.1	Gender-wise Participation in Agriculture in Gujarat	137
6.2	Share of Women Landholding in Gujarat	138

6.3 Operational Holding by Women by Caste in Gujarat
for 2010–11 139

8.1 Socio-economic Profile of Kharia Respondents 199
8.2 Patterns of Landownership Among the Kharia
Respondents ($N = 100$) 199
8.3 Familiarity with Inheritance and Succession
Rules and Practices Followed in Land Distribution
and Transfer ($N = 100$) 200
8.4 Opinion and Assessment with Regard to Land Rights
to Women ($N = 100$) 200
8.5 Socio-economic Profile of Munda Respondents ($N = 100$) 202
8.6 Patterns of Landownership Among the Selected Munda
Respondents ($N = 100$) 202
8.7 Familiarity with Inheritance and Succession Rules
and Practices Followed at the Time of Land Transfer and
Distribution ($N = 100$) 202
8.8 Opinion and Belief with Regard to Land Rights to
Women (Whether Land Should Be Registered in
the Name of Women; $N = 100$) 203
8.9 Socio-economic Profile of Santhal Respondents
($N = 100$) 203
8.10 Patterns of Landownership in Residential Plots
and Agricultural Land ($N = 100$) 204
8.11 Nature of Land Registration ($N = 100$) 204
8.12 Familiarity with Land Inheritance and Succession
Laws and Practices ($N = 100$) 205
8.13 Opinion with Regard to Land Rights to Women 205

9.1 Gendered Landholdings Pattern for 2000–01 and
2010–11 (in Actual Numbers) 214
9.2 Gendered District-level Landholding Pattern for
2000–01 and 2010–11 (Numbers and %) 216
9.3 Maharashtra Gendered District-level Land Area
Pattern for 2000–01 and 2010–11 (in Hectares and %) 217

10.1 Number of Men Women Owning Land in Their
Names (1976–2010) 244

13.1 Demographic Characteristics of Sikkim for 2011 326

13.2	Distribution of ST Population and Individual Tribes for 2011	327
13.3	District-wise Beneficiaries Allotted Agricultural Land *Patta* in Sikkim (Since Inception till Date; Area in Ha)	340
15.1	Demographic Profile of Uttarakhand for 2011	381
15.2	Gender-wise Distribution of Number of Operational Landholdings in Different Categories in Uttarakhand for 2010–11	390
15.3	Division- and Gender-wise Distribution of Number of Operational Landholdings in Different Categories in Uttarakhand for 2010–11	390
15.4	Hill and Plain Areas and Gender-wise Distribution of Number of Operational Landholdings in Different Categories in Uttarakhand for 2010–11	391
15.5	Year-wise Status of IAY and Deendayal Uttarakhand Awas Yojana from Financial Year 2001–02 to 2014–15	392
15.6	Total Cases Pursued by Women for Their Land Rights	395
15.7	Details of Land Deeds Done in Favour of Women in Uttarakhand	397

Annexure Tables

A2.1	Percentage of Households Having Land and Women Having Land from Family in Selected Sample Sites	50
A2.2	Characteristics of Women-accessed Land from Family in All Situations	50
A2.3	Characteristics of Women-accessed Land from Natal Family in All Situations	51
A12.1	Panchayati Raj Department Information for Land *Pattas* for the Year 2007–08 to 2014–15 (Progress and Achievement Against Targets)	319
A12.2	Allotee Type-wise Number of Houses Sanctioned Under IAY for Financial Years 2011–15	321

List of Figures

5.1	Size-class of Total Holdings (Goa) for 2000–01 and 2010–11	112
5.2	Gendered Landholding Pattern for 2000–01 and 2010–11	114
5.3	Gendered Land Area Pattern for 2000–01 and 2010–11	115
8.1	Classification of the Tribal Communities in Jharkhand	185
8.2	Area of the Study	198
9.1	Gendered Number of Holdings (Maharashtra and India) for 2000–01 and 2010–11	214
9.2	Gendered Pattern of Area of Landholdings for 2000–01 and 2010–11	215

Foreword

This volume, titled *Understanding Women's Land Rights: Gender Discrimination in Ownership*, raises issues of gender and land at a juncture when the New Economic Policy is in force and vast agricultural lands are getting diverted to development projects making land market volatile.

The changes in land policy have a direct bearing on women's position and ability to take advantage of the existing land laws. The volume focuses on the changes taking place in the area of land and gender issues in relation to the fast-changing agrarian society, and recommends ways to counter the existing gender inequality.

The volume contains 14 essays. The essays make special efforts to evaluate critically the existing state laws/legislation, statutes, and customary laws with regard to women's land rights after taking into consideration the diverse viewpoints regarding the status of landownership and rights of women in their respective communities/states. The volume is a pioneering work as it combines both the fieldwork and existing literature on the land rights of women written so far. This is a broad-based issue; hence, it transcends disciplinary boundaries and can be found useful for a variety of readers. It also lays down the future course of corrective action.

One of the important activities of the Centre for Rural Studies is to conduct research studies on various aspects of land reforms, land administration, and rural development programmes. I am thankful to the Ministry of Rural Development, Department of Land Resources, Government of India, for providing financial support to conduct this research study. It will be an important contribution in the area of women's struggle for gender equality particularly in land rights.

I am thankful to Professor Prem Chowdhry, editor of this volume, for writing an editorial introduction for the volume. Contributors of the papers are well-known social scientists; I acknowledge their contribution. I appreciate the initiative of Mr C. Sridhar, IAS, Centre Director; Dr Saroj Arora, Senior Research Officer, and the staff of the Centre for Rural Studies of LBSNAA in bringing out the volume. Special thanks are also due to SAGE Publications for bringing out the volume under the *Land Reforms in India* series.

Upma Chawdhry, IAS
Director and Chairperson
Centre for Rural Studies
Lal Bahadur Shastri
National Academy of Administration
Mussoorie, Uttarakhand

A Note from the Centre Director

India is an agrarian society where 69% of its population lives in rural areas. Agriculture is the main source of livelihood for a large number of rural populations including women. Women contribute significantly to agricultural production, yet they do not enjoy significant landownership rights. Women's lack of ownership of productive resources such as land weakens their bargaining capacity within the household as well as in the public sphere. This further excludes them from sociopolitical and legal institutions and they continue to be discriminated against. Studies have shown that the land and inheritance laws in most of the states in India are biased. Similar situation may be seen in northeastern states where customary laws are in practice. There is a need to revisit the land laws in order to remove the existing anomalies.

For women's empowerment and emancipation, feminist movements have been gathering strength in various parts of the world in the 20th century. Most of these countries have signed the Convention on the Elimination of All Forms of Discrimination Against Women (CEDAW)—an international treaty adopted in 1979 by the United Nations General Assembly—and expressed their concern and commitment for establishing gender parity. To ameliorate the condition of women, India has also taken several measures and launched various programmes. During the Ninth Five-year Plan, women and their land rights emerged as an important agenda. To ensure accessibility and grant ownership of land rights to women, the Government of India, Department of Land Resources, during the Ninth Five-year Plan (1997–2002) issued instructions to all the states that 40% of agricultural land settled under land reform programme should be exclusively in the name of women. In the remaining cases, the allotment may be jointly in the name of husband and wife. This programme has benefitted a large number of women. During the Tenth Five-year Plan (2002–07), various states introduced a scheme of providing concession in registration and stamp duty to women property buyers. This scheme has benefitted millions of women across the states. Delhi was one of the pioneering states which implemented the scheme in 2002. Later on, Andhra Pradesh, Assam, Gujarat, Haryana, Madhya Pradesh, Rajasthan, Union territory of Puducherry, Punjab, Uttar Pradesh, and Uttarakhand also introduced this scheme. Further, the Hindu Succession Act was amended in 2005. To make women self-reliant, Andhra Pradesh Government launched a scheme in 2009 to lease land to women members of self-help groups.

The present study titled *Understanding Women's Land Rights: Gender Discrimination in Ownership* has been conducted on behalf of the Department of Land Resources, Ministry of Rural Development, Government of India. The objectives of the study were to review different statutes, laws and customary laws relating to land from a gender perspective, and to assess the extent, conditions and forms of landownership, the nature of law (customary/formal) operational in relation to landownership of women, and the historical background of land systems. The present volume brought out under the *Land Reforms in India* series contains 14 articles covering 14 states of the country. These states are Andhra Pradesh, Goa, Gujarat, Jammu and Kashmir, Maharashtra, Rajasthan, Tamil Nadu, Uttarakhand, and the tribal-dominated states such as Arunachal Pradesh, Chhattisgarh, Jharkhand, Mizoram, Nagaland, and Sikkim. Three states, namely Chhattisgarh, Jharkhand, and Uttarakhand which came into existence in 2000 have been studied extensively. It would be pertinent to mention that the Centre for Rural Studies, Lal Bahadur Shastri National Academy of Administration, Mussoorie, had conducted a similar study in 13 states, namely Assam, Bihar, Haryana, Himachal Pradesh, Karnataka, Kerala, Madhya Pradesh, Meghalaya, Manipur, Orissa, Punjab, Uttar Pradesh, West Bengal, and a union territory of Puducherry; this study was published by SAGE in 2009 under its *Land Reforms in India* series.

Our attempt has been to lay down the groundwork which may be built upon by future research. I hope this volume will be found as useful as the earlier one by different sections of society including policy makers, planners, administrators, academicians, social scientists, women's organizations, students of gender studies, non-government organizations, and researchers, and will pave the way for millions of women who are denied land rights.

C. Sridhar, IAS
Deputy Director (Senior) and
Centre Director
Centre for Rural Studies
Lal Bahadur Shastri National Academy
of Administration
Mussoorie, Uttarakhand

Acknowledgements

This study would not have been possible without the kind support and collective contribution of various individuals and organizations. I am grateful to Mr Padamvir Singh, IAS, former Director, Lal Bahadur Shastri National Academy of Administration (LBSNAA), Mussoorie, for the administrative support. I owe my sense of gratitude to Mr C. Sridhar, IAS, Deputy Director (Senior), LBSNAA, and Centre Director, Centre for Rural Studies, for his cooperation, guidance, and motivation to complete the project.

I am extremely thankful to Dr. Prem Chowdhry for writing an editorial introduction for this volume. Renowned academicians from multidisciplinary backgrounds were invited to write on the issue of gender and land rights. I feel indebted to each one of them for their contributions. I am thankful to Professor Lalneihzovi, Head, Department of Public Administration, Central University, Aizawl, for sharing her experiences on women's movements in the northeastern states including Mizoram to establish a gender-just society. Extensive work done by Dr Toshimenla Jamir, Dr Lanusashi Longkumer, and Dr Rosemary Dzuvichu has helped in building a framework on gender and land relations in Nagaland.

I am grateful to district magistrates/commissioners and revenue officials of the states for their support and for providing data without which contributors of this volume could not have completed their articles. I am grateful to each of them for their immense cooperation. I express my heartfelt thanks to Mr P. Singthanga, Mizoram Judicial Service (MJS), former Secretary, Department of Law and Judicial, Government of Mizoram (GoM), for his cooperation. His colleagues Mr Zahmingthanga Ralte, Joint Secretary, Mr H. Lalthlangliana, the then Deputy Secretary, Mr Vincent Lalrokima, Deputy Secretary, and

xx • UNDERSTANDING WOMEN'S LAND RIGHTS

Ms R. Lalmuankimi, Under Secretary, all from MJS, and Ms Annette Lalrinsangi, Law Officer, GoM, have explained the significance of customary laws in tribal society and how these laws influence gender and land relations. I am also thankful to Mr R. Lalhmangaiha, Mizoram Civil Service (MCS), Director, and Mr Dawngkima, Joint Director (Survey), Directorate of Land Revenue and Settlement (DLR&S), GoM, for providing data and making logistic arrangements. I am also thankful to Mr Biaklawma, MCS, former Director, Local Administration Department, GoM, Mr Lawrence Lalrammawia, Revenue Department, and Mr Joseph Darrothanga, Urban Development and Poverty Alleviation Department, Aizawl, who gave their valuable feedback on the initial draft. Special thanks to Mr Zuala, Senior Surveyor, District Revenue Office, Aizawl, for acting as an interpreter during field visit and Mr Malsawmdawngliana, computer operator, DLR&S for filtering gender-wise data on landownership.

I am indebted to Mr L. T. Konyak, IAS, Secretary (retd.), Mr K. Nzimongo Ngullie, IAS, Commissioner and Secretary to the Government of Nagaland (retd.), who have shared their valuable experiences on gender, land, and customary laws practised among various tribal communities in Nagaland. I am also grateful to Mr Wezopo Kenye, Dimapur, Mrs Angau I Thou, Mon, Mr W. Honje Konyak, Kohima (all from Nagaland Civil Services and Former Deputy Commissioners (DCs) of the respective districts), and the officials of the Directorate of Land Records and Survey, Dimapur, namely, Mr E. N. Kithan, Director, Mr Vilarietuo Kire, Additional Director, Mr Neilhoutru Teruno, Joint Director, Mr L. Khuming, Deputy Director (Sr.), and Mr Khunenchu Magh, Deputy Director, sparing their valuable time to discuss the land management system in the state. I am also thankful to Ms Lithrongla Tongpi, NCS, Additional DC, Kohima, and Mr Longasen Lotha, Extra Assistant Commissioner, Dimapur, for making logistic arrangements. Mr Mohammed Ali Shihab, IAS, former SDO (Civil), Kohima, and presently ADC, Mon district, Mr Zibenthung Kithan, Revenue Officer, Mr Zhaphizo, LRSO, and Mr Sedu Zulza, Kohima, actively participated in Focus Group Discussion (FGD). Mr Pakon Phom, SDO (Civil), and Mr Hamdok M. Konyak, Block Development Officer, both from Phomching, Mon District, organized a meeting with the village council members of Longwa village, located at the international border of Mynmar and India, and the *Ang*—traditional village chief of Konyak tribes in Mon district. Discussions with Mr Wato Konyak, *Dubhashi*,

Dimapur, helped in understanding the role of *Dubhashi* in land administration in Nagaland. I truly feel indebted to each one of them for their contribution.

Mr Shivam Verma and Mr Sachin Jaiswal, both the then IAS officer trainees (OTs), professional course, 2013 batch, attached with Mon and Kohima districts for their respective district training programme, have shared their experiences on land system, customary laws, and gender. Dr Naveen Aggarwal and Dr Ankita Chakravorthy Aggarwal, the then IAS OTs of professional course, 2013 batch, AGMUT cadre, and attached with Aizawal district, and Ms Grace Lalrindiki Pachuau, the then IAS OT of professional course, 2013 batch, remained instrumental in one way or the other. I am grateful to these young Indian Administrative Officers for their cooperation and enthusiasm.

No words would be enough to acknowledge the contribution of the members of the civil society, village council (VC), HoHo groups, and village authorities such as *Gaon Buras*. They have shared rich experiences and also expressed their concern towards the development model. During FGD, they participated actively and patiently, and gave meaningful suggestions. Though it is not possible to mention all, it is important, however, to mention some of them: Mrs Tokheli Kikon and Mr Longhukun, Chairpersons of their respective VCs, Mrs Vekhosayi Nyekha, President, Western Chakhesang Hoho, Mr Weios Butsa, Chairman, Mr Dietho Rhakho, Treasurer, Naga Council, Dimapur, and Mr T. L. Angami, former *Gaon Bura*. Mr Zeihlem and Mr Hosea Konyak General Secretaries, Konyak Union, Mr Chingden Konyak, Vice President, Konyak Union, Naga Council, and Mr Nyuputlt Sheko Khong, Mon district, have actively participated in FGDs and shared their knowledge about the functions of their respective organizations and women's relationship with land in their respective tribal communities. I am also thankful to the villagers and the VC members of Lungleng village, Aizawl district, for their cooperation and active participation in FGD. I acknowledge their contribution in the knowledge-building exercise.

Last but not least, I would like to express thanks to my colleagues in CRS and the Academy. Had it not been for the active cooperation of the employees of the Centre for Rural Studies, LBSNAA, Mussoorie, the work would not have completed. I sincerely acknowledge the contribution of Mr Adesh Kumar who worked relentlessly till the completion of the project. Mr Alok Pandey and Mr Virendra Virodia from the computer section have helped in handling computer-related issues. The staff of the Gandhi Smriti Library has extended all possible support. I am thankful to each one of them.

Saroj Arora
Senior Research Officer
Centre for Rural Studies
Lal Bahadur Shastri
National Academy of Administration
Mussoorie, Uttarakhand

1

Editor's Introduction: Persisting Gender Discrimination in Land Rights

PREM CHOWDHRY

There has been and continues to be a great deal of governmental and non-governmental emphasis on 'empowering women'. What does empowerment of women entail? At a very rudimentary level, it means gaining control over sources of power like material assets and self-assertion, and ability to take part in the making of decisions that affect their lives. For this, women must have equal opportunities, equal capabilities, and equal access to resources. Such a manifestation would ultimately mean a redistribution of existing power relations and finally a challenge to the patriarchal ideology and male dominance, as the concept of women empowerment is associated with gender equality. Many sociologists and political thinkers have written and will continue to write on women's empowerment and reach the same conclusion as stated above.

But what do the women want themselves? This question has to be thought through with the concerned categories of women and in this case that of rural women. What is it that the rural women may find empowering in their negotiation with their daily devalued and powerless life? What I am going to state here is gathered from my extensive fieldwork conducted in 2011 in various regions of rural Haryana, involving several rounds of interviews with women of varying ages, social class, caste, and professions, and also focus group discussions held in different villages with women.[1] On the basis of these interactions, three areas emerged important which in the opinion of women themselves were crucial and needed to be strengthened for their empowerment. Among the options emphasized by women, land/property scored highest in their vision of empowering themselves. This was followed by education and employment. Possessing means of production entails possessing not only a source of income but also a source of authority/power/status and mobility—leading to having access to other facilities like education and health. Having a right to land or other productive assets gives women a sort of bargaining power[2] that they would not normally have, and in turn they gain the ability to assert themselves in various aspects of their lives, both in and outside of the home. The case studies that I undertook also show that the first thing that women do after acquiring some money (by inheritance or through earning, etc.) is to acquire some productive resources as means of generating income.

It is not as if women in India do not have the legal right to inherit land and other property. They have had this right for more than 66 years, since the adoption of the Indian Constitution on 26 January 1950. Since its inception, the government of India is obliged to confer equal rights and opportunities on men and women in the political, economic, and social spheres and to prohibit discrimination against any citizen on the ground of sex, religion, ethnicity, caste, etc. In other words, the government is committed to safeguard the rights and privileges of women as per its constitution. At the international level, India is a signatory to the Convention on the Elimination of All Forms of Discrimination against Women (CEDAW) adopted in 1979 by the United Nations. With this it reasserted its commitment to remove discrimination against women in all forms, including the legal sphere, by suitably modifying gender-biased laws. Guided by these constitutional principles and directives as well as international commitment, the government has been periodically involved in attempting to enforce them. For example, a National Perspective Plan for Women (1988–2000) was drafted with the aim of providing equity and social justice for women. The Ninth Five-year Plan (1997–2002) similarly included a section on removal of gender discrimination in accessibility and ownership of resources such as land by advocating a need to change land-related laws, and emphasized the need for landownership by women. It also pointed out the gender inequalities inherent in land inheritance laws as well as ceiling laws, and suggested corrective measures.

Despite all this recognition, good intentions, and willingness of the government, women continue to encounter tremendous barriers to arrogate what should be rightfully theirs. It is undeniable that there is a difference between the legal recognition of a claim and its social recognition and between recognition and enforcement. There is also a distinction between ownership and effective control. For women's empowerment, it is essential to enhance their ability to claim and retain control over their rightful inheritance shares.

I

This is the second volume for understanding land rights of women covering 14 out of a total of 29 states. In alphabetical order those included in the present volume are Andhra Pradesh, Arunachal Pradesh, Chhattisgarh, Goa, Gujarat, Jammu and Kashmir, Jharkhand, Maharashtra, Mizoram, Nagaland, Rajasthan, Sikkim, Tamil Nadu, and Uttarakhand. The 11th volume titled *Gender Discrimination in Land Ownership* with a similar thrust was published in 2009 (Chowdhry 2009). It had covered 13 states and a union territory, namely Assam, Bihar, Haryana, Himachal Pradesh, Karnataka, Kerala, Madhya Pradesh, Manipur, Meghalaya, Orissa, Punjab, Uttar Pradesh, West Bengal, and Puducherry (union territory). Except for the recently created state of Telangana (2014) and the state of Tripura (1972) as well as the six union territories out of a total of seven (namely, Andaman and Nicobar Islands,[3] Chandigarh,[4] Dadra and Nagar Haveli,[5] Daman and Diu,[6] Lakshadweep,[7] and Delhi—the national capital territory[8]), the whole of India has been covered by these two volumes. These volumes together offer an in-depth analysis of the existing ground situation in order to explain why the post-independent law makers, political leaders, judiciary, and the administrators fell short of fulfilling the high intentions of the constitution makers. Why is it that the gender-based discrimination in the accessibility and ownership of productive resources including land considered to be embedded in the social, legal, economic, and political structures has continued to prevail, thereby defeating all stated intentions and moves made towards acquiring the proclaimed goal of gender equality in different states of India? Why is it that in practice, few women own land and even fewer effectively control it?

With a view to understanding this problem the authors in this volume, like that of the previous one, have analysed the situation prevailing on the ground by undertaking rigorous studies of their chosen states, and recommended certain crucial steps so that matters may be rectified. They have reviewed and examined different statutes, laws/legislations, and customary practices relating to landownership by women, and assessed the extent of women's ownership of land resources in rural areas, based upon the conditions and forms of landownership existing for women in a particular state. The diverse social/cultural/ethnic groups and the nature of law, whether customary or codified, have been studied to determine how far these factors determine the outcome for women in relation to exercising their land rights.

What emerges clear from such a study is that in view of land being a state subject, the response to land rights of women is multifaceted and varied given the heterogeneity of India, its different geographical terrains, multiple religions, ethnicity, and enormously varied cultural and customary patterns existing within a state. In fact, the different state laws have worked towards negating the effects of the constitutional makers and early legislative measures brought by the parliament. This response emanated out of the fact that in post-independent India, agriculture- and land-related legislation were put under the state list, while laws relating to property and succession were put on the concurrent list. As this aspect has been very comprehensively dealt with in the previous volume (ibid.), I shall very briefly recapture here the main arguments only. With the states empowered to enact laws which they deem necessary for their respective regions, such a categorization has had the effect of promoting rather than negating gender-discriminatory land practices. All states have taken important measures in relation to agricultural labour, tenants and other farmers, land ceilings, allocation of surplus lands, distribution of *pattas* (official documents stating land title and the terms on which land is held), and other land reforms but, as the essays in this collection reveal, none have accommodated women as such. On the other hand, the concurrent list which includes laws passed by the parliament cannot be touched upon by the state legislatures; any modifications suggested by the states need assent of the President of India. Consequently, the first and the most far-reaching gender-equitable law that the states have not been able to abolish or alter is the Hindu Succession Act passed by the parliament in 1956. Repeated attempts at amendment of this Act, made by certain state governments, have been effectively blocked by the centre.

The 1956 Act related to the 'Hindus'—a term which included in its scope Sikhs, Jains, and Buddhists. This still left vast numbers of religious communities such as the Muslims, Christians, Parsis, and Jews, comprising about 24% of the total population of India, out of its ambit. These remained governed by their personal laws and local customs which are still, in large parts of India, uncodified. Today, inheritance for Hindus is governed by the Hindu Succession Act of 1956 and inheritance for the Muslims is governed by the Muslim Personal Law (Shariat) Application Act of 1937, which accommodated the daughter by giving her half the share of the son. However, there is a considerable gap between scriptural dictates and actual practice. Many Muslim communities follow customs similar to those prevalent among Hindus in their region of residence, which means an exclusion of a daughter from inheritance of landed property, except among the Mappilas of Kerala where customary practice means matrilineal inheritance. The Parsis, on the other hand, are governed by the Indian Succession Act of 1925. Amended specifically for Parsis in 1991, this Act gives them greater gender parity in inheritance; Christians (other than Christians in Punjab, Himachal, and those falling under uncodified laws in the northeastern states) are likewise governed by the relevant provisions of the 1925 Act, which treats a son and daughter's share equally, but has no restriction on testation.

A progressive Act, the Hindu Succession Act of 1956, introduced for the first time the notion of a woman, as a daughter (obliterating any distinction between married and unmarried daughters), sister, widow, and mother, as an equal and absolute owner of property, with full rights to its disposal. Earlier, women could inherit as widows (and very rarely as daughters), and that too only in the absence of four generations of agnatic males. Also, this inheritance was limited. She could enjoy property only during her lifetime, and after her it reverted to her husband's heirs. She could not alienate property except in highly restricted circumstances of legal necessity, benefit of the estate, for religious or charitable purposes, and finally with the consent of the reversioners.

There were, however, certain significant pockets of matrilineal and bilateral inheritance in southwestern India (especially Kerala and also in pockets of Karnataka, and Northeast India, e.g., in Meghalaya, where women's property rights were not the exception but the rule). Such communities received special considerations under the Hindu Succession Act, just as the tribal communities of Arunachal Pradesh, Mizoram, and Nagaland (also Meghalaya), which were also not covered by this Act. The essays on the northeastern states in this collection indicate how this region continues to be ruled by local customs which remain uncodified in large part and are given to differing interpretations that discriminate blatantly against women.

Although the 1956 Act was a substantial move forward, it still fell woefully short of introducing equal inheritance rights for women, and significant inequalities remained. One of its major limitations, apart from other shortcomings, lay in the non-inclusion of females as coparceners in joint Hindu family property. They enjoyed only maintenance rights as wives, widows, or unmarried daughters. The male, however, becomes a coparcener at birth. The other glaring shortcoming in the Act was in relation to tenurial laws. In the woman's right to inherit agricultural land, exception was granted to 'tenancy' land. The devolution of such land was subject to the state-level tenurial laws which differ from state to state and are governed by customs. Similarly, the 1937 Shariat Act which governs inheritance for the Muslims left out agricultural land, owned or tenanted, from its purview. Subsequently, some of the southern states extended the provisions of the 1937 Shariat Act to also cover agricultural land. For instance, legislation in 1949 covered Tamil Nadu and parts of Andhra Pradesh (as also parts of Karnataka, with Kerala following suit in 1963). In all other regions, the treatment of agricultural land for Muslims depends variously on customs, tenurial laws, or other pre-existing laws. The 1956 Act also gave unrestricted testamentary right to Hindu males in their separate and self-acquired property, as well as in their share of the joint family property, which can and has been used to deprive females of their rights.

It has taken India nearly 50 years to rid the Hindu Succession Act of some of its major gender anomalies. An amended Act was passed on 29 August 2005 in the parliament, removing some of the most glaring inequalities faced by women on several fronts. Briefly speaking, the Act granted women equal rights as men in all property, including agricultural land (also land under tenancy), owned or tenanted, ancestral or self-acquired. This amendment abolished the highly gender-unequal inheritance of land, which was earlier subject to state-level tenurial laws. It further made daughters, married or unmarried, equal to sons in joint Hindu family property, with right to claim partition and, by presumption, to become *karta* (manager) while also sharing the liabilities. Making daughters, especially married daughters, coparceners in joint family property had already been effected in some of the southern states. This amendment reiterated the understanding that women are co-sharers in inheritance as a matter of their right; they are not left to the good will of men of the family. Having a birthright in joint family property also means that it cannot be willed away by male members.

The amendment also gave daughters, both married and unmarried, the same rights as sons to reside in or seek partition of the family dwelling house. The earlier 1956 Act had not allowed a married daughter (unless separated, deserted, or widowed) even residence rights in the parental home; the unmarried daughters had residence rights but could not demand partition. The amendment has also removed the bar placed on certain widows such as those of predeceased sons from inheriting the deceased's property if they had remarried. Under the amendment they can now inherit. The amendment underlines that daughters and sons are equally important members of the parental family. However, certain anomalies persist relating to unequal status of women beneficiaries and state laws concerning the fixation of ceilings and fragmentation of agricultural holdings. The amended law also fails to take into account the unrestricted testamentary right which can and has been used to disinherit women from self-acquired property. Women's groups are fighting to seek relinquishment of this right.

It may be remembered that the Hindu Succession Act governs most of India and a majority of Indians, but not all of India or all the Indians. Several communities and areas lie outside its scope. As pointed out earlier, most of the northeastern states, comprising parts of Assam and Tripura, and Arunachal Pradesh, Meghalaya, Mizoram, Nagaland, and Manipur, remain governed by customary laws, which as the essays in this volume argue are gender discriminatory. For these areas, a special case had been made out in the constituent assembly advocating preservation of life and customs of these tribal areas, which was incorporated in the sixth schedule of the Indian Constitution. The sixth schedule has provided autonomy to the areas and allowed the tribes to frame their own rules in accordance with their customary practices.[9] The state and union legislations are not enforceable in these regions unless approved by the district councils. Most of the customs followed in these areas are highly anti-women, except for certain strands of the tribal tradition which are comparatively more favourable to women than caste societies. The essays in this volume argue how such traditions are now fast deteriorating, under the impact of extensive commercialization, industrialization, coming in of individual ownership, deforestation, and wide-scale displacement. These changes are leading towards strengthening of patriarchy, and at times to patriliny even in matrilineal societies like that of Meghalaya, as covered in the previous volume.

II

As the states emerge gender biased and discriminatory, this volume attempts to analyse the state laws and state response to this discrimination which need urgent and focused attention everywhere. To facilitate an understanding of this problem spread across differing regions, the states undertaken for this collection have been notionally grouped into three separate categories for the purpose of this editorial note. Roughly speaking these are: the regular states, such as Andhra Pradesh, Gujarat, Maharashtra, Rajasthan, and Tamil Nadu; the tribal states, such as Arunachal Pradesh, Mizoram, Sikkim, Nagaland, Chhattisgarh, and Jharkhand; and the special category states such as Goa and Jammu and Kashmir.

The current state of Andhra Pradesh came into existence in June 2014 after the state of Telangana, with 13 districts, was carved out of it. There was, however, a continuation of the land-related policies and programmes that were operative in the earlier united state of Andhra Pradesh. In this, according to the author of Chapter 2, Revathi, the state amendment of the Hindu Succession Act, in 1986, had been a major step towards introducing gender-just inheritance law. Famously called the 'Andhra model', it made daughters coparceners in the joint family property same as the sons. The 2005 amendment of the Hindu Succession Act by the parliament furthered this right by enabling them to inherit agricultural land on the same basis as sons. Several other measures followed like the wasteland distribution to women. However, lack of implementation as well as cultural inhibitions made all of them fall short of their targeted aims regarding women. According to the author, the implementing agencies of the state such as the revenue department, the land survey, and land registration departments have not been fully geared to implement these laws. Appropriate actions have been advocated to ensure that women have a platform to claim their share of the family property.

An important highlight of the chapter on the state of Gujarat is the extensive feminization of its rural economy. This is however not exclusive to this state but is a fact of rural life that it shares with many other states. Emphasizing this aspect, Itishree Patnaik (Chapter 6) shows the participation of women in agriculture to be around 65% in Gujarat when their ownership of land is only 14%. In fact, the declared aim of the state to provide 'land to the tillers' stands defeated as women despite their extensive involvement with agricultural work are still not accommodated as the title bearers of land. The land-related laws have hardly been operative here. The existing instances of women inheriting land show such women to be inheriting in their capacity as widows, who have benefited on the basis of their customary rights rather than being beneficiaries because of the government policy. Even where women have come to enjoy ownership rights, they do not exercise effective control over land. Women emerge as either not aware of their rights or so steeped in patriarchal culture that despite their awareness, these rights either remain unclaimed or do not end up in giving them any control over the land. This control would depend, according to the author, upon changes being made in political, legal, religious, and social domains.

Just like Gujarat, in Maharashtra also extensive feminization of rural economy has taken place. Giving figures, Ritu Dewan (Chapter 9) observes how the landholdings in this state over the years have declined as compared to the other parts of India, and this decline is noticeable especially in relation to women. The implication being that the process of attaining land rights has been slower for women in Maharashtra than in the rest of India. Within the state, the process of marginalization of women is further visible in the changes across size of holdings within the gender categories. The only answer to this, maintains the author, is a strict enforcement of gender parity in the agrarian sector.

Tamil Nadu, unlike several states, especially of the north, had given coparcenary rights to daughters along with sons under the Hindu Succession (Tamil Nadu Amendment) Act of 1989. However, other communities like the Christians constituting 6.12% of the population and the Muslims constituting 5.86%, as pointed out earlier, continue to be governed by the colonial Acts which were highly discriminatory against women. Ranjani K. Murthy, writing about Tamil Nadu (Chapter 14), argues that as the number of landless rural households in 2005–06 was very high, that is, 64.3%, the chances of women inheriting land rights were extremely limited. This was specially so in relation to the Scheduled Castes, Scheduled Tribes, and the Muslims. However, the state has a number of self-help groups (SHGs) and non-governmental organizations that are active in helping landless women to file petition with the district administration and in accessing land individually or collectively under certain governmental schemes.

Similarly, in Rajasthan, despite state policies and interventions, gender gaps continue to exist. Kanchan Mathur (Chapter 12) holds the patriarchal ideology and practice along with sociocultural factors responsible for not only inhibiting women from participating at the community level but also for not claiming their land rights. The operation of strong cultural bias against women's rights is also evident in their inability to lease, mortgage, or dispose of land and its produce. The gender issues in land/property ownership in the state of Uttarakhand are examined by Indu Pathak (Chapter 15). As in other states, despite laws guaranteeing equality to women regarding their property rights, the wholly ineffective implementation in this state has negated them. In the hilly regions of this state, however, the out-migration of rural men has created a situation in which the responsibility of rural household economy has fallen on women, allowing them far greater control than they would have had under normal circumstances. In order to empower women and make them socially and economically independent, the author considers it necessary to break the patriarchal mindset that has a negative attitude towards women's property rights.

The authors' recommendations to enhance and ensure women's ability to claim and retain control over their rightful inheritance shares have certain common threads running through them. These could be located in establishing the social legitimacy of women's claims, reducing gender bias in village-level registration practices and village council rulings, enhancing women's legal knowledge, providing women with legal aid, improving women's fall-back position so that they are able to deal with the ensuing intra-family conflicts, including providing external support structures that would reduce women's dependence on brothers and close kin. In all this, the role of collective action is considered to be primary, which in return can be bolstered by providing encouragement and support to local and state-level women's movement and women's associations.

Further, efforts are recommended to be made to increase women's representation in local bodies, thus, improving local authorities' ability to improve gender equity; emphasize on the positive impact of literacy and education on women in understanding, claiming, and realizing their rights in family property; encourage women to undertake land lease in order to strengthen their livelihoods options and enhance food security; take special measures to include and ensure livelihood for landless poor households; and above all, create a sociocultural environment supportive of the implementation of pro-women legal measures and legislative Acts. Active steps are also recommended to be taken towards generating the much-needed social acceptance of women's right to land cutting across the inter-sectionalities of caste, class, and religious groups.

Editor's Introduction: Persisting Gender Discrimination in Land Rights • 11

III

Apart from the above-mentioned states, India has a fairly large number of tribal populations spread over many of its states and union territories. The 2011 census figures show that except for the states of Punjab and Haryana, and union territories of Chandigarh, Delhi, and Puducherry, all other states of India have varying percentage of Scheduled Tribe population in relation to its total population.[10] The tribal-dominated states taken up in this volume are Arunachal Pradesh, Mizoram, Nagaland, and Sikkim from the northeastern region, and Chhattisgarh and Jharkhand from Central India. However, the tribal population is also found in varying degree in the states of Andhra Pradesh, Gujarat, Maharashtra, Rajasthan, and Tamil Nadu, as well as in the states of Goa and Jammu and Kashmir.

For historical reasons, land in the hill areas under tribal domination was accorded protection and even now continues to lie outside the ambit of formal legislative enactments.[11] However, certain encroachments from different quarters have taken place leading to a tense and conflictual situation (Bhaumik 2010; Subramanian 2015). Various factors are responsible for it which in the opinion of the observers and writers, including those in this volume, are related to the increasing pressure on land from population growth, rising land demand for development projects, pressure of the market forces, and immigration. An encroachment of community forest land and other natural resources by the local bigwigs as well as by the outside agencies is also noticeable. Acquisition of community land for various development projects, displacing a large number of tribal families, has been steadily on the rise.

The tribal areas in nine states of India, namely Andhra Pradesh, Gujarat, Maharashtra, Chhattisgarh, and Rajasthan (as also Jharkhand, Madhya Pradesh, Himachal Pradesh, and Orissa), are covered by the Fifth Schedule, whereas certain parts of Mizoram, Assam, and Tripura and the complete state of Meghalaya in the northeastern region of the country are covered by the Sixth Schedule. Arunachal Pradesh, Mizoram, Nagaland, and Sikkim do not fall under any special schedule[12] but land in Arunachal Pradesh and Nagaland is governed by the customary laws, whereas Sikkim has its land revenue laws. Though Nagaland and major portion of Mizoram are not covered under the Sixth Schedule, yet land, forest, and customs in Nagaland are protected under Article 371G, and similarly land, forest, and customary laws in major parts of Mizoram excluding the Sixth Schedule areas are protected under Article 371A of the Indian Constitution. This heterogeneity has resulted in a mosaic of land tenure systems which not only differ widely from the other non-tribal regions but also show a variety of landownership patterns co-existing within these regions. For instance, in some tribal regions the landownership is community based and tribals have customary rights, whereas at other places, an individual landownership pattern prevails. Land laws of many states do not permit tribals to sell the land to the non-tribals.

Yet land acquisition from the tribals has emerged as a very significant issue. The early post-Independence projects of the Centre such as the Heavy Engineering Corporation at Ranchi, Bhilai Steel Plant, Hirakud dam, Mayurakshi, and Tenughat projects were all built on tribal land. In the estimate of the human rights activists, over 80% of the people displaced were tribals who were not rehabilitated (Dungdung 2016). Such examples can be multiplied. Commercial interests in timber, which first penetrated these areas 150 years ago with the colonial demand for railway sleepers, have intensified over the years, reflecting capitalism's spreading ethic of profiting. The new economic policy has further opened vistas for establishing development projects in the country. More and more private companies, national as well as international, are venturing in these areas which are rich in minerals and forest and are predominantly inhabited by the tribal communities. Various industries and projects related to mines, minerals, coal, and sponge iron are being launched in a big way. Similarly, several government-led development projects such as dams, irrigation and hydel power plants, economic development projects, wildlife sanctuary protection programmes, national parks, and tiger or sea bird projects are also moving on in a big way. This implies that more land would be required for the development projects in the years to come.

Any attempt to acquire land in these areas requires deep understanding not only of the tenurial system but also of the sociocultural ethos of the tribal community as their lives revolve around natural resources, and land is pivotal to these. There is also a need to determine whether tribal rights are in consonance with the spirit of constitution when such projects are undertaken. Thus, it is important to assess the impact on the socio-economic and cultural lives of the tribals when land is acquired for any development project.

The execution of developmental projects has involved an influx of non-tribals from other states such as Bihar, Uttar Pradesh, West Bengal, Odisha, and elsewhere to work in the tribal areas. This has created a massive problem of tribals and non-tribals with such a force and political colouring that women's empowerment is all but thrust into the background. Currently, for example, in Jharkhand, the non-tribals are taking over the state, side-lining the tribals on the question of state domicile policy of the present government as to who constitutes a 'resident' of the state and from which cut-off year (Shekhar 2016). Consequently, the government policies followed in the tribal regions may well reveal themselves to be discriminatory rather than empowering for the tribals—both men and women.

The tribal areas are also conspicuous by the absence of land records, especially as the tribal population is heterogeneous in nature and each tribe has a specific character of its own. This factor makes the acquisition of land easy, leading to land alienation of the tribals and shrinking of their livelihood sources. Currently, a debate is gathering momentum whether to relax protective land legislation for tribals and bring them in the mainstream by including them under the central Acts or to adopt a 'museum approach' and maintain status quo. In the two emerging contrary opinions, one opinion holds that the protection given to the people is an impediment to development projects much needed by the tribals. Contrary to this, the other opinion holds that in the absence of the special protection, these indigenous communities will be lost forever. The different authors in this volume reflect this divergence of opinion. Rimi Tadu, for example, underscores the importance of land to the indigenous communities of Arunachal Pradesh (Chapter 3), which she considers integral to their identity, cultures, and customs, and details how under the modern capitalistic development paradigms introduced by the state, the tribal living patterns and mutual relations are going through severe stresses and strains. Despite divergence of opinion, there is also an emerging consensus that the land issues of Scheduled Tribes need to be dealt with from an overall perspective of the tribe vis-à-vis non-tribe and the restoration of tribal lands from the non-tribal control.

The large-scale projects in the tribal areas involve huge displacement of population. The resettlement aspect of this population shows land to be usually allotted to the adult male head of the household. This is a gender-discriminatory practice and needs to be corrected. Also, those women, particularly the marginalized, who are affected/displaced by the development programmes, need to be given priority in land allocation/ compensation under resettlement and rehabilitation packages. The government of India in its national policy on displacement and rehabilitation should ensure that the policy is gender sensitive and takes into account the interest and rights of women. Moreover, under the land acquisition law, only those households who own titled land are compensated, whereas those households who own community land are not considered for any compensation. In view of this problem, the study on Mizoram in this volume suggests that community land may not be acquisitioned for developmental projects. Clearly, the existing land acquisition law needs to be thought through and amended.

In view of the fact that the tribal customs are neither documented (except for Mizoram) or codified, serious questions are being asked about them, especially from a gender perspective as most customary laws of the tribal region are clearly regressive and anti-women. The existing customs also contradict the basic tenets of the constitution. Consequently, the concerned states, with the help of women's organizations, should identify and examine the prevailing customary laws on land and inheritance, and redefine and modify them to make them gender just. Apart from application of customary laws in tribal areas, there are also instances in the tribal belt, for example in Rajasthan, where the government functionaries apply provisions of the Hindu Succession Act in certain places and the customary law and practices of the Hindu law in other places, which give inheritance rights only to the male members. There is an urgent need to send the official guidelines regarding the correct application of law, which is gender just.

A barbarous way adopted in these areas to silence a 'demanding woman' or a 'would-be demanding woman' is to label her as a witch and punish her most severely and even kill her (McCoy 2014; Singh 2015). Violence is adopted in order to disinherit women from their land, settle family and clan disputes, punish women for resisting sexual advances, or even to discourage women from participating in local politics and elections. There are many instances of such labelling. Disturbingly, the witch hunting is now observable not only among the tribal women but also has come to have a visible presence among the non-tribal regions with no tribal population like that of Haryana, with male members attempting to deprive widows of their rightful share of land by stigmatizing them as 'witches'.[13]

Writing about Jharkhand, M. N. Karna (Chapter 8) shows how customs were inhibiting women's rights in the state. The majority of the respondents that he interviewed from the tribal communities did not favour the idea of registering land in the name of women. The only way out of this, according to him, was not to leave any community and area out of the purview of land reforms and to base institutional reconstruction on the democratic principle of gender equality and justice. Likewise,

Saroj Arora writing on Mizoram (Chapter 10) describes how patriarchy-embedded customary laws deny women inheritance rights and restrict their participation in the public domain. Also commercialization of agriculture has meant, according to her, a shift from community land to settled land. As a result of which women are gradually losing access and control over community land and common property resources. However, in view of a strong women's organizations in Mizoram, the state, after much resistance, recently brought certain changes in the socio legal system by enacting two laws, namely the Mizo Marriage, Divorce and Inheritance of Property Act, 2014 and The Lushai Hills District (Village Council) Act, 2015, both of which are deemed favourable to women.

Similarly, the study on Nagaland for this volume by three authors, namely C. Sridhar, Saroj Arora, and Khunenchu Magh (Chapter 11), shows the land, customary laws, and practices as well as other traditional institutions being protected under Article 371A of the Indian Constitution. In this tribal state, no union law is applicable unless approved by the state assembly. More than 98% of the land belongs to the community, which consists of 90% of Scheduled Tribes, almost all Christians by religion. Both men and women work on the community land but women have no entitlement to ancestral land. The authors advocate a review of the land-related customary laws in order to make them gender just. They also emphasize the need for women's reservation at grass-roots level institutions. These demands have a strong echo in the Nagaland women's movement.

Apart from Mizoram and Nagaland, the other state that has similar women's movement making identical demands is Sikkim. Analysed by Sohel Firdos (Chapter 13), this state shows a strong women's movement capable of pressurizing the state to eliminate gender discrimination especially in relation to land rights and inheritance of property. This discrimination comes blatantly to the surface as a Sikkimies woman if married to a non-Sikkimies cannot purchase land, neither can she transfer land to any of her children born out of such a wedlock. As this is a glaring discrimination, a number of women activists as well as women organizations have raised their voice against it.

IV

The state of Goa and that of Jammu and Kashmir fall into a special category as both have certain features that set them apart from the other states. Goa is the only region in the entire country that has a Common Civil Code earlier known as the Portuguese Civil Code which governs all rights of women, whatever their creed, caste, or ethnicity; this includes women's right over property, both natal and marital. Jammu and Kashmir, the only Muslim-majority state in India, enjoys a special status under Article 370 of the Indian Constitution. This provides a fairly high degree of autonomy to the state and enables it to have its own constitution (adopted in November 1956). The union government[14] jurisdiction extends over limited matters in this state.

For Goa, despite having a Common Civil Code, Ritu Dewan's (Chapter 5) analysis shows land rights for rural women that are curtailed or restricted and often denied in various ways, just as they are in other states of India. Being regulated and mediated through a vast cluster of laws, regulations, and schemes, covered in detail by the author, they still negate gender equality in terms of inheritance or in terms of holding the matrimonial property in common. Consequently, although the ownership of matrimonial property vests in both the spouses, it is managed by the male spouse, except in case of some impediment. The male spouse can alienate property, provided he obtains the consent of his wife, which can be obtained post facto, whereas the wife can alienate only if she has the authorization of her husband. In reality, therefore, the equality of rights in parental or matrimonial property stands severely compromised. Goa requires, as the other states do, to negate the right given to a male to either sell, mortgage, or give away the landed property without the consent of his spouse. These extensive reforms in the family laws of Goa are advocated by the author in order to ensure land rights for rural women and bring about gender parity, equality, and empowerment.

Gender issues in landownership in Jammu and Kashmir (including Leh and Ladakh) discussed in Chapter 7 authored by Abha Chauhan, similarly, show a malady of land-related laws of inheritance which include the customary laws, personal laws, statutory laws, and those codified into statutory laws as part of the democratic institution, land-reform legislations, as well as the recent efforts by the state in making gender-sensitive and inclusive land laws. Despite all this, the situation remains discriminatory for women as in other parts of India. The most glaring example of discrimination is the special privileges given by the state to its 'permanent residents'. One such special privilege is that only a permanent resident can buy land in the state. Just like in the state of Sikkim, women of Jammu and Kashmir, if married to the non-state subjects, as well as their children, are discriminated against. They do not have the same rights as other women marrying the state subjects. Although this state has seen some successful land laws and tenancy reforms, the gender inequalities in the land ceiling laws remain glaring. Replacement of customs with the personal law for Muslims in 2007 has been beneficial for women to a certain extent but the state needs legal intervention to rectify several other gender-unjust laws which, as the author delineates, continue to assail the Kashmiri society. To rectify matters, the author strongly recommends the extension of the Hindu Succession Act (Amendment) 2005 as well as the land ceiling laws to the state.

V

In conclusion, we may state that the regions undertaken to study in this volume underline three major contentions that may unitedly work in arresting gender discrimination in land rights and make way towards women empowerment. These are legal enactments, their implementation, and the societal acceptance. Some of the regions show that they are not entirely deficient in gender-just laws, although it is also undeniable that several additions can be made to the existing laws and also new laws can be introduced to supplement the existing ones or provisions can be made to extend these laws to regions where they do not exit. Many of the authors in this volume recommend that the need is to bring a law which would be applicable uniformly to all regions, religious and ethnic groups, and communities, who are now governed by a diversity of laws. This demand was in fact first put forward in the form of a Uniform Civil Code (UCC) in the 1930s by the All India Women's Conference. For a variety of reasons, extensively analysed in the previous volume (Chowdhry 2009), this demand was not granted legal recognition and was only incorporated within the directive principles of state policy, which the states would endeavour to secure. From time to time this demand has come to be echoed from different sides. It came to be debated, criticized, appreciated, and condemned—all at the same time. Even the judiciary raised it up in no uncertain terms.[15] All revived attempts proved highly contentious and split the women's movement in India into 'pro- and anti-UCC' contending streams of opinion. Today, in the volatile sociopolitical climate, the issue of reforming 'personal laws' has become entwined with questions of religious and community identity, and with the politicization of identity issues. Promoted as a means of effecting national unity and integrating diverse communities, it has become associated with the agenda of the Hindu right-wing political groups.

In the debate that has followed the desirability of introducing UCC for the whole of India, three major positions have emerged. Briefly speaking, these are, first, that personal law reform should proceed from 'within' each religious group, with each group left to pursue legal reform separately; second, that gender-just laws which apply to all citizens by birth should coexist with personal laws, so that on adulthood each person can choose whether to be governed by the one or the other; and third, a gender-equal code should be applicable to all citizens without distinction of community, religion, or custom. Although so far no consensus has been reached, this debate has helped in creating a lot of awareness among women from different strata about gender issues and their rights, as well as about the role played by custom and religion in negating these rights.

However, where the actual deficiency lies and may continue to lie even after fresh enabling laws, etc., is in their implementation. We can wholeheartedly agree with a recent May 2016 pronouncement of Raghuram Rajan, the then Governor of the Reserve Bank of India, that 'Policy making may be easy but its implementation is harder.'[16] The detailed analysis of various papers emphasize virtually the same: the attainment of land rights for rural women is curtailed, restricted, and often denied in various ways and requires interventions to assure implementation in order to bring about gender parity, equality, and empowerment for women. For this, urgent legislative, administrative, and judicial reforms are needed.

What interventions can assure implementation of the laws? Regarding this, certain suggestions may be put forward. For example, the state administration may issue a standing order regarding the execution of such laws, and in the case of non-implementation or ineffective implementation of the programme make bureaucrats legally accountable. Some observers have gone to the extent of recommending that a violation of the law of succession should be made a cognizable offence.

Steps may also be taken to redefine terms such as 'land to the tiller' or 'kisan' (a male term) introduced during the inception of land reforms programme—a term that stands for and is often taken to refer and relate to male cultivators only. In fact, the language of the land reform acts similarly prioritizes males over the implicit exclusion of the females in matters of inheritance. Social justice demands elimination of all such implicit and explicit language usages. In reality, with the increasing feminization of agricultural activity, a large number of rural women in

India are engaged in the agricultural sector, but they have no accessibility to, and ownership rights in, land or any other productive resources; they are not referred to as cultivators. This lack of owning productive resources, such as land, also creates hindrance in having accessibility to various government programmes. The recent government policy of issuance of 'Kisan credit cards' usually to male farmers is one such instance. This is based on the definitional notion that only the male head of the household is the owner of the agricultural land.

The states should also move towards certain restrictions on the rights of testation as the existing provisions fully ignore the interest and rights of women. A part of the testation should be made mandatory for women. It may also be ensured that if women relinquish their claims, the relinquishment is done through a formal deed of law rather than informally. Even formally the process whereby women (daughters, sisters, and mothers) forego their share in the holding in the name of their fathers, brothers, or sons is a relatively simple procedure. Signatures are taken on a ₹100 stamp paper in the presence of a government functionary like *tehsildar* to transfer the land. Enactment of stricter laws relating to release and transfer of land as well as involvement of higher administrative and judicial staff is required to deal with this situation. The implications of such a relinquishment should be made clear to the woman signatory. This would at least provide a rethink and even some protection to women against signing away their shares due to their ignorance or misinformation and their shares being taken over by their relatives.

For understanding such matters, the need for education of women cannot be overstated. For example, very often the relinquishment of their rights by women is effected by default, because they are unable to read or comprehend the legal document. Not only this, but the land acquisition itself requires payment of registration fee, filling of forms, and gaining a certificate of landownership from the local government body, to name just a few steps. Most often women, particularly in rural areas, are unable to fulfil these requirements due to low literacy rates and lack of awareness regarding obtaining ownership titles.

There is also a great need to appoint women functionaries at the grass-roots level in the revenue and agricultural departments. It is a well-known fact, and I have observed it myself, that more than anyone else women are very effective in motivating other women. The local-level institutions like the panchayats are the lowest tier of democratic institution at the village level and play a significant role in land-related issues. The insertion of Article 243D of the Indian Constitution has assured the reservation of one-third of the seats for women in Panchayati Raj institutions. However, women are hardly equipped to handle the panchayat and related activities. Active measures must be undertaken to educate and equip them with proper training and information, especially on land-related issues. This should also extend to the village *pradhan* (headman) and other panchayat members so as to make them accountable for their decisions and actions. It should be made mandatory for the administrators at all levels from panchayat onwards to educate women about their land rights and encourage them to exercise these rights. The panchayati raj institutions may also be linked with legal aid cells or other legal redressal forums, so as to ensure that women who bring their land-related problems to the gram panchayats have ready access to legal advice and services.

Creation or strengthening of the available gender disaggregated database with details of public, private, and also institutional holdings across all castes and communities is a dire necessity. This is one factor which finds its recommendatory echo in all quarters. In fact, the maintenance of such a sex-segregated data should be mandatory for all types of land records of the revenue department. This would not only offer a clear picture of gendered practices in landownership, land use pattern, area operated, and extent of tenancy, etc., but also help in assessing the impact of land reform policy on women's status. Computerization of land records would further facilitate this process.

The targeted women for providing and assuring land rights should be those, as already mentioned, from socially vulnerable and marginalized groups and landless women. To these may be added the categories of single women (unmarried, widows, divorced, or separated) and women heading their households, as well as women from innumerable farmer-suicide-affected households. They all need to be prioritized for special attention. The public land distribution programmes including leasing of all unused, potentially cultivable land, ceiling surplus land, and illegal land occupied by trusts and religious institutions should be identified and made available to such women on priority basis. In order to strengthen the move towards giving land rights to women, the recommendation emerging from most of the authors is in favour of putting a stop to the land acquisition by private or governmental agencies or the conversion of agriculture land for industrial, real estate, and other purposes.

An important incentive of transferring land to women that needs to be greatly encouraged and publicized is to be found under the government scheme in which land transferred to women's names attracts much less taxation.[17] This scheme of giving concession in the stamp duty to women property buyers introduced recently is a move towards empowerment of women. However, being a state subject, this scheme has been introduced by less than half the states and union territories. Out of 29 states and 7 union territories, only 10 states and 1 union territory have implemented this scheme. Such states, included in this volume, are only three, that is, Gujarat and Rajasthan (implemented in 2004) and Uttarakhand (implemented in 2006, amended in 2009). Goa on the other hand has a sliding scale of stamp duty on women property buyers starting from 2% only. Significantly, official records and reports show a sharp increase in the number of agricultural land deeds registered by women since the introduction of this scheme. In Rajasthan, for example, more than two lakh women registered agricultural land in their names in a single year, that is, from January 2004 to December 2005. Even if transferred by male owners, either as a gift deed or purchase of immovable property in the name of a family female like the wife or the mother for tax purposes, the very act of ownership gives the woman at least a fair degree of independence, a partial say in decision-making, and also a certain level of economic authority. I found this to be true of Haryana, where women gave instances of changes that could be witnessed among such women, leading them to assert themselves in a variety of ways (Chowdhry 2012a, 2012b).

It is undeniable that the forces against equality and empowerment of women may still devise newer ways to defeat the attempts at reform. The above recommendations may be counted as enabling steps in safeguarding the rights and privileges conferred upon women by the Constitution of India. A third requirement towards attaining land rights for women is the societal acceptance of these changes. Societal acceptance is as essential as the other two, that is, law and its implementation. Unless there is societal acceptance, these changes will continue to be ignored, sidelined, and resisted—even violently—as can be witnessed in the cases cited in this volume.

This crucial step towards halting gender discrimination, that is, societal acceptability, is perhaps the most difficult to attain. It would undoubtedly take a very long time and concerted efforts from all the stakeholders to effect a change in the mindsets of people, regardless of their gender. Let us not forget that the strength of a nation lies in assuring equal rights and opportunities to both men and women in the political, economic, and social spheres, and prohibiting discrimination against any citizen on the ground of sex, religion, race, and caste. How may this social acceptability be achieved would need another volume of work.

NOTES

1. In 2011, I had undertaken an extensive study for UN Women on determining effects of women's property ownership and economic independence on reduction of violence against them in rural Haryana. See Chowdhry (2012a and 2012b).
2. See https://en.wikipedia.org/wiki/Bargaining_power (accessed on 20 March 2017).
3. See https://en.wikipedia.org/wiki/Andaman_and_Nicobar_Islands (accessed on 20 March 2017).
4. See https://en.wikipedia.org/wiki/Chandigarh (accessed on 20 March 2017).
5. See https://en.wikipedia.org/wiki/Dadra_and_Nagar_Haveli (accessed on 20 March 2017).
6. See https://en.wikipedia.org/wiki/Daman_and_Diu (accessed on 20 March 2017).
7. See https://en.wikipedia.org/wiki/Lakshadweep (accessed on 20 March 2017).
8. See https://en.wikipedia.org/wiki/Delhi (accessed on 20 March 2017).
9. See for example, Lalneihzovi (2006), Prasad (2004, 1987, 1979), and Rao, Thansanga, and Hazarika (1987).
10. In terms of percentage of the total population, Arunachal Pradesh has: 68.8; Andhra Pradesh: 7; Andaman and Nicobar islands: 7.5; Assam: 12.4; Bihar: 1.3; Chhattisgarh: 30.6; Dadar and Nagar Haveli: 52; Daman and Diu: 6.3; Goa: 10.2; Gujarat: 14.8; Himachal Pradesh: 5.7; Jammu and Kashmir: 11.9; Jharkhand: 26.2; Karnataka: 7; Kerala: 1.5; Lakshadweep: 94.8; Madhya Pradesh: 21.1; Maharashtra: 9.4; Manipur: 35.1; Meghalaya: 86.1; Mizoram: 94.4; Nagaland: 86.5; Odisha: 22.8; Rajasthan: 13.5; Sikkim: 33.8; Tamil Nadu: 1.1; Tripura: 31.8; Uttarakhand: 2.9; Uttar Pradesh: 0.6; West Bengal: 5.8. See GoI (2013).
11. Colonial and immediate post-colonial discourse on the tribals in India centred around the issues of assimilation, integration, and separate development in the context of emerging nation. For details, see articles included in Das Gupta and Basu (2012).
12. Scheduled Areas are autonomous areas within a state, administered federally, usually populated by a number of Scheduled Tribes. The Fifth Schedule falls under Article 244(1) and the Sixth Schedule under Articles 244(2) and 275(1) of the Indian Constitution. See the Constitution of India (https://india.gov.in/my-ernment/constitution-india/constitution-india-full-text); see under 'Schedules'. Also see Chatterjee (2010), Patnaik (2008), Lalneihzovi (2006), Singh (2006), Prasad (2004), Ekka and Sinha (2004), Munda and Bosu (2003).
13. Persecution and murder of women, especially widows, in the name of witchcraft is not limited to states with a certain specific demographic profile or

geographical contiguity. According to the National Crime Records Bureau from 2008 to 2013, Haryana witnessed 57 'witchcraft' murders in 2010, the maximum among states that year. Other states were also not far behind. In 2011, Karnataka reported 77 'witchcraft' murders, and Andhra Pradesh shows a steady stream of such murders, averaging 24 every year for the last six years. NCRB report cited in *Indian Express*, daily newspaper, 19 August 2015.
14. See https://en.wikipedia.org/wiki/Government_of_India (accessed on 20 March 2017).
15. From time to time, this demand has come to be echoed from different sides. Even the judiciary raised it up in no uncertain terms. The latest attempt was in October 2015 when Justices Anil R. Dave and Adarsh K. Goel of the Supreme Court gave a renewed call for enactment of a UCC (Agnes 2016).
16. Cited in *The Indian Express* (13 May, 2016).
17. The implementation of the scheme by certain state governments has motivated a large number of families in registering property in women's name in these regions. For details, see Arora and Singh (2016).

REFERENCES

Agnes, Flavia. 2016. 'Muslim, Women's Rights and Media Coverage.' *Economic and Political Weekly* 28 (LI): 13–16.

Arora, S. and Singh, P. 2016. Concession in Stamp Duty: A Tool for Women Empowerment: An Empirical Assessment. In *Women Empowerment and Development* edited by Sameera Maiti. Jaipur: Rawat Publications.

Bhaumik, Subir. 2010. *Troubled Periphery: The Crisis of India's North East*. New Delhi: SAGE Publications.

Chatterjee, Sarajit Kumar. 2010. *North East India—Dispersion & Discontent Historical, Cultural and Socio Political Perspectives*. Vol. 1. Delhi: Abhijeet Publications.

Chowdhry, Prem. 2009. *Gender Discrimination in Land Ownership*. New Delhi: SAGE Publications.

———. 2012a. *Reduction of Violence Against Women: Property Ownership and Economic Independence in Rural Haryana*. UN Women. Available at: http://www.unwomensouthasia.org/economic_security.html (accessed on 24 May 2011).

———. 2012b. 'Infliction, Acceptance and Resistance: Containing Violence on Women in Rural Haryana.' *Economic and Political Weekly* 15 (37): 43–59.

Das Gupta, Sanjukta, and Raj Shekhar Basu, eds. 2012. *Narratives from the Margins: Aspects of Adivasi History in India*. New Delhi: Primus Books.

Dungdung, Gladson. 2016. 'Ask No Questions.' *Indian Express*, 16 May, 13.

Ekka, William, and R. K. Sinha. 2004. *Documentation of Jharkhand Movement.* Kolkata: Anthropological Survey of India.
Government of India. 2013. 'Table 1.1—State wise Scheduled Tribe Population and Decadal Change by Residence: 2001–11, 2013.' In *Demographic Status of Scheduled Tribe Population of India.* Available at: http://tribal.nic.in/WriteReadData/userfiles/file/Demographic.pdf (accessed on 27 May 2016).
Lalneihzovi. 2006. *District Administration in Mizoram—A Study of the Aizawl District.* Delhi: Mittal Publications.
McCoy, Terrence. 2014. 'Thousands of Women, Accused of Sorcery, Tortured and Executed in Indian Witch Hunts. *The Washington Post*, July 21. Available at: https://www.washingtonpost.com/news/morning-ix/wp/2014/07/21/thousands-of-women-accused-of-sorcery (accessed on 27 May 2016).
Munda, R. D., and Bosu S. Mullick. 2003. *The Jharkhand Movement Indigenous People's Struggle for Autonomy in India.* Copenhagen: International Work Group for Indigenous Affairs.
Patnaik, Jagadish K. 2008. 'Autonomous District Councils-A Study of the Implications of the 6th Schedule in Mizoram.' In *Mizoram Dimensions and Perspective Society Economy and Polity*, edited by Jangkhongam Doungel. Delhi: Concept Publishing Company.
Prasad, R. N. 1987. *Government and Politics in Mizoram.* New Delhi: Northern Book Centre.
———. 2004. 'Sixth Schedule and Working of the District Councils in North-Eastern States.' *Dialogue*, 6 (2): 149–64.
Rao, V. Venkata, H. Thansanga, and Niru Hazarika. 1987. *A Century of Government and Politics in North-East India.* Vol. 3. Mizoram/New Delhi: S. Chand and Co.
Shekhar, Hansda Sowvendra. 2016. 'The Adivasis Will Not Dance: An Adivasi's View of the New Domicile Policy in Jharkhand.' *Indian Express*, 14 May, 15.
Singh, M. K. 2006. *Jharkhand Development and Politics Avenues and Challenges.* Delhi: Gangandeep.
Singh, Santosh. 2015. 'Jharkhand: 5 Tribal Women Lynched for Being "Witches".' The Indian Express, *August 9, 14.*
Subramanian, K. S. 2015. *State, Policy and Conflicts in Northeast India.* Delhi: Routledge.
The Indian Express. 2015. *The Indian Express*, New Delhi, 19 August.
———. 2016. *The Indian Express*, daily newspaper (13, 14 and 16 May 2016; 19 August, 2015) New Delhi.

2

Land Rights and Land Access to Women in Andhra Pradesh

E. REVATHI

The present state of Andhra Pradesh came into existence on 6 June 2014 with 13 districts after Telangana was carved out of the undivided state of Andhra Pradesh as the 29th state. Andhra Pradesh has six agro climatic zones: the North coastal region consisting of Srikakulam, Vizianagaram, and Visakhapatnam districts; the Godavari zone comprising East Godavari and West Godavari; the Krishna zone comprising Krishna, Guntur, and Prakasam districts; the Southern zone comprising Nellore, Kadapa, and Chittoor districts; the scarce rainfall zone comprising Kurnool and Anantapur districts; and High Altitude and Tribal Area Zone of Srikakulam, Visakhapatnam, and East Godavari districts. The contribution of the agricultural sector to state GSDP is 29% in 2015–16 at current prices (GoAP 2016), which is substantially higher than is the case for all India. The rural population constitutes around 70% of the total population. About 41.5% of rural households in the state are agricultural households, a figure which is lower than the all India figure of 57.8% (MOSPI, GoI 2013).

Land policies in the state can be classified into two phases—the first phase focused on redistributive land reform, and the second phase on distribution of government land to the landless and also market-assisted land reforms. As elsewhere, women did not figure in the first phase of land reforms but were targeted during the second phase. The former state of Andhra Pradesh was unique in many ways in the country: It was the first state to be formed on a linguistic basis; many social movements involving marginalized and disadvantaged people's groups and regions took place in the state; movements for land were taken up by extremist or radical Left groups to Left parties such as the Communist Party of India (CPI) and the Communist Party of India (Marxist) (CPI-M); it had experimented with economic reforms, where, ultimately, a strong and thriving regional movement for statehood resulted in the bifurcation of the state.

It was also a state which had pioneered a vibrant self-help group (SHG) movement as a platform for women's livelihoods, access to assets—very importantly, land for poor women, and social mobilization of women for individual and collective issues. Undivided Andhra Pradesh had also implemented land reforms around the mid-2000s during the Congress regime in the context of peace talks with the Leftist groups which paved the way for giving land rights (titles) to women for the land distributed by the government; and, as part of market led-land reforms, the state also implemented the Land Purchase Programme (LPP) aided by the World Bank.

A distinctive act of the undivided state was the amendment of the Hindu Succession Act (HSA) in 1986 which was a major step towards a just inheritance law to empower women. In the present context of analysing land policies in general and gender-related land laws in particular, this chapter has analysed the laws which prevailed in the state of Andhra that was merged into the state of Andhra Pradesh[1] and also the policies taken up by the state of Andhra Pradesh after 1956 till 2014. The first phase of land reforms (abolition of intermediaries and tenancy legislation) taken up in post-independent India in the undivided state reflected the different legal systems of Andhra (having roots in the erstwhile Madras State) and Hyderabad state, while the subsequent land policy pertains to the undivided state.

I

OBJECTIVES AND METHODOLOGY

This chapter, thus, begins with an analysis of the policies that addressed the concerns of women in the state within the overarching framework of land policies, and their implication for providing access to women to land. Secondly, it analyses the various programmes taken up by the state to give women access to land. Thirdly, it attempts to examine empirically the conditions under which women access land considering different climatic and social factors such as irrigated or dry land and tribal areas (for details of the sample, see Table A2.1). Irrigated and dry lands represent different levels of socio-economic development and demonstrate the enabling or disabling conditions for better outcomes of the Hindu succession law. The underlying hypothesis is: 'Better socio-economic conditions facilitate women to access land, especially through the family.' However, in tribal areas, where the Hindu succession law is not applicable, the issues are different. Access to land in this context is used in a less rigorous sense which denotes not only rights of ownership and use but also informal concessions granted by individuals to kin and friends.

The chapter is based on secondary sources for a review of legal policies and programmes undertaken by the state in making land accessible to women. Further, it also draws from an empirical study done earlier by the author (Revathi 2012). The ongoing section is Section I which details the objectives and methodology. Section II deals with land legality and women and the empirical study related to women's access to land from the family. The various programmes taken up by the state in making land accessible to women is dealt with in section III and section IV gives a summary, conclusions, and policy implications.

II

LAND LEGALITY AND WOMEN

The first phase of land reforms in the 1950s and 1960s focused on redistributive land reform, the abolition of intermediaries, tenancy reform, ceiling on landholdings, and consolidation of landholdings. The abolition of intermediaries in the Andhra area was effected through the expropriatory legislation of the Madras Estates (Abolition and Conversion into Ryotwari) Act 1948 and the AP (Andhra area) Inams (Abolition and conversion into Ryotwari) Act in 1956, converting the tenurial system into ryotwari system and bringing tenants into direct contact with the state. Later, the protection of tenancy was taken up by enacting the AP (Andhra Area) Tenancy Act in 1956. The law permitted tenancy but it was regulated by strict terms regarding duration of lease, rents, and renewal.

Sections 4 and 10 of the AP Tenancy Act provided for the resumption of land by the owner to the extent of two-thirds of the 'ceiling area' and ensured that the tenant had possession of at least half the area he was cultivating before the resumption of land by the landlord. Further, Section 10(1) of the Act laid down that there should be a written lease agreement and the minimum period of the lease should be six years in perpetuity and the rent should be 25%–30% of the gross produce. The Act also provided for the right to purchase land by the tenant in case the land was sold by the landlord. Though the Act seemed to give considerable rights to tenants, the eviction of tenants was easy due to the right of resumption and other loopholes in the Act. An amendment was brought to this act in 1970 with provisions for fixing fair rent, automatic renewal of lease, and pre-emptive rights. However, the land could be taken back for the purpose of 'personal cultivation' subject to land ceiling limits. Parthasarathy and Raju (1971: A45–A47) have rightly pointed out,

> [T]enancy is high in Andhra Pradesh (undivided AP) because the state has not followed the spirit of guidelines issued by Government of India regarding fixation of fair rent; and also the suggestion of the Planning Commission that personal cultivation be defined (by the criterion of residence in the village in which the land is located for a greater part of the agricultural year).

Though tenancy was not prohibited, because of the regulatory provisions tenancy became the least governed by tenancy Acts giving rise to informal tenancy in the state (Subramanyam 2000; Vakulabharanam et al. 2011).

The trend in tenancy shows that the share of tenant holdings in all holdings has come down over a period of time while the share of leased-in area has remained almost the same. NSSO estimates in 2002–03 for the undivided state showed that while 12.9% of all holdings were reported as tenant holdings, the leased-in area constituted only 9% of the cultivated area. The share of reported tenant holdings for the divided state of Andhra Pradesh is 26.5%, while the share of leased-in area is 37.5%. Moreover, the percentage of leased in households to all rural households is 37% (MOSPI, GoI 2013). This shows the high prevalence of tenancy in the new state. The extent of land under tenancy is even higher when informal tenancy is taken into consideration. According to the Land Committee Report, through a primary study done in five villages in five districts in coastal Andhra Pradesh, 55% to 60% of the land surveyed was under lease. Moreover, all the lands were leased on an informal basis because of the stringent rules of the tenancy Act (Land Committee Report 2006). The more recent legislation of the Andhra Pradesh Licensed Cultivators Act of 2011 (one of the recommendations of the Land Committee) has attempted to register tenants and make them eligible for loans and other benefits from public institutions without tweaking tenancy legislation.

The AP Ceiling on Agricultural Holdings Act was passed in 1961 in Andhra Pradesh as in other states in the country. This land ceiling law was weak because of the provisions of higher ceiling limit of land, the individual as the unit of application, definition of family holding, and the possibility of separate holdings for a wife or daughter in the name of *stridhan*.[2] Very little land was declared surplus and, hence, available for distribution due to the many exemptions given in this Act. As the land ceiling legislation in terms of the limit on land, the type of crops, and the unit of application differed across states, a new national policy and guidelines were evolved in 1971 to bring uniformity and stringency. The AP (Ceiling on Agricultural Holdings) Act was passed in 1973 in line with the national guidelines. The limit of a standard holding in the state ranges between 10 and 27 acres for the wet land category and between 35 and 54 acres for the dry land category. The estimated surplus land initially was 20 lakh acres, but later, by 2007–08 it was estimated at 8.43 lakh acres. Of this estimated surplus land, 6.52 lakh acres were taken over but only 5.97 lakh acres were distributed among 5.40 lakh beneficiaries till the end of 2008, which amounted to just 1.45% of the net area sown. The implementation process of the land ceiling legislation brought to the fore the several shortcomings of the Act due to which large landholders could circumvent the land ceiling law in many ways, like appeals made to various courts of law (appellate courts, high courts, and the Supreme Court). The appellants could obtain exemptions from the land ceiling law in different ways. There were many well-identified methods for avoiding declaration of surplus land: by claiming that a child below the age of 18 years was a major; exemption under the clause of 'adverse possession'; undertaking unregistered sale of land and making private sale deeds; deletion of areas under the tenancy Act; and obtaining the Occupancy Rights Certificate under the Inam Abolition Act (Kodandaram and Laxmaiah 2007).

The surplus land appropriated through land ceiling legislation was redistributed to the landless which was a constituency that did not include women until the mid-1990s. A mention was made about women in one of the provisions of the programmes of action for land reforms in the Approach Paper to the Ninth Five-year Plan that 'Preference to women will be given in the distribution of ceiling surplus land and legal provisions shall be provided for protecting their rights on land' (Planning Commission n.d.: 61).

Land reform had always been slow and its outcomes were not effective according to expectations in the state of Andhra Pradesh. Discontent centred around landownership time and again. The report of the Land Committee[3] submitted to the GoAP in 2006 addressed three major concerns after reviewing the land issues in the state:

1. How to augment the 'surplus' land under the possession of the government?
2. How to encourage investments by tenants in order to raise land productivity and incomes from land?
3. How to restore tribal lands appropriated by non-tribals?

WOMEN AND LAND RIGHTS: THE LEGAL FRAMEWORK

Discrimination against women pervades economic and social spheres, though social discrimination emanates mainly from economic discrimination. This discrimination is evident in property rights. Women are not treated on a par with men in inheriting coparcenary (family) property. The idea of making women and girl children coparcener in joint family property in the same way as a son was first proposed in 1945 and again in 1956 at the time of the drafting of the Hindu Succession Amendment Act (HSAA). But the *Mitakshara* form of joint family was retained which was amended firstly by south Indian states like Kerala, Andhra Pradesh, Tamil Nadu, Karnataka, and Maharashtra on the argument that women needed to be treated equally both economically and socially (Law Commission of India 2000). It was also felt that the denial of property rights to women would lead to the pernicious dowry system (Singh and Reddy 2004). The 1956 HSA was amended by Andhra Pradesh in 1986, making daughters coparceners in the Hindu Joint Family property by amending Section 6 of the Act. These amendments are typified as Andhra model and Kerala model. The Andhra model was also adopted by the other states of Tamil Nadu, Karnataka, and Maharashtra, while the Kerala model abolished the joint family system itself, thereby nullifying any claims to rights based on birth in the joint family.

The HSA of 1956 had exempted tenancy rights in agricultural land from its purview. There are three types of situations regarding the devolution of rights over tenancy land across the country. States such as Rajasthan, Madhya Pradesh, and the Telangana region of undivided Andhra Pradesh explicitly hold that devolution takes place according to the customary or personal law. In Rajasthan and Madhya Pradesh, personal law applies to all communities but, in Telangana, it is applicable only to Hindu tenants. The second set of states such as Gujarat, the Andhra region or the present state of Andhra Pradesh, Tamil Nadu, West Bengal, Karnataka, Kerala, and the Bombay region of Maharashtra do not mention any order of devolution in the case of tenancy rights but it is assumed that personal law is applied. In the third set of states—Delhi, Haryana, Himachal Pradesh, Punjab, Jammu and Kashmir, and Uttar Pradesh—the tenurial laws specifically mention inheritance rules and these rules are highly gender biased.

In the state of Andhra Pradesh, a lease is heritable under Section 10(5) of the AP (Tenancy) Andhra Area Act, 1956. It holds that all rights of a cultivating tenant subject to the provisions of Sections 8–13 of the HSA 1956 are heritable in the order of class 1 heirs, class 2 heirs, agnates, and lastly cognates, without any distinction between males and females. Thus, there is no scope for gender bias as such in the inheritance of tenancy rights as all descendants, including widows, have the right in case of absence of other heirs. Moreover, Section 6 of the 1956 HSA has already been amended in the State Amendment Act of HSA 1986 (Saxena 2013).

The Andhra Pradesh Land Reforms (Ceiling on Agricultural Holdings) Act 1973 defines a family excluding minor married daughters or deserted minor daughters, thus incorporating a gender bias against them. The law minister's observation during the discussion on the 1956 Hindu Succession Bill was that

> [D]ue to variations across states and even across regions within states in laws dealing with tenancy land or other land related laws which impinge on women's right to equality land has been kept outside the jurisdiction of central law and that any future legislation will not be affected in any way by the provisions of this bill.

This perspective shifted only after the Centre urged the states to take up gender equity land reforms since the mid-1980s[4] and until the HSAA of 2005 was passed by the union government which brought into its purview all agricultural land (including land under tenancy), overriding state laws inconsistent with the Act.

HINDU SUCCESSION (ANDHRA PRADESH AMENDMENT) ACT, 1986, AND THE HINDU SUCCESSION (AMENDMENT) ACT, 2005

The Hindu Succession (Andhra Pradesh Amendment) Act, 1986, gives the daughter a share in the coparcenary (inherited) property by amending Section 6 of the 1956 Act. The Act extends succession by survivorship and gives equal rights to daughter in coparcenary property. The important features of the Act are that a daughter shall by birth become coparcener in her own right with all claims and liabilities as the son; at partition equal shares are allotted to daughter and son, and in the case of death of the daughter, share would be allotted to the surviving child; property held by a Hindu female shall be disposed by her by will or other testamentary disposition. The Hindu Succession (AP Amendment) Act 1986 is prospective including that the Act is also retrospective from 5 September 1985, the date a daughter who is not married or who is subsequently born gets an interest in the coparcenary property as a son gets. The Act had limited impact due to the fact that the concept of coparcenary is patriarchal, and fitting women into this framework becomes problematic; moreover the socio-economic cultural institutions were not conducive for the enforcement of the Act. Further not many claims are made by women for fear of disturbing customs and family norms (Singh and Reddy 2004).

Notwithstanding the amendments made by a few states (especially the southern states) to the 1956 Act, it remained applicable all over the country till the passing of the HSAA in 2005. The discriminatory provision as in Section 6 of the HSA 1956 has been deleted by the 2005 Act whereby daughters get equal rights in Hindu *Mitakshara* coparcenary property. Section 23 of the HSA 1956 which precludes daughters from claiming a dwelling house until the male heirs want a partition also has been deleted. The HSAA 2005 of the Government of India overrides any inconsistent state laws and brings parity in male and female rights in agricultural land, thus facilitating women's access to land as farmers. Besides, it also empowers women to claim a share in the natal dwelling house.

EFFECTS OF INHERITANCE LAWS

In terms of legality, the land laws in the state have been gender just. This is evident from the amendment of the HSA in 1986 which included the inheritance of tenancy rights. However, the ceiling on agricultural landholdings has not yielded much surplus land as the landed class could exploit the provisions of the Act and gender equality as a tool to retain ownership of land 'within the household'.

What has been the effect of inheritance laws on women's access to land from the family? What is the direct effect and what are the indirect effects of the inheritance law on women's welfare? These questions are addressed in the literature in the Indian context. The first set of studies which focused on measuring the direct effects of the inheritance law on women accessing land concluded that the state-level HSAA significantly increased the probability of women inheriting land, although it did not bring about full gender equality (Goyal, Deininger, and Nagarajan 2009). Further, the law has been effective in women's perceived ownership of household land and the probability of women inheriting land (Brule 2010). Another set of studies analysed the various outcomes of women's access to land through inheritance. Some of the positive outcomes were that when women got land through inheritance, the degree of autonomy enjoyed by them in their marital home increased, which in turn might have led to positive economic outcomes (Roy 2008). HSAA also led to a large and significant increase in the education of daughters (Goyal et al. 2009); granting property rights to women provided them with a permanent source of income and enhanced the value of lifetime income and also increased the investment incentive because of better management of resources and finances (Roy and Tisdell 2002).

WOMEN'S ACCESS TO LAND FROM FAMILY UNDER DIFFERENT SITUATIONS IN ANDHRA PRADESH: STATISTICAL ANALYSIS

This section attempts to empirically analyse women's access to land from the family in the state of Andhra Pradesh. Female participation in agriculture historically has been high in Andhra Pradesh. The labour force participation rate in the current daily status for rural women was high at 375 per 1,000, while it was only 180 for all India for 2011–12. Female agricultural workers (FAL) in total female workers constituted 66% (in both principal and subsidiary status) in 2011–12, while it was 63% for all India (NSSO 2014). Around 42% of FAL were self-employed (cultivators) in 2011–12, and 90% of them worked as unpaid family workers. According to the data provided by the Agricultural Census, women operated 25% of all holdings in 2010–11 which was an increase over 2005–06 at 22%. Similarly, they operated 22% of the total cultivated area in 2010–11, while it was only 18% in 2005–06 (GoI 2010–11). The size distribution of the holdings shows that at least 50% of the holdings operated by women are small and marginal holdings. However, this does not indicate the ownership status of women's operational holdings. Micro studies on women's access to land in Andhra Pradesh do provide evidence about their ownership in agricultural land. Around 33% of households in the districts of Krishna and Adilabad of undivided Andhra Pradesh reported land in the name of women from the natal family (Galab and Revathi 2011). Another study conducted in the districts of Vizianagaram and Visakhapatnam reported that 34% of women whose parents owned land, inherited or expected to inherit land from them (Landesa 2013).

The conditions under which women access land from the family have been tested empirically in three geographical situations of irrigated land, dry land, and forest in the present state of Andhra Pradesh.[5] It is hypothesized that women's access to land or land inherited from the family depends to a great extent on the level of socio-economic conditions, community-specific culture, and state and civil society interventions.

The three sample sites consist of seven villages in three *mandals*[6] in three districts denoting different situations. Households listed in all the selected sample sites are 1,539, of which 40% own land received from family. Overall, 58% of landed households have land which is obtained from family in the name of women (Table A2.1). We have used the sample of households listed in our survey for the present purpose. However, we have not considered the households that received land from the government to isolate the determinants for women's access to land from the family. The binary logistic model used is as follows:

Logit $(p) = \log(p/1-p) = b0 + b1X1 + b2X2 + b3X3 + b4X4 + b5X5 + u$

Dependent Variable: Women accessing land from family = 1, otherwise = 0
  Independent Variables:
  X1 = Irrigated land situation = 0, Dry land situation = 1, Forest situation = 2
  X2 = Landholding size of household (continuous variable)
  X3 = Number of years of education (continuous variable)
  X4 = Age of the woman (continuous variable)
  X5 = Marital status: Married = 1, otherwise = 0

Table 2.1
Determinants of Women Accessing Land Under Different Situations

Independent Variables	Situation (Dummy)	Land Effect	Education Effect	Age Effect	Marriage Effect
Dry Land Situation	1.167*** (3.21)	1.412*** (4.11)	1.684*** (5.39)	1.831*** (6.24)	1.832*** (6.25)
Forest Situation	0.711*** (2.04)	0.923*** (2.52)	1.414*** (4.11)	1.668*** (5.30)	1.626*** (5.09)
Household Landholding		−0.173*** (0.84)	−0.178*** (0.84)	−0.184*** (0.83)	−0.172*** (0.84)
Years of Education			0.171*** (1.19)	0.261*** (1.30)	0.262*** (1.30)
Age of Woman Respondent				0.044*** (1.05)	0.042*** (1.04)
Marital Status					−0.252 (0.78)
Constant	−1.833	−1.782	−2.545	−4.864	−4.579
Chi Square	72.77	88.87	125.77	202.02	203.80
Log Likelihood	1,572.57	1,556.46	1,519.56	1,443.31	1,441.54
Cox and Snell R-Square	0.046	0.056	0.078	0.123	0.124
Nagelkerke R-Square	0.07	0.085	0.119	0.187	0.189
Number of Observations	1,539	1,539	1,539	1,539	1,539

Source: Field survey 2011–12 (Galab and Revathi 2011).
Notes: Values in brackets indicate odds ratio = p/1−p;
Levels of significance (%): *** 1–5, ** 5–10, * 10–15.

The irrigated land situation is the reference category and the other two situations are analysed with reference to it. Women accessing land from family (natal and marital) is more possible and significantly different in both the dry land and forest situations compared to the irrigated land situation. Among the three situations, the irrigated land situation had the lowest percentage of women having access to land from family—13%. In comparison, the forest situation had the highest percentage of women accessing land at around 33%, while it was around 24% in the dry land situation. The independent variables were introduced into the model one by one. As the landholding size of the household rises, the possibility of women accessing land lessens, but it is higher in the dry land and forest situations compared to the irrigated land situation. In other words, in both these situations, women tend to access more land as the landholding size increases, indicating the positive influence of the coefficient of landholding of household on women's access to land. Land is scarce in the irrigated land situation which might be the reason for women's limited access to land. The level of education of women also has a significant effect on women's access to land which is positive in dry land and forest situations. A higher percentage of women tend to access land as their level of education increases. However, the marital status of women has not made a significant difference in women's access to land. To sum up, the possibility of women accessing land is more in dry land and forest situations in comparison to the irrigated land situation. Household landholding size and the level of education of women also have a positive influence and women tend to get land when they are older (Table 2.1 and Table A2.2).

Does this pattern change when women access land from their natal family? If so what factors matter in women's access to land from inheritance? To probe this dimension, we have taken the sample of women who obtained land from their natal families. The binary logistic model fitted is as follows:

$$\text{Logit}(p) = \log(p/1-p) = b0 + b1X1 + b2X2 + b3X3 + b4X4 + b5X5 + u$$

Dependent Variable = Women accessing land from natal family = 1, otherwise = 0

Independent Variables:
X1 = Irrigated land situation = 0, Dry land situation = 1, Forest situation = 2
X2 = Landholding size of household (continuous variable)
X3 = Number of years of education (continuous variable)
X4 = Age of the woman (continuous variable)
X5 = Marital status: Married = 1, otherwise = 0

The dependent variable is binary taking value 1 when women access land from the natal family and 0 if otherwise. The independent variables are introduced one after the other. The reference is with the irrigated land situation. When compared to the irrigated land situation, the possibility of getting land from the natal family is less in both the dry land and forest situations. Daughters are not given land in these two situations even when the size of the family landholding rises. Though the level of education positively influences women's access to land from the natal family it has no significant impact in both the dry land and forest situations. Age and the marital status of women also do not improve the possibility of getting land from the natal family in the two situations. Overall, the results show that the possibility of women getting land from their natal family is better in the irrigated land situation and the lowest in

Table 2.2
Determinants of Women's Access to Land from Natal Family Under Different Situations

Independent Variables	Situation (Dummy)	Land Effect	Education Effect	Age Effect	Marriage Effect
Dry Land Situation	−2.182*** (0.11)	−2.221*** (0.11)	−2.01*** (0.13)	−2.011*** (0.13)	−1.984*** (0.14)
Forest Situation	−1.199*** (0.30)	−1.086*** (0.34)	−0.604 (0.55)	−0.527 (0.59)	−0.558 (0.57)
Household Landholdings		−0.15 (0.86)	−0.165 (0.85)	−0.199* (0.82)	−0.165 (0.85)
Years of Education			0.119** (1.13)	0.152** (1.16)	0.155** (1.17)
Age of Woman Respondent				0.021** (1.02)	0.019* (1.02)
Marital Status					−0.321 (0.73)
Constant	0.66	0.88	0.262	−0.818	−0.503
Chi Square	65.73	67.66	71.77	75.63	76.52
Log Likelihood	391.16	389.23	385.12	381.26	380.38
Cox and Snell R-Square	0.167	0.171	0.181	0.19	0.191
Nagelkerke R-Square	0.232	0.238	0.251	0.26	0.266
Number of Observations	360	360	360	360	360

Source: Field survey 2011–12 (Galab and Revathi 2011).
Notes: Values in brackets indicate odds ratio=p/1−p;
Levels of significance (%): *** 1–5, **5–10, *10–15.

the dry land situation which is not significantly altered by other factors like landholding of the household, and characteristics such as the level of education, age, or marital status of women (Table 2.2 and Table A2.3).

Pattern of Land Access: Irrigated vis-à-vis Dry Land Geography

Challapally (irrigated land situation) is part of the Krishna delta, and paddy is cultivated in two seasons. Historically, Challapally Samasthanam was ruled by Kamma zamindars. Even now the Kamma community is dominant in terms of landholding and political power. Traditionally, women own land as '*stridhan*' which is passed on to daughters among the upper castes of Kamma and Reddy. Historically, female landownership started in 1903. Landownership by women rose subsequently. For example, in Nandivada, a major panchayat in Krishna district, it was around 8% in 1932 but increased to 33% of the total landownership by 2001. This marked rise was predominantly among the Kamma and Reddy castes (Srinivas 2008). Our study shows that 60% of women received land as daughters. Women accessed land as part of dowry and especially among the upper castes it also paved way for an equal share of the property. Close kin marriages are preferred in irrigated land situation in order to avoid land fragmentation but this practice had started to decline to some extent by the 1970s among the upper castes. The source of accessing land has important implications for a woman's control and management of land. Female empowerment was high because of landownership which was reflected in higher education for women. Land given to the daughter is mostly taken care of by the parents and the proceeds are sent to the daughter. The practice of giving share to daughters in family land has also been followed to some extent by other middle-order landed communities such as Kapu and Balija. Strong natal ties exist in the irrigated geography which is manifested in women accessing land as daughters.

On the other hand, in the dry land geography of Yellanur in Anantapur district, the Reddy community is predominant, economically and politically. Historically, there has been an on-going factional feud between two Reddy families which have tried to have an edge over one another, both by physical annihilation and economic appropriation. Often women are interlocked into the factional politics and economics. The marital family is the predominant source of obtaining land for women in the dry land situation where 85% women received land as wives. Two factors have contributed to the rise in women's access to land from the marital family. The prevalence of the factional feud in the dry land situation may be one reason for women getting land as wives and as widows. Households having higher landholdings are more involved in factions and in such households land is owned by women. Our study shows that 80% of the women in the Reddy community involved in the factional feud have land in their name, whereas in the non-faction households, only 59% women have land in their name. At the same time, daughters are not given land but cash dowry, and they also do not ask for land due to the strong family norm of adequately compensating the daughters with dowry, and asking for a share in land would jeopardize their ties with their natal family. The perception is that giving land to daughters would diminish the economic power of the landed class. But land was put in the name of women to circumvent the Land Ceiling Act of 1973; after 2004, land was increasingly put in the name of women in the Reddy community in order to avail bank loans and crop insurance (FGD in Vennapusapally and Yellanur). Though land is not registered in the women's name, their name is entered in Revenue of Records (RoR) as cultivator and a title deed or 'Pattadar Passbook' (PPB) is issued which facilitates availing of all the government benefits in place for small and marginal farmers. Currently, married women do predominate in accessing land in this situation. There is a caste class convergence in women's access to land in both the irrigated and dry land situations. It is the upper caste women from medium and big farmer households who obtained land from the family though the source varied.

Economic Deprivation and Disempowerment of Koya Women in the Forest Geography

The Koya tribe is dominated and exploited in its own land (Singh 1993). In the forest situation, Koya women are disempowered in the sense that they are not given land at the time of marriage according to their customary law as descent is from the male line. Women have chances of obtaining land from their marital family only as maintenance. Koya girls do not have the right to inherit either the property of their parents or husbands (as the HSA does not apply to the Schedule V areas); they are only entitled to maintenance. Koya girls suffer from insecurity due to the community (Koya) laws of inheritance of property. The insecurity caused by these laws push Koya women into standing on their feet economically. As a result, they are drawn into the public sphere and are exposed to non-tribal situations and, hence, tend to get into marital relations with non-tribal men (Singh 1993). Women have been used as a means for accessing resources through the guise of fictitious marriages by non-tribal men. They make *benami* (fictitious) transactions in land in the form of lease, purchase, or mortgage, and access government programmes for the development of tribals through tribal women. Tribal women are exploited and disempowered at two levels—as women and as individuals (Rao, Bhushan, and Revathi 2001). Traditionally, the 'kulam' panchayat is the dispute settling institution with regard to law but the authority of this institution has been significantly eroded because of various factors, important among them being the challenge from outside through the women. The customary laws have lost their effectiveness because of the penetration of the Indian Penal Code into Koya customary laws and women often lack the skills to negotiate with modern laws when they are cheated. In mainstream situations, land in the possession of a woman results in positive outcomes for the woman, household, and community but in the tribal (Koya) situation, the resources in women's name in most cases would deprive the community and enrich the non-tribal community.[7] More women in this context received land from the marital family as widows.[8]

III

GOVERNMENT INITIATIVES IN ACCESSING LAND BY WOMEN

The AP Occupants of Homesteads (conferment of ownership) Act (Act number 21 of 1976) was passed in 1976. The main objective of this Act 'is to provide for the conferment of right of ownership on landless agriculturists, agricultural labour, and artisans in respect of sites occupied, adjacent to their dwelling houses or huts in rural areas of the state'. This Act empowers the landless and homeless poor to claim rights over occupied sites, but the poor have rarely availed themselves of its benefits due to lack of awareness. Andhra Pradesh had a higher proportion of people without homestead land compared to all India. While the 11th Five-year Plan document fixed the area of homestead land as 10 cents, in Andhra Pradesh the government had been giving homestead plots varying between 3 and 5 cents. The average area of homestead land per household in the state is 3 cents (MOSPI, GoI 2013). The state has witnessed movements for homestead land by the poor, predominantly by women, under the leadership of Left parties during 2005–06 which also resulted in the occupation of agricultural and habitable land.

DISTRIBUTION OF GOVERNMENT WASTELAND

The programme for distribution of government wastelands[9] was taken up with enthusiasm in the post-Independence period and particularly in Andhra Pradesh. Under this programme, 1.7 million hectares of land was distributed (GoI 2008). Andhra Pradesh is one of the states with substantial areas of wasteland under its control and which has also redistributed large areas of government-held land. Most of such allocations took place in the decades of the 1970s and 1980s, and the average land distributed ranged between 2 and 3 acres. By the middle of the decade of 2000, it became evident that the status of land distribution remained on paper. In some cases, it was distributed without formal legal documentation; more powerful interests took possession or encroached on land or a big parcel of land was assigned but not surveyed and partitioned (Akella, Hanstad, and Neilson 2007; Balagopal 2007). Yet a fresh round of land distribution of 'unallocated wasteland' had started in the mid-1990s after it became a major issue in the political agenda during the Congress regime which returned to power under the leadership of Y. S. Rajashekhara Reddy in 2004 (*Business Standard* 2004). The government has taken up 'assignment of government lands to the landless poor' in a big way under the banner of 'One Lakh Acres Land Distribution to Landless Poor' in five phases during 2005–10, constituting nearly 12.5% of the net sown area. Land was distributed in the name of women in III, IV, and V phases. By the end of 2010, 5.4 million acres of government land was distributed among 3.15 million beneficiaries or 2.9 million poor rural households, of whom 24% were Scheduled Castes (SCs) and 28%, were Scheduled Tribes (STs) (CCLA 2011). However, field investigations indicate that perhaps as many as 30% of the reported beneficiaries did not have both legal and physical possession of the allocated land (Hanstad, Nielson, and Brown 2004). Though the alienation of land distributed by the government is prohibited according to the AP Assigned Lands: Prohibition of Transfers (PoT) Act of 1977, government estimates show that at least one million acres of assigned land had been alienated, predominantly by way of white paper transactions or what is called 'Sada Bainama'.

LAND PURCHASE PROGRAMME (LPP)

The then government of Andhra Pradesh had designed its strategy for poverty alleviation with a larger space for women SHGs and women's empowerment (Galab and Chandrasekhar 2003). The strategy was to strengthen women's SHGs and their federations by linking them to credit institutions. It was expected that these institutions would generate micro processes to influence both formal and informal institutions and also policies for betterment of the livelihoods of the poor. This programme earlier called Velugu is now called Indira Kranti Patham or the IKP.[10]

In order to address rural poverty SHG women have been given access to assets of which land is a major component. The IKP land component enables poor women in the rural areas access to land through two programmes, the LPP, and the Land Access Programme (LAP). While the LPP, which the SERP launched in 2004, negotiated the purchase of agricultural land by SHG members from willing private sellers, the LAP launched in the same year facilitated resolving land problems for the poor lacking secure legal rights, in convergence with the Revenue Department.

Land Purchase activity was taken up in 190 villages of 128 *mandals* in the undivided State of Andhra Pradesh with the help of World Bank funding. By 2008–09, 4,539 acres of land was purchased at an expenditure of 293.75 million rupees which benefited 5,303 landless poor women. Of these beneficiaries, 53% belonged to the SC and 37% to the ST communities (SERP 2009).

The LPP made four improvements over earlier reforms: It helped the rural poor to obtain ownership of a 'micro plot' measuring 1/2 to 1 acre, negotiated purchase of lands from willing private sellers, involved the stake of beneficiary families, and involved ownership of the land in the name of the wife or female head of household (SERP 2009). However, the programme could not be taken forward because of less effective community participation and the prohibitive purchase price of land due to collusion, and the programme was wound up by 2009.

In the four years of implementation of the LPP in the present state of Andhra Pradesh, 3,161 women could obtain 4,463 acres of land for a total outlay of 52.38 lakh rupees. Nearly 55% of the beneficiaries were SC women and 37% ST women. The LPP of SERP has shown better agricultural outcomes compared to the land distribution programme and earlier LPPs taken up by the Andhra Pradesh Scheduled Caste Cooperative Finance Corporation in terms of cropping intensity and irrigation facility, which yielded a higher income per acre. The beneficiary households could improve their credit worthiness and could improve their socio-economic status in the village (Rani 2013). The beneficiary households experienced food security, improvements in health and education and lesser migration (Panth and Mahamallik 2008). Women became decision-makers at the household level along with men, which had positive implications for girl children.

Box 2.1

Impact of IKP LPP: Nandigama Mandal in Krishna District

Thirty-one landless women were given land under IKP in Nandigama Mandal in Krishna district. The impact of the LPP was evaluated vis-à-vis the control group of non-beneficiary women from landholding households. Women beneficiaries under LPP were given registered land *patta* (official document stating land title and the term on which land is held). The purchased land was of good quality but only 11% of land was irrigated. About 90% of the land was under food crops. About 20% of women could access agricultural programmes which benefited them. 81% of the women got credit from banks and the average credit accessed was around 22,000 from formal sources. Their financial credibility improved so that they could borrow from non-formal sources of credit also. Women could find a larger space within household. At least 65% said that their spouses helped them in care activities such as cooking, cleaning, and caring for children, ill, and elderly. They could liberate themselves from household drudgery by using improved services and household appliances. In terms of decision-making, women could participate in farm-related decisions and also have effective control by undertaking farm-related activities. Around 70% women have control over the income from land. A higher percentage of women could take strategic decisions related to the family such as the number of children that they should be having, decision on spacing between children, and decision on girls' education. Among the livelihood choices, women were more involved in saving due to their enhanced income from land and dairy activities. The livelihood-related empowerment also percolated to other domains—decision-making in the private domain and also in public domain in terms of participation in collective actions and acting against discrimination.

Source: Field Survey 2010–11 (Galab and Revathi 2011).

LAND ACCESS PROGRAMME

The potential for land access activity arose due to the gap between acclaimed government land distribution and actual possession of land by beneficiaries as noted above. The huge gap between land allocation and possession is clear from the number of land dispute cases stalled in the revenue courts[11] (Hanstad, Neilson, and Brown 2004). In fact, the land distribution programme was mostly target driven and lacked adequate ground work (Rani 2013).

The LAP implemented by SERP is built on a community-based paralegal model.[12] It primarily aims at making the poor aware of their rights, ensuring title and tenure security of lands to the poor by identifying and resolving land issues, and socially empowering the poor to assert their rights. The overriding objective is to transfer knowledge and information to rural communities so that ultimately they are empowered to handle their land issues. The strength of IKP's Land programme is due to the incorporation and penetration into the formal structures which it accomplished through the training of select employees of the district land administration department in every district. The IKP LAP has scored impressive results. Between 2006 and 2010, paralegals and community surveyors identified six lakh land problems of the rural poor involving 11.8 lakh acres of land, of which they helped to resolve 4.3 lakh land problems involving 8.7 lakh acres of land (SERP 2013).

Around two-thirds of the land cases identified pertain to SC and ST families. SERP had also taken an inventory of SC and ST land problems during 2010–12. It identified 21.6 lakh land problems pertaining to 14.6 lakh SC and ST families involving 24.1 lakh acres of land. Of these, around 10 lakh land problems were resolved by organizing village courts in 2012 (SERP 2013). The major land issues are: regularization of government lands distributed, mutation, issue of PPBs (title books), and checking discrepancies in land records (Table 2.3). As a result of its efforts, land issues have become a part of the 'agenda of the poor women's federation'.

There is a long history of problems relating to land in the tribal areas in the state of Andhra Pradesh, with non-tribals occupying lands in scheduled areas and denying access to land to tribals. In spite of protective laws, 48% of lands in V scheduled areas[13] in the state are in the hands of non-tribals (GoAP 2006). The land component of IKP has also extended its reach to tribal land problems through the Legal

Table 2.3

Major Land Issues Identified and Resolved Under LAP

S. No.	Land Issues	No. of Issues	Percentage Poor Involved	Percentage Resolved
1.	Regularization to the eligible sivaijamadars	26,149	99	77
2.	Mutations (succession/purchase/gift/ partition/mortgage/exchange, etc.)	175,554	99	92
3.	Issue of PPB/ title deeds(TD)	59,360	99	82
4.	Correction/entry/discrepancies in revenue records (RoR 1B/PPB/TD)	696,959	88	95
5.	All	1,060,640	92	92

Source: Progress Report, Land Access. Available at: www.gov.ap.in (accessed on 20 June 2015).

Note: Sivaijamadar is government wasteland and title deed given on this land is called Sivaijamadarpatta.

Assistance Programme working in close coordination with Integrated Tribal Development Agency (ITDA).[14] The 'strategy of IKP of evolving Tribal youth/women as paralegals to map and address land issues of the tribals has been proved to be correct provided they are trained adequately and they worked continuously' (Sastry 2006). The physical inventory[15] of lands prepared by the paralegals and community surveyors has resulted in identifying the problems that restrict effective rights on land and its utilization by tribals. Some of the issues identified have been resolved through village courts and the cases pending in civil courts have been resolved through *lok adalats* (people's courts) conducted with support from the District Legal Services Authority. IKP has been successful in giving title to land under the occupation of tribals, getting land titles under the Forest Rights Act,[16] and fresh assignment of land to landless tribals. In the much hailed case of Kumra Manuku Bai of Adilabad district, the family got land assigned to their father by the government after a prolonged legal battle invoking the provisions of the Andhra Pradesh Assigned Lands (Prohibition of Transfers) Act 1977 by the Mandal Samakhya.[17] Though the Mandal Samakhyas are determined to restore lands lost to non-tribals, it is indeed a hard battle due to the fact that the orders of lower courts or local government are not implemented on the plea that cases are pending in upper courts. Restoration of land is delayed by revenue officials even in cases decided in favour of tribals. Mandal Samakhyas need to be more empowered with institutional infrastructure, knowledge, and finances to review all cases decided in favour of non-tribals, and to resolve all land issues faced by the tribals in general and tribal women in particular (Ledger, Kumar, and Mitchell 2011). Thus, LAP appears to have been successful in resolving issues pertaining to the SCs but only to a limited extent in the case of STs as their land is involved with more powerful non-tribal occupants.

The whole experience of land access shows that women are more vulnerable than men in securing formal rights to land. They face a number of difficulties in the process of mutation of records: they face apathy from the officials when approached, and lack of awareness of procedures. Widowed women are particularly vulnerable as the fear of eviction is higher. On the other hand, effective rights on land by having secure title deed has benefited them in a number of ways like access to formal credit, crop insurance, availing government subsidies, and social benefits (ibid.).

WOMEN AS TENANTS OF AGRICULTURAL LAND

The Government of Andhra Pradesh made an intervention in 2004 through the Community Managed Sustainable Agriculture (CMSA)[18] in order to reduce the cost of cultivation as a response to increased agrarian distress in the state, especially in the dry land zones. A separate line of credit has also been earmarked for leasing land to the extent of half an acre by the poorest of the poor women members of the SHGs to undertake paddy cultivation, adopting the system of rice intensification (SRI) in 25 cents of land and vegetables in the remaining 25 cents based on sustainable practices[19] (Note about CMSA). Women were able to lease land without much difficulty as farmers realized the strength of the women backed by collective institutions and readily leased out land to them (SERP n.d.). The increasing number of poor women having access to land through leasing demonstrates strong demand for leasing land (Table 2.4).

The SHG network served as the institutional base for women to lease in land, take up cultivation, and address poverty and household nutrition security through sustainable resource management practices.

The experience of women from SHGs leasing land has in a way led to the proposition of legislation by the GoAP titled 'Andhra Pradesh Women Self Help Groups (Leasing of Agriculture Land) Bill 2009' to provide access to agricultural land for the poor SHG women without land through leasing as well as protecting the interests of lessors and lessees of the agricultural lands. The appropriate policy and legislative framework for leasing (as a group or individual) by SHG members at

Table 2.4
Number of Women Leased Land Under PoP Strategy in CMSA (2005–08)

S. No.	Name of the District	Number of Villages Surveyed	Number of PoP Families Who Have Taken Land on Lease from Resource-rich Families			
			2005	2006	2007	2008
1.	Vizianagaram	44	20	41	63	67
2.	Nellore	50	23	352	287	496
3.	Vishakhapatnam	3	0	12	15	14
4.	Chittoor	15	0	4	8	14
	Total	112	43	409	562	891

Source: Season-end Report, SERP.

market rates and terms, and the support extended for land leasing activities through IKP have the potential to realize positive outcomes (Karuna, Vhugen, and Hanstad 2012).

IV

CONCLUSION

The legal framework in Andhra Pradesh related to land reforms brought women into its focus by the 1986 amendment, popularly called the Andhra Model. According to this, daughters were made coparceners in the joint family property on a par with sons. The HSA 2005 has made women's inheritance rights in agricultural land equal to men's for all states. Given the legal enactments, the question remains as to the actual status of women's access to land. Empirical study shows that in the irrigated land situation, women accessed land from the natal family, whereas in the dry land situation, women accessed land predominantly from the marital family. Though the possibility of women getting access to land from the family is high among upper castes, women's share is yet to be equal to that of men. Women are given land either to circumvent the land ceiling law or to obtain benefits as farmers from different government programmes. The empirical study concludes that geographic and cultural conditions along with the level of socio-economic development to a large degree determine the extent of land obtained from the family. The divergence in the source of the land accessed through the family (natal and marital) in the irrigated and dry land is more related to culture and geography than to socio-economic development. While this is so, the situation in the forest ecology (scheduled areas) of the state has become complicated with the interfacing of gender and land. The interface between women and land in the Koya tribe throws up issues of resource conflict between tribes and non-tribes and women's empowerment.

The limited success of redistributive land reforms has prompted the undivided state of Andhra Pradesh to take up target-oriented distribution of government wastelands in a big way. Another distinctive action of the state was to pioneer a massive social mobilization programme for women which could create an institutional base to play a positive and creative role in taking forward livelihood activities of which land has been recognized as a critical resource. However, the outcome of the government land distribution has been that at least 30% of reported beneficiaries did not have either legal or physical possession of the allotted land. The LAP assumes importance in this context which strives for resolving land issues of various natures and aims at securing land rights for women and others. Another distinct programme taken up by the undivided state was the LPP which met with reasonable success but could not be continued due to its structural limitations. Women's SHG institutions met with success in dealing with tribal land cases regarding title deeds and Recognition of Forest Rights (RoFR) deeds. However, they are not equipped to deal with land lost to non-tribals and its restoration. Targeted government intervention has resulted in a convergence between the landed and landless and women accessing land.

POLICY IMPLICATIONS FOR THE STATE OF ANDHRA PRADESH

The present state of Andhra Pradesh has a very high percentage of landless rural households. A fallout of high landlessness is high incidence of tenancy, especially in the irrigated zone or the Krishna–Godavari delta zone.

A relatively high proportion of women inherit some piece of land, not equivalent to a share in the agricultural land of the family among the upper caste. The implementing agencies, the revenue department, the land survey, and land registration departments are not fully geared to implement the HSAA of 2005. Issuing the required guidelines for the implementation of the Act and ensuring that a gender cell is created in each mandal revenue office with the services of the survey and registration departments available at this single window would ensure that women have a platform to claim their share from family property. Along with this it is also important to ensure that at least 30% of personnel in all these three departments are women, which is already in practice in few states such as Madhya Pradesh and Rajasthan. Research studies have shown that the accountability of local officials in men versus women can either improve or diminish the access of daughters to land inheritance. Moreover, institutional changes that increase the representation of women in local bodies would improve the responsiveness of local authorities to women and contribute positively to the effectiveness of the inheritance reform to improve gender equity (Brule 2012).

In the case of targeted land distribution, the government should attempt to resolve all land issues faced by the beneficiaries to obtain secure land rights and ensure that the land records are kept clean. The recent initiatives of the government of Andhra Pradesh in this direction are noteworthy. SHG institutions can be made more effective in this regard. The land issues of STs should be dealt with from an overall perspective of the tribe vis-à-vis non-tribe, and the state should strive for the restoration of tribal lands from non-tribal control as also emphasized by the Land Committee. The present system of Mandal Samakhya along with District Legal Services and other support systems is ineffective in resolving the tribal land issues vis-à-vis non-tribals. The community-based paralegal programme is a cost-effective system for providing free and legal assistance to the poor and vulnerable on land issues. It needs to be strengthened.

In view of the high prevalence of informal tenancy, there could be an attempt to formalize it by strengthening the Licensed Cultivator Act of 2011. Women may be encouraged to participate in the lease market by enacting the Andhra Pradesh SHG Women (Group Leasing of Agriculture Land) Bill (2009). As the debate is now centred on production-enhancing land reform which encompasses liberal reform of the tenancy market, the proposed enactment would result in a win-win situation for both lessees and lessors. Women inheriting a small piece of land on the supply side and landless and land-poor women on the demand side can participate in the lease market effectively, thus strengthening their livelihoods and enhancing food security. The model pursued by the Deccan Development Society in the state of Telangana for the dry land regions or the Kudumbashree model stand as a few successful examples of women's lease contracts.

In view of the scarcity of land, the homestead land programme could be taken up where landless poor households are given 10 cents of land for carrying out livelihood activities. A homestead act can be enacted for this. Women from the vulnerable households need to be prioritized in the allotment of land by the government.

APPENDIX

Table A2.1
Percentage of Households Having Land and Women Having Land from Family in Selected Sample Sites

Agricultural Situations	District	Mandal	No. of Villages Selected	No. of Listed HH	Landed HH	% of Landed HH to Listed HH	HH Having Land on Woman's Name	% of HH Having Land on Women's Name to All Landed HH
Irrigated land	Krishna	Challapally	3	689	233	34	95	41
Dry land	Anantapur	Yellanur	2	609	270	44	208	77
Forest–Tribal	East Godavari	Chintoor	2	241	119	49	57	48
All			7	1,539	622	40	360	58

Source: Household Listing Data, Field Survey 2011–12 (Galab and Revathi 2011).

Table A2.2
Characteristics of Women-accessed Land from Family in All Situations

Description	%
Number of observations	1,539
All women having land	22.61
Women having land in irrigated land situation	13.21
Women having land in dry land situation	23.65
Women having land in forest situation	32.84
Women having land in age group 18–32	11.28
Women having land in age group 33–47	23.71
Women having land in age group 48–62	32.89
Women having land in age group 63–77	28.23
Women having land in age group 78–92	14.29
SC women having land	7.14
ST women having land	22.89
Backward Caste women having land	14.17
Other Caste women having land	36.46
Women not literate	21.34
Women who can read and write	17.34

(*Table A2.2 Continued*)

(*Table A2.2 Continued*)

Description	%
Women with two years of formal education	21.33
Women with three years of formal education	20.89
Women with four years of formal education	29.48
Women with five years of formal education	29.29
Women with six years of formal education	40.63
Women with seven years of formal education	27.27
Married women	21.12
Widowed/Divorced/Separated	31.65
Women from landless households who got land	7.63
Women from marginal farmer households who got land	50.76
Women from small farmer households who got land	38.28
Women from semi-medium farmer households who got land	21.36
Women from medium farmer households who got land	9.00
Women from big farmer households who got land	44.44
Male-headed households	40.23
Female-headed households	71.45

Source: HH listing data, field survey, 2011–12 (Galab and Revathi 2011).

Table A2.3

Characteristics of Women-accessed Land from Natal Family in All Situations

Description	%
Number of observations	360
Women who got land in irrigated land situation	65.93
Women who got land in forest situation	36.84
Women who got land in dry land situation	17.92
Women who got land in all situations	33.06
Women who got land in 20–34 age group	30.77
Women who got land in 35–49 age group	31.03
Women who got land in 50–64 age group	37.82
Women who got land in 65–80 age group	29.03
Women who got land among SC community	23.33
Women who got land among ST community	38.60
Women who got land among Backward Caste community	22.22
Women who got land among Other Caste community	35.62
Illiterate women who got land	23.40
Literate women who got land	19.57

(*Table A2.3 Continued*)

(*Table A2.3 Continued*)

Description	%
Women with one year of formal education	50.00
Women with two year of formal education	40.43
Women with three years of formal education	47.06
Women with four years of formal education	60.47
Women from landless households who got land	61.70
Women from marginal farmer households who got land	24.39
Women from small farmer households who got land	39.22
Women from semi-medium farmer households who got land	30.43
Women from medium farmer households got land	33.33
Women from big farmer households who got land	75.00
Married women	30.82
Widowed/Divorced	42.65

Source: HH Listing Data, Field Survey, 2011–12 (Galab and Revathi 2011).

NOTES

1. The undivided state of Andhra Pradesh was formed in 1956 by combining the state of Andhra and the Telugu-speaking districts of the erstwhile princely state of Hyderabad. Madras (of which Andhra was a part till 1953) and Hyderabad had different legal and administrative setups regarding land.
2. According to the Hindu Law, *stridhan* is any property belonging to a woman, especially property absolutely at her disposal and going to her heirs upon her death intestate.
3. The Land Committee was constituted by the Government of Andhra Pradesh with Koneru Ranga Rao, the then Minister for Municipal Administration and urban Development, as its chairperson in 2004 'to assess the overall implementation of land distribution programmes of the government, suggest measures for their effective implementation, suggest required changes and amendments to the Acts/Rules for improved enforcement of land related legislations'.
4. The department of Women and Child Welfare, GoI, asked all the states to carry out suitable amendments to Section 6 of the HSA 1956 to give daughters their due share in coparcenary rights. Further, by the mid-1980s, there was a consensus in making policy decisions to provide greater access to land resources to rural women. Among them the important provisions were that at least 40% of eligible women should be given *pattas* for allotment of government land/ceiling surplus land and house sites, all new homestead land distributed to landless families should be only in women's name, and title deeds to be registered jointly (Conference of Revenue Ministers, GoI n.d.).

5. The study was conducted during 2010–12. All households were listed to know the proportion of households owning land and also the proportion of households in which women owned land according to socio-economic categories. The empirical study was conducted in Challapally *mandal* in Krishna district (irrigated geography); Yellanur *mandal* in Anantapur district (dry land geography), and Chintoor *mandal* which is predominantly a Koya tribal *mandal* in East Godavari district[1] which is a V Schedule area (forest geography).
6. *Mandal* is part of a district within a Revenue Division. Revenue Divisions are administrative divisions in the district.
7. The study by Rao et al. (2001) in three *mandals* of Bhadrachalam of Khammam district in undivided Andhra Pradesh selected 313 women who had marital relations with non-tribal men and examined the extent of alienation of tribal resources through women. According to the study, only 1.6% of these 313 women had a proper marital relationship with non-tribal men. The rest were either first or second wives or the marriage was fictitious. Some of them had purchased land (3%) or leased land from tribals (8%) and they also possessed their own house and land in such areas, which is violation of the LTR Act.
8. Of the women who received land in the Koya community, 24% were widows, compared to around 15% in the irrigated and dry land situations.
9. Wastelands are either entirely barren or produce below their economic potential.
10. There is a long history of evolution of the IKP. The AP District Poverty Initiatives Project (APDPIP) and the AP Rural Poverty Reduction Project (APRPRP) culminated in the IKP programme which focuses on rural families through the women's SHG and their federations. The IKP is implemented by the Society for Elimination of Rural Poverty (SERP), an autonomous institution set up by the Government of undivided Andhra Pradesh as part of the state government's rural development department for elimination of rural poverty. SERP is actively functioning under the Panchayati Raj and Rural Development Department in the new state of Andhra Pradesh.
11. An estimated 50,000 land dispute cases had been stalled in revenue courts by 2011, and thousands of other claims and disputes did not enter the formal system because claimants are unaware of their rights and/or are unable to pursue their claims.
12. The LAP was part of a large state rural livelihoods programme, the IKP, implemented by the SERP. The institutional arrangement is that SERP institutes a Land Rights and Legal Assistance Centre at the district level manned by a land manager who is a retired revenue officer and a legal coordinator and is a law graduate. The Centre handles all activities relating to ensuring secure land access to the poor and works in close coordination with the Zilla Samakhya, which is a federation of SHG women at the district level.

13. In the post-Independence period,

    [The] geographical areas designated in V schedule are the same as Scheduled areas as delineated by the British as scheduled areas. The V Schedule applies to the excluded and partially excluded areas (where the agent governed in the name of the Crown but left the local self governing institutions untouched) in states other than the North Eastern states under Article 244(i) of the Constitution. It provides protection to the people living in the scheduled areas from alienation of their land and natural resources to non-tribals. (Bijoy 2003)

14. Land Rights and Legal Assistance Centres have been set up in the ITDAs as support mechanisms in 65 *mandals* in the tribal areas.
15. Physical inventory is a method by which the information available in office records can be verified with people concerned in the *gram sabha* or in one-to-one discussion. *Gram sabha* is a meeting of all adults living in the area covered by the Panchayat.
16. The Scheduled Tribes and Other Traditional Forest Dwellers (Recognition of Forest Rights) Act 2006 is an 'act to recognize and vest the forest rights and occupation in forest land in forest dwelling Scheduled tribes and other forest dwellers who have been residing in such forests for generations but whose rights could not be recorded' (Asian Indigenous and Tribal People Network 2006).
17. See www.rd.ap.gov.in/IKPLand/Manukubai (accessed on 24 July 2015).
18. CMSA is a paradigm shift in moving from an input-centric model to a knowledge- and skill-based model. It involves making the best use of locally available natural resources and takes best advantage of the natural processes.
19. PoP Strategy in CMSA aims to facilitate landless labour to lease land and promote CMSA in this land. The poorest of the poor households will lease 0.5 acre land, and cultivate paddy according to the SRI method on 0.25 acre and adopt the 36×36 model or poly crops on the remaining 0.25 acres. It was, thus, designed to achieve two objectives. One, the PoP family should earn a net income of ₹50,000 in a year and, two, by growing all crops, that is, paddy, vegetables, and pulses, the PoP family will have food security. Apart from selling their produce, they can save something for their own consumption.

BIBLIOGRAPHY

Agarwal, Bina. 2002. *Are We Not Peasants Too: Land Rights and Peasant Claims in India*. SEEDS. New York: Pamphlet series published by the Population Council.

Akella, Karuna, Tim Hanstad, and Robert Nielson. 2007. 'New Life for Land Reform: The Potential in a Decentralized approach.' Unpublished manuscript.

Asian Indigenous and Tribal People Network. 2006. 'India's Forest Rights Act of 2006: Illusion or Solutions.' The Occasional Briefing Paper, New Delhi.

Balagopal, K. 2007. 'Land Unrest in Andhra Pradesh-I Ceiling Surpluses and Public Lands.' *Economic and Political Weekly* 42 (38): 3829–33.

Bijoy, C. R. 2003. 'The Adivasis of India—A History of Discrimination, Conflict and Resistance.' Indigenous Affairs, International Working Group for Indigenous Affairs (IWGIA), Copenhagen, Denmark 1/10, March 2001, pp. 54–61.

Brule, Rachel. 2010. 'Changes in India's Property Rights Regime and the Implementation for Improved Gender Parity.' Available at: http://ssrn.com/abstract (accessed on 24 July 2015).

———. 2012. 'Gender Equity and Inheritance Reform: Evidence from Rural India.' Available at http://rachelbrule.files.wordpress.com/2012/brule_paper/final.pdf (accessed on 10 May 2017). *Business Standard*. 2004. 'AP Government Announces Distribution of One Lakh Acres of Surplus Land.' *Business Standard*, November 11.

Centre for Economic and Social Studies. 2006. 'Andhra Pradesh District Poverty Initiative Project/Indira Kranthi Patham.' End Term Appraisal Report, Hyderabad.

Chief Commissioner for Land Administration (CCLA). 2011. *Land Administration Report*. Hyderabad: Government of Andhra Pradesh.

Conference of Revenue Ministers, GoI. n.d. *Theme Paper on Enhancement of Property Rights Including Land Rights of Women*. Annexure XI.

Deininger, Klaus, Aparajita Goyal, and Hari Nagarajan. 2009. 'Can Change in Inheritance Legislation Improve Women's Access to Physical and Human Capital? Evidence from India's Hindu Succession Act.' Available at www.isid.ac.in/pu/seminar/16_04_2010, Paper.doc (accessed on 20 July 2015).

Galab, S., and N. Chandrasekhara Rao. 2003. 'Women and self-help groups: Poverty Alleviation and Empowerment.' In *Andhra Pradesh Development: Reforms and Challenges Ahead*, edited by C. H. Hanumantha Rao and S. Mahendra Dev, 462–87. Hyderabad: Centre for Economic and Social Studies.

Galab, S., and E. Revathi. 2011. 'Existing State Policies, Programmes, Interventions and Processes and Their Impact on Women's Access to Land.' Report submitted to the Ministry of Agriculture, New Delhi.

Government of Andhra Pradesh (GoAP). 2014–15. *Socio-economic Survey Report*. Hyderabad: Planning Department.

———. 2016. *Socio-economic Survey Report*. Hyderabad: Planning Department.

Government of India (GoI). 2000. *National Agricultural Policy*. New Delhi: Government of India.

———. 2007–08. *Annual Report*. New Delhi: Ministry of Rural Development.

Government of India (GoI). 2008. *Report of the Committee on State Agrarian Relations and the Unfinished Task in Land Reforms*. New Delhi: Department of Land Resources, Ministry of Rural Development.

———. 2010–11. *All India Report on Number and Area of Operational Holdings 2010–11*. New Delhi: Agricultural Census, Department of Agriculture and Cooperation Ministry of Agriculture.

Goyal, A., K. Deininger, and H. K. Nagarajan. 2009. 'Can Changes in Inheritance Legislation Improve Women's Access to Physical and Human Capital? Evidence from India's Hindu Succession Act, Development Economics Research Group, World Bank, Washington DC. Available online http://www.researchgate.net/publication/228552917 (accessed on 10 May 2017).

Groppo, P., ed. 2003. *Land Reform Land Settlement and Cooperatives*. Special Edition, World Bank and Rural Development Division, FAO. Available at: http://www.fao.org/sd/ltdirect/landrf.htm (accessed on 15 June 2015).

Hanstad, Tim, T. Haque, and Robert Nielson. 2008. 'Improving Land Access for India's Rural Poor.' *Economic and Political Weekly*, 43 (10): 49–56.

Hanstad, Tim, Robin Nielson, and Jennifer Brown. 2004. 'Land and Livelihoods: Making Land Rights Real for India's Rural Poor.' FAO of the United Nations, Livelihood Support Programme Working Paper 12, Rural Development Institute, USA.

Kodandaram, M. and M. Laxmaiah. 2007. 'Land Reforms—Promising Much, Delivering Little.' In *Rekindling Hope? Access, Retention and Development of Land—A Dalit Perspective*, edited by Thomas Pallithanam. Hyderabad: Andhra Pradesh Social Watch.

Land Committee Report. 2006. Report submitted to the Government of Andhra Pradesh, Hyderabad.

Landesa. 2013. 'The Formal and Informal Barriers in the implementation of the Hindu Succession (Amendment) Act.' Report of Rural Development Institute. Available at: www.landesa.org/wp-content/uploads/hsaa-study-report.pdf (accessed on 20 June 2015).

Law Commission of India. 2000. 174th Report on 'Property Rights of Women: Proposed Reforms under the Hindu Law'. D.O.No.6 (3) (59)/99-LC (LS). New Delhi: Law Commission of India.

Ledger, Deena, Sunil Kumar, and Robert Mitchell. 2011. 'Land Rights, Paralegals, and Poverty: How Paralegals in Andhra Pradesh Improve the Lives of Rural Poor—A Study Report.' Report of Rural Development Institute, Hyderabad.

Mitchell, Robert, and Tim Hanstad. 2008. 'Innovative Approaches to Rural Landlessness in Andhra Pradesh: A Report on the Experience of the IKP Land Activities.' Report prepared for the Andhra Pradesh Department of Rural Development and the Society for Eradication of Rural Poverty, Hyderabad.

MOSPI, GoI. 2013. 'Key Indicators of Situation of Agricultural Households in India.' NSSO Report of 70th Round, MOSPI, GoI.

National Sample Survey Office (NSSO). 2014. National Sample Survey Report Number 554. Employment and Unemployment Situation in India, 68th Round 2011–12. National Sample Survey Office, Ministry of Statistics and Programme Implementation, Government of India.

Note about Community Managed Sustainable Agriculture (CMSA), Society for Elimination of Rural Poverty, Government of Andhra Pradesh. Available at: 65.19.145.141/cmsa/ui/cmsamodules/Home Page.Html (accessed on 24 July 2015).

Panth, S. Ananth, and M. Mahamallik. 2008. 'Impact Assessment of IKP Land Purchase Scheme in Andhra Pradesh.' Report submitted to Society for Elimination of Rural Poverty (SERP), Government of Andhra Pradesh, Hyderabad.

Parthasarathy, G., and K. Suryanarayana Raju. 1971. 'Andhra Pradesh (Andhra Area) Tenancy (Amendment) Act, 1970: A Critical Review.' *Economic and Political Weekly*, 16 (13): A45–A47.

Planning Commission. 2008. *Approach Paper to the IX Five Year Plan (1997–2002)*. New Delhi: Planning Commission.

———. 2011. *Report of the Twelfth Plan Working Group on Disadvantaged Farmers Including Women*. New Delhi: Planning Commission.

Rani, Ch. Radhika. 2013. *Empowerment of Landless: An Analysis of Land Distribution and Land Purchase Programmes of Andhra Pradesh*. Research Report Series 99. Hyderabad: National Institute of Rural Development, Ministry of Rural Development, GoI.

Rao, Janardhan B., Bharath Bhushan, and E. Revathi. 2001. 'Deserted Adivasi (Koya) Women in Godavari Valley in Andhra Pradesh.' Unpublished manuscript, KRUSHI, Warangal.

Revathi, E. 2012. 'Land Access to Women and Women Empowerment Under Different Situations in Andhra Pradesh.' Report submitted to ICSSR under Senior Fellowship Programme, Kakatiya University, Warangal.

Roy, K. C., and C. A. Tisdell. 2000. 'Property Rights in Women's Empowerment in Rural India: A Review.' Working Paper No 14, Working Papers on Social Economics, Policy and Development ISSN, University of Queensland.

Roy, Sanchari. 2008. 'Female Empowerment through Inheritance Rights: Evidence from India.' STICERD Working Paper, London School of Economics, London.

Sastry, V. N. V. K. 2006. 'Study on Indira Kranthi Patham's Work on Tribal Land Issues.' Report submitted to Rural Development, Government of Andhra Pradesh, Andhra Pradesh.

Saxena, N. C. 2013. *Enhancement of Property Rights and Land Rights of Women*. Theme Paper. Delhi: Planning Commission, Government of India.

Singh, Kumar Suresh. 1993. *Tribal Ethnography, Customary Law and Change*. New Delhi: Concept Publishers.

Singh, Ranbir, Vijender Kumar, and Vidyullatha Reddy. 2004. *Coparcenary Rights of Women in Andhra Pradesh*. Project Report. Hyderabad: NALSAR University of Law.

Society for Elimination of Rural Poverty (SERP). 2002. *Operational Manual: Increasing the Rural Poor's Access and Rights to Rural Land*. Hyderabad: Andhra Pradesh Department of Rural Development.

———. 2008–09. *IKP Annual Report*. Hyderabad: Andhra Pradesh Department of Rural Development.

———. 2009. Indira Kranthi Patham: 'Land Purchase and Land Access for the Poor.' Available at www.rd.ap.gov.in/ikpland/ikp-note-mar-2010.pdf (accessed on 12 February 2015).

———. 2013. Indira Kranthi Patham, Annual Report 2013–14, Department of Rural Development, GoAP, Hyderabad.

Srinivas, DBN. 2008. 'Land Caste and Economic Mobility: A Village in Coastal Andhra.' In *Rural Transformation-perspectives from Village Studies in Andhra Pradesh*, edited by G. N. Rao and D. N. Reddy, 351–402. New Delhi: Daanish Books.

Subramanyam, S. 2000. 'Agricultural Tenancy in India: Growth Promoting or Growth Retarding.' *Arth Vijnana* 42 (4): 360–66.

Vakati, Karuna, Darryl Vhugen, and Tim Hanstad. 2012. 'Land Leasing by Women in Andhra Pradesh: Seeking Security and Reducing Risk.' In *Land Policies for Inclusive Growth*, edited by T. Haque, 370–400. Delhi: Concept Publications.

Vakulabharanam, Vamsi, N. Purendra Prasad, K. Laxminarayana, and Sudheer Kilaru. 2011. 'Understanding the Andhra Crop Holiday Movement.' *Economic and Political Weekly* XLVI (50): 13–16.

3

Engendering Tribal Land Rights for Gendering the Land: A Case Study Among Apatani and Nyishi Communities[1]

RIMI TADU

Understanding land relations among ethnic communities can be a complex and an overwhelming exercise because of the sheer diversity in their practices and land relation. Arunachal Pradesh, the easternmost Himalayan region of India, hosts diverse geological, ecological, climatic, and topographical conditions making it conducive to host equally diverse ecologies. Arunachal is considered as one of the 18 'biodiversity hotspots' in the world (Compensatory Afforestation Fund Management and Planning Authority 2013–14).[2]

However, very often it is its strategic geo-political location which largely determines the course of development policies in the state. The post-Independence period was marked with the militarization of the state with slow rate of development interventions and strong national integrative activities. But post-economic liberalization in India, there was a shift in policy for Northeast India, in general, and for Arunachal, in particular. These changes created unique social realities in the state. As Southeast Asia became the new 'West', the 'Look East Policy' (the present government in the centre calls it 'Act East Policy') was formulated for the northeastern region.

Any structural economic planning requires a 'political stability' (state control) and conducive environment (infrastructure) on the ground. This is creating newer pressures on redefining the land relations in these states. Under the circumstance people are becoming conscious and are reasserting their claims and rights on their land; and within the communities, women are negotiating for their land rights. Nevertheless, it is leaving a distressing footprints on the tribal lands and correspondingly on their lives.

The chapter is based on field interviews with men and women from Apatani and Nyishi communities of Arunachal Pradesh. Both are among the prominent communities in the state and have very different or opposing economies of land relation and social customs. While Nyishis, the largest group in the state, practise *jhum* cultivation and occupy the largest area in the state, Apatanis, valley-based settled cultivators, have elaborate land use practices. The detailed discussion will show that both the communities broadly represent the diverse range of land relations existing in the state and are going through similar experiences and struggles under the standardized development plans.

The chapter attempts to draw attention to overarching intersections and gaps in the academic and policy approaches, formulations regarding the land relations within these communities, and new emerging trends. It will outline its arguments by proposing two interconnected approaches: first, by engendering the urgent need for ethnic and ethnographic understanding of land and not merely statistical and materialistic evaluation which means evaluation and assessment of land based on more organic or native terms, secondly, by introducing work towards the formation of 'tribal feminism'[3] with an approach with special focus on women's land relation and their economy. This further leads to the larger question of women's status in tribal societies, already under wide debate.

The predominance of women's role in the agricultural economy of tribal communities makes women as the main provider of the household (though this is hardly getting recognized), the land being the primary resource, upon which women labour is controlled by men due to the traditional customs. Thus, women hold a subjugated status. However, under the current political economy of developments policy governing the formal land laws, the women's situation can become more precarious (IWBN 2007; IWGIA 1999, 2004).

The study draws from various interactions with members of women's organizations, village headmen, lawyers, etc., and by using participant observation in the field. Being an Apatani woman, one can recognize the possibilities of subjective biases, and might carry and acknowledge the unique advantages. It gives one a unique access to a particular world view and subjective lived experience as an insider. Finally, the chapter looks at such conflicting pitching of women's rights versus tribal rights and argues instead that both the processes should be seen as complementary and embedded within each other.

READING LAND

The policy makers use their own framework to understand the land or the territories. One of such most remarkable works is the government gazetteers. They work through abstract maps created by field-level surveyors with names indexed to grid-like units of scales superimposed over it. Then the people are categorized, numbered, and described in groups over laid out maps. Nature and environment are identified as resources (material capitals). Such processing of land gives an abstract, ordered, fixed, and standardized visual schema which make regulation, interpretation, control, and manipulation for a planned development easier for planners.

This does two things to the cognitive capability of the policy makers and development planners on the one hand, and thus creates a conflicting situation between the administrators and field implementers and the people on the other hand.

The first thing such process of abstraction does is that it de-naturalizes[4] the perception of land. Abstracting and co-modifying land merely into a resource disassociate land from its natural qualities, characteristics, and cultural meanings embodied in it. As a result, the natural characters of terrains and their ecological environment tend to be seen as obstructions to development plans. For instance, the Border Road Organization, with its military origin, ironically uses the metaphor of 'enemy' for the nature; hence, one often notices self-declarations such as 'We have conquered the nature' or 'We are Mountain Tamers' on the roadside. The nature, after the 'conquest', is then feminized with another set of double-meaning laden sexist signposts such as 'Be gentle on my curves' and 'Enjoy the beauty of Hill Queen'. Secondly, such abstraction alienates the land from its people. It sees people and land as separate entities and their relation as a utilitarian one, where people are to exploit land. The problem with such abstraction is that after a certain level of abstraction, even people become a mere demographic category and the 'development' becomes the primary focus. Thus, displacing and dispossessing a category of people from their land for development projects to benefit another category of people becomes a requisite.

On the other hand, the people in the traditional communities are very ontologically related to their land (D'Souza and Changmi NA: 13).[5] Land forms part of people's environment, their lived reality, culture, source of identity, and framework for their worldview. Land as terrain had bounded them to an area, separated them from others, provided them refuge, resources, and occupation. It is through such engagement and investment in their land that their sense of familiarity and belongingness to their land and the landscape are formed. This in return recreates the sense of a homeland and a heritage centrally located in their distinct identity formation (Leo 2015; Narzary 2015; Xaxa 2008). Therefore, in order to understand these relations one has to ethnicize the land by determining its sociocultural meanings and values rather than abstracting it out as mere resource or material. Alienating people from their land which they are so intricately related to is not a mere economic extradition but it tantamount to ethnic genocide—not by physical extermination but by destroying their identity.

It is only after such exercise of ethnically redefining the land that one should move into a deeper exploration of understanding the gendered roles and relations to land.

Women's situation in these communities could be one of the most important critiques of patriarchy in general, and of a form of patriarchy masked in the communitarian system in particular. In Arunachal, women's claims on land rights and communities' claims for recognition of customary rights are often set in opposition. Attempts to claim women's land rights under the customary laws by women's organizations get opposed in the name of customary rules and systems. While on the other hand, the demands for the recognition of customary laws and people's land rights as legal rights by several indigenous groups and political leaders in the state were blocked by women's rights organization in past. Such situation easily gets polarized to be pitched against each other and find logjam from where none move forward.

STATUS OF LAND RIGHTS IN ARUNACHAL PRADESH

Among the northeastern states, the Sixth Schedule (in tribal dominant districts in Tripura and Assam and whole of Meghalaya) or Articles 371A (Nagaland) and 371G (Mizoram) gives formal recognition of customary laws and institutions, and confers the land rights to the tribal communities. However, in Arunachal, the subject remains ambiguous as there is no comprehensive and coherent land law or legal status that categorically confers land rights on the people. Instead, there are numbers of both national and state policies, regulations, and laws that are synonymously interpreting and delimiting the land laws and relations in the state creating further ambiguity and dilution of people's control over their land and land-related resources.

For instance, considering the diverse and complex land relations in the region, according to the Assam Frontier (Administration of Justice) Regulation 1945 (Amended in 2005), the traditional councils were left to deal with land issues according to customary laws. According to the Act, the village councils such as Mel among the Nyishis, Kebang among the Adis, or in other cases, government appointed *Gaon Buras* (government's agent) in the village to deal with land-related issues. Then there are similar provisions under National Forest Rights Act 2006 and Scheduled Tribes and Other Traditional Forest Dwellers Act 2006 which recognize and guarantee people's control and access over their land and its resources.[6] But such provisions are then equally nullified by contradictory provisions such as the Balipara, Tirap, Sadiya Frontier Tracts Jhum Land Regulation, 1947, and the draft Arunachal Pradesh Forest Amendment Act, 2014, which establish the deputy commissioner (DC) as the legitimizing authority at local level. The DC is 'advised' to follow the customary and local norms in exercising his/her authority; yet again it is his or her 'discretion' whether to adhere or legitimize any traditional custom or councils. Similarly, under the Arunachal Pradesh (Land Settlement and Records) Act, 2000, it is the department rather than the community who is to identify or redefine the land either as community land, individual land, forest land, or government revenue land. The department is supposed to consult the respective community but there is hardly any land called 'Forest Land' or 'Government Revenue Land' as a separate entity of land. Such provisions erode communities' agency in upholding their practices and rights as the owner of the land.

There are other sets of Acts and policies such as the National Forest Policy, 1952; the Forest Conservation Act, 1980; the State Land Acquisition Act, 1990; the National Highway Act, 1956; Arunachal Pradesh Industrial Policies, 2001 (amended in 2008); Arunachal Pradesh Public Premises (Eviction of Unauthorized Occupants) Act, 2003; and State Rehabilitation and Resettlement Policy, 2008, that authorize the government to acquire any patch of land either from a community or from an individually owned land for 'public purpose'. Many of these Acts do have procedures for public meetings and compensation packages but largely these are procedures that ensure one way transfer of land from people to state. On 29th January 2015, the Ministry of Environment & Forests (MoEF) granted general approval for 35 defence infrastructure projects in border areas of which 11 projects are alone for Arunachal which is going to affect 11,667 acres of forest area (*Indian Express* 2015). The project includes diversion of forest areas for highways and other road projects for Indo-Tibetan Border Police, Border Security Force, and Shashakt Seema Bal. Prioritizing these projects for better military functions the MoEF relaxed and bypassed several norms guaranteeing tribal land rights such as the mandatory public hearing process. The Defense Ministry even sought exemption from the purview of Forest Rights Act and Forest Clearance Act.

These policies meant for people's welfare end up competing and encroaching against the people in claiming land, and, ironically, term people's assertion as illegitimate or anti-development. It is evident that the ongoing land ordinance bills are only making such state assertions unquestionable.

JHUM CULTIVATION VERSUS DEVELOPMENT-INDUCED DISPLACEMENT

In Arunachal, except for few communities such as Apatanis and Khamptis, most communities are traditionally practising shifting or mixed form of cultivation.[7] Their sociocultural matrices and economies are woven around agriculture. The Jhum Land Regulation Act, 1947, acknowledges the intrinsic relation between *jhum* practices and people. Yet the same Act also establishes the position of a 'land conservator' or DC or forest ranger as the ultimate authority to notify the land use and give permissions for *jhum* cultivation. Further, Section 10 says,

> [T]he government can acquire any Jhum land required for public purpose. *No formal* acquisition proceedings shall be necessary but an opportunity shall be given to those having rights in the land to show cause against such acquisition and reasonable compensation shall be paid for all land required under this section. (Emphasis added)

The underlying belief of the state was that *jhum* cultivation is destructive for forest and environment and cause wastage of land. Several studies have debated against such assumptions and criticized such policies as colonial and biased. Yet increasingly people are dissuaded from *jhum* practices and encouraged to take up settled cultivation or alternative land use. Inducements such as ₹200–300 for per bigha paid to families for developing irrigated land, tied funds under the watershed programmes, Panchayat funds, and MGNREGA hold funds for 'land development' activities (Maithani 2005: 21). In 2013, the state agriculture department reported that between 2003 and 2013, the total area under *jhum* cultivation had declined from 110,000 hectares to 84,000 hectares. The recent draft bill Arunachal Pradesh Forest Act, 2014, Section 10(4) says, 'This practice of Jhum cultivation shall in all cases be deemed to be a *privilege* subject to (be) control(led), restriction and abolition by the State Government and *not to be (considered as) a right.*' Such laws are increasingly restricting and redefining the traditional controls over land and by circumvention, they establish the state as the ultimate authority over all the land.

As a result of large-scale transformations, new socio-economic stresses are emerging with varying effect on people's lives and attitudes, as they are gradually moving away from their traditional occupation as cultivators. As new livelihood 'choices' compel people to migrate from their traditional areas, a new cycle of vulnerabilities such as landlessness is set on (Fernandes 2009: 350–63). People in interior Nyishi villages migrate to more urban localities where the modern formal laws and institutions have not yet set any mechanism to receive or settle the new settlers. Often it leads to a conflicting situation whereby people who are still following their traditional norms and customs find themselves on the wrong page of the formal laws.

The following case study might highlight some of these aspects.

Nabam Yana,[8] a 48-year-old woman with a son and a daughter, lives in the Pakhe Panchayat segment near the capital city, Itanagar. She is originally from Talo village. Her eldest sister was promised to her husband for marriage but she died as soon as she joined the husband's family. As a bride was promised from the family, the second eldest daughter was given for marriage as per the custom. But same happened with her as well. Finally, Yana's now mother-in-law decided to bring and raise Yana as a toddler by herself. Later, a feud broke in the village and Yana's husband's family had to go down to the plains of Assam where some of the Nyishi families were settled. After sometime, they returned to the hills and settled near Yazali where she joined her husband. The new land was not as productive. Her husband came down to Itanagar in search of some work. She joined the husband too with children left in the village.

Itanagar was a newly emerging town and many non-local communities were settling there. They lived in a rented house; while her husband found some labour work, she tried some odd jobs such as selling vegetables, local drinks, firewood, etc. But soon as they were planning to bring their children along for their proper schooling, the landowner asked them to vacate the place. So they, along with a few other families, started looking for a place to construct their own houses. They found a patch of land little in the outskirt of the main town as most areas were already occupied by earlier settlers. The land was under the forest department. The department had earlier tried to bring this patch of land under some utility. Once there was a tea garden, then a children's park cum forest garden, thereafter, it was converted into a vegetable greenhouse farm, etc., with forest reclaiming it in intervals. Finally, it was left fallow when Yana and her husband and other families started levelling the land. At first, a group of people from a nearby village came and claimed their rights over the land. Three rounds of *Mel'* were called whereby the claimant proved their ownership based on their oral tradition; the new settlers (Yana's family and others), thus, requested their permission to settle there. The case was amicably resolved and houses were constructed. It was only after then when the forest department started intervening to vacate the land and claimed that the land belonged to the government.

But the families were determined not to budge; for them the matter had already been settled with the 'original owners'. This led to several harassment meted by the families as they were often threatened, beaten, and even jailed. The case was taken to the court where they won the case. However, in the meantime they also managed to manoeuvre political support from a local MLA who helped them to get the area recognized as a panchayat constituency. Initially, there were some 20 families who took the Land Possession Certificate (LPC) and constructed their houses. Soon, several newer families joined and took on the adjacent lands. At present there is a panchayat office, a primary school, a few poultry farms under a government scheme, road connections, rice fields and vegetable garden, churches, etc.

The area got expanded into two more new villages. These villages, unlike the traditional one, are heterogeneous villages consisting of Nyishi, Apatani, Adi, Gallong, and Miri from different parts of the state. They have formed their own village development committee to look after the welfare and development of the village and land. Though this is a new institution, it has traditional characteristics. Whenever a new family joins, they informally organize a small feast and invite the committee members to introduce themselves. Yana asks if government lands are not for the benefit of the poor people like us, of what use are they?

People are innovative and actively engage with their environment. Their customary laws are always responsive (and contextual) to their conditions and times. Thus, the customary laws and traditional agreements hold more sense and legitimacy to them than the alien formal laws. In the above case, as soon as the new village emerged, the traditional structures and customs automatically came into being as unsaid norms. Though the village composition changed, as all settlers were from different regions and different ethnic groups, their response and conformation towards the customary laws were similar.

On the other hand, despite the formal, fixed, and authoritative bearings of the formal laws, people have actually managed to mould and negotiate/reinterpret it to their benefits according to their situation. The ambiguity within the formal laws (as discussed earlier) and the narrow scope of understanding the customary laws and lived realities of the people had rendered formal laws irrelevant and ineffectual in dealing with complex local situations. With nothing to lose, such situations compel people to either overlook the laws or to reinterpret them. Thus, the interface between the traditional people and the formal law is much fluid than it is believed.

Also, there are few trends which are newly emerging, especially among the communities practising shifting cultivation, due to the new political economy of the state-led development paradigm. First, as more and more people are opting for a permanent settlement, the community lands are getting divided into individually owned lands. With this, there is a gradual exclusion of women from land economy as individual-based inheritance is drawn on the male lineage system, though traditionally the land was commonly owned without gender division. Further, the commercialized farming and market-based production activities are largely male dominated, unlike in traditional economy where women have more roles, showing a regressive trend for women's status (Fernandes and Barbora 2002).

Secondly, increasing individualization of community land also leads to accumulation of land in fewer elite hands as new politico-economic classes are emerging. As people are becoming more and more conscious of land as a 'property' the land relations are taking a major shift. This is a common phenomenon across the region as individual-based formal laws are being superimposed over the customary community common land system (Fernandes 2009; Fernandes, Pereira, and Khatso 2005).

Third, the state has emerged as a strong competitor to the people. Without specifying the actual ownership and terms of rights over the land, the people and the state are competitors for acquiring and controlling the land. Here, in Arunachal, people's land rights hang thinly on their ability to assert their rights on customary grounds or in innovative engagement with the ambiguous formal laws (discussed further in more detail). People's assertion to be recognized as the primary owner of the land (Ete 2014) and hence their demand to be consulted and involved in negotiations between the state and the companies/contractors/investors, whenever development projects are planned, is seen as an unnecessary obstruction, and as an anti-development and even anti-government move.

Thus, there is a need for a newer understanding of land—the ethnic identity of land. Land, as a terrain has been interpreted by development policy makers as an obstruction that has kept its people isolated and backward. However, it is only a perceptive insider who can tell that such distances were actually carefully maintained by these communities. It was necessary for maintaining sociopolitical autonomy of their respective homelands. To sustain their resources, the surrounding hills, forests, streams, and rivers formed traditionally and mutually agreed buffer boundaries. Nevertheless, this seldom restricted inter-village and intra-village interactions. Marriages, sociopolitical alliances, economic exchanges, and even encroachments and several blood feuds were carried across communities and villages. Therefore, the land has a very ethnic location to their identity. It should be understood in terms of people's perspective of their land as a homeland, a heritage—the artefacts of their past earmarked across their land, a sacred geography—the land and mountains where the spirits of their ancestors dwell, and a life sustaining resource.

For instance, the Apatani community which occupies a single area has uniquely engaged with their land and surrounding environment over the centuries to create their unique homeland with its unique ecology and economy that has become part of their distinct identity. According to Betsy Taylor (2009), their valley is 'one of the most intensively cultivated and ecologically sustainable economies ever achieved anywhere in the world'. In a way, their entire culture and traditional practices are embodied in their relation to their lands. It brings the context to their ethnicity and ethnic identity. This land is irreplaceable. Any drastic change either to the land or to the people will automatically affect other's identities and lifestyle. Therefore, these lands are ethnic lands.

NYISHI COMMUNITY

According to the 2011 Census, Nyishi[10] is the largest community in the state with a population of 121,475. They live in seven contiguous districts: Upper Subansiri, Lower Subansiri, West Kameng, East Kameng, Papumpare, Kurung Kumey, and Kra Dadi districts. According to their oral traditions, after entering the present Arunachal from the North in time unknown, they followed two migration routes along two river systems: the Subansiri (running north to south) and the Kurung (running north-west to east) river. The migration took place in waves. As a result, the entire region was under constant movement of settling communities in search of fertile and suitable land. As some earlier settlers found their fertile land, they decided to settle permanently and hence practised settled cultivation and soon evolved their own niche with their environment and neighbouring communities. They have a distinct sense of exclusive clan villages occupying permanent, individual, and inheritable land location. They maintain the communitarian and cooperative systems where even though the land is owned individually, its sociopolitical management is done by the clan collectively. *Jhum* cultivation, the only suitable form of cultivation in hilly terrains, is a labour-intensive practice. It requires more collective and cooperative work. Irrespective of who owns the particular plot of land, the entire clan decides upon the area where the *jhum* cycle is to be carried out. After the clearing done collectively, the land plot then gets divided among the entire village households to be cultivated individually. In the *jhum* fields, the households grow all necessary items such as millet, rice, maize, green vegetables, sweet potatoes, tapioca, chilies, ginger, pumpkins, beans, cucumber, yam, tobacco, and cotton, unlike in terrace fields where only rice is grown. The remaining household requirements such as bamboo, cane, wild fruits and vegetables, herbs, hunting games, firewood, wood for constructions are all collected from the surrounding community forests.

The latter settlers had to come down to further lower belts. Here the villages are more fluctuating due to frequent migration necessitated by less fertile land and shifting cultivation. In the hilly terrains, the fertile soil cover is thin and loose, the soil fertility depletes soon and so the nearby forest resources cause the groups to shift their settlement every four to eight years. Sometimes, it is the inter- or intra-village feuds, sometimes some epidemic, and sometimes inspiration comes from spirits to leave a certain place.[11] As a result, permanent, absolute, and individual-based landownership was never practicable. The community is in constant move. Yet it is seldom a random process. They are guided by their customary practices and institutions and village elders and priests who would organize the shifting process. Recent studies have shown how shifting cultivations are ecologically most suitable in fragile forest and soil environment. The land is though commonly owned by the community, yet each land area is distinctively recognized as belonging to respective clans and villages. Their oral traditions also keep the records of the earliest or the original settlers and the subsequent settlers. The new settlers pay tributes to original settlers and acknowledge their original ownership. As land is commonly owned, there is no distinction between men and women to its access.

APATANI COMMUNITY

Apatanis present a very different context with their permanent settled villages and cultivation fields (population 43,777, Census 2011). They are virtually surrounded by their Nyishi neighbours with whom they share common origin and migration myths. According to their oral traditions at the time of creation, unlike their Nyishi counterpart, they chose the settled rice cultivation. The centuries of settled way of life afforded by their permanent cultivation practice have two significant implications for their land relation: first, the advancement of an energy-efficient cultivation method making it possible to repeat cultivation on the same plot without affecting its productivity which otherwise would have compelled shifting cultivation; secondly, the development of elaborate land use, ownership, and customary norms and laws related to property ownership. Their landlocked valley compelled a kind of involution where they had to limit their expansion and reorganize their land use more conscientiously by evolving elaborate cultural systems and defined customary laws that could sustain the entire population within the limited area, and allaying any possible friction within the densely populated valley.

There is individually owned (*Ato Kiidi*) land, with absolute rights of the owner to control, use, dispose of, and manage, and the common clan land (*Boot Kiidi*) used and managed by community, though available for individual reclamation whenever necessary by the following rules. The common land Acts like a land reserve which any needy person fallen out of fate can utilize and rebuild their life. The individual land includes the housing sites located within the clan colony or village,[12] the bamboo gardens, the nurseries, wet rice fields, dry fields, pine groves, and maintained forests. The community land includes burial ground, grazing ground, rivers, and sacred alter sites which are commonly used. The forest lands which are located farther away also form the part of common land as they require more collaborative efforts for maintenance. Thus, the ritual sanctity and clan exclusivity of a clan village is maintained through laws of inheritance by the following strict primogeniture where the eldest son inherits the ancestral/traditional properties (*Alo Khu*) including the ancestral house site within the village (if any) and the younger one gets the land property acquired by the father during his lifetime. This is also a way of retaining one's location (lineage) within the clan and ancestral village. Thus, the land becomes the centre of one's identity and through the customary laws of inheritance the sanctity of ancestral village lands are maintained. Therefore, landholding is not only associated with one's wealth and social status but also with one's stakeholdership within the clan and the community.

FEMINIZING TRIBAL AGRICULTURAL ECONOMY AND RE-LOOKING AT WOMEN'S 'STATUS'

Even at the risk of being repetitive, it is worth reiterating that the status and well-being of women is very much embedded in the sociopolitical and economic realities and well-being of their community. Women's experiences of land alienation and dispossession due to the state and market interventions are because of their identity as a community. However, often we see that the call for women's land rights is pitched against the efforts for the legal recognition of customary laws and rights by various indigenous groups, which as a result impedes both the processes. Experiences from indigenous feminist movements gave rise to a very compelling argument (see Eikjok 2004; Mithlo 2009; Ramirez 2008). One of the reasons behind such conflicting views comes from the misplaced opposition created between women's rights and tribal's rights or between women's rights and human rights.

Compared to academic discourses on the indigenous people's rights in the state, the subject of women's rights has drawn wide attention both from within the state and from outside. These writings can be broadly identified into two groups with two objectives concerning women in the state. The first objective has been to have a critical understanding of the 'status' of women in communitarian societies and the second objective deals mostly with providing insights and policy recommendations to improve women's situation in the state. Both the groups differ in their approaches and, hence, in seeking the solutions. One group comes mostly from the policy background; they generate and analyse varying statistical data and gender development indicators such as on health, education, work participation, participation in decision-making bodies like Panchayati Raj Institution, and sex ration. There are several problems with the ways and kinds analysis they draw. For instance, the sex ratio of the state is considered to be one of the poorest in the region at 938 females per 1,000 males. Often this is taken as indicative of the level of gender disparity existing in the state. The same method is used in data generation and, thus, problematizing other indicators such as health and education status. However, it does not take into account the large influx of non-tribal populations coming into the state in search of livelihood or those who are posted on various government services and who are largely male. The actual sex ration of the ST population is 1,032 females per 1,000 males (see Table 3.1).

Another set of work (though rare) comes from feminist scholars. Analysing the day-to-day reality of women in a traditional society and the gender disparity instituted within the customary laws of the communities, they shun the egalitarian tag on tribal society. Feminist scholars like Sumi Krishna, quoting Tiplut Nongbri, argue that 'gender inequality

Table 3.1

Sex Ratio in Arunachal Pradesh

Year	Sex Ratio for Arunachal Pradesh for Total Population	Sex Ratio for ST Population in Arunachal Pradesh
1961	894	1,013
1991	859	998
2001	901	1,003
2011	938	1,032

Source: Census of India (various years).

(in tribal society) is obscured by their poor economic conditions which forces men and women to cooperate and share in joint economic activities', terming this as 'superior status' of women is an erroneous conclusion (Krishna 2001, 2005). They try to raise the critical consciousness about subjugations ingrained in the day-to-day life of women. The only problem with these scholarships is that they have narrowed their objectives and framework by focusing only on women's situation to explain the functioning of the entire community. They tend to treat women as an exclusive group separate from their communitarian location. As a result, it not only fails to capture the lived reality of tribal women but also puts their interests in a conflicting situation vis-à-vis their community.

In this section, we will try to relook at the existing discourses and concepts. The idea is not to merely critique them but to build upon them by negotiating a space for what could be termed as tribal feminism. In these sections, we will try to outline the field realities (natural and political) and interlinkages between socio-economic relations and structures of communitarian societies that create a unique lived reality of a tribal woman, hence, trying to open up the new spaces and illuminating newer understanding of what does it means to be a tribal woman living a communitarian life and what contributes to the status of women or of men per se. It would be undue and erroneous to exclude her from her community to analyse her situation.

1. **Men Own Property, Women Manage Economy?**

There is something unnerving about this dichotomized analogy of men as the landowner and women managing land as a resource.[13] It seems to fix the binary of role as well as the binary of 'rights'. The paradox comes with the term 'manager' which seems to convey a privileged responsibility. The underlying understanding being that women exercise some decision-making and control over the process of Common Property Resource (CPR) management.[14] Women organize the entire cultivation plan and implement the same. They decide on the labour force, how the field is going to be used, what crop to grow, and which plot is to be used; after harvesting, they takes care of storing the harvest and, to a large extent, of how it is used. However, a group of women told me that there is nothing much actually left to take decisions upon as most of these activities are already predetermined. The climatic condition, the terrain, the season, household needs, availability of seeds, traditional norms, and knowledge are the factors that determine the planning process. In a way, every cultivation activity is predetermined and so are the roles of women. It means their engagement in cultivation is basically a mechanical task and involves pure labour. Then how these activities, which are basically mechanical tasks and are about pure labour, are equated with exercise of power in decision-making? How they represent women's status in the society.

Through my long-term engagement with the subjects among Apatanis, I have realized that status, role, resource, economy, control, and power are a complex arrangement. To understand and explain their interlinkages, one has to understand the binary or dual household economy of these communities functioning simultaneously to sustain the household needs and production. This dual economy of household comprises the domestic economy (DE) managed by women and public economy (PE) managed by men. DE being the base economy due to its direct engagement with primary resources—land and labour—serves for *subsistence*, while PE being the derivative from DE deals with the *surpluses* produced by DE. The PE of the household interacts and transacts with the public sphere of social systems and economies. Under traditional economy, these interactions and transactions were carried out through social relations or to form newer relations. These relations in return attributed status to the head of the household, the male head. This indirectly enhanced the value of the women in the household. There is a difference between 'status' and 'value', while the former attributes power and influence, the latter only enhances women's worth as a commodity (the bride price or gifts during marriages).

So how do women contribute to DE and PE indirectly? During my fieldwork an elderly Apatani woman showed me cane baskets of varying sizes which were used for measuring rice grain for barter. They exchanged everything with rice grains they produced in field, for example, eggs, vegetables, fowls, labour, ornaments, servants, land, and even Mithuns (Bos Frontalis). Christopher von Furer Haimendorf (1980: 49–53) in his account of Apatani and Nyishi economy has equated *Mithun* as the cash of the tribal community. But now it can be easily argued that it was the rice, instead of *Mithun*, which functioned as the most accepted exchange money.

A woman plays a superseding role in organizing household cultivation activities. While very often men's tasks in cultivation are heavy ones, such as clearing the plot, cutting the bunds, fencing, and building water canals, they are largely seasonal or a one-time activity in a cycle, whereas women's work are perennial and more back breaking. Several scholars engaged with the subject believe that cultivation, especially shifting/*jhum* cultivation, has a better scope for women's agency and decision-making power, say in terms of choosing the plot for cultivation, what to grow, how to organize labour, and how to use the produce. Geeta Menon (1995: 151–52) says that traditionally in *jhum* cultivation, after men select and clear the plot, women take over from there. The argument is that this makes *jhum* cultivation more 'gender-friendly' because women get the control and manage the entire procedure after men finish their task. However, during my own field interviews among the Nyishi communities from different regions, many shared that the division of labour is determined by the traditional norms and by rather more practical issues. Heavier works like cutting and clearing of main forest and fencing are done by men; it is a taboo for men to do any plantation or ploughing work as these are to be done by women. Even the decisions regarding the crops selection and consumption do not arise as it is already predetermined by household necessities and the environmental conditions. It is only the surplus which is utilized for more personal necessities such as buying ornaments, land, livestock, or organizing some ceremonies/festival. This ultimately adds to the capital of the head of the family/men; women also gains indirectly from such transactions.

It is usually this role played by women that is being presumed and presented as women managing, controlling, and taking important decisions in the economy. They are said to buy ornaments, beads, and household help. Though, in practice, they can be conditioned into prioritizing men's economy (or PE) and necessities before their own. In a traditional society, men would use the surpluses to spend on or to bring another wife while the same is not true for women. During field interviews, women shared about cases where the wife would pay 'bride price' for her husband's subsequent wives and she would even take it as a matter of pride.[15] Later, such wives become her co-wives who can be her co-worker. They would maintain their own respective separate fire-hearts within the Nyishi longhouses and have their own agricultural plots and separate granaries.

Among Apatanis, the entire cultivation activity is increasingly entirely shouldered by women who are covering up for the labour deficit created by men who shifted to non-agricultural livelihoods and younger women who are pursuing education and other jobs. The flip side of this economy is that under the present economy, when agriculture has taken the backseat as meaningful and profitable livelihood source, women, especially poorer women, are economically and traditionally compelled to continue with this uneconomic activity. This by default reflects upon and even reproduces the economic devaluation of women and her labour.

On the other hand, as both the binary household economies are closely but hierarchically linked, there are interrelated implications on the status of women under the modern form of economy.[16] While DE continues to be bound within the household, PE opened up to modern economy and started engaging with surplus production. Thus, in most of the household, PE became the main site of production or income generation, further marginalizing DE. Here, women's role then merely reduces to the role of a caretaker/housewife as discussed earlier. However, there is also an opportunity for women. As modern economy is not largely dependent on traditional means of production, that is, land, controlled by men, there is a scope for newer social relations and autonomy for women.

2. Women and Landownership

Both Apatani and Nyishi societies are patriarchal, patrilineal, and patrilocal societies which also delimit the scope for women's land inheritance. It means that men dominate every sphere of social life including control over land as the genealogical lineage and inheritance rights are drawn on male line, and after marriage wife has to relocate herself to join the husband. Among the Apatanis, the ritual sanctity, social cohesion, and political strength of each clan village largely depend on the exclusivity of their exogamous clan colonies or villages. Therefore, as the Apatani maxim goes, 'As leaves are to the ground, so are women to others', women are debarred from land inheritance, especially the ancestral land called *Alo Khu* to avoid its transfer to other villages.

As a result, a woman's identity, position, and status are drawn from her relation to the land but through the male members of her family. Her access to the land is also dependent on these relations. Thus, by traditional custom, a widow with a son can retain her social position, shelter, and livelihood within the husband's village as a caretaker of her son's landed property. If a woman is barren or do not bear male heir, her position withers in the family and society, and so do her rights to claim access to the fields. In this case, the property reverts to husband's nearest kin. Now, it depends on the goodwill of the male relatives to support her living. Therefore, women are advised to forgo their claims on land to their brother to keep on good terms with him. The brother is then under obligations to see sister's well-being in all eventuality.

Thus, there is a tremendous pressure on women to be reproductive (to give male heir) and to be economically productive (manage DE). In olden days, Apatani women would dread being seen lazing around.

It could stigmatize them, even leading to divorce or shattering their prospects of marriage. Among Nyishis, the bride price is paid to bride's parents in exchange for the 'labour/resource' embodied in her. Under traditional economy, one of the main reasons behind the practice of polygamy was cited to be for expanding one's *jhum* fields (Mishra 1991: 48) and wealth. While each wife could maintain her own independent sub-households (represented by different fireplace), *jhum* plots, and granaries, the labour and resources could be pooled from these sub-households and co-wives; the husband being the head of the family could use the collective resource for his own benefits or for 'PE', which consequently would enhance his social status and influence.

Thus, this leads to the paradoxical situation of women and their DE. As discussed earlier that women being the main cultivators are the main producer and provider of the household in a traditional economy. However, 'how the produces and surpluses are used?" and 'to what end?' are conditioned in such a way that they only supplement the PE or men's economy. The storable surpluses like rice are stored and used for organizing festivals and ceremonies which are associated with status enhancement of the male head in the family, and of women indirectly. Despite the fact that women play a major role in the main production process (agriculture), status or rights are not attributed. It draws a close resemblance to classical Marxian adage that the one who owns the source of production (land) controls the society where the working class (women) produces without owning or enjoying any control and power. Women's access to the land is limited only till the production process. Without owning and engaging only in the production process her situation is rendered forever vulnerable despite the fact that society has far moved ahead of natural and traditional environment. Therefore, landownership rights to women whenever land is individually owned are absolute for bringing structural changes and gender justice.

However, many times the outcry made by groups who head the demands for constitutional recognition of customary laws sees such move as destructive. Not only they are biased in their argument and understanding about women's position in tribal society but they also seem to ignore certain aspects of traditional tribal societies and the way customary roles function. They do not realize that they are not fixed rules and neither they are as tangible as they are being made to be. Much of the norms are determined by the actual day-to-day practices and environmental demands. For instance, traditionally the patriarchal, patrilineal, and patrilocal system makes it impossible for an Apatani woman to own land but in practice there are few cases where women inherit land and the practice is in increase. It is interesting to note that the customs laws prohibit the *Alo Khu* from being given to daughter but customs do not say that land cannot be given to women. The economic bases, social relations, political institutions, and land relations are changing. The land rights to women will only help in diversifying the livelihood opportunity of the household, without which women (especially poor women) face a serious livelihood disadvantage and poverty risk (Agarwal, Sivaramayya, and Sarkar 1997).

3. Re-visiting Women's Status in Communitarian Society

In the economy of women, social status and identity of women in traditional agricultural tribal society are determined by two factors. Firstly, her value as resource embodied in her body self: its productive ability as labour and reproductive ability (giving birth). Secondly, the process and structure of production: the social institutions and customs that produce relations which in return attributes membership and status in the community. These factors determine her roles and rights in accessing, 'managing' and utilizing the resources as we have discussed above. As her role is largely reduced only as a labour, she is structurally excluded from the actual controls of the resources and capital produced. Her scope and opportunities from exploring, using and expanding her own resources are also delimited by the mere fact that she does not control the resources. As Agarwal et al. (1997) argue that even a small plot of land in her hand enhances better chances of some livelihood-generating activities. To take a small example, the government loans and access to certain schemes, which are believed to be gender neutral, are given only on the production of LPC. Now, women who are traditionally not allowed to own land have to look for other less secure livelihood activities. On the other hand, the gendered roles as a caregiver and homemaker affect the scope of various opportunities that is otherwise available. It is this absence of women in the actual production process that by default excludes women from the actual structure of production. Thus, even though there have been changes in the mode of production, such as the other monetary income-generating livelihood activities replacing the sustenance-based agricultural production, there has been no change in the status of women. Among the Apatanis, their settled way of life and unabridged production activity allowed emergence of various socio-economic stratifications within the community over the period of centuries. But it has hardly affected patriarchy and women's status in the society, a woman has always been treated lesser than man across the classes.

However, having said so there are several (liberating and egalitarian) aspects of the communitarian societies that provide several axes that act as cushions or safety nets for both women and men from abject exploitation, for instance, the practices of CPR, among Apatanis the customary obligations on maternal uncles and brothers to look after women's well-being even after their marriage, no taboo against remarriages, no sacrosanctity associated with virginity, common land reserves and access, kinship systems of cooperation and sharing, etc.

Apart from this, there is another realm which has a significant impact on their status as well as on their understanding of self. This realm, which is generally not accessible for an outsider (male/non-tribal), is the realm of the lived reality of tribal women within their communitarian society. Their society and village is composed of her family members and relatives, and people with familiar, similar, and shared lived reality. The feminist discourse contextualized on northeastern societies argues that 'the greater visibility, freedom of mobility and participation in economic activity' are a compulsion and not because of the egalitarian nature of the tribal communities (Krishna 2001, 2005). The question to be raised here is, What is the lived reality of that 'participation' and 'visibility'?

In traditional tribal villages (and even in urban spaces), a woman can be seen sitting, walking, talking, and working in almost every public space—village, fields, gardens, houses veranda, forests, river, etc. She is not needlessly conscious of her visibility or body in public. Her body is an appendage, instrument, and a labour resource to her; she is not unnecessarily concerned about hiding or covering it. Except for certain social and formal norms, there are tangible barriers to interaction between men and women. They work in fields, walk to forests for firewood, and sit on veranda or bamboo porch or around fire heart and talk. There is tremendous amount of constant and open sharing and communication taking place between men and women. They share, consult, joke, fight, argue, gossip, learn, flirt, romance, think, solve problem, and plan. Such communications are based on more egalitarian and power-free interactions as they take place in informal spaces which are not determined by traditional formal rules. Among Apatanis in the past, men and women, and boys and girls used to work together in their respective labour gangs (*Patangs*), and throughout the day while working together in fields they would share about their life, gossip, exchange folk stories, compete in singing traditional verses, etc.

In tribal societies, both hard-core political and economic power, and soft power such as age, virtue, knowledge, oral skills to influence opinion, and spiritual power are the sources for social capital. Together they all form power sources within a communitarian society which ascribe status to a person/an individual. A woman with astute sense of leadership within her limited sphere is well respected. Thus, the status of women is based on her social capital and on organic and soft relations, and not necessarily only on institutions and structures.

While the customary laws define the formal norms of landownership, they are the less formal, less structured norms and practices that delineate its management. For example, there are women who own land, inter-class marriages, a wife who commands more respect than the husband in the village, a woman priest among the Nyishis, girls performing better academically and in employability, etc. Often the customs and norms are bent or ignored on daily basis when it comes to day-to-day convenience. Therefore, these practices are more accommodative while formal laws and rules might not be.

4. Interface with State and Market-driven Modernization and Precarity of Women's Economy

Modernization has led to several structural transformations in traditional economy. As people are moving towards newer economies, the economy itself is getting integrated to regional and national economy (Krishna 1998: 23–61, 2000). In the process, several lifestyle changes are coming, there are more livelihood options, the level of literacy is increasing and so in general sense of law and order, health facilities, amenities, and market options are better. This has many implicit effects on the women's situation too. While on the one hand they are better equipped in negotiating their spaces and legally assert it, yet on the other hand, there are several regressive trends that are emerging.

For instance, introduction of modern agricultural technologies was one of the prime programmes of the policy makers since the first Five-year Plan. Thus, allied programmes for agriculture, such as horticulture, floriculture, and animal husbandry, along with trainings, exposure visits, introduction of high-yielding variety seeds, fertilizers, financial loans and subsidies, were introduced to encourage modern agriculture. However, there were several underlying biases in these programmes. It looked at agriculture as merely 'livelihood' and assuming men as the sole breadwinner, the programmes were designed for men. While on the other hand, due to the cultural context of subsistence-based agricultural economy, men could not take it as a meaningful livelihood source. Instead, they were looking for job opportunities in government (agriculture) departments as employees. Thus, women were gradually excluded from their age-old agricultural activities.

According to Fernandes and Barbora (2002: 123),

> Change in its (land) use through alienation, deforestation, and commercialization affects them negatively since by and large men control the new technology and marketing systems. With it, women run the risk of losing their traditional control over their livelihood, strengthening the patriarchal ethos, weakening their equity-based culture and becoming only housewives.

There is a tendency of individualization of property which restricts common access of land; hence, it reduces women's access to land. On the other hand, there is an increasing trend where families are opting out from agriculture-based economy to other options now possible due to modern economy and education. They argue that the modern interface with the community has been counterproductive in women's empowerment and gender equality.

Though this discussion requires a more critical examination, yet I would caution from drawing such an easy conclusion. The feminization of agriculture as it was traditionally practised has more patriarchal underpinnings than it is generally construed. In dealing with the subject, one needs to uncover those underpinnings and lay them bare for a more critical analysis and it is only then that one should try to reclaim women as the original/actual agriculturists and their role as the provider of the household. Without attributing and acknowledging such roles played by women, the entire system otherwise would seem like a labour-extracting system where such self-imposed conformity to norms and degradation could be achieved only through a patriarchal ideology. Though it is important to acknowledge and re-evaluate women's contribution or contributions made by DE to household economy to highlight how traditional and communitarian society and economy had been discriminatory against women, there is also no need to unnecessarily romanticize feminization of agriculture.

One needs to keep in mind that these transformations afforded through modern economy (which are still highly state-funded) were superimposed over the pre-existent economy which was still largely run on patriarchal principles. One is not trying to completely negate the advantages and positive transformations that modernity had brought in women's life in general, yet there have been few regressive impacts on women's status as the larger communities itself are going through transformations.

CONCLUSION

Imposition of common uniform formal laws would be a regressive development for a diverse range of communities in the state. And so the codification of customary laws based on patriarchal norms would be detrimental for women. Therefore, there has to be a clear balance between the basic tenets and principles of both customary laws and formal laws on the one hand, and on the other hand there should be land policies that are context specific and sensitive to the value system of the communities. It should be progressive rather than regressive in all aspects. Recognition of the communitarian way of living and cooperative production process are a must. This way breaking and privatization of community land can be prevented. This should reduce the practice of shifting cultivation, poverty-driven migration, and internal land alienation.

There should be constitutional recognition of customary laws, community land, and tribal people's rights over the tribal land—in another words, the recognition of traditional institutions such as the traditional village councils as it is done in other Fifth and Sixth Schedule areas. And that such policies and laws should have embedded objectives of ascertaining gender parity and land rights for women.

In conclusion, few points which need to be re-stressed as the main discussion points in the chapter are:

First, tribal women should be identified as integral to their community and its identity, not in their exclusion. Their vulnerability and prosperity, both are interlinked to their identity as a community.

Second, in a traditional labour-intensive agricultural society women shared equal, if not more, responsibility with men in providing for the sustenance of the family and household, especially the DE. Ensuring land rights to her would provide necessary security to the household as well as to her.

Third, women are the main cultivators or agriculturists in terms of the amount of labour and time women devote to the activity, the amount of agricultural knowledge they hold, and traditional roles they perform during the agricultural cycle.

Fourth, under patriarchy, despite women's significant role in household/DE, women are excluded from its benefits. However, it does not lead to abject exploitation of women because of several other non-economic social and organic relations that are the hallmark of the communitarian society that supports its members.

Fifth, while a man's status and identity are very much dependent on his relation to land and social structures, a woman is excluded from land rights, her status and social identity is ascribed from her social relation to men, and it is directly dependent on her economic (labour) and social (reproductive) role/function.

Sixth, modern economy, which brought structural transformation in the socio-economic and political relations within the community, largely remained the same for women's situation as it remains disconnected with these (production) structures. Exclusion of women from any meaningful share and control of power structures entrenches patriarchal subjugation of women.

Seventh, it is important to note that the socio-economic and political transformations that have taken place in these societies have failed to improve or affect women's status. In many ways the transformations that are taking place at present in Arunachal Pradesh among these communities are regressive for women in various ways. Any meaningful transformation to women's life can be brought only by connecting her to these structures and then transforming these structures to make them more just and egalitarian.

Eight, land is integral to these communities (for both men and women); they are ontologically connected with each other. The culture and traditions of these communities including their customary laws embody these relations. One can always meaningfully negotiate with these. Any sweeping changes to any of these aspects would irrevocably affect these communities.

Ninth, there are differences between what is defined under 'formal' customary laws and norms, and what are practised in day-to-day lives. While customary laws and norms could be a more per-formative behaviour, the daily acts are practice based. Thus, practices are more accommodative, while laws and rules might not be.

As we have seen that for traditional tribal/communitarian societies of Arunachal Pradesh in general and among Apatanis and Nyishis in particular, land is not merely a property. To their society, the land has been the author of their sociocultural practices and customs. Thus, beyond the concept of land as a productive asset, it has a crucial ontological role in determining one's location, identity, and status within their respective villages and clans. It determines a member's economic security, which in turn enhances one's influence and sociopolitical status within the community. It is at this juncture that women's status becomes an important subject for our consideration. It is inherently related to women's economy. A woman is in precarious situation, more so because of modern and formal legal interventions that are taking place in the state without defining any land right for women, and for the community altogether. Just like the land rights and access, a tribal women's status is also hanging fluid and complex waiting to be defined. Land as property defines the physical boundaries loaded with legal, legitimate, formal, and tangible sanctions.

NOTES

1. The working paper was presented in a workshop on 'Codification of Land Related Customary Laws: Challenges and Prospects' held at Guwahati on 19th–20th February 2015 organized by LBSNAA, Mussoorie. I would specially like to thank Dani Sulu, Duyu Laji, Kalpana Kannabiran, Saroj Arora, Subeno Kithan, and Walter Fernandes for their valuable comments on the earlier drafts of the paper. It tremendously helped me in finalizing this paper.
2. Annual Plan of Operation 2013–14 by Arunachal Pradesh State Compensatory Afforestation Fund Management and Planning Authority.
3. 'Tribal feminism' should be understood in the similar line of the 'Dalit feminism', 'Black feminism', or 'indigenous feminism', which is a critical re-look on the West and often elite-dominated feminism on the one hand, while on the other hand exposes the double subjugation experienced by tribal or Adivasi women due to their social location within a certain community. I am using the term 'tribal' in a very limited sense to represent the communitarian societies in the region.
4. As similar to the concept of 'de-humanizing' by Herbert C. Kelman (1976) where 'humanness' embodies identity and experience and expression of being human, and de-humanizing would be by taking them away.
5. Concept borrowed from D'Souza and Changmi (NA: 13), which says that land is central to the ethnic identity and cultural forms of tribal communities. I further extend the concept through various discussions here based on my own observations.
6. The total land area of the state is 83,743 sq. km; of this 67,321 sq. km, which is 80.39% of the total geographical area, is declared under forest cover according to State Forest Report 2013 by the Forest Survey of India (MoEF 2013) and of this 20.46% is Reserved Forests, 18.49% is Protected

Forests, and 61.05% is declared as Unclassed Forests as per the State Forest Report 2011 published by the Forest Survey of India (MoEF 2011).
7. According to the Inter-ministerial National Task Force on Rehabilitation of Shifting Cultivation Areas reports in the year 2008, 54,000 families practise *jhum* cultivation in Arunachal Pradesh.
8. The names of individuals and places are changed in order to protect the anonymity of the interviewee.
9. Traditional council meetings.
10. Census 2011 enumerates three ambiguous communities with very similar names, spelled differently: Nyishi (249,824), Nishang (2,849), and Nissing (32,479).
11. One of the common sign they see is of a particular mythical snake which becomes visible only to a person to whom the sign was directed at.
12. Apatani villages are organized into five traditional major village clusters: Biila, Diibo, Hangu, Hari, and Hiija. Each village cluster is divided into clan colonies or village with compact housings to save space.
13. Their main argument being that women play an important role in cultivation as cultivators; hence, they are considered as assets to economy, which in turn contributes to their status. Thus, under modern economy, when women are getting excluded from their access to land as cultivators, it has a regressive effect on women's status (see in D'Souza, Alphonsus, and Christina 2002; Fernandes and Menon 1987; Fernandes et al. 2005).
14. 'The men clear the land and women take over thereafter' (Fernandes et al. 2005).
15. Polygamy is no more a common practice among the Nyishis, especially among the younger generation.
16. Binary household economy is the one in which women work in a private domain and men in a public domain.

REFERENCES

Agarwal, B., B. Sivaramayya, and L. Sarkar. (Committee members). 1997. Report of the 'Committee for Gender Equality in Land Devolution in Tenurial Laws.' Centre for Rural Studies, LBSNAA, Mussoorie.

Compensatory Afforestation Fund Management and Planning Authority. 2013–14. *Annual Plan of Operation by Arunachal Pradesh State.* Itanagar: Compensatory Afforestation Fund Management and Planning Authority.

D'Souza, Alphonsus, and Kekrieseno Christina. 2002. *Coping with Social Change in North-east India. A Comparative Study of Three Ethnic Groups in North-east India: Aka, Angami and Dimasa.* New Delhi: SAGE Publications.

D'Souza, V., and Sunumi Changmi. NA:13. Unpublished working paper.

Eikjok, Jorun. 2004. 'Gender in Sapmi: Socio-cultural Transformations and New Challenges.' *Indigenous Affairs*, 1-2/04, International Working Group for Indigenous Affairs, Denmark. Available at: http://www.iwgia.org/iwgia_files_publications_files /IA_1-2-04.pdf (accessed on 15 December 2012).

Ete, Mibi. 2014. 'Hydropower Development in Arunachal Pradesh: A New Narrative in Natural Resource Politics?' In *Heinrich Boll Stiftung* on 10 November 2014. Available at: http://in.boell.org/2014/11/10/hydropower-development-arunachal-pradesh-new-narrative-natural-resource-politics (accessed on 26 March 2017).

Fernandes, Walter. 2009. 'Land Relations and Conflicts in Northeast India: A Look at Modernization, Immigration and Livelihood Loss.' In *Agrarian Reforms, Land Markets and Rural Poor*, edited by D. Narasimha Reddy. Mussoorie: Centre for Rural Studies, Lal Bahadur Shastri National Academy of Administration.

Fernandes, Walter, and Sanjay Barbora. 2002. *Modernization and Women's Status in North Eastern India: A Comparative Study of Six Tribes*. Guwahati: North Eastern Social Research Centre.

Fernandes, Walter, and Geeta Menon. 1987. *Tribal Women and Forest Economy: Deforestation, Exploitation and Status Change*. New Delhi: Indian Social Institute.

Fernandes, Walter, Melvil Pereira, and Visalenu Khatso. 2005. *Gender Impact of Tribal Customary Laws in North Eastern India*. Guwahati: North Eastern Social Research Centre.

Haimendorf, Cristopher von Furer. 1980. *A Himalayan Tribe: From Cattle to Cash*. Berkeley, CA: University of California Press.

Indian Express. 2015. 'The Ministry of Tribal Affairs Refused to Relax the Norm.' *Indian Express*, April 23.

Indigenous Women's Biodiversity Network (IWBN). 2007. Opening Statement Montreal, Canada, October 8, 2007. Available at: http://www.biodivnetwork.de/upload/papers/positionspapiere/Montreal/IWBN_statement_ABSWG5.pdf (accessed on 15 December 2012).

Inter-ministerial National Task Force. 2008. *Inter-ministerial National Task Force Report on Rehabilitation of Shifting Cultivation Areas*. New Delhi: Inter-Ministerial National Task Force.

International Working Group on Indigenous Affairs (IWGIA). 1999 and 2009. 'Gender and Indigenous Women, Position and Strategy Paper.' Available at http://www.iwgia.org/images/stories/sections/aboutwgia/documents/strategy-papers /Genderstrategy.pdf (accessed on 10 March 2013).

Kelman, C. Herberst. 1976. 'Violence Without Restraint: Reflections on the Dehumanization of Victims and Victimizers.' In *Varieties of Psychohistory*, edited by G. M. Kren and L. H. Rappoport, 282–314. New York: Springer.

Krishna, Sumi. 1998. 'Gender and Biodiversity Management.' In *Gender Dimensions in Biodiversity Management*, edited by M. S. Swaminathan. New Delhi: Konark.

Krishna, Sumi. 2000. 'The Impact of the Structural Adjustment Programme on Gender and Environment in India.' In *Shifting Sands: Women's Lives and Globalization*, edited by CWDS. Calcutta: Stree.

———. 2001. 'Gender, Tribe and Community Control of Natural Resources in North-east India.' *Indian Journal of Gender Studies*. Available at: http://ijg.sagepub.com/content/8/2/307 (accessed on 26 March 2009).

———. 2005, June 18–24. 'Gendered Price of Rice in North-eastern India.' *Economic and Political Weekly* 40 (25): 2555–62.

Leo, Dominic. 2015. 'Reclaiming the Foundational Value of Land: A Poumai Naga Narrative.' In *Identities and Their Struggles in North East*, edited by Alex Akhup. *Tribal and Adivasi Studies: Perspectives from Within*. Vol. 2 of Tribal Intellectual Collective India. Kolkata: Adivaani.

Maithani, B. P. 2005. *Shifting Cultivation in North East India: Policy Issues and Options*. New Delhi: Mittal Publication.

Menon, Geeta. 1995. 'The Impact of Migration on the Work and Tribal Women's Status.' In *Women and Seasonal Labour Migration*, edited by Loes Schenken-Sandbergen. New Delhi: SAGE Publications.

Ministry of Environment & Forests (MoEF). 2011. *State Forest Report*. New Delhi: Forest Survey of India (MoEF).

Ministry of Environment & Forests. 2013. *State Forest Report*. New Delhi: Forest Survey of India (MoEF).

Mishra, Kiran. 1991. *Women in Tribal Community*. New Delhi: Vikas Publishing House.

Mithlo, Nancy Marie. 2009. 'A Real Feminine Journey: Locating Indigenous Feminisms in the Arts.' *Meridians* 9 (2): 1–30. Available at: http://www.jstor.org/stable/40338781 (accessed on 26 March 2017).

Ramirez, Renya K. 2008, June. 'Learning Across Differences: Native and Ethnic Studies Feminisms.' *American Quarterly* 60 (2): 303–07. Available at: http/:www.jstor.org/stable/40068539 (accessed on 10 September 2013).

Taylor, Betsy. 2009. 'Grounds for Democratic Hope in Arunachal Pradesh: Emerging Civic Geographies and the Reinvention of Gender and Tribal Identities.' In *Beyond Counterinsurgency: Breaking the Impasse in Northeast India*, edited by Sanjib Baruah. New Delhi: Oxford University Press.

Xaxa, Viginius. 2008. *State, Society and Tribes: Issues in postcolonial India*. New Delhi: Pearson Longman.

4

Gender Issues in Landownership in Chhattisgarh: Existing Land Laws, Policies, and Practices

RAMESH SHARMA

India is rapidly emerging as one of the global leaders in terms of economic growth. Recent analyses of growth in India, however, reveal that in terms of its sector composition, agriculture's contribution has steadily declined from close to 26% of GDP in 1996 to about 16.7% in 2005. Industry's contribution has hovered at around 25%, with services increasing to over 50% (Chandrasekhar and Ghosh 2007). Herein lies a major contradiction: 68.84% of the population continues to live in rural areas, and those dependent on agriculture for making a living have only marginally declined from 61% to 57% over this period. Low agricultural growth rates of a little over 2% per annum over the Tenth Five-year Plan period (2002–07), compared to the overall growth rates of over 7.5%, have not led to a process of 'de-agrarianization' or a shift away from agrarian modes of livelihood (Bryceson 1997), but rather have contributed to deepening social inequalities, in terms of rural–urban inequalities, as well as inequalities based on caste, ethnicity, and gender. Women and also the Scheduled Castes (SCs) and Scheduled Tribes (STs) are increasingly confined to agriculture and excluded from engagement in the high growth sectors (Food and Fertilizer Technology Center for the Asian and Pacific Region 2010; Rao 2011).

The Approach Paper to the Eleventh Five-year Plan highlights some of these concerns, drawing attention to both the rural–urban divide and the gender divide as critical barriers to growth (Government of India 2006). Women have a critical role in agriculture and with increasing out-migration among the males; this now means that more and more women are farming the land. But except a few stray examples, they are not recognized as 'farmers'. The government does not see the need to increase investments in agriculture where a very large number of women continue to work, and instead investments for women are made in the social sector. Where the focus should be on bringing about a change in land entitlements and securing land tenures for women, the focus is on diverting gains from 'high growth rates' to welfare and protection programmes for women ensuring that they continue to be seen as dependents. The government programs still fail to take into account the fact that women face ideological and material constraints that prevent them from freely participating in production and markets.

In India, 68.84% of the population lives in rural area (Census 2011). A large population is dependent on the agriculture sector. Agricultural land continues to be one of the most important forms of property and productive assets in rural areas even today. Land is a critical factor not only in the well-being of the family but also in its socio-economic status. It has been sufficiently established that landownership reduces the risk of poverty, increases access to credit, enhances bargaining power, and is a valuable asset during crisis.

WOMEN'S LAND RIGHTS IN CHHATTISGARH

Chhattisgarh is one of the youngest members of the Indian Union, born on 1st November 2000. The raison d'être of Chhattisgarh was economic and social underdevelopment of this region in undivided Madhya Pradesh. The formation of the new state has thrown both challenges and opportunities for its development. These challenges assume a new dimension in the backdrop of the fact that around 32% of the population of Chhattisgarh belongs to STs and another 12% belongs to the SCs.

IMPORTANCE GIVEN TO WOMEN'S LAND RIGHTS IN CHHATTISGARH

The state created a Department of Women and Child Development in 2000. The Chhattisgarh Policy for Women (2010) was however the first attempt of the department to formulate a comprehensive policy for the empowerment of women. The policy cites the gender gap in control over property as the 'single most important factor affecting women's position', and aims to promote an increase in women's control over land, property, and other common resources through:

- Ensuring land rights to the women and encouraging co-ownership of the property like house, etc.;
- Public advocacy and swift legal redressal where women are deprived of rights that are already secured by law;
- Creating mass consciousness and providing legal awareness about women's rights;
- Providing concessions in court fees for poor and landless women litigants;
- Encouragement and recognition of women as farmers;
- Encouraging research and technical innovations to reorient the administrative machinery of agriculture to cater to the needs of women;
- Encouraging women farmers to practise mixed farming including cereals, pulses, oil seeds, roots, tubers, etc.;
- Promoting development of dairy, sericulture, fisheries, horticulture, and floriculture under the management of active women's groups by providing training in processing, value addition, and marketing.
- Encouraging the use of common lands in rural areas by women groups to cater to the fuel and fodder needs of the villages;
- Encouraging women to pursue higher studies in agriculture and agricultural management;
- Encouraging inclusion of women's perspectives in planning of housing and provision of shelter in rural and urban areas so as to ensure that the benefits of housing, essential services, and community facilities are directed to women in general;
- Preferential allotment of plots and houses to women by public agencies;

- Encouraging setting up of safe accommodation for working and single women.

Whilst the policy was a step forward, several problems remain. The intention to give all future government distributed land in the name of women alters within the same document to become 'all land distribution and redistribution undertaken by the government will be made in future in the name of the wife along with her husband'. The policy commitments remain largely on paper and the only case where women have received entitlements along with their husbands is the case of land titles under the Forest Rights Act (FRA).

CHHATTISGARH LAND REVENUE CODE, 2000

The Chhattisgarh Land Revenue Code was enacted in 2000. In the specific instance of legal aspects of landownership, in the Chhattisgarh Land Revenue Code 2000, women were either non-existent or regarded merely as an appendage to men, even when they may be the lawful owner of land. The Chhattisgarh Land Revenue Code by default presumed that the *Bhumiswami*, the owner of land, was male. The entire code was designed with the basic presumption in mind that it is men who own the land and work it. The term, *Bhumiswami*, referring to owner, lord, master, keeper of land, itself is masculine; its appropriate feminine form, which would have been *Bhumiswamini*, was disregarded by the lawmakers.

Two important components had gone into the framing of the Chhattisgarh Land Revenue Code. One, it was a broad reiteration of the general practices that had already been in place pertaining to landownership, rent, and the role of the state in deciding associated matters. Two, it included within itself some of the reformist ideas of national movement vintage regarding prohibiting absentee landlordism, imposing land ceilings, protecting landholders from exploitative usury, and making special provisions to ensure that tribal lands did not pass into the hands of non-tribals through the play of usury and other market forces. There was no stated bias as such against women holding land. For most part, the new land law was gender neutral. Yet, there was no sensitivity, so on numerous occasions the law seemed as if it had been designed only for men landowners and tenants. Thus, on the one hand, the Chhattisgarh Land Revenue Code talks of persons owning land, persons cultivating land, and persons owing rent to the government, and on the other hand, it frequently refers to these persons as 'he' and 'his'. It could be said that reading too much gender bias through such linguistic usage from the previous decades is unfair. However, the noticeable presumption remains that the Chhattisgarh Land Revenue Code took it for granted that men owned and worked the land.

'All lands belong to the state government' says the Chhattisgarh Land Revenue Code 2000 (Section 57) and all others held the land in tenure from the government. The tenure holders were called *Bhumiswamis*, and there was only one class of them, irrespective of their social, political, or official status. So a person holding less than an acre, as also the Rajas and Nawabs who had merged their states into India at the time of Independence, was a *Bhumiswami* in the eyes of the law, with equal obligations—'his' duties, and 'his' rights that were laid down in the Chhattisgarh Land Revenue Code 2000. Any improvement that a *Bhumiswami* has on the land was taken to be on 'his' holding, through 'his' efforts and so on. The government allocated to itself the task of reassessing land revenue and land usage pattern of any land. It would also maintain a record-of-rights in which the names of all the *Bhumiswamis*, occupancy tenants, and government lessees would be recorded along with specific identifiers of the pieces of land held by them.

The issue of land rights for women should be a priority concern for the Government of India given that the Indian Constitution grants 'equal right to livelihood'. Whether all women would be able to exercise this right (to hold land) is a secondary issue given the state of landlessness in the country. The pertinent issue is that of ensuring land rights for women so that their vulnerability and dependency can be reduced, especially when there is marital discord and breakdown of the family.

This study aims to discuss four key points: (a) importance of land rights to the women, (b) men and women's perceptions on different types of land rights, (c) benefits of joint and independent titles, and (d) barriers that exist for women in claiming their land rights.

For the purpose of this study, 100 respondents were identified in the state of Chhattisgarh for seeking household-level information. The survey was conducted in two districts, namely Mahasamund and Surguja, and covered seven blocks in these districts (two blocks in Mahasamund and five blocks in Surguja).

METHODOLOGY

The study was undertaken with the objectives of (a) collecting primary data on landownership pattern among women, (b) understanding people's perception on land rights for women, and (c) making recommendations for policy makers.

For this purpose, interviews were conducted in 50 villages across two districts (Table 4.1). Two households in each village were covered through random sampling. Interviews were conducted on the basis of an open-ended questionnaire.

For the purpose of the study, it is important to understand that both the districts, Surguja and Mahasamund, are predominantly tribal. The Oraon and Gond tribes reside in the forested areas of these districts.

For primary data collection, interviews were conducted with women in each selected village. The collected information was supplemented by observation and household survey.

Secondary information analysis was done from multiple sources such as books, articles (published and unpublished), government records, journals, and reports from civil society organizations like Ekta Parishad.

LIMITATIONS OF THE STUDY

There are obvious limitations in the study such as non-availability of respondents due to various reasons, leading to repeated visits to the village. Dominance of male members at the time of interviews prevented the women from expressing themselves freely. Interviews were

Table 4.1

Field Area and Respondents

S. No.		Study Field Area	
1.	State	Chhattisgarh	
2.	District/s	Mahasamund	Surguja
3.	Blocks	Bagbahara, Mahasamund	Udayapura, Sarguja, Prem Nagar, Surajpur, Ramanuj Nagar
4.	Respondents	50	50

Source: Author.

only conducted with women; majority of them belonged to the tribal communities. They represented different social and economic strata, but primarily the tribal society.

OVERVIEW: TRIBAL WOMEN IN CHHATTISGARH

Both Surguja and Mahasamund are predominantly tribal districts. In Surguja district, among the STs, women comprise 49% of the total population, while in Mahasamund district, women comprise 50.87% of the total population. The trend amongst the SC communities is also similar for both districts. In Surguja, sex ratios for ST and SC communities were 987 and 979, respectively, while in Mahasamund, the same were 1,035 and 1,027, respectively. Literacy rate for women was also higher in Mahasamund than Surguja at 53% and 41%, respectively. Overall, 43% of the women were engaged in agriculture, 31% in animal rearing, and 15% in fishing. In Surguja, 14% of the total government employees were women, while in Mahasamund this percentage was 13%.

According to Census 2001, Chhattisgarh had 450,000 women-headed households. This comprised 11% of the total households. ST households were having greater numbers of women-headed households than SC and others. It was found that 66.13% of women-headed households comprised of widows, 3.36% of divorced and separated women, and 3.45% of never married women. In women-headed households, 54.36% women were found to be working as farmers, fisherwomen, hunters, loggers, etc. In rural areas, this rose to 70%.

In tribal communities which believe in egalitarian value system, the gender roles are defined and complimentary to each other. Men plough the land, women plant and gather food, and both contribute to the family and the community. Traditionally, tribal men and women had equal access to land, cattle, and forest resources but due to growing influences of dominant culture, capitalism, and emphasis on individual property ownership, tribal women now have less opportunities to access to land and resources. Gender relations within the tribal society are experiencing change and not necessarily for the better. Since the *patta* (official documents stating land title and the term on which land is held) became the norm for landholding, power has transferred to the man and through him to the son. Women who marry a non-tribal loose the right to own land. Traditionally, tribal women have been exclusively in charge of gathering, storing, processing, and marketing forest produce but this has changed significantly with the control of the forest department and a market system based on contractors and middlemen who are invariably men.

Various researchers have established that tribal women suffer adversely due to loss of community resources, evictions, displacement, and the rapid degradation in forest resources. All of these have contributed to the loss of their status. Recent research indicates that violence against tribal women is increasing while kinship bonds are decreasing (Panda and Snehlata 2008). The practice of 'witch-hunting', superstitions, and increasing social taboos for the women seem to be gaining ground.

LANDHOLDINGS AMONG WOMEN IN CHHATTISGARH

Table 4.2 provides an insight into the landholding status in Chhattisgarh. In the marginal landholding category, 14.56% landholders were women, while in the small landholding category, they were at 10.83%. Their percentage reduced significantly in the semi-medium, medium, and large landholding categories with 9.34%, 7.92%, and 7.14%, respectively. Overall, 14.41% landholders were women.

Table 4.3 shows that amongst the tribal communities, 14.47% landholders in the marginal landholding category were women; this was slightly less than the total percentage of women. Their numbers reduced

Table 4.2

Operational Landholdings Status in Chhattisgarh

Social Category	Marginal	Small	Semi-medium	Medium	Large
All	2,183,000	831,000	503,000	202,000	28,000
Men	1,865,000	741,000	456,000	186,000	26,000
Women	18,000	90,000	47,000	16,000	2,000

Source: Agriculture Census, 2010–11 (Ministry of Agriculture, Government of India, 2014).

Table 4.3
Operational Landholdings Amongst the STs in Chhattisgarh

Schedule Tribe	Marginal	Small	Semi-medium	Medium	Large
Total	532,000	296,000	228,000	104,000	16,000
Men	455,000	261,000	205,000	95,000	15,000
Women	77,000	35,000	23,000	9,000	1,000

Source: Agriculture Census, 2010–11 (Ministry of Agriculture, Government of India, 2014).

Table 4.4
Operational Landholdings Amongst the SCs in Chhattisgarh

Schedule Caste	Marginal	Small	Semi-medium	Medium	Large
Total	326,000	84,000	35,000	9,000	1,000
Men	273,000	74,000	32,000	8,000	1,000
Women	53,000	9,000	3,000	1,000	NEG

Source: Agriculture Census, 2010–11 (Ministry of Agriculture, Government of India, 2014).

significantly in other categories. In the small, semi-medium, medium, and large landholding categories, their percentages were 11.82, 10.08, 8.65, and 6.25, respectively. Overall, 12.4% landowners amongst the tribal communities were women.

Table 4.4 shows that amongst the SC communities, 16.25% landowners in the marginal landholding category were women, which was higher than the percentage for the tribal communities. In the small and semi-medium categories, percentage of women owners was lower than that for the STs; however, in the medium landholding category, the percentage was higher than among the tribal communities. In the large category, unlike the tribal women, SC women had no land. Overall, 14.48% of landowners among the SC were women, which was more than the percentage among the ST communities.

The above discussion clearly shows that the total percentage of women landowners was the lowest amongst the tribal communities. While land rights were important for women across all social groups, they were critical for tribal women because of various other distress compounding factors such as loss of control over natural resources, evictions, displacement, and low literacy rates.

FINDINGS OF THE STUDY

Ownership of Homestead Land

Ownership of homestead land is viewed as a significant benchmark of land reforms. Absence of a secure tenure over homestead land is a significant symptom of deprivation. The study indicates that 74% of the respondents did not have a secure tenure for their homestead land.

Out of 74% of the respondents living on government land, only 8% have land entitlements. Of the respondents, 26% have legal ownership of their homestead land. This includes government land on which 8% have ownership and inherited land on which 18% have ownership. Among the respondents, 4% told that they were living on landlords' land. Another 4% told that they were living on leased land. In both cases, they did not have any legal safeguards.

In 1985, the Government of India started a Rural Landless Employment Guarantee Programme (RLEGP) in order to secure homestead rights of the rural poor. The Indira Awas Yojana has been the only government scheme for promoting rural housing but barely 22% of the eligible population has received benefits of this scheme. In 2011–12, the Government of Chhattisgarh utilized only 44% of the outlay for this scheme. According to Chhattisgarh Land Revenue Code (2000) Section 244, the state government should acquire any land for the extension of habitat (*abadi*). Section 244 also provides legal space for regularization of adverse possession on government land and further declares it as *abadi* land. Nevertheless, in Chhattisgarh, the study clearly shows that a very large number of people were living on land to which they have no secure rights. The Government of Chhattisgarh should address the issue at the earliest and specifically ensure that entitlements include women as owners.

Ownership of Agricultural Land

Ownership of agricultural land among tribes is ruled by the tribal customary law under which women lack any right to own land. The rights of women are further compounded by their marital status and ability to bear children. Women who are of older age may be consulted in matters of property but they do not have any rights per se.

The study indicates that of the 100 households surveyed, 49% have no legal entitlement to the land cultivated by them. Neither men nor women have any entitlement. Of the respondents, 38% have received their agricultural land through inheritance but none have entitlement in the name of a woman. The argument offered by the respondents for not including women as inheritors was that women leave home after marriage and the practice of giving them land would lead to fragmentation in landholdings.

Only 9% of the respondents said that women have entitlement of agricultural land. The average landholding of these women was 2.0–2.5 acres.

Women in Cultivation

Women are primarily seen as providers of labour in the cultivation process and not considered as 'skilled labour'. However, the study indicates that 94% women were involved in the cultivation process that included sowing, weeding, and harvesting. Some women respondents also said that they ploughed the land too. However, men viewed women's role as insignificant and claimed that majority of the work was done by men. Women participated only in sowing, weeding, and harvesting. The women more or less echoed similar views but stated that women played a significant role in sowing, weeding, and harvesting, while men played greater roles such as providing capital for inputs and hiring tractors and labour. Both men and women said that cultivation of land was now expensive. Women said that they had little or no say in matters of borrowing money for cultivation, buying or renting of land, selection of crops, and buying of inputs such as seeds and fertilizers from the market. Only 3% women in the study said that they had a voice in decision-making pertaining to matters of cultivation and production. Even in matters such as schooling of children and health care, women credited men with having the ultimate responsibility and control.

The study clearly indicates that women were primary stakeholders in the cultivation of land. They worked as labourers on their own land and on others' land but their contributions were not considered primary. Men viewed themselves as 'cultivators' but their roles were largely limited to ploughing and buying of inputs. Men in both Surguja and Mahasamund migrated, for several months in a year, for better work opportunities and cash income, while women took care of the land. Nevertheless, the men were the 'cultivators' and the women 'labourers'. This appeared to be the accepted norm as has emerged out of this study.

Land and Decision-making

The study indicates that women have little or no control over decisions related to the sale, mortgage, or leasing of land. Of the six respondents who said that they had sold their land in the past, only in two cases the women said that they were consulted before the land was sold.

Of the women respondents, 28% told that they were consulted when land had to be leased. In most of these cases, the land was leased in places where both men and women migrated for working on land, such as the agricultural zones of Bilaspur, Raipur, Durg, and Rajnandgaon.

Majority of the women reported that they participated in discussions related to the choice of crops to be grown and in the usage of land. However, they said that their role were very limited in matters pertaining to mortgage, purchase, and bequeathing of land. In all such matters, the decisions were taken by men of the household, and since harmony in the household was important, hence, women acquiesced even though they may have wanted to disagree with the decisions.

The results show that women lack control over land. Women work on land but do not own it. This reality is reflected in the decision-making related to land. Men control cash/income and all that pertains to the market, whether it was buying of inputs or selling of land. Given that the state of Chhattisgarh is rapidly industrializing, this has led to the emergence of a critical situation for rural households, particularly in tribal areas such as Surguja and Mahasamund, where large tracts of land are being bought by the corporate or being acquired by the government for the corporations. Lack of ownership of land by women is leading to serious consequences for the tribal households.

Common Property Resources and Land

Findings of the study reveal that 4% of the respondents were aware of their common property rights as described in the legal documents of the village. About 55% respondents stated that the FRA needed effective implementation and that its effective implementation would lead to recognition of tribal customary laws pertaining to common property resources.

Common property resources play a significant role in tribal households. Largely pertaining to the forest tracts, these resources provide fuel, fodder, building materials, and cash incomes through sale of Non-timber Forest Products (NTFPs). In tribal societies, women are inclusively involved in the collection, storage, processing, and marketing of these resources. Women also play a significant role in the conservation of forests. However, as is in the case of land, women's forests rights are insecure. The FRA, 2006, emphasizes community ownership of forests and its forest produces but in Chhattisgarh the provisions made under Community Forest Rights remained largely unimplemented. Both the *Nistar Patrak*, which is a revenue record at a village level, and the Chhattisgarh Land Revenue Code recognize this fact under Sections 234–237 but in reality, the government and its agencies such as the Forest Department have usurped these rights.

Denied ownership of the agricultural land and systematically barred from accessing common property resources, the tribal women of Chhattisgarh face serious challenges, often leading to their exploitation. A number of studies have established the importance of women's rights, particularly among tribal community, in improving their status in society. The Government of Chhattisgarh needs to take an urgent action to ensure women's rights; mere making of women's policy is not likely to change the situation.

Land Allotment on Joint Entitlement Basis

The survey and settlement process form an important and critical aspect of any revenue system. These processes allow physical correction of records and provide the parameters for corrections. They also provide remedies for eligible entitlement and mutations. The Chhattisgarh Land Revenue Code also has these provisions in Sections 70 and 104 but there is no space for joint entitlements or ownership for women. The state of Orissa issued an order in 1989 that enables issuing of joint entitlements in the names of husband and wife, and in the case of widows, in the name of women; but neighbouring states such as Chhattisgarh and Jharkhand have made no such enabling provisions.

The FRA, 2006, is the only instrument that recognizes joint entitlement and ownership of agricultural land. The Act also recognizes community ownership of forests and forest resources. However, this Act is silent on the issue of entitlement of single women, whether through divorce, not getting married, or widowhood.

The study indicates that 9 out of the 100 respondents have benefitted from the implementation of the FRA. Women who benefitted under FRA said: 'this joint entitlement recognizes that we have value and that we are also farmers who cultivate land.'

Inheritance of Landed Property

In a time when land has high monetary value and is in short supply, women face not only legal constraints in operationalizing their land rights but are also subject to a variety of sociocultural constraints. In both Surguja and Mahasamund districts, women respondents opined that their land rights were subject to both legal and customary laws. Of the respondents, 44% said that both the laws apply to them in matters of inheritance and transfer of land, and 35% said that largely it is governed by customary laws. In either case, exercising land rights for woman is a formidable proposition because society is not in favour of recognizing their rights.

While the Hindu Succession Act covers inherited land, other types of interests in agricultural land such as 'tenancy rights' are exempted. The Chhattisgarh Land Revenue Code is silent on the matter of tenancy rights. Section 190 of the code that deals with conferral of *Bhumiswami* rights on occupancy tenants does not specify the gender factor in tenancy. According to an estimate (EPW 2002), majority of the labourers (29%) categorized as 'occupancy tenants' have a very informal status in the revenue system of Chhattisgarh.

The Chhattisgarh Land Revenue Code does not take into account the parameters of the Hindu Succession Act or any other personal law in prevalence. Registering the names of women in mutation records is not defined as compulsory duty of the revenue officials. With such neglect it is not surprising that women find it difficult to exercise their land rights.

Factors Restricting Land Rights for Women

The study reveals that men play a decisive role in matters related to land, whether it is related to family land or cases coming to the village council. In both Oraon and Gond village councils in Surguja and Mahasamund, respectively, they were men who decided matters related to land.

Only 3% respondents were somewhat aware of the legal and customary provisions pertaining to land inheritance and ownership. Majority of the respondents said that they only knew of such things through experience and observation. They shared that usually widows were given half of the land that the husband held, while women who married outside the community were divested of all property rights. The daughters did not inherit land as it was not the practice in the society they live.

Given that control lies with men and ignorance of law was the norm, women's land rights remained a grey area. Even though the Hindu Succession Act has been amended to include women as inheritors of ancestral property, it is not likely to have an impact on land rights of women in the absence of knowledge of the law.

Dowry and Land Rights

It is often believed that the dowry system does not exist among the tribal communities, but in the present study, 68% respondents reported that there was a practice of dowry in their communities. Respondents reported that cash ranging from ₹500 to 50,000 has been given as dowry. They further said that considerable amount of money was also spent on marriage celebrations depending on the economic status of the household. Jewellery, household goods, and cattle also form part of dowry. Respondents told that after marriage both man and woman share the dowry; however, in the case of separation or death of husband, woman rarely gets anything, as the dowry is taken by the husband's family.

Despite this, dowry is seen as equivalent of inheritance and as woman's share in her parents' property. The majority of respondents in the study admitted that dowry compensated their share in the land.

Resolution of Disputes

According to the customary laws of both Oraon and Gond tribes, a widow loses her right to share in her husband's property if she remarries, gets unchaste, or leaves her husband's village on his death. If she is childless or has only daughters, then she gets maintenance.

Of the respondents, 85% told that in their knowledge, no case of dispute related to matters of inheritance has come before the village council in recent times. The respondents said that nowadays such disputes were taken to the police, court, gram panchayat, or *tehsildar*[1]. About 85% respondents also said that the village council was not capable of solving such disputes. About 18% of them said that they participate in the meetings of the village council for the resolution of the disputes brought before it.

KEY FINDINGS

- There is an increasing alienation among tribal women in the state as far as land resources and forests are concerned. This alienation is decreasing their bargaining power and increasing the possibility of their exploitation. Custom laws that supported the better status of tribal women have eroded extensively and the newer practices copied from the dominant culture are leading to women's disempowerment. Dominance of outside culture favours men more than women. For example, 'bride price' practised in the tribal society in Chhattisgarh has now been replaced by dowry. While 'development' by the state brings industry and mining to the tribal districts of Surguja and Mahasamund, often displacement and migration become the results to be borne by the people. In this process women are severely affected. The fact that women do not have land titles means that they have little option except to migrate or work as labourers in 'development' projects.
- Despite framing of progressive policy for women, their land rights are not the agenda of the state. Through implementation of the FRA, tribal women have received joint land titles to an extent, yet in matters of inheritance or in cases where land falls outside the purview of the FRA, women remain without land titles.

- Women are not aware of their legal rights. Their focus remains on maintenance of the family and for this they strive to maintain the gender roles status quo, while customs recede into the background and the judiciary and the revenue officials become the norm for resolution of land disputes. Women lack information and the resources to access justice so much so that they don't even want to discuss the subject.
- Last but not the least, women admitted the importance of land titles. Also women who have been able to get land titles under the FRA programme, found themselves more secured and important. Women want to have land in their names but do not know how it can be possible.

RECOMMENDATIONS

1. The land Revenue Code of Chhattisgarh should be reviewed and corrected from a gender perspective. Other land-related laws such as land leasing laws should also be revisited and corrected with the similar intention.
2. The Revenue and Forest Departments should take steps to enhance the understanding of gender vis-à-vis landownership possibilities for women. To begin with, the departments need to realize and accept that women are also entitled to own land.
3. The gram panchayats should be linked to legal cells so that women who take their case to the panchayats have ready access to legal advice and services.
4. A Land Commission should be established for women, on the lines of the State Women Commission, to ensure that women have a single window opportunity for the resolution of cases pertaining to land entitlement.
5. A cadre of para-legal workers should be created at the village level to assist and advise people, particularly women, who seek resolution to land-related issues.
6. Women groups should be mobilized and trained at the village level to recognize issues that lead to loss of land entitlement for women and the methods by which they can protect their rights.

NOTE

1. Revenue official at sub-divisional level. *Tehsildar* is directly responsible for supervision of lower-level officers for revenue purposes and provides general supervision of land records in a sub-district.

REFERENCES

Bryceson, D. F. 1997. 'De-agrarianisation in Sub-Saharan Africa.' In *Farewell to Farms*, edited by D. F. Bryceson and V. Jamal. 3–20. Aldershot: Ashgate Publishing.

Chandrasekhar, C. P and J. Ghosh. 2007. 'What Explains the High GDP Growth?' *Businessline* 11 September. Available at http://www.thehindubusinessline.com/bline/2007/09/11/stories/2007091150360900.htm (accessed on 4 May 2017).

Food and Fertilizer Technology Center for the Asian and Pacific Region. 2010. 'Globalization and International Development.' Available at http://www.agnet.org/situationer/stats/21.html (accessed on 23 January 2010).

Panda, P. K. and B. Agarwal. 2005. 'Marital Violence, Human Development and Women's Property Status in India.' *World Development* 33 (5): 823–50.

Rao, N. 2011. About Grain to Grind: Gender, Rural Development and Food (ed). Conference Proceedings in Gender and Development. Berne: DDC–Swiss National Commission for UNESCO.

5

Women and Land Rights in the Context of Legal Propertied Equality in Goa

RITU DEWAN[1]

The fulcrum of gender equality in all its myriad manifestations is the ownership and control over resources, and specifically in a developing economy, primarily and essentially land. However, these manifestations and also the intensity of inter linkages between gender equality and resources are, to a deeply significant level, determined by historical and regional specificities relating to economic as well as extra-economic factors and forces. Nowhere in India are these direct and indirect interconnections between gender equality and resources so intricate, nuanced, and simultaneously complex as in the state of Goa.

The analysis in this study has of course been located within the overall context of India being a signatory to Convention on the Elimination of All Forms of Discrimination against Women (CEDAW) and other conventions that make a commitment to gender equality, including the ensuring of land rights. As is known, CEDAW has given women the right to own and administer property without discrimination (CEDAW, Article 15), as well as right to equal treatment in land and agrarian reform (CEDAW, Article 14[2] [g]). Also, Article 16 ensures that both spouses have equal rights in the 'ownership, acquisition, management, administration, enjoyment and disposition of property'. Additionally, Resolution

15 (paras 1 and 3; 1998) of the Sub-Commission on the Promotion and Protection of Human Rights on 'Women and the Right to Land, Property and Adequate Housing' states that discrimination against women with respect to acquiring and securing land constitutes a violation of human rights law and urges governments to amend and repeal discriminatory laws and policies.

The decades after the Eighth Five-year Plan have witnessed increasing policy support to gender equality. These include, to name but a few, the 1995 guideline to issue *patta* land in the joint names of husband and wife; individual as well as group distribution of land titles to women; gendered distribution of surplus land; the granting of homesteads; enhancing women's land access through direct government transfers, purchase or lease from the market and inheritance, etc.—rather a long and encouraging list. The result has been rather laudatory—an almost 2% increase in the share of women landholders over the last decade, reflecting the relative success of a gender-sensitive policy and a strong women's movement.

The examination of the issue of land rights and gender in the state of Goa has been conducted through a dramatically different perspective and structure than that existing in other regions of the country. This is because, as is known, Goa is the only state that applies Article 44 of the Indian Constitution that 'the State shall endeavour to secure for the citizens a uniform civil code throughout the territory of India'; the Common Civil Code which was instituted in Goa in 1867 still exists and applies to virtually all facets of life in the state, including property rights.

STRUCTURAL LOGIC

In the context of the fact that this is the only region in India where women are guaranteed equal property rights, the structural logic of this chapter will of necessity differ widely and also wildly from other such state-level analysis. We begin by giving a short economic and administrative background of the region, followed by an overview of the status of women determined by educational and health indicators. To understand the very different and unique land rights pertaining in Goa, a somewhat detailed presentation of both the Uniform Civil Code and the relevant land laws and legislations is essential. Related components are the nature of women's schemes as operative in the state. The demystification of gendered land patterns will, therefore, be built on the prevailing intermixes of land, property, and matrimonial rights.

It must be noted that prolonged and multi-pronged strategies were used to avail of secondary data, some of which have borne fruit. We were also able to interview several government officials and women's rights practitioners who have been involved with this issue for several decades. Case studies are crucial to such a seminal analysis, and are therefore integrated. Recommendations, if they can be thus termed, are in-built into analysis, apart, of course, from being identified separately.

GENDERED ECONOMIC OVERVIEW

Goa, which became the 25th state of India in 1987, was under Portuguese rule for four and a half centuries, from 1510 till its liberation in 1961. It consists of two districts—North and South Goa, the former with six blocks (Bardez, Pernem, Bicholim, Satari, Ponda, and Tiswadi), the latter comprising of five (Mormugao, Salcette, Quepem, Canacona, and Sanguem). There are 359 villages and about 50 urban centres and towns.

Goa has the highest per capita income in India, reporting an astounding ₹224,138 (at current prices) in 2013–14, much higher than the national average of ₹143,677 (PIB 2015). The state has also had a constant and consistent growth rate of about 8% per annum as per quick estimates of gross state domestic production (GSDP) for 2012–13, in spite of a decline in the mining sector and also in registered manufacturing. The sector-wise composition of GSDP at constant prices (2004–05) shows that the tertiary sector accounted for 64.80%, followed by the secondary sector with 30.55%, and predictably and lastly the primary sector at 4.65% (Government of Goa 2013–14).

Goa also boasts of several other human developmental achievements. We take a critical look at some of the more crucial indicators.

1. Goa has a relatively better sex ratio of 968 as compared to India's 940, and a child sex ratio of 920, just a little above India's pathetic 914 (Census 2011).[2] What is extremely problematic is that the child sex ratio is much lower than the sex ratio; that this divergence has been increasing over time is an accepted fact. The sex ratio has witnessed a secular decline, from 981 in 1971 to 975,

967, and 960 in the subsequent censuses (Government of Goa 2003–04). What this trend can also imply is that preference for boys is somewhat disconnected with the three major components of income levels, literacy rates, and also property rights.
2. Literacy figures too are commendable. Of Goan's, 87.4% are literate as compared to India's 74.04%; its male literacy rate is more than 10 percentage points higher at 92.81% as compared to the nation's 82.14%. What is indeed laudable is Goa's female literacy rate of 81.84%, almost 15 percentage points more than the national average of 65.46%; thus, over four-fifths of Goan women are literate as compared to not even two-thirds at the national level.[3]
3. Health data reveals that the infant mortality rate achieved in Goa is highly commendable—9 per 1,000 live births, less than even one-fourth of the national average of a rather shameful 40 (NSS 68th Round 2011–12). However, along with low maternal mortality rates that the state has achieved is the fact that almost two-fifths of Goan women have been recorded as being anaemic by NFHS III (as quoted in Almeida and Correa 2008: 1).

The NFHS III reported universal knowledge of contraception at 99%; yet, its use is apparently less than half. Several NGOs suspect that the family size is being controlled by means other than contraception. Given the evidence that there is a male child preference, and the low fertility rate is leading to a falling family size, it is not unlikely that the choice of children (both number and sex) is not happening randomly but by means of sex selective techniques and abortions/female foeticide (De Souza 2009: 108–09).

What is essential to the analysis of land rights for women in the regional reality of Goa is the location of this issue in the levels of involvement in the labour force. Thus, it would be pertinent to examine gendered participation in economic activity, particularly in the rural context. The labour force participation rates and the worker–population ratio are quite identical for both 2011–12 and 2012–13, as can be seen from Tables 5.1 to 5.3; significant differences, however, emerge in the workforce participation rates.

We examine the above at different levels. First, all three measurements of rural women's economic participation in Goa are lower than that at the all-India level, which is not surprising given the fact that the

Table 5.1

Gendered Rural Labour Force Participation Rate for 2011–12

Region	Female	Male
Goa	21.2	58.6
India	25.3	55.3

Source: http://mospi.nic.in/Mospi_New/upload/man_and_women

Table 5.2

Gendered Rural Worker Population Ratio for 2012–13

Region	Female	Male
Goa	21.0	54.7
India	24.8	54.3

Source: http://mospi.nic.in/Mospi_New/upload/man_and_women

Table 5.3

Gendered Rural Workforce Participation Rate for 2011

Region	Female	Male
Goa	22.6	55.5
India	30.0	53.0

Source: http://mospi.nic.in/Mospi_New/upload/man_and_women

level of urbanization in the state at 62.17% is double that of the country's 31.16% as per the 2011 Census. Second, rural males in Goa report consistently higher rates than the national averages, especially in labour force participation. Third, in seeming contradiction, this is exactly where rural Goan women report the largest difference from their national counterparts. These issues become quite intriguing once they are linked to the right of Goan women to property as guaranteed in the Portuguese Civil Code operative in the state.

GENDERED LANDHOLDING PATTERNS: DECADAL ANALYSIS

We now lay out the basic fundamentals in quantitative terms so as to understand the levels and nuances of the changing landholding patterns in the state of Goa. This is essential in order to examine the actual situation before critiquing it from the perspective of the specificity of women's property rights in the only region in the country that has historically had at least de jure equality in land rights. It should of course be noted at the outset that the agricultural census, on which this section is based, gives data on operational holdings and not landownership. Be that as it may, the gendered patterns emerge quite sharply.

As can be seen from Table 5.4, landholdings located in Goa as a proportion of the national total remained static across the decade between the two Agricultural Censuses of 2000–01 and 2010–11, at 0.05%, with Goan men and women accounting for a consistent share of 0.04% and 0.01%, respectively.

The overall pattern is quite interesting in that the process of marginalization appears to have reversed, with the share of marginal holdings falling from 81.7% to 76.84% over the decade, although the area remained the same at 32.29%. This change has been offset by an increase partly in small but mainly in the number of semi-medium size holdings, as can be clearly seen from Figure 5.1.

What are most fascinating are the gendered patterns of land operated across the various size classes of holdings. In 2001, Goan women accounted for 22.4% of all landholdings in the state, rising less than one percentage point a decade later to 23.19%; however, the land they operated rose at a somewhat higher proportion during this period, from 15.56% to 17.75%. This, thus, does represent at least a partial improvement in women's property status, even though to a rather insignificant

Table 5.4

Gendered Operational Holdings (Goa and India for 2000–01 and 2010–11; Actual and %)

	Total Holdings			
All India/Goa	2001 (number)	(2001) (%)	2011 (number)	(2011) (%)
All India	119,658,738	100	138,109,893	100
Goa	63,956	0.05	77,895	0.05
All India (Male)	106,668,599	100	120,327,121	100
Goa (Male)	49,625	0.04	59,825	0.04
All India (Female)	12,990,144	100	17,682,772	100
Goa (Female)	14,331	0.1	18,070	0.1

Source: Agricultural Census 2000–01 and 2010–11.

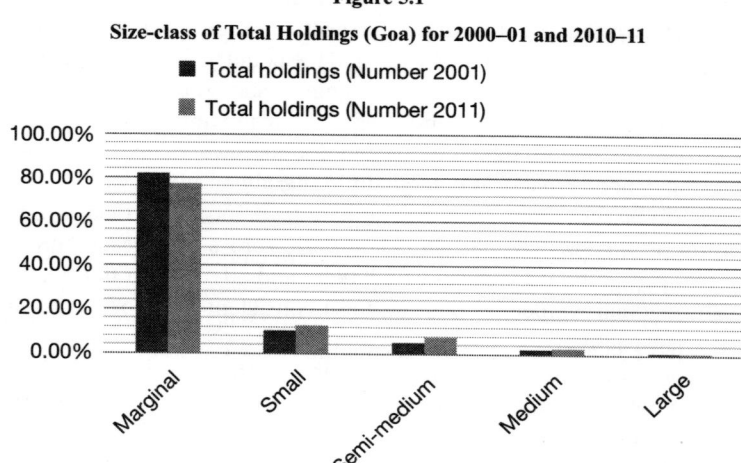

Figure 5.1

Size-class of Total Holdings (Goa) for 2000–01 and 2010–11

Sources: Agricultural Census 2000–01 and 2010–11.

extent, keeping in mind that woman according to the Common Civil Code operative in the state should own half of all land.

The gendered nuances of changes in both the number of operational holdings and the area operated are even more fascinating. We examine each size class separately. Women accounted for 24.09% of all marginal landholdings in Goa in 2000–01, rising to 25.19% a decade later, the area they held under this size class increasing almost proportionally from 22.72% to 23.85%.

Predictably, women appear to have lost out in the property hierarchy, the number of holdings they operate as well as the area declining as the size class increases for at least another two categories. Women accounted for a virtually identical 15.3% of all small and semi-medium holders in Goa, the proportions changing rather interestingly to 19.6% and 13.68% a decade later. Simultaneously, the area changed from 15.08% and 14.89% to 22.27% and 14.66%, respectively, in 2010–11. That is, women smallholders appear to have gained somewhat more than the semi-medium holders, both in terms of number and area.

Interestingly, the proportion of women holding above 10 hectares of land rose from 10.93% to 12.29% of all large landholders in the state, the area they account for increasing simultaneously from 7.97% to 10.87%. This intriguing trend needs to be demystified in terms of absolutes—the number of such holdings today is accounted for by 69 women, their number increasing by merely 15 from 54 a decade ago.

The current pattern of land rights is as follows.

Gendered Landholding Patterns

- Of all landholders in Goa, 23.19% are women, operating 17.75% of land.
- The overwhelming majority of women landholders at 83.44% have marginal holdings, accounting for 43.39% of the total land they own.
- Of the land women own, 22.27% is held by the 1,879 women smallholders.
- The semi-medium and medium size class comprise of 5.77% of all female holders and 25.61% of land.
- Large holdings of women constitute barely 0.38% of female holders, operating merely 8.7% of all land held by women in Goa.

As of today, as it can be seen from Tables 5.5 and 5.6, there are 18,070 women-operated holdings in Goa extending over 15,436 hectares of land compared to 59,825 male-owned holdings, which cover 71,507 hectares. The gender inequalities are sharp, both in relation to numbers and area, as well as to size of holdings (Figures 5.2 and 5.3). The problematique is clear—women do not get equal property rights even in a region that legally guarantees them an equal share in property.

Table 5.5

Gendered Landholding Pattern for 2000–01 and 2010–11 (Actual Numbers and %)

S. No.	Size of Holding (in ha)	Male (2001)	Male (2011)	Female (2001)	Female (2011)
1.	Marginal	39,668	44,779	12,590	15,078
2.	Small	5,578	7,923	1,010	1,879
3.	Semi-medium	2,683	4,909	487	778
4.	Medium	1,256	1,722	190	266
5.	Large	440	492	54	69
6.	All Classes	49,625	59,825	14,331	18,070

Sources: Agricultural Census 2000–01 and 2010–11.

Figure 5.2

Gendered Landholding Pattern for 2000–01 and 2010–11

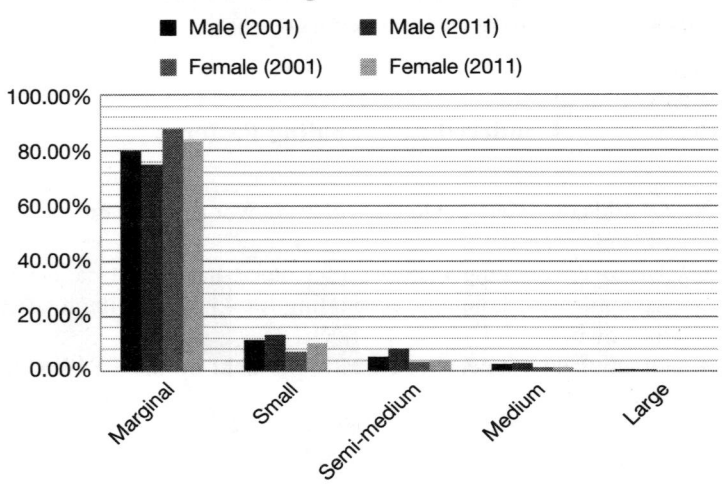

Sources: Agricultural Census 2000–01 and 2010–11.

Table 5.6

Gendered Land Area Pattern for 2000–01 and 2010–11 (Actual Area and %)

S. No.	Size of Holdings (in ha)	Male (2001)	Male (2011)	Female (2001)	Female (2011)
1.	Marginal	13,055	21,384	3,839	6,699
2.	Small	7,080	14,128	1,228	3,439
3.	Semi-medium	6,881	14,449	1,213	2,264
4.	Medium	7,153	10,539	997	1,691
5.	Large	10,001	11,005	867	1,343
6.	All Classes	44,172	71,507	8,143	15,436

Sources: Agricultural Census 2000–01 and 2010–11.

WOMEN, LAND RIGHTS, AND THE COMMON CIVIL CODE: A RECOMMENDATORY CRITIQUE

Women, Land Rights, and the Common Civil Code

Goa is the only region in the entire nation that has a Common Civil Code which governs all rights of women, including that of property, both

Figure 5.3

Gendered Land Area Pattern for 2000–01 and 2010–11

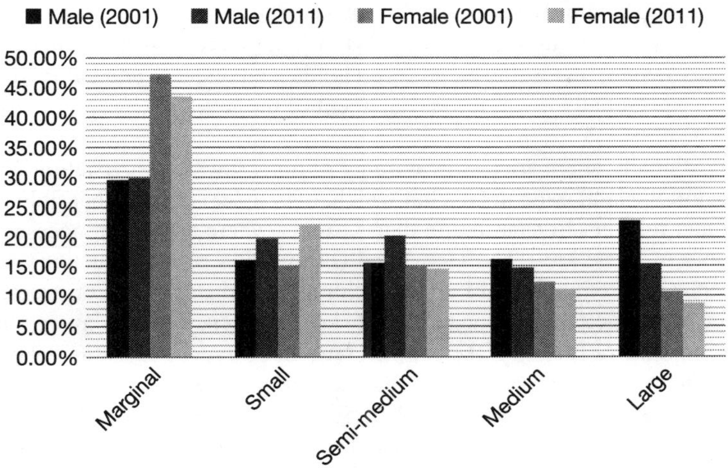

■ Male (2001)   ■ Male (2011)   ▓ Female (2001)   ▓ Female (2011)

Sources: Agricultural Census 2000–01 and 2010–11.

marital and natal. Any analysis of gendered land rights in the state must, therefore, interrelate land laws and legislations with the Portuguese Civil Code. Consequently, this rather long section examines the three tightly interwoven structures of the Common Civil Code, the Family Laws, and the Land Laws so as to arrive at a holistic perspective within which the gendered nature and implementation of land rights must necessarily be perceived. It must also be pointed out at the outset that this section is not merely a laying out of what is termed as salient features, but contains within a critical and hence recommendatory analysis.

Land rights for rural women in Goa are regulated and mediated through a vast cluster of laws, regulations, and schemes; we list them below for purposes of clarity.

1. Family Laws, that is, a group of laws which, among other things, also embody the concept of matrimonial property rights.
2. Code of communidades (village community): The village community law by which the land and the resources of the area are commonly managed by the villagers.
3. Goa Land Revenue Code, 1968.
4. Goa Mundkar (Protection from Eviction) Act of 1975, governing Mundkars, that is, those who lawfully reside with a fixed

habitation in a dwelling house with or without obligation to render any services to the family, with the consent of the *bhatkar*, that is, the landlord.
5. Goa Agricultural Tenancy Act, 1964, governing the agricultural tenant, that is, the person who holds land on lease and cultivates it personally up until the enactment of the Act.

Additionally, there are a large number of other laws and legislations that govern the land issue in Goa but which, of course, is neither possible nor in fact relevant to examine in detail except where and when necessary. Some of these are—The Goa Land (Prohibition of Construction) Act, 1995, Goa Regulation of Land Development and Building Construction Act, social welfare and social security laws and schemes, the law relating to cooperative societies, the contract law, the relevant provisions relating to banking laws, insurance laws, partnership laws, corporate laws, exclusionary laws which negate people's rights such as the Special Economic Zones Act of 2005, Information Technology Policy, Biotechnology Policy, creation of industrial estates, land acquisition laws, and the absent laws relating to evolving forms of property holdings such as time shares in which several joint owners have the right to use a property as a holiday home under a time-sharing scheme.

Considering that land has value from the point of view of its utilization value and from the point of view of ability to use land to have access to critical amenities of life and to services that are essential for the development of the full potential of a woman, land rights for rural women are also regulated through another set of laws such as the procedural laws for access to water, transport, electricity/power, credit, and access to tapping general beneficial legislation, and rights to exercise choices on the use of the land. In that sense, land rights only get translated into land rights for women, if the referred critical access is available.

Therefore, any move to ensure land rights for rural women invariably requires an analysis of the content of several interrelated laws from a gender perspective and so also an analysis of the procedural laws of access and the social circumstances of the various sections of rural women that enable or disable or half-heartedly able a use of these laws, which is what this section of the chapter proceeds to do.

At this point, it is pertinent to note that the rural woman in the context of Goa could range from a Goan woman residing in a town/village, which in turn includes women from families at different stages of landedness and landlessness, to a migrant woman who has migrated from other parts of India, and at this point of time, who resides in one of the villages/towns of Goa, particularly those that skirt the highway, or a Goan rural woman who has migrated solely for employment to any other state in India, and mainly outside India, out of social and economic compulsions, or women who stayed back while their spouses/children migrated to the Gulf countries. At a time when migration is a reality of many a people's worlds, and also Portuguese passports and citizenship are available to Goans born of children of parents born prior to 1961, but who have their roots in India, as persons of Indian origin or overseas citizens of India, this is as critical a factor which cannot be ignored.

It is useful at this juncture to hark back to Goa's legislative history to appreciate the context and content of the different trajectory of the laws relating to land rights for women in Goa. Goa perched on the West Coast of India, post its liberation in 1961, is touted as the model location for women's rights, because it possesses what is called a 'Uniform Civil Code', a phrase not used during Portuguese rule. The Portuguese had what is called a Portuguese Civil Code, a Portuguese Civil Procedure Code, a Portuguese Code of Civil Registration, a Portuguese Commercial Code, a Portuguese Criminal Code; life in Portugal and its colonies was to be legally regulated by the above codes. Even during the Portuguese rule, these codes were not without their implications for land rights. For instance, women who were widowed and had to lead an isolated existence and were lined up for tonsuring of their heads were often even induced to enter a liberated world with the promise of not tonsuring their heads, and accompanied with land rights.

However, it is to be remembered that the Portuguese Civil Code is a code of 1867, and what is now Goa was colonized by the Portuguese in bits and parts from different kingdoms. Therefore, the areas that were conquered from 1498 onwards through the period up to 1543 are referred to as the Old Conquests, and those conquered thereafter as the New Conquests. There are distinct cultural differences, and population indicators which still persist with reference to the two sets of areas of what is now called Goa.

Prominent among these indicators is the difference in density. Consequently, the ecological footprint hides the completely uneven terrain and footprint within Goa. Similarly, Goa has the lowest poverty head count ratio at 5.09%, according to the report submitted by India as regards compliance under the Millennium Development Goals, but that again hides the vast differences which are camouflaged in the guise of being a 'topper'. The statistics do not afford a gender break-up, the caste break-up, the place of origin break-up, or the break-up for old and new conquests or any such relevant and essential details.

Although the Portuguese Civil Code of 1867 has since been amended several times, the version of the code as amended in 1936, along with the amendments consequent to the Concordat (a treaty between Portugal and the Holy See) in 1940, is the legal foundation for what are called the Family Laws of Goa, in that by a regulation for its administration after it joined India, that is, the Goa, Daman and Diu Administration Act, 1962, the parliament extended most of the central laws prevalent in pre-1961 in the rest of India to Goa, but did not extend some laws and maintained that only those provisions of the Portuguese laws, on subjects which were not extended from India, or on subjects not covered by the laws of India, would be retained. So it was that none of the various Family Laws—what are often referred to as personal laws—were extended to Goa from the rest of India, and consequently those portions of the Portuguese Civil Code which related to Family Laws were retained. This was, therefore, primarily a kind of residual provision and there was no special notification as to which laws were retained. It, hence, became rather problematic for both the judiciary and the administrators to interpret what of the Portuguese law could be said to be retained as applicable to Goa by the said parliament regulation. This position continues to this day. Until recently, most of the laws were not officially translated from the Portuguese to English and much less so in the languages set out as official languages of Goa in the Official Language Act, 1987.

So we return to what is being touted as the Uniform Civil Code, and it begs the question: Is it uniform and to the extent that it is uniform, is uniformity the password for equality for women, and to what extent the concept of equality as substantive equality and human rights enshrined in the constitution finds favour in this 'Uniform Civil Code' which is now locally called the Family Laws of Goa?

The Family Laws encompass the following: the portions of the Portuguese Civil Code dwelling on marriage, dissolution of marriage, separation of persons and properties, annulment of marriage, succession, inventory proceedings (initiated in court to determine the devolution of properties of a Goan deceased with properties in Goa), guardianship, and adoption of children—the Code and Customs of Gentile Hindus. The term 'Gentile' is a rather derogatory one, the literal meaning being a pagan or heathen, that is, a person who does not acknowledge a particular god or belief.

From the very face of it, one can see that there is one section of the law, namely, the Code and Customs of Gentile Hindus, which nails the lie about uniformity and even contains provisions for bigamy/polygamy, if there is no male child, which in turn has implications for land rights for women. Critics of those who raise this often state that this chapter is not applicable—something which is left to the courts to interpret as people, including women, negotiate through the vast maze of the law. The critics also state that the provision is not used and, hence, best simply laid to rest on that account. The contention that the provisions are not used, may largely be true, as one does not come across cases that are hinged on this law, though it is salaciously eyed by many who wish to tap the sexist provisions of this law.

There is also the fact that the law classifies marriages into canonical marriages and civil marriages, that is, non-canonical marriages. This means that there are two kinds of marriage registration: that for Catholics who opt for canonical marriages and that for non-Catholics and those who do not opt for canonical marriages. The procedure for registration of marriage is that a couple should declare their intent to get married by filling a form duly signed by them and two witnesses and affirmed before the civil registrar of the taluka in which either one of them resides. Post this declaration, after 15 days and before one year, the couple has to confirm their intent along with the witnesses before the civil registrar or the celebrant of the nuptials of the couple in the Catholic Church. The location of confirmation depends on whether the person is Catholic or non-Catholic and whether the registration as a canonical marriage is opted for by the Catholic, so that the marriage is written into the marriage registration books. If the marriage is a canonical marriage, the parties have the additional option of bringing it to an end through annulment before what is called the Patriarchal Tribunal of the Catholic Church. Earlier, it was the only option available for Catholics until a Catholic woman approached the then Judicial Commissioner's Court, which was the highest court in the then Union Territory of Goa, to get the benefit of Article 14 of the Constitution, upon which the courts threw open the doors of civil law remedies in civil courts for Goans. So, as of now, there is still the option of a party seeking annulment under the canon law from the Patriarchal Tribunal after which the order of the said tribunal is sent for confirmation to the High Court of Bombay at Goa, to confirm the annulment, which then has civil effects as far as the marital status of the persons goes. The ecclesiastical authorities maintain that their order, on confirmation by the high court, only has civil effects when it comes to the union of the spouses, and that it is for the courts to decide on the separation of properties. However, when the courts deliberate on separation of properties in terms of the law on separation of properties or in terms of the inventory proceedings, it is the high court approved order of the Patriarchal Tribunal that will end up being considered when it comes to determining a fault-based system of division of property.

The rights relating to succession and separation of properties are said to be equally applicable to all, irrespective of religion or whether their marriages are canonical or non-canonical, in that sons and daughters have equal rights to parental properties, in the absence of a will, and the default system of holding property upon marriage is the regime of communion of assets which means that upon marriage, unless an option is made to the contrary, all assets, including land, whether inherited, or acquired before or after marriage, are held in common by the couple. There is also a limitation on parents to be able to alienate only half of their property by will, which in a sense in some ways takes care of the son preference and ensures that its attendant consequences do not prejudice the rights of women.

But rights are different for parties whose marriage has been annulled as against parties whose marriage has been dissolved by divorce or death or who are separated by a decree of separation of persons and properties. In the event of a divorce, the properties are divided in equal shares. In the event of separation, if the separation was sought both of persons and properties, then the properties will be divided equally. However, there is no clarity even on this account. For instance, annulment of a marriage means that the marriage never was and, therefore, it would follow that there is no concept of matrimonial property rights, because there cannot be such rights if the matrimonial status of the couple itself is negated. However, technically, the law provides that the party who is at fault shall not secure any of the benefits of a marriage which is annulled, while a party who is not at fault shall.

Hence, when the civil law is circumvented by utilizing the Patriarchal Tribunal which grants annulment on the grounds such as non-consummation of marriage which is not a ground for annulment under the Family laws of Goa, it will be the tribunal's grounds of determining fault that will be upheld in the division of properties.

It is quite another thing that in a judgement of the Bombay High Court, references to provisions of the Portuguese Civil Code, which do not find place in the translated portions of the law, now suggest otherwise and cast a fault-based system on the division of properties upon divorce or separation. This brings us to the implications of the certainty of substantive and procedural rights in the law, so that valuable time and resources are not lost in proceedings that ultimately get challenged on technicalities for which the vulnerable has neither the time nor the resources and not even the possibilities to go through such a labyrinthine maze of justice, which can begin with issues of jurisdiction and applicability of laws and end up with conflicts around fault or no-fault divisions of properties, and which is the law that actually applies. This does no good for a woman in a generally patrilocal society who is struggling to start a new life and pick up the threads of her marriage.

Vishranti's mother Maria is a Goan who after the dissolution of her marriage with Vishranti's father married Simon, a person of non-Goan origin not governed by local Goan family laws. He was governed by the Indian Succession Act. Simon had a daughter who was named Serena by Vishranti. Serena was, after Maria's death, living with Vishranti.

Shortly after Vishranti's mother died, Simon made an application to the panchayat to transfer the house tax records of a house standing in Maria's name to his name. He never once mentioned the existence of Serena or Vishranti who were basically the rightful holders of that property as they were the legal heirs of Maria. Yet, by a mere application where Simon represented that he was the husband of Maria and presented his marriage certificate, the house tax record was transferred in his name.

Simon later got married to Natasha after Maria's death and applied to add Natasha's name on the house tax record. As Vishranti got wind of the application, she went to the panchayat to make inquiries and learnt that her mother's house in which she and Serena were staying had already been transferred to Simon's name and was on its way to being considered for transfer to Natasha's name. It was then that Vishranti put her objection on record, pointing out that under the Indian Christian Marriage Act, there was no provision of communion of assets as there is in Goa's family laws and, hence, the heirs of the deceased are entitled to the shares in the assets. That aside, she and Serena as heirs had not been notified. She placed her objections, and as the transfer was allowed, subject to revocation if misrepresented, the panchayat obliged and revoked the transfer, but not before Simon had already transferred the electricity and water connection records in his name on the strength of the transferred house tax record in his name. Simon was not asked for any documents re succession to Maria.

As a result, Vishranti had to move the panchayat first and, thereafter, the electricity and water supply departments to set the record right, all of which could have been avoided if Vishranti had been intimated in the first instance and given a hearing before the decision in the matter of transfer of house tax record was taken.

The confusion about applicability of rights compounded matters. Crystal clear procedures must be in place, so that there is little or no room for arbitrary actions.

A question that is of even more significance, assuming that the aforestated issue of divorce is applicable only to a few members of society who have pursued the dissolution of their marriages, a number which is increasing, but which is by no means a significant number in comparison to the entire population, is what about landholdings during marriage. Is it the principle of unity of persons in marriage, and therefore the property being the marital property and property of neither the husband nor the wife but of the marital union? Apparently this is the case; but how does that translate into administration of the marital property? Apparently at the time of the Code of 1867, which was located in a feudal patriarchal age, non-hierarchical administration could not even be imagined. Hence, one of the couple was seen as having to manage the property and, needless to say, in that feudal age, the person capable of doing so was invariably seen to be a male.

Consequently, all the sense of equality in terms of inheritance or in terms of holding the matrimonial property in common gets reduced to almost naught with a provision to the effect that although the ownership of matrimonial property vests in both the spouses, it shall be managed by the male spouse, except in the case of impediment. What this means is that the property will be administered by the male spouse, and will only be administered by the female spouse in the event the male spouse is unable to manage in situations such as his being abroad. Further to this, there is another provision that the male spouse can alienate property provided he obtains the consent of his spouse, which can be obtained post facto, whereas the female spouse can alienate only if she has the authorization of her husband. Thus, together these three articles in themselves render nugatory all the provisions relating to equality of rights in parental or matrimonial property.

Women in Goa from among those families that own some land are brought up to believe that their signature is of great significance and that their signature on the conveyance document, along with that of their spouse, can alone give proper title/interest in the marital property and determine whether the marital properties held in common are alienated or not. However, the article discussed above renders this nugatory. What it in effect says is that if a male should choose to alienate property, whatever he has alienated is to be adjusted against his moiety (half) share. But what if he alienates more than half his property claiming that what he is alienating is part of his half? There is no system in place to compute what constitutes the total asset value of the couple at the time of drawing up any conveyance or will wherein the male spouse states that he is disposing of only his legitimate share. So whatever action the woman can take is post facto the transaction when she finds that her husband has alienated more than half of the marital properties without her consent. The result is generally a long struggle for justice with third parties having acquired rights by virtue of the husband's acts of alienation of the properties through execution of conveyance documents by himself alone. However, this privilege of so alienating properties even when the husband is not contributing towards maintenance is not available to the female spouse as the law clearly stipulates that she cannot alienate properties without the authorization of her husband to do so.

Vimala was palmed off in marriage by her parents to a purportedly rich man who ran a business in a locality in Maharashtra. Neither she nor her parents knew at the time of her marriage that her husband was a chronic alcoholic and gambler. The marriage actually lasted for but a few years, though there was no formal divorce or ongoing proceedings for divorce. As she learnt that her husband had begun selling their marital properties, she moved the court under the Protection of Women from Domestic Violence Act, 2005, to restrain her husband from selling the marital properties and was granted interim reliefs. While the matrimonial and domestic violence proceedings were on, her husband died.

Soon after his death Vimala was served with a legal notice from her nephew that the properties had been willed to him. These were properties that constituted marital properties. Her consent had not been taken at the time of willing. Furthermore, as it turned out, several major properties had already been sold. In reality, therefore, there was no inheritance and the husband had exceeded his quota of half of his half share, which constituted the disposable property.

Vimala was left with no option but to challenge the sale deeds by which the properties were sold without her consent and also the will by which all the remaining properties were willed. She has successfully challenged some of the sale deeds, and some litigation persists, thus pointing to the difficulties with post facto remedies.

Also, there is a provision for relinquishment of rights by any child who wishes to waive off the inheritance. This provision is often used to browbeat the sisters into relinquishing their rights to parental property stating that they were given some dowry and it is not done to make claims to their parental property.

We interviewed Stella from Betim village in Bardez tehsil of North Goa who was compelled by her two brothers to relinquish her rights under this clause. Even though she is married to a man who is not financially well off and has three children and a mother-in-law to support, her brothers repeatedly harassed her over several years to give up her share of the property. Finally, unable to cope with the family pressure and also the endless visits to several administrative offices to clarify her rights, Stella gave in and signed over her property rights in the sub-registrar's office in Mapuca. Predictably, both her brothers who are now substantially better off have suddenly become rather 'generous', condescendingly visiting her twice a year and 'gifting' her coconuts from their recently appropriated property. Both Stella and her brothers term this as 'maintaining peace in the family'.

Sumati, married to a rather rich businessman in Verna village in South Goa, has seven siblings, of which only one is a brother. She and her five sisters have all 'voluntarily' relinquished their shares in favour of their brother. She states categorically that as the parents have arranged marriages of all the six sisters in large landowning families, none of them need to 'deprive' their brother of what should be his rightful share under their religion. Sumati's husband, when interviewed, stated proudly and predictably that he earned enough to take care of his family's needs, and did not need any share of his wife's parent's property to support his 'historically sumptuous lifestyle'.

Special safeguards are, hence, needed to ensure that rights of ownership and control are not wrested out of women, that there is a future for real land rights for women. Furthermore, there is also the aspect of harmonization of laws. After the liberation of Goa and its joining India in 1961, there were laws enacted for Goa Union Territory and subsequently set out to be State laws, once Goa attained statehood. In the first round immediately after 1961, these included The Land Revenue Code, The Goa Mundkar Act, and the Agricultural Tenancy Act. At this point it becomes necessary to state that initially IAS officers from India were appointed to run the administration. Hence, they had little or no grasp of the law, and in the turbulent period of the 1960s, when the exploited and oppressed sections of society were demanding real independence, the laws that had been crafted in those contexts were simply imported into Goa, without taking into account the family laws prevalent in Goa or even the concept of substantive equality.

The Goa Land Revenue Code 1969 is operated as if from a separate compartment, without any linkages to the Family Laws. First of all, when the survey and Record of Rights was carried out in the late 1970s and early 1980s, the practice was to allot survey numbers according to holdings and to set out the names in the records as told to them by the people on the site. The Land Mutation System, that is, the system by which the record of devolution and conveyance of land is made, presupposes a smooth functioning of the administrative and legal systems. This, however, is often not the case. Tribal populations, particularly, were distinctly disadvantaged by the survey and mutation processes in that their births were not registered and their names as incorporated in Forms I and XIV which is the Record of Rights were at variance with the pet names which were at variance with their real names as reflected in any identity documents. Furthermore, *Nav* Hindus (meaning new Hindus), who converted from Christianity to Hinduism, bore the Catholic names in their birth certificates and Hindu names in Forms I and XIV in the Other Rights column.

Any devolution of rights was made doubly difficult even for Catholic women whose names do not stand automatically changed upon marriage in the marriage certificate and, therefore, if their names were to be entered in the land records in situations where their spouses or son-less parents are dead, which is what happened during the survey, then their names were entered as their first name and the husband's surname. In the case of tribal women, there are a range of other issues of lack of reading and writing capacity which resulted in the names entered in the marriage certificates being based on whatever the officials understood to be their names on the strength of their narration, and no birth registration records to fall back upon. This is further compounded by the fact that in issuing a divergence certificate, only the names in identity documents are taken into account and the names as they figure in documents pertaining to the Record of Rights.

This is apart from the gender insensitivity of many officers and officials manning the mutation systems who do not consider including the wife if the occupants/rights-holders are married. This again gets reflected in the land acquisition notices, where it is the men folk who are notified about the acquisition of land, as the women's names do not figure in the Record of Rights which is taken as the document for determining the persons to notify.

In this context, we are hereby appending Forms I and XIV given to us by the relevant administrative authorities, and which are being currently used as Record of Rights. It is indeed surprising that there is no column whatsoever for the definition of inter-familial relationship, whether natal or marital, nor is there an age column—gender, of course, is not even considered as an issue.

The dwelling houses of the Mundkars, which have undergone a sea change from the time the original Mundkar constructed the house in the landlord's property, do not figure in the survey plans, thus, further compounding the case especially for women from the marginalized sections who comprise the numbers that constitute the illiterates of Goa.

Consequently, the Goa Mundkar (Protection from Eviction Act), 1975, sets out that the member of a family of a Mundkar means his spouse, son, unmarried daughter, and includes father, mother, grandson, widowed daughter, and widowed grand-daughter, solely dependent on the Mundkar for maintenance. There is also a provision that Mundkarial rights are heritable. Read with the other sexist provision which automatically assumes patrilocality after marriage, this provision has been interpreted to mean heritable by those who are defined as members of the family under the Mundkar Act and not as heritable by those who qualify as heirs in the Family Laws of Goa.

There are, thus, two sets of laws in operation when it comes to inheritance. Following a challenge to the law for breach of Article 14 of the Constitution, the High Court of Bombay at Goa in *Henriqueta D'Souza vs Manguesh Mishal and others* and *Rama Hegde vs Diogo Piedade Rodrigues* together held: On a fair construction of Section 3 of the Act (the section that provides for heritability), in our view, the heritability of the Mundkar in a dwelling house would devolve upon the successors who are living/residing in the dwelling house along with the Mundkar at the time of opening of the inheritance.

The High Court tried to reconcile the rights of residence with the rights of inheritance and held that a married daughter who resides with her parents would be entitled to inherit Mundkarial rights, but if she did not reside with her parents she would not be entitled to inherit from her parents. However, given the gender bias in implementing the law, the interpretation given to fixed habitation in the case of married daughters can assume several overtones and it is necessary that legislative amendments are carried out to give legislative sanctity to the spirit of the judgement.

Sandra married a man whose family of the 'raised castes' did not accept her in the family and soon the harassment reached such an extent that she had to return to her parental home. Sandra and her husband later reconciled, and for her as well as her parents, it was a case of once bitten, twice shy. So they all decided that she would stay in her parental Mundkarial home. She and her brother lived with their parents, and her brother, after his marriage, began living with his wife at the location where she ran a thriving business. The brother eventually died, but not before he had got the house tax record transferred in his name at the panchayat level stating that he is the only son, taking care not to commit perjury by the commission by stating that he was the only child.

However, the Panchayat did not think it necessary to notify the daughter of the deceased Mundkar, though they were well aware about the stay of one of the daughters with fixed habitation in the Mundkarial house, and in any event at that premature stage, they could not have predetermined the case without notice to the daughters and giving an opportunity to them to have their say. Sandra only learnt later that the transfer was affected in the house tax records. It was by mere chance that she heard whispers about this transfer, and moved an application to the panchayat under the Right to Information Act to ascertain about the transfer, and confirmed the same. With this began her long road to justice, where her sister-in-law would not accept that she is not the one exclusively entitled to the house. Complaints of all sorts were lodged and continue to be lodged against her. Sandra had to challenge the transfer before the block development officer, who appears to have been set in his mind that daughters must go to their husband's houses upon marriage, and hence rejected her appeal against the panchayat's decision to transfer the house tax exclusively in her brother's name without even giving her a hearing. She was left with no option but to challenge the order of the block development officer, even as she continued to face cases of eviction filed against her by her sister-in-law who repeatedly maintains that married daughters do not constitute heirs to their parental home even if they reside with their parents. This, she maintains, with the tacit support of many in the administration.

As for the Buildings (Lease, Rent and Eviction Control) Act, 1968, when it comes to the tenanted house, the member of the family includes the daughter, but it is qualified that the married daughter shall be excluded from claiming the right if her husband has claimed the tenancy right in another house as a member of his parental family.

In relation to the Agricultural Tenancy Law, again, the provision of heritability exists, but the rights of a married daughter are not as convoluted in this case, because there is no definition lurking anywhere in the law, of members of the family, which in any way circumscribes the heritability. But the fact that the survey records included the names of males generally as the tenants has set a wrong precedent by not setting out the female spouse's name.

Shares in cooperative housing societies governed by the Goa Cooperative Societies Act, 2001, which are about rights to the housing and/or along with the proportionate share in land, are not required to be issued in the names of both the parties and hence transfers are effected by transfer of the shares by the person in whose name they stand; this is usually the male spouse by dictates of social practice, unless the said male spouse has an impediment or is no more. This also holds for time shares, as there is no separate law governing time shares. It is important to consider this aspect, given that Goan women migrate to other countries in search of livelihoods and may invest in time shares to fall back on when they can no longer work.

With the rise in real estate businesses, many persons in difficult marriages shrewdly got their property transferred to the name of the company or acquired property in the name of the company, which is a separate entity even if their spouse is in a controlling position over the assets of that company. The Family Law, thus, cannot be extended at this level and is not at all synchronized with this law, that is the Companies Act, or with the laws relating to partnerships.

This is also the case with banking laws, insurance laws, etc., which do not consider Goa's inheritance or matrimonial property rights in the matter of nominations, and dispense monies to whosoever is listed as the nominee. The nationalized banks also did so initially but later received instructions about the different position in Goa vis-à-vis Family Laws. Other banks that have been established thereafter have not followed suit.

According to Section 4 of the Goa Land Prohibition on Construction Act, 1995, no person shall on and from the date of commencement of this Act, undertake any work of construction of any structure, building, hut, or any part thereof, on any land belonging to the government, a local authority, or a communidade, except under the authority of written permission granted by the concerned authority. This was the law on the strength of which, for instance, arbitrary evictions from land at the village of Baina were effected without giving the parties residing there any notice, thereby depriving them of the basic due process of law, apart from rendering them homeless. A significant proportion of these evicted women are single and often migrants.

Housing schemes, such as Indira Awas Yojana and Rajiv Awas Yojana do not have any special offerings for women such as women in difficult circumstances, and to the extent that women tap these schemes through applications in their names, the onus has been on them to run from pillar to post, and if provided assistance by any male, they remain at the mercy of the male family member, who on some occasions has even extorted the amounts allotted and left the woman to find her own means to repair. With the imposition of a tax on a new construction without any relaxation for a BPL family and documentation, required for the Town and Country Planning clearance, hardly any rural persons are found to be applying for construction under these schemes.

The C&AG's Performance Audit Report No. 37 of 2014 on Indira Awas Yojana was laid on the table of both houses of parliament on 19 December 2014. The main findings that have emerged in relation to Goa are as follows:

- The actual housing shortage (essential for identification of beneficiaries) was not assessed in Goa.
- No quality inspections/technical supervisions were conducted by the concerned authorities/technical experts at any level in Goa.
- As part of the Indira Awas Yojana, a scheme for providing homestead sites to those rural BPL households who neither possessed agriculture land nor a house site was launched in 2009. Audit found that this scheme was not implemented in Goa.

The Goa Housing Board has made available allotment of plots of land on payment of reasonable prices, and again there have been no special provisions for homeless women so rendered on account of social factors. Furthermore, these schemes cannot by definition be tapped by the local population, as it requires that people should declare that they do not have any land, whereas by and large, every person has land or entitlements to land in some form or the other in the state of Goa. It may be quite another matter that the amount of land they have may be miniscule and not able to ensure any dwelling or livelihood rights to them. Thus, the only persons who have been able to get the benefits of that land, which was usually communidade land acquired by the government for housing for the poor, are people from outside Goa, with only a few takers from Goa, some of whom have allegedly manipulated documents to be able to benefit from these allotments despite their high sources of income.

The centuries-old Village Community Laws also subsist side by side with the Family Laws. In a place like where large tracts of land are owned by the Communidade, women have no rights except limited rights in case they are widowed without male children, or are the unmarried daughters of son-less parents, and consequently have no say on the way these lands are being wantonly appropriated at the cost of destruction of people's lives and livelihoods.

Several exclusionary laws such as land allotted under special economic zones and Biotechnology Policy, etc., further compound the predicament of women as they are dispossessed of or not accorded property rights for the setting up of such areas.

RECOMMENDATIONS AND SUGGESTIONS

The specificity of the central issue of ownership and control over land by the women of Goa is unique in that it is the only region in the entire nation that ensures—de jure—equal property rights in both marital and parental property via the Common Civil Code or what is also called the Portuguese Civil Code. However, as we have found through our detailed analysis, the attainment of these rights is curtailed, restricted, and often denied in various ways, and requires urgent legislative, administrative, and judicial reforms in order to ensure land rights for rural women in Goa and bring about gender parity, equality, and empowerment. These suggestions should not be considered as being exclusive but inclusive and suggestive.

1. In order to formulate policy to ensure land rights for women, it is of prime importance that sex-disaggregated data be maintained. It is indeed surprising that although the Record of Rights has existed for so long, there is no gender column in Forms I and IX.
2. Gender factoring studies especially at the micro level be conducted generally and more particularly in the area of the uses that the land is put to by women and so also the control that women have over the land.
3. Data relating to relinquishment of rights by Goan women are available at the sub-Registrar's Office; it should therefore not be too difficult to collate the information, even though painstaking.

4. Administrative measures have to be taken to popularize the existing family laws and land laws among women, particularly those from marginalized sections of society—for this, a module needs to be developed and the assistance of taluka legal aid committees functioning at the court level can be sought.
5. Family laws of Goa need to be reviewed to ensure that gender discriminatory provisions are deleted and special safeguards are instituted for women, so as for women to be able to access the laws and in order to counter pressures on women to relinquish their rights.
6. Legislation such as the Goa Land (Prohibition on Construction) Act, 1995, has to be repealed. Long-residing people, that is, those living for more than a year, on Government, Communidade, or local authority land, must be provided adequate rehabilitation, prior to any displacement, if the displacement is inevitable.
7. There must be special measures to elicit the say of women from all sections of society in the determination of how the land in their village is to be used, given that the overall nature of land usage has a bearing on the use value of their land and consequently on their land rights.
8. The various related laws and regulations that have a bearing on land rights must be synchronized with the Family Laws in the matter of property rights and the same principles must reflect in the operationality of land rights without discrimination, except of course for positive discrimination where and when necessary.
9. All concerned stakeholders must be specifically gender-sensitized through orientation in their training academies and refresher courses on the concept of substantive equality, and how it translates in the matter of land rights, so that laws contrary to the grain of substantive equality as enshrined in the Constitution are not enacted and so also enforcement of the laws is not contrary to the spirit of the law, where the laws are gender-sensitive.

NOTES

1. This paper would not have been possible without the involvement of Dr Albertina Almeida, Advocate, Goa. Acknowledgement is also due to Radha Sehgal, Research Associate, Centre for Development Research and Action.

2. http://nrhm.gov.in/nrhm-in-state/state-wise-information/goa.html (accessed on 19 March 2017).
3. http://nrhm.gov.in/nrhm-in-state/state-wise-information/goa.html (accessed on 19 March 2017).

BIBLIOGRAPHY

Almeida, Albertina and Mariette Correa. 2008. *Women's Rights to Land and Housing in Goa.* Goa: Sandarsh (mimeograph).
De Souza, S. 2009. 'Status of Women in Goa.' Unpublished PhD thesis, TISS, Mumbai. Available at: www.shodhganga.com (accessed on March 19, 2017).
Government of Goa. 2003–04. *Economic Survey*. Bardez: Directorate of Planning Statistics and Evaluation, Government of Goa.
———. 2013–14. *Economic Survey*. Bardez: Directorate of Planning Statistics and Evaluation, Government of Goa.
Khalap, Ramakant. 2012. 'Reports on Law Commission, Goa.' April 2009–March 2012, Chairman, Law Commission, Goa (mimeo.).
———. 2014. 'New Interpolations in Tenancy Laws Not so "Manohar".' *Navhind Times*, November 9. Available at: http://www.navhindtimes.in (accessed on 10 March 2017).
Press Information Bureau (PIB). 2015, July 22. New Delhi: Government of India, Ministry of Statistics & Programme Implementation.
Ramakant Khalap. 2010. 'Land Title Messy Affair in Goa.' Available at: http://www.goanews.com (accessed on 19 March 2017).
Usgaocar, M. S. 2013. *Family Laws of Goa, Daman and Diu*. Vol. I. Goa: Vela Associates.

INTERNET SOURCES

goalawcommission.gov.in/goa (accessed on 15 September 2015).
http://nrhm.gov.in/nrhm-in-state/state-wise-information/goa.html (accessed on 19 March 2017).
mospi.nic.in/Mospi 'Natural Accounting in Goa: Ministry of Statistics Government of Goa.' Available at: mospi.nic.in/Mospi (accessed on 30 August 2015).
www.dwcd.goa.gov.in (accessed on 19 March 2017).
www.http://rdagoa.nic.in/ruralhousing.htm (accessed on 19 March 2017).
www.http://www.saiindia.gov.in (accessed on 15 September 2015).

6

Women Empowerment Through Landownership Rights: Critical Assessment of Their Status in Gujarat

ITISHREE PATTNAIK

Empowerment refers to women's role or perceived ability to control or change different aspects of their personal, social, political, and economic development. Empowerment is a relative measure, not an absolute one. It is a non-linear process of change rather than one with a targeted or defined outcome. Its interpretation is subject to complex contexts of culture, values, knowledge, relationships, and behaviours; it is constantly negotiated and contested on an individual basis and at household and community levels. In sum, it is a measure of relative social status that is difficult to catalogue and compare (ActionAid 2013: 9). However, studies have established a close correspondence between women landownership and indicators of economic and social development (Cross and Hornby 2002; Datt, Simler, and Mukherjee 1999). Women's ownership of farm land is seen as a critical step not only for increasing their empowerment but also for improving farm productivity (Rao 2007). Women landownership is linked with the improvement in both individual and family nutrition (Allendorf 2007; Jose and Navaneetham 2008; Katz and Chamorro 2002), children's education achievement (Katz and Chamorro

2002), improvement in the ability to participate in decision-making (Allendorf 2007; Datt et al. 1999), increased representation at community group meetings (Datt et al. 1999; UN Women 2013), and reduction in physical and psychological domestic violence (Gupta 2006; Panda 2006). It is nothing short of an irony that though women have the same legal rights to own land like men, in reality they hold less than 10% of privately held land (RDI 2009).

According to Census 2011, as many as 65% of the total women workforce is engaged in agriculture-related activity either as cultivators or agricultural labour compared to just 49% of men. Yet only 14% of landholdings are in the names of women. In the absence of the landholding title, woman are deprived access to a number of other benefits such as institutional credit and bank loans, and barred from further government schemes for agricultural benefits, which can help in alleviating poverty (Saxena 2012: 7). Lack of property rights lead to sub-optimal decisions and missed opportunities to increase productivity (RDI 2009). Thus, landownership is a step towards enhancing women's economic and social empowerment and reducing multi-layered discrimination. In other words, women's empowerment can be understood as an important factor for reducing gender discrimination and improving nutritional outcomes for women (Jose and Navaneetham 2008; Sethuraman and Nata 2007).

OBJECTIVE AND METHODOLOGY

In this background, the chapter attempts to critically assess the status of women land rights in the state of Gujarat in a changing legal and socio-economic scenario. The major part of analysis is drawn from the secondary sources, namely articles published in journals and books, government reports, private reports (published by Working Group for Women and Land Ownership [WGWLO] that address women's land rights in Gujarat), and Acts such as the Hindu Succession Act (HSA) and Muslim Personal Law. This data is complimented by primary information collected through the series of interview sessions with lawyers practising in Gujarat courts, and state government officials in various departments, namely (a) revenue, (b) women and child development, (c) rural development, and (d) tribal development. Besides holding interviews with resource persons from the Gender Resource Centre, and with a number of non-government organization (NGO) representatives working on women-related issues, focus group discussions (FGDs) targeting women were also moderated in two villages, namely Balda and Ankhol in the districts of Ahmedabad and Mehsana, respectively.

I

ANALYSIS

WOMEN LANDOWNERSHIP STATUS IN GUJARAT

Background

On 1 May 1960, the state of Bombay bifurcated into Gujarat and Maharashtra. The new state formed the Land Ceiling Act, 1960, that provisioned a fixed ceiling on future acquisitions as well as for existing holders. The main aim of the reform policies was to provide land to the tillers. But there has been hardly any focus on distributing land to single women in Gujarat because the aim of these land reform policies was to transfer the land to the tillers, mainly men, who were recognized as the sole cultivators, and women were least recognized as farmers/cultivators. The issue of women's landownership could come to light only after land reform and redistribution policy was long over. It was only after the Eighth Five-year Plan that the government raised concern about the joint *patta* (official documents stating land title and the terms on which land is held) of land between spouses. The central government directed the states to register government-allotted wasteland and ceiling surpluses in joint names. However, they remained indifferent on the inequalities in devolution laws regarding women. Thus, gender equality in regard to the land title has been limited only to the land redistributed by the government. The Tenth Five-year Plan raised concern about increasing women's access to land after the NSSO data highlighted the increasing participation of women in agriculture. The Eleventh Five-year Plan gave importance to women group farming; especially single women through joint ownership or leasing of land. However, none of these government plans and policies raised the issue of discriminatory inheritance laws against women.

Even when women participated in peasant movements like Pardi Satyagraha in 1953–65 (Desai 2002) and tribal-led movement in the eastern belt of eastern Gujarat in 1980s and 1990s (Jani 2002), focus on gender issue was completely lacking. Similar was the story when Mahuva Andolan was staged, in which involvement of women was very prominent during the *andolan* (movement) to protect the ecologically sensitive wastelands against the construction of a cement plant by Nirma. The aim of the protest was to provide land to the landless so that the land could be retained with the community. When the plant construction was stopped after Supreme Court's intervention, no effort was seen to consider women for their ownership over the wasteland (Ganguli 2014).

The above discussion on land reform movements for land rights only reiterates that the land is always seen as family assets and only men are perceived to be the head of the household. Hence, even if the allocation of land titles takes place, it is always in the name of men. There are not many evidences of allocation of land to women. Even the women receiving land in rare circumstances have to put up with harsh opposition from the male-dominated society. The kind of situation was the reason why even women holding any amount of land could not assert themselves either in economic terms or in terms of enhancing their social status. This was mainly because of lack of an institutional support system. Sadly, neither the land reform Acts nor the civil society movements seem to have taken women's land rights issue seriously to make any positive difference.

Current Status

As per Census 2011, around 65% of women work in agriculture (as cultivators and agricultural labourers) compared to 44% of males. The share of women in agriculture is almost similar with the national figure, whereas the share of male workers in agriculture in Gujarat is less than the All-India Share (49%). Female representation further increases when we consider the rural population alone (80% of workers in agriculture) and the share has almost remained stagnant over the period 1991–2011. The share of women workers in agriculture is higher than that of male workers, which reflects the important role of women in agriculture in rural Gujarat. The share of women as agricultural labour is 57% which is significantly higher than that of cultivators, which is only 22% (Table 6.1).

Table 6.1

Gender-wise Participation in Agriculture in Gujarat

Total	Cultivators		Agricultural Labours		Females in Agriculture	Males in Agriculture
	Male	Female	Male	Female		
Total						
1991	26.3	30.5	14.2	44.7	75.2	40.6
2001	27.0	28.0	17.3	39.1	67.1	44.3
2011	23.6	17.8	20.3	47.1	64.9	43.9
Rural						
1991	34.0	32.8	17.7	47.3	80.0	51.7
2001	42.3	31.5	26.5	43.4	74.9	68.8
2011	40.1	21.7	33.5	56.9	78.6	73.6

Source: Census of India (2011).

Despite high participation of women in agriculture, there is no gender-disaggregated landownership data available in the state or at national level. However, the closest information of landownership that could be gathered is through operational holdings.[1] As noted by Rao (2011), the information on operational holding reflects the extent to which women have authority or autonomy to make agricultural decisions. When the officials of the revenue department were inquired about the absence of gender-wise record maintenance and its usefulness in formulating policy specific to women, they could only respond that collecting gender-wise data was never practised.

Based on the operational landholding information, women in Gujarat appear to be operating over only 10.3% of land, while men are the owners of over 89.7% of the land (Table 6.2). This unequal landholding between men and women is marginally more in Gujarat as compared to the national average of 13.5% among women who operate 11% of land. However, women's share in the total landholding (both individual and joint) in Gujarat is higher than all India (12.8% operate 10.3%). When it comes to the actual average landholding in hectares, land operated by women in individual ownership in Gujarat is less than 2 ha as compared to 1 ha at All-India level.

Although there are not many studies specific to this issue, couple of studies that endorse the skewed ownership of land between men and women are illustrated in the following lines (WGWLO 2004). Their study covered 23 villages across 15 talukas and 10 districts in Gujarat. The result shows that in a sample of 4,749, as high as 88% of land was owned by men and only 561 (11.7%) by women, highlighting the continued

Table 6.2

Share of Women Landholding in Gujarat

	Individual Holding		Joint Holding		Total Holding	
	Female	Male	Female	Male	Female	Male
India						
Number (share)	13.5	86.5	8.7	91.3	12.8	87.1
Area (share)	10.9	89.1	8.1	91.9	10.3	88.7
Gujarat						
Number (share)	10.3	89.7	20.1	79.9	14.1	85.9
Area (share)	9.1	90.9	20.2	79.8	13.2	86.8

Source: Calculated from Agricultural Census Database (Agricultural Census 2010–11).
Note: Share of women landholding to the total landholding in number (as the actual number) and area (in ha).

gender inequality in landownership in Gujarat. The recent study (exploring the question 'Do women own land?') was conducted (ongoing) by the author[2] in eight villages covering four districts in the state. Out of 3,235 households surveyed across eight villages (two villages each from four districts, covering Saurastra, North Gujarat, South Gujarat and Tribal-East region), only 3% of women were found to be the landowners. This was highest in Rajkot (North Saurastra) followed by Patan (North Gujarat) and Valsad (South Gujarat), respectively. Women landownership was the lowest in tribal areas of Panchmahal. Most of the women in Rajkot and Valsad owned land title in their name either due to widowhood or since their husbands transferred land in their name in order to get concession from stamp duty.

Scheduled Tribes (STs) constitute around 15% of Gujarat's total population. The gender ratio of STs is 981 which is higher than the state average of 919 (Census of India 2011). In terms of work participation among the Dalits (Scheduled Caste [SC]) and Adivasis (STs), around 46% and 81%, respectively, are engaged in agriculture (ibid.). The share increases to 60% and 86%, respectively, when we consider total women workers engaged in agriculture among these sections. The incidence of poverty is dominant among both Adivasis and Dalits, which is linked to their low productive asset status and low education[3] (Desai and Kulkarni 2008; Velayudhan 2012). In Gujarat, poverty reduction remains lowest among

Adivasis (Mehta 2006; Shah 2014). If the position of women operating landholdings is considered, it could be observed that 85% of land is in the control of women belonging to general caste, whereas Adivasis and Dalits (SCs) possess only 15% (Table 6.3). Between them, operational holdings are lowest among the Dalits, implying further deprivation of the SC women compared to general and tribal categories. Nevertheless, the incidence of disparity in landholdings was higher among the Dalits and the Adivasis, mainly because of the low level of education, lack of awareness, and access to other productive assets base (Kulkarni et al. 2008; RDI 2009).

If average landholding size is worked out for the different caste groups in Gujarat during 2010–11, Adivasis find themselves lowly placed (1.50 ha) compared to others (Dalits and general caste—1.91 ha and 2.05 ha, respectively). Here, it is important to note that most of their lands are not in the records of the revenue department as yet despite the Forest Rights Act (FRA) implementation started in 2008 (Bandi 2014). Though gender disparities are less pronounced in tribal areas having the highest sex ratio in Gujarat, tribal woman face certain discrimination in areas of wages and access and control over land, credit, income, technology, education, health, and skilled work. The property rights of the tribal women are poor as they continue to be ruled by an obsolete system of customary law under which they lack rights of succession or partition of ancestral property. In the tribal areas, the *varsai* (inheritance) has not been conducted for last two to three generations. There are many cases of widows and other single women who are deprived of their rightful share of land (Chauhan 2007). In the tribal region, women's entitlement to own land or other assets is decided by the community *panch* (traditional decision-making bodies). In the absence of property right, most of the decisions favour men since the composition of *panch* members is invariably constituted of men.

Table 6.3

Operational Holding by Women by Caste in Gujarat for 2010–11

District	Individual Holdings		Joint Holdings		Total Holdings	
	Number	Area	No.	Area	No.	Area
SC	3.1	3.0	4.1	3.5	3.7	3.3
ST	7.2	5.6	14.3	15.5	11.2	11.3
Gen	89.7	91.4	81.6	81.0	85.2	85.4

Source: Calculated from Agricultural Census Database.

> **Box 6.1**
>
> **Tribal Women and Land Inheritance Customs**
>
> There are around 20 major ST groups in Gujarat and among them Bhil, Dubla, Dhodiya, and Gamit are prominent groups. In the Gamit tribe, unlike other tribal communities, the system of joint family still exists. As per rule followed among Gamits, the land is not divided until the father or the head of the family is deceased. The property is inherited equally by the male children, and it is the eldest son who becomes *equigeniture*[4] head of the household on the death of father. There also prevails the system of *gharjamai*[5] among the Gamits and the land is distributed among the daughters of the family (Vaghela 2011). Another prominent ST of Gujarat is Kotwadias, who are concentrated in the districts of Surat, Valsad, Bharuch, and the Dangs. Nuclear family is more common among the Kotwadias. Sons inherit the property equally, while the eldest son succeeds the authority, and women land inheritance is not allowed.
>
> *Source:* Interviews with the officials of Tribal Development Departments, Government of Gujarat.

II

UNDERSTANDING THE IMPLEMENTATION OF LAND RELEVANT ACTS ENSHRINED IN THE CONSTITUTION

HINDU SUCCESSION ACT (HSA), 1956/2005

Inheritance rights to land, particularly agricultural land, have been most difficult to enact in India (Agarwal 1994). After almost 50 years, the HSA, 1956, was amended in 2005 to recognize the inheritance right of daughters and married women. The law recognized daughters and married women as coparceners of joint family property (Property Rights of Women: Proposed Reform Under the Hindu Law 2000). First, the 2005 Act by deleting a major gender-discriminatory clause—Section 4(2) of the 1956 HSA—has made women's inheritance rights in agricultural land equal to men. Section 4(2) excluded from the purview of the HSA significant interests in agricultural land, the inheritance of which was subject to the succession rules specified in state-level tenurial laws. Particularly in the north-western states, these laws were highly gender-biased and gave primacy to male lineal descendants. Women came very low in the succession order and got only limited estate. The new legislation brings male and female rights in agricultural land at par for all states including

Gujarat, overriding any inconsistent state laws. However, the Supreme Court set the year 2005 (9th September to be precise) as a cut-off date for women's right to ancestral property.

CUSTOMARY LAWS AND INHERITANCE RIGHTS

Nonetheless, the moot question remains, whether the incidences of women claiming their rights in a joint family property after the enforcement of HSA, 2005, are on increase or made no impact at all? Answer to this important query was discouraging if the accounts of Gujarat High Court Advocates are to be believed. According to them, there are hardly any cases registered as an after-effect of the HSA amendment. The registered cases for landownership in Gujarat are less than 2%. Even the advocates proclaimed that most of the times the family and the society discourage women from claiming their rightful inheritance of land rights. To illustrate this, one of the advocates narrated a case of a woman. This woman, despite being well-educated (in the profession of medicine) and settled abroad, could not pursue her case against her brother to inherit her share of property from her parents. She could sustain for about only two years after which she has to yield to the pressure and harassment from her relatives who have ostracized her out before finally withdrawing the case against her brother. Through intervention from her maternal uncle she could get a paltry sum as share in lieu of a larger share of the land.

The practical status of HSA 2005 is revealed further from the FGD moderated in Ahmadabad where total nine women (three belonging to Patel, two from Thakur, and four from Dalit communities) shared their experiences. The group as a whole was not aware about landownership laws in regard to women's entitlements such as in the HSA. The Patel women were not bothered about land inheritance and whether it is in their favour or not. They were strongly confident that their community would definitely take care of their needs. They asked questions such as, 'why we need land in our name? Why it is required?' Most of the women from the Patel community were from a higher economic class and better educated as compared to the others. The Thakur community was mainly conservative in nature and women were not allowed to take part in any kind of family discussions. Hence, when they were asked about landownership for women, they expressed their unawareness saying neither they knew the laws nor they were interested to know, as their community would not allow them to be involved in decision-making. The thought process of landowning in women's name might not have ever struck them as it is difficult for them to think above the caste and community. One woman of the Thakur caste was found owning land in her name, but she informed that her husband bought the land in her name in order to get concession in stamp duty. She did not know how much land was in her name or when the land was bought. The four Dalit women who participated in the FGD belonged to the lower economic strata. These women hardly knew about the land laws but they sincerely expressed their interest in understanding the issue. Some of them reported problems of domestic violence and felt that if they had land in their names they would not have faced such kind of violence. A divorced Dalit woman said, 'Had the land been in my name, I would have at least something to fall back on, rather than working as a daily wage labour.'

It clearly shows a link between domestic violence and ownership of land assets.

In another study, FGD involving seven women belonging to Koli Patel (OBC) (2), Ahir (2), Brahmins (2), and Dalit (1), shed some more light on the reality on ground with regard to HSA. The group consisted of two widows who owned land in their name. One Dalit woman was found owning land as her husband applied for joint ownership. She was very active in the agricultural field and when her husband migrated seasonally, she took care of all the land-related decisions. She was an active worker in the local NGO and with the help of the NGO, she tried to spread awareness among Dalit women regarding their rights. She reported that the consumption of alcohol was quite high among men in their community. She observed that there were many incidents of men selling land for alcohol consumption. Thus, had the land been in women's name, the husband would have sought the permission before selling or the woman has the right to intervene. Another widow from Brahmin community had inherited land after her husband's death had to face severe criticism from her relatives. She expressed that she was often called a 'family breaker', '*dayan*' (witch), and 'a selfish and characterless women' as she demanded land on her own name. Among the Brahmins in the village, it was a big issue when she demanded her right over land. However, she expressed that for inheritance purposes, she had to transfer the land in her son's name even though she wanted to transfer the same land to her daughter. This woman was quite independent in all household- and farm-related activities, yet she has to depend on her in-laws for selling the farm produce. She has to share the small income with her in-laws as they helped her to sell the farm produce. Feebleness to deal with the market and lesser bargaining power excludes women from the process of value chain.

In the FGDs conducted by Ragor and Rajgor (2008) in Kutch, most of the women participating in discussions had participated in the 'Kutch Zamin-bachao-Andolan'. Some of them also had land in their names. These women were positive about the women's landownership. Most of them were of the view that land title in their names gives security, respect, and independence. Women with landholding in their names among this group were also active in the public life by associating themselves with various NGOs. However, for land transfer, they preferred daughter-in-law rather than daughter. According to them, as daughters marry outside of the village they will not directly work on the land. Besides, land transfer to daughters was not a socially accepted norm. Such views of women were strongly influenced by the patriarchal relations. Most of the women from the Ahir caste (OBC) in Rapar taluka of Kutch had joint ownership of land. According to practices in their communities, when a husband opts for the second marriage, the first wife gets a share in his property. However, the woman is not allowed to choose her daughter as the inheritor. Sharing the land with the daughter is not possible, as the community may not allow the son-in-law to till land in the in-law's village. In their community, when women agree to marry a disabled, they get some portion of land or property in her name, showing that women will receive land title only when they do some sort of sacrifice.

MUSLIM PERSONAL LAW

There are very few studies available on Muslim women's land inheritance system in Gujarat. This section is mainly drawn from the discussion with the advocates regarding Muslim laws. It is well known that the Muslim women are governed by the Muslim Personal Law (Shariat) Application Act, 1937. In 1986, the Muslim Protection of Rights on Divorce Act was enacted with the aim that Muslim women could avail maintenance under Section 125 of the Code of Criminal Procedure (crPC). This law initiated debate on personal law, gender, and identity and the interaction between personal law and the civil law. Unlike in Hindu religion, in Islam, the principles of inheritance are narrated in detail. The heirs include mother, father, husband, widow, daughter, uterine brother and sister, and consanguine sister. Females inherit half of the portion of males. Thus, the share of daughter depends on what share the son receives. The wife's share is one-quarter in the absence of child and one-eighth in the case of existence of a child. All wives receive an equal share. Muslim population in

Gujarat comprised of about 9% in 2001 and this has increased to 11.5% in 2011 (Census 2011). The 2011 Census shows that Muslims in Gujarat have the highest child sex ratio of 927 girls per 1,000 boys as compared to 917 in Christians and 885 in Hindus.

Land inheritance for women has never been a practice among the Muslims in Gujarat. Cash, jewellery, and sometimes cattle are promised as *Mehr* (an amount promised during marriage that a husband gives to wife) but not share of land. There are evidences that women may receive a share of the farm produce but not a portion of land. According to the law, women cannot own land when the husband is alive. The practice of oral divorce (*talaq*) and polygamy further complicates the property distribution, as the second wife receives priority while the first wife's right is neglected. According to a Gujarat High Court lawyer, there are almost no cases of Muslim women fighting for property. The lawyers and judges hardly know the integrity of the Muslim Personal Laws. The revenue officers at the block and district levels dominantly being Hindus have only a limited understanding of Muslim Personal Law. Concerning inheritance, there are few evidences where the judge has accepted the deceased's multiple marriages and ordered for the equal division of property among wives and children (Velayudhan 2006).

III

WOMEN LAND INHERITANCE AND SOCIETAL IMPEDIMENTS

The study conducted by WGWLO in 2004 states that around 50% of the total landholding women members had the land transferred in their names due to widowhood, implying the major cause of land transfer as an effect of the husband's decease. Situation in India makes it difficult to draw genuine reason since about 41% of women own land due to voluntary land transfer by husband, providing a positive signal and suggesting changing social dynamics. But in reality, most of the transfers take place to reap the advantage of government policies such as receiving tax benefits, saving expenses on entry through the *talathi*[6] (registration fee exemption), and escaping the Land Ceiling Act, 1960. Further, most of such women who own land are not actually aware about their ownership status. This raises a serious question about the nature of the 'ownership'.

It is doubtful whether the ownership has translated into authority/control, including decision-making about the use of land. Thus, ownership and control are two different things and should not be used interchangeably. The study also found that around 4.5% of women owned land because their husbands did not have the farmer status so they could not buy land in their names, hence, wives' names. Same percentage of women inherited land from their maternal side because their parents had no male inheritors. No evidences of daughters owning a share of land along with the sons was found.

It is important to mention that there are two types of landownership—one is 'recorded ownership', which is a formal transfer, and the other one being 'informal ownership', which is verbal in nature. According to the study by Velayudhan (2008), ownership was mainly informal, irrespective of regions and caste. The study made a comparison of tribal and non-tribal regions on women landownership. In the tribal region, social customs allow daughters to inherit land in the case of *gharjamai*. In the non-tribal region, in the absence of a male inheritor, the land goes to the nephew. There were few cases of *gharjamai* getting the share in the non-tribal villages where the land got transferred in the name of a *jamai* (son-in-law), but never in the name of a daughter. Basically, land can only be owned by men is this area. In the case of tribal villages, remarriage of widows is considered an alternative option for livelihood support contrary to landownership. However, in the non-tribal villages, remarriage is not a socially accepted norm. There were rare evidences of small piece of land being transferred to the daughter on her return to parents' home after broken marriage in the tribal village. Whereas in similar situation, in the non-tribal villages, the girl might be given livelihood support, but not land.

The study by WGWLO (2004) found that around 20% of women claimed to own land without *pattas* in their name and these cases were mainly prevalent among widowed women. This type of informal land transfer raises a serious concern as women do not have legal rights over this land and it could be transferred to anyone over a period of time. As the claim can be withdrawn at any time and is not legally binding, this kind of arrangement does not help woman either economically or socially. Bigamy is another social custom, which is prevalent amongst tribal and Muslim communities in Gujarat. This arrangement allows small pieces of land transfer in the name of women in the case of her husband marrying the second time. This decision about first wife receiving a portion of land is most often decided by the village panchayat. It is doubtful how far women are aware of their land entitlement after the husband's remarriage. Women's awareness of this entitlement within bigamy is essential since its practise is a socially accepted norm. However, not many studies have reported cases of bigamy.

Another important aspect is that of 'ownership versus authority'; as noted, landownership through either inheritance laws or government policies would solve only a part of the larger issue as ownership also needs to translate into control over decision-making regarding the land. Landownership and control on decision-making could be measured by indicators such as decision on cropping pattern, input use, health, and education of children. The study by WGWLO (2006) revealed that around 40% of the women reported changing the cropping pattern. Changed cropping patterns could be linked with control over the land or authority of the women on her own land. Nevertheless, the major reason was that most women were unable to take care of the land and maintain self-cultivation. As a result, most of them preferred to cultivate either one crop per year or shifted to food-grain cultivation—thus, clearly exposing the weak position such women are into. Lack of awareness amongst women regarding effective practices of farming in the absence of support either from relatives or society at large following their ownership of land only adds woes. During the recent survey by the author,[5] it emerged that 65% of the women in the sample reported that they preferred to work on their farm as labourers, while major decisions regarding farming are taken by in-laws or elder male members in the house since they do not want to face criticism from relatives if anything goes wrong. The lack of exposure to the market is another major reason that restricts women from taking control over land and limits their farming. These women found self-cultivation risky as the age-old beliefs and patriarchal society do not allow them to make decisions independently.

IV

INITIATIVES BY THE STATE GOVERNMENT FOR GENDER EQUITY IN LANDOWNERSHIP

'Nari Gaurav Niti—2006' is one of the important policies initiated by the Government of Gujarat to promote gender equity. The policy aims at providing human rights and fundamental freedom to women on equal terms with men in all spheres, such as personal, political, economic, social, cultural, and civil (Dave 2014). Moreover, the policy also suggests the formulation of the Women's Right to Matrimonial Home and Property Act and a special provision in the existing laws to ensure that any property bought after marriage must be bought jointly in both spouses' names. The action plan also suggests an amendment to Sections 145 and 146 of CrPC to promote buying of property in the joint names of both husband and wife. The state government has exempted women from registration fees by 1.5% and around 1.76 lakh women benefitted from just this provision in 2008. According to official records, 30% of the total documentation of land and property was done solely in women's names.[8]

To promote land registration in the name of women in either single or joint ownership, the Department of Rural Development (DoRD) exempted women from registration fee, transfer fee, and stamp duty. On March 2008, the DoRD had sent notice to all the district collectors to provide data on land allotments. By 2008, 5.05 lakh documents were registered in the name of 4.17 lakh women and around ₹129.6 crore was remitted in terms of registration fees by the government under this programme. However, the record shows that in the three districts of Amreli, Junagadh, and Banaskantha, only 55 women were allotted land in their individual capacities, whereas 60 had joint ownership. It shows that during two years, only a handful of women have benefited from the programme in these three districts. There has also been an attempt to include women as occupants through the settlement survey,[7] in all the lands where women are also cultivating under this programme. The progress of the programme is yet to be known. Though the programme is a positive step, it needs to be lunched at a larger scale and a more rigorous action needs to be taken by the department.

In order to further illustrate the discrimination of ownership rights towards women, an example of claims of the Forest Rights Act (FRA) in Gujarat and the issues of forest dwelling communities are presented. Under the Act, it was claimed[8] that the distribution of *jamin pattas* (title to land) will help the holders to have all rights and benefits from the government similar to those of farmers residing in mainstream revenue villages. Further, the conservative practice of maintaining a landholding entitlement in the revenue record in the name of the head of a family is now extended to the spouse of the family head too. This positive legislation places the woman member on an equal footing alongside their male counterparts, essentially recognizing her as the owner of the land if the husband is deceased. Earlier, forest dwellers could not inherit land, but this path-breaking initiative will make inheritance possible. However, the impact of the FRA does not appear to be materializing as initially envisaged. Recent studies by Bandi (2013, 2014) on the implementation of the FRA in Gujarat do not present a very encouraging picture. In these studies, it is observed that the overall poverty followed by poor awareness among tribal communities is contributing to their poor situation. In such a scenario, discussing separately about women entitlement in land is rendered less significant. However, the study mentions the measures being taken by the authorities to correct the implementation of the FRA in Gujarat.

Taking note of the working of government measures, what comes out glaringly is that various government departments are making constructive efforts towards the issue but the department and centres, which are working in these issues, operate in isolation with limited interdepartmental interaction. There is absence of coordination between the departments like Women and Child Development, DoRD, and Department of Revenue. In order to achieve common goals, the integration of the departments is essential as they can plan comprehensive efforts in these issues.

WAY FORWARD

The above analysis has emphasized the persisting gender inequality in both land inheritance and land reform policy by the Gujarat Government. The participation of women in agriculture is around 65% but the landholding is only 14%. One need not talk about land ownership, which is negligible. Without titles to lands, women are not recognized as farmers, even by the state, by the extension of service providers[9], or as candidates for membership in institutions such as cooperative societies. But by providing land title to women and extending them with infrastructural support could increase output by increasing their access to credit and agricultural extension information services, both of which are hindered by class, caste, and gender bias. However, there are evidences of women attaining landownership through government policy, though such incidences are quite marginal. In most cases, women are not aware about their rights. Legal knowledge regarding various laws and changes in laws is minimal amongst rural women (RDI 2009). Many of the women are not aware about their rights and even if some of them are aware, influence of patriarchal culture appears to shape women's social position and decisions resulting in rights remaining unclaimed. Hence, women's land rights could be protected through steps such as creating awareness among women about their legal rights, formalizing land-related documents, changing the mindset of the society, and empowering women through the provision of land rights. Efforts could be channelized and executed as in the following in pursuit of achieving these objectives:

- Creating awareness among male members, relatives, and the village heads is equally essential. This could be done through the means of audiovisuals, comic strips, posters, and skits for information dissemination and increased awareness amongst the women. Skits and role-plays were used extensively since these tools are very accessible.
- Training the *talathis* (village-level officers) regarding their role in maintaining land title records and regarding measures to be taken when the *varsai* takes place.
- The language of law is difficult to understand for ordinary people, thus for the translation of the law into common language, the role of para-legal workers (PLWs) is important. In Gujarat, with assistance from the Centre for Social Justice, a legal support organization was started for building a cadre of PLWs. Quarterly training programs were designed for the PLWs and this training enabled them to take up cases for women regarding land title. Though the initiative by the group has positively impacted women's landownership in rural areas where they work, their project is limited to certain areas. The government departments need to work with them for a more fruitful result.
- The 7/12 form (land record form) which records the land details should essentially record such inputs gender-wise.
- Including the picture of the plot in the land record is also essential. Most of the times women are not aware about the specific plot allotted to them. The *talathi* narrated during the interview that there were some cases where women claimed that they have been promised a different plot and given an inferior one or may be a smaller size plot. Thus, including the plot size and the picture of the plot would help for the formal documentation.
- During the ongoing project of the author, most of the women landowners reported that the major decisions regarding crop choice, inputs purchase, marketing credit, and mortgage or sales are taken by others even if they own the land. Thus, simply changing the laws might not be the solution, rather it is essential to change the societal mindset. Women's control over land depends upon many actors in political, legal, religious, and social domains.

NOTES

1. Operational holding in the Agricultural Census (http://agcensus.nic.in) is defined as all land which is used for agricultural production and is operated as one unit by a person alone or with others without regard to the title, legal form, size, or location. An operational holding comprises: (a) land owned and self-operated; (b) land leased; and (c) land otherwise operated. An operational holder is the person who has the responsibility for the operation of the agricultural holding and who exercises the technical initiative and is responsible for its operation. The person may have full economic responsibility or may share it with others. The operational holder may be individual, joint, or institutional. An individual holding is defined as one that is operated by one person, either alone or by a group of persons, who are the members of the same household. By far, the largest proportion of agricultural holdings in the country is individual holdings.
2. The project 'Challenges of Feminized Agriculture in India' is in progress (Commenced in July 2015).
3. As per the 2011 Census, the effective literacy rate is 62.5% in ST population compared to 78% of Gujarat. Female literacy rate is 53% for the STs compared to 70% of the state.
4. *Equigeniture*: Property is inherited by the male children. The eldest son becomes the head of the household after the death of the father.
5. *Gharjamai*: Son-in-law who stays at his wife's residence after marriage.
6. The 'Nari Gaurav Niti' of the Government of Gujarat promotes registration of land and property both in sole name of women as well as under joint ownership of wife and husband and to 'totally exempt women from transfer fees and stamp duty if land or property is in the name of women singly.'
7. The author is working on a research project (ongoing) titled 'Challenges of Feminized Agriculture in India', supported by the Australian Research Council and Indian Council of Social Science Research, New Delhi. The fieldwork is in progress.
8. The author had consulted the Gender Resource Centre of Gujarat Government in order to get updated data on land transfer from the 'Nari Gaurav Niti'. The data published with respect to land transfer under the programme is eight years old. The staff of the centre reported that even after constant efforts to collect the data on land transfer, they lacked information. This could be due to the fact that 'the *Mamlatdar* and the government officials are male members and thus do not take the matter seriously'.
9. The Department of Revenue, Government of Gujarat, has started a re-survey after 25 years with the aim of integrating survey records.
10. The Chief Minister of Gujarat in her announcement made in August 2015 claimed that the state would be the first to register the names of forest-dwellers who have been given land rights under the FRA in 7/12 (Land Record of Rights) (NITI Central 2015).

11. Knowledge transfer among the women farmers was minimal despite the innovative 'door-to-door extension service—Krishi Mahotsav' by the Gujarat government (Pattnaik et al. 2012).

REFERENCES

ActionAid. 2013, February. *From Marginalization to Empowerment: The Potential of Land Rights to Contribute to Gender Equality—Observations from Guatemala, India and Sierra Leone.* Johannesburg: ActionAid.

Agarwal, Bina. 1994. *A field of One's Own: Gender and Land Rights in South Asia.* Cambridge, UK: Cambridge University Press.

———. 1995. 'Women's Legal Rights in Agricultural Lands in India.' *Economic and Political Weekly* 30 (12): A39–56.

———. 2002. *Are We Not Peasants Too? Land Rights and Women's Claims in India.* SEEDS. The Population Council. Available at: http://ccc.uchicago.edu (accessed on 5 April 2010).

Agricultural Census. n.d. Available at: http://agcensus.dacnet.nic.in (accessed on 1 August 2015).

Allendorf, Keera. 2007. 'Do Women's Land Rights Promote Empowerment and Child Health in Nepal?' *World Development* 35 (11): 1975–88.

Bandi, Madhusudan. 2013, October. 'Implementation and Outcomes of Forest Rights Act: A Critical Assessment of Two States in India.' Monograph No. 31 (RULNR Monograph No. 17), Centre for Economic and Social Studies, Research Unit for Livelihoods and Natural Resources, Hyderabad.

———. 2014, January–February. 'Forest Rights Act: Towards the End of Struggle for Tribals?' *Social Scientist* 42 (1–2): 63–81.

Census of India. 2011. 'Primary Census Abstract.' Census of India, Government of India. Available at: www.censusindia.gov.in/DigitalLibrary (accessed on 19 March 2017).

Chauhan, Dharmishta. 2007. *Working with Widows: Experience from AKRSP (I).* Ahmedabad: AKRSP (I).

Cross, C., and D. Hornby. 2002. 'Opportunities and Obstacles to Women's Land Access in South Africa.' A Research Report for the National Land Committee of South Africa and South Africa's Department of Land Affairs. Available at: http://www.gov.za/sites/www.gov.za/files/landgender_0.pdf (accessed on 20 March 2017).

Datt, G., K. Simler, and S. Mukherjee. 1999. 'The Determinates of Poverty in Mozambique.' Final report, International Food Policy Research Institute (IFPRI), Washington, DC.

Dave Kapil. 2014. 'Govt to Revise 2006 Policy for Greater Gender Equality.' *Times of India* (Ahmedabad), http://grcgujarat.org/pdf/Nari-Gauravniti-news-artical.pdf (accessed on 5 May 2015).

Desai, Kiran. 2002. 'Land Reforms through People's Movements, Land Reforms in India.' In *Land Reforms in India: Performances and Challenges in Gujarat and Maharashtra*, edited by Land Reforms through People. Vol. 8. New Delhi: SAGE Publications.

Desai, Sonalde, and Veena Kulkarni. 2008. 'Changing Educational Inequalities in India in the Context of Affirmative Action.' *Demography* 45 (2): 245–70.

Ganguly, Varsha Bhagat. 2014. 'Mahuva Andolan of Gujarat.' *Economic and Political Weekly* 49 (40): 104–10.

Gupta, J. 2006. 'Property Ownership of Women as Protection for Domestic Violence: The West Bengal Experience.' In *Property Ownership and Inheritance Rights of Women for Social Protection—The South Asia Experience: Synthesis Report of Three Studies*, edited by ICRW. Delhi: ICRW.

Jani, Indukumar. 2002. 'Land Struggle in the Eastern Belt of Gujarat.' In *Land Reforms in India: Performances and Challenges in Gujarat and Maharashtra*, edited by Ghanshayam Shah and D.C. Shah. Vol. 8. New Delhi: SAGE Publications.

Jose, S., and K. Navaneetham. 2008, August 16–August 22. 'A Factsheet on Women's Malnutrition in India.' *Economic and Political Weekly* 43 (33): 61–67.

Katz, E., and J. S. Chamorro. 2002. 'Gender, Land Rights and the Household Economy in Rural Nicaragua and Honduras.' Paper prepared for USAID/ Broadening Access and Strengthening Input Market Systems (BASIS) Collaborative Research Support Program (CRSP), Madison, Wisconsin.

Krishnaraj, M., and A. Shah. 2004. *Women in Agriculture*. Delhi: Academic Foundation.

Kulkarni, Seema, Sara Ahmed, Chayya Datar, Sneha Bhat, Yuthika Mathur, and Dinesh Makhwana 2008. 'Water Rights as Women's Rights Assessing the Scope for Women's Empowerment through Decentralized Water Governance in Maharashtra and Gujarat.' Report submitted to International Development Research Centre, Canada, prepared by SOPPECOM- Utthan-TISS, https://www.soppecom.org/pdf/Water-rights-and-women%27s-rights-report.pdf (accessed on 5 January 2014).

Mehta, Niti. 2006, January–June. 'Imbalances in Development Between Regions and Social Groups: Evidences from Gujarat.' *Anvesak* 36 (1): 1–12.

NITI Central. 2015. 'Anandiben Takes the Lead on Right to Property for Tribals.' Webpage available at: http://www.niticentral.com/2015/08/19/gujarat-becomes-the-first-state-to-give-land-under-fra-329772.html (accessed on 19 November 2015).

Panda, P. 2006. 'Domestic Violence and Women's Property Ownership: Delving Deeper into the Linkages in Kerala.' In *Property Ownership and Inheritance Rights of Women for Social Protection—The South Asia Experience: Synthesis Report of Three Studies*, edited by ICRW. Delhi: ICRW.

Pattnaik, Itishree, Tushaar Shah, G. G. Koppa, and Amita Shah. 2012, November. 'Agricultural Extension Service Through Krishi Mahotsav in Gujarat: A Preliminary Assessment.' *Occasional Paper* Series, No. 2, Gujarat Institute of Development Research (GIDR), Ahmadabad.

Property Rights of Women: Proposed Reform Under the Hindu Law. 2000. 174th Report of the Law Commission of India. Available at: http://www.lawcommissionofindia.nic.in/kerala.htm (accessed on 5 May 2017).

Rajgor, Gouthami and Meena Rajgor. 2008. 'Women's Perceptions of Land Ownership: A Case Study from Kutch District, Gujarat, India.' *Gender & Development* 16 (1): 41–54. doi:10.1080/13552070701876144.

Rao, N. 2007. 'Custom and the Courts: Ensuring Women's Rights to Land, Jharkhand, India.' *Development and Change* 38 (2): 299–319.

———. 2011. 'Women's Access to Land: An Asian Perspective.' Paper presented in the Expert Group Meeting 'Enabling rural women's Economic Empowerment: Institutions, Opportunities and Participation', Accra, Ghana, 20–23 September. Available at: http://www.un.org/womenwatch/daw/csw/csw56/egm/Rao-EP-3-EGM-RW-30Sep-2011.pdf (accessed on 15 September 2015).

Rural Development Institute (RDI). 2009. *Women's Inheritance Rights to Land and Property in South Asia: A Study of Afghanistan, Bangladesh, India, Nepal, Pakistan, and Sri Lanka*. Seattle, WA: RDI. Available at: http://www.landesa.org/wpcontent/uploads/2011/01/RDI_Report_WJF_Womens_Inheritance_Six_South_Asian_Countries_ December_2009.pdf (accessed on 10 June 2015).

Saxena, N. C. 2012. 'Women Land and Agriculture in Rural India.' Delhi: UN Women. Available at: www.unwomensouthasia.org/assets/UN_Women_Land_ Agriculture_in_Rural_India.pdf (accessed on 5 January 2015).

Sethuraman, K., and D. Nata. 2007, November. 'The Nexus of Gender Discrimination with Malnutrition: An Introduction.' *Economic and Political Weekly* 42 (44): 49–53.

Shah, A. 2014. 'Poverty and Livelihood among Tribals. In *Tribal Development in Western India*, edited by Amita Shah and Jharna Pathank. Delhi: Routledge.

UN Women. 2013. 'Challenges and Barriers to Women's Entitlement to Land in India.' Available at: http://www.landesa.org/wp-content/uploads/UN-Women-Barriers-to-and-Impact-of-Womens-Entitlement-to-Land.pdf (accessed on 20 March 2017).

Vaghela, P. D. 2011. 'Impact of Tribal Sub plan Schemes on the Tribal Communities.' Thesis of the Dangs Sardar Patel University. Available at: http://hdl.handle.net (accessed on 20 March 2017).

Velayudhan, Meera. 2006. 'Muslim Women and Land Rights in Gujarat: WGWLO Experience. *WGWLO Paper Series* 1. Ahmedabad: WGWLO.

———. 2008. *Women's Right to Land: Voices from Grassroots Movement and Working Women's Alliance in Gujarat*. Ahmedabad: Aga Khan Rural Support Program (India).

———. 2012. 'Contextualizing Women's Rights and Entitlements to Land: Insights from Gujarat.' *Social Change* 42(4): 505–26.

WGWLO. 2004. 'Study on Status of Women and Agriculture Land Ownership in Gujarat and Strategies Derived by NGOs to Enable Women Own Land Based on Study Findings. Working paper Series 2, WGWLO, Ahmedabad.

———. 2006. *Reports of Para-legal Action Research*. Ahmedabad: WGWLO.

7

Gendering the Landownership Question in Jammu and Kashmir

ABHA CHAUHAN

Gender inequality exists and perpetuates across the globe in varied forms, an important aspect being unequal access to and control over productive resources between women and men. This large-scale discrimination against women in the economic sphere is a reflection of hierarchical society that embodies other forms of social, cultural, political, and legal inequalities. Land is an important economic asset in any society and its unequal distribution in rural India, where the bulk of the population still lives (68.84%, 2011 Census), leads to income inequality and lower standard of living and quality of life. This consequently results in unequal access to decision-making processes, institutional facilities, and development programmes (Bhatt 2000: 139–40). Correspondingly, ownership and control of land by women contribute significantly towards reducing poverty and promoting their well-being, as well as having access to political power and improved social status in society.

A large number of women in India depend on agriculture, constituting nearly 40% of agricultural workforce in the country. In all, 75% of all female workforce and 85% of all rural female workforce in the country is involved in agriculture (GoI [Government of India] 2013b).

Around 11% households in India are headed by females; this situation arises due to widowhood or desertion, male out-migration, men's entering into non-farm activities, and other livelihoods. Absorption of a larger number of rural men in the non-agricultural labour force is leading to increasing concentration of women in agriculture or what is termed as the 'feminization of agriculture'. During 1988–94, while 29% of rural males added to the labour force in the over-14 age group were absorbed into non-agriculture, less than 1% of the additional female workers were similarly absorbed (Agarwal 2003: 192). As a result there is greater dependence on women for agricultural production, besides the burden of all other forms of subsistence work and household chores in rural areas.

However, few women own land and even fewer have effective control over it (Agarwal 1995). In India, less than 10% of landowners are women. It is estimated that the total area owned by the households in the rural sector during 2003 was 107.23 million hectares, wherein average area owned per household was 0.73 hectares and the percentage of landless households was about 10.04% (GoI 2006: 22). In the state of Jammu and Kashmir (J&K) and in other northwestern states in India, the ownership of land by women is highly skewed.

Agriculture plays an important part in J&K's economy. Around 70% of the population here gets livelihood, directly or indirectly, from agriculture and allied sectors (Govt. J&K Ninth Agriculture Census, 2010–11: 10–11). The total area of the state is 2,416 million hectares, of which 745 hectares (i.e., about 31%) is the net sown area (Govt J&K, *Digest of Statistics*). Though there has been an increase in the number of operational agricultural landholders between 1976–77 (9.71 lakh) and 2010–11 (14.49 lakh), the individual and joint operational landholdings decreased from 1.02 hectares to 0.53 hectares during the same period (Govt J&K, *Ninth Agriculture Census*: 10–11). Therefore, it can be said that as the average size of holdings declined in J&K over the years, the number of landholders increased. The area operated upon also decreased between 1976–77 and 2010–11 (ibid.).

According to another estimate, the average area owned per household in J&K reduced to 0.43 hectares in 2013 from 0.99 hectares in 1992 and the percentage of landless household increased from 2.80 to 3.06 during the same period (GoI 2013a: 22). This shows that in the state of J&K though land reforms have benefitted people in terms of land distribution, the average size of landholdings is declining and the number of landless people is increasing, thereby widening the gap between the landless, small and large landowners.

In J&K, women play an important role in the agriculture sector. Female cultivators constitute 54.66%, while males are 37.48% of the total workers in J&K as per the 2001 Census. This is better than the scenario at the all-India level where female cultivators are 32.93% while male cultivators constitute 31.06% of the total workers for the same period (GoI, *Statistical Profile on Women Labour, 2009–2011*). This suggests a larger participation of women in agriculture in J&K with little ownership rights on land. The revolutionary land reforms in the state, it is believed, did not significantly help women to become landowners, though no gender-disaggregated data on distribution and ownership of land could be sought. However, the data available on operational landholders in agriculture suggest that there are women operational landholders and their number, though marginally, is increasing over the years in J&K.

Of the total operational landholders (14.49 lakh) in J&K, the share of males is 92.55% and that of females is only 7.32% as per the data from the Ninth Agriculture Census (2010–11). This depicts a huge gender discrepancy, but there has been a decrease of 1.06% and an increase of 0.16% in male and female operational holders' shares, respectively, between the two agriculture censuses of 2005–06 and 2010–11, suggesting greater control of women on agricultural land (Govt J&K, *Ninth Agriculture Census*: 17–18).

Of the total operational landholders in 2010–11 in J&K, the share under 'Scheduled Castes' (SC) category was 7.13% and that under 'Scheduled Tribes' (ST) category was 12.51%. Of the total operational holdings of the SC, males constituted 96.38% and females 3.62% (ibid.). During the same period, the percentage of total ST operational holdings for ST males was 92.17 and that of ST females was 7.88, thus suggesting better condition of ST women compared to the SC women. Regarding the 'other' category, the percentages for male and female are 92.38 and 11.51, respectively; women here are better off than both SC and ST as well as for all classes. This depicts the gender gap within the marginalized communities, as well as between them and the general category (ibid.: 21–23).

The notion that land laws are not gender-neutral either in their formulation or in their implementation is supported by women's organizations, activists, and lawyers (Agarwal 1994: 4). The issue of women's land rights started becoming important in the 1980s as it acquired attention in policy making and among the grass-roots organizations and women's groups. The Sixth Five-year Plan (1980–85) mentioned that the government would make efforts to give joint titles to spouses when distributing agricultural land and home sites. The *National Perspective Plan for Women: 1988–2000 AD* also made several substantive recommendations to reduce the gender gap in access to land (Agarwal 2003: 186). In the Ninth Five-year Plan (1997–2002), a full section on 'Gender and Land Rights' was included which provided detailed recommendations including distributing titles to women and providing women farmers with related information and support. It emphasized the need to collect gender-disaggregated data on landownership, use them in official records, and also amend the Tenurial Laws to ensure equality of inheritance in agricultural land (ibid.: 199).

In November 1997, the Ministry of Rural Areas and Employment, GoI, set up a three-member committee, the Committee for Gender Equality in Land Devolution in Tenurial Laws to reform the rules governing the inheritance of agricultural land. Since agriculture is a state subject, changes in Tenurial Laws are undertaken by state legislators. The committee's report while highlighting the gender inequalities in laws affecting inheritance suggested measures for promoting gender equality in inheritance laws and recommended the amending of Tenurial Laws of different states, particularly those in the northwest of India. In the case of J&K, recommendations were made for amending the Jammu and Kashmir Tenancy Act, 1980, Section 67, to ensure gender equality in matters of succession (Agarwal, Sivaramayya, and Sarkar 1998: 14–15).

The Eleventh Five-year Plan (2007–12) also recognized that much of the agricultural productivity is becoming dependent on women's ability to work as farmers, and thus, made recommendations for ensuring effective and independent land rights. The Twelfth Five-year Plan (2012–17) emphasized increasing women's land access from different sources such as direct government transfers, purchase or lease from the market, and inheritance, through a series of initiatives such as joint land titles in all government transfers, credit support to poor women to purchase or lease land from the market, increase in legal awareness and legal support for women's inheritance rights, and government schemes, among others (GoI 2013b).

Steps are being taken to incorporate gender concerns in state policies and programmes related to allotment and distribution of land. The problems are immense as women remain at the margins in the process of making land laws in India. Even where significant changes have ushered in giving women the rights in landownership, many of them do not or are not in a position to claim these rights.

Legal inequalities in relation to women's land rights in India are by and large related to inheritance laws on the one hand and land-reform-related legislations on the other. In the federal democratic political system of India, the laws concerning property and succession are placed in the concurrent list, while agriculture- and land-related legislations are in the state list. The laws in the concurrent list that are passed by the parliament cannot be modified without the assent of the President of India, such as the Hindu Succession Act (HSA), 1956, codified to make provisions for Hindu women's property rights or the Muslim Personal Law (Shariat) Application Act, 1937 (Government of India, Act No. 26 of 1937) passed to abrogate customs or usages that governed a considerable proportion of Muslim population in India. Such laws could not do away with the gender inequalities completely. The HSA, 1956, specifically exempted tenancy rights in agricultural land, and the 1937 Shariat Act explicitly excluded from its purview agricultural land depriving women of the rights in all kinds of property (Chowdhry 2009: xv–xix).

Most of the states took important land-reform measures, such as distribution of agricultural land above ceiling, allocation of surplus lands or wastelands and assigning of joint *pattas* (an official document of landownership), but women were not accommodated in these. The laws differed from state to state and in many places were governed by customs among Hindus, Muslims, or other religious communities (ibid.). In J&K, like in many states of the northwest of India, there exists a major disjunction in state land enactments affecting the devolution of certain categories of agricultural land and the personal laws affecting the devolution of all other property. In the tenancy laws of J&K, the rules of devolution show a strong preference for succession in favour of agnatic males. The gender inequalities also arise from land-reform enactments relating to the fixation of ceilings and in assessment and distribution of surplus land (Agarwal 1994: 216–18). Here, the inheritance laws are in disjunction with the land reforms and the related Acts of the state.

Land reforms cannot be challenged on constitutional grounds as they come under the Ninth Schedule of the Constitution. Therefore, it was required that the laws at the state level be amended to make them gender sensitive just as agricultural land is a state subject. The state of J&K took certain revolutionary steps in land and tenancy reforms to reduce the gender gap. It also passed the HSA in 1956 as well as the Shariat Act in 2007 governing Hindus and Muslims of the state, respectively. These brought significant changes as the two communities were governed by customary laws for a long time. However, there are certain discrepancies existing in laws governing women's land rights and their implementation is a far more formidable task in the J&K state owing to its unique situation and strategic location.

It analyses the relationship between gender and land rights in the state of J&K by reviewing and examining the existing land laws in the state. It focuses on the historical background of the state of J&K with special status under Article 370 of the Indian Constitution; the laws of inheritance including the customary laws, personal laws and statutory laws, and those codified into statutory laws as part of the democratic institution; land-reform legislations; and the recent efforts by the state in making gender-sensitive and inclusive land laws.

JAMMU AND KASHMIR: ITS SPECIAL STATUS AND LOCATION AFFECTING LAND LAWS

J&K is located in the northwestern corner of India sharing international border mainly with Pakistan and China. It is the only Muslim majority state with nearly 68.3% Muslim population; and Hindus (28.4%), Sikhs (about 2%), and Buddhists (nearly 1%) constitute significant minorities. The state comprises of three very diverse regions namely Kashmir, Jammu, and Ladakh. The total geographical area of the state is 222,236 sq. km. It has 22 districts, 82 tehsils, 142 blocks, 6,551 villages (4,128 panchayats), 2 cities, 86 towns, and 7 urban agglomerations. The total population of J&K, as per the 2011 Census, is 12,541,302, with male population being 6,640,662 and female population 5,900,640. The rate of literacy for the state is 67.16%, with male literacy at 76.75% and female literacy at 56.43%. The sex ratio of the state has declined over the years and at present it is appalling at 889 suggesting the declining status of women and girls in J&K (Census of India 2011).

J&K is the only state in India that enjoys special status under Article 370 of the Indian Constitution. It has its own constitution known as the Constitution of Jammu and Kashmir (came into effect in 1957), and the laws formulated or amended in the Parliament are not automatically extended to the state of J&K except in matters of defence, external affairs, communication, and finance. The President of India under Article 370(1) is conferred with the power to extend any provision of the Constitution to the state with such 'exception and modifications as may be deemed fit subject to consultation or concurrence with the State government' (GoI 1950: 243–44).

This special status of J&K has to be understood in the context of its strategic location at the border between the two countries, India and Pakistan, and the contestation between them over its territory. The genesis of this situation can be traced back to 15 August 1947 when India got independence from the British Rule and was partitioned into two nations—India and Pakistan. At that time, the ruler of the princely state of J&K, Maharaja Hari Singh, after initial dithering, agreed to accede to India and signed the 'Instrument of Accession' on 26 October 1947 (Samaddar 2004).

As a consequence of this dispute, the state of J&K has faced a long-drawn conflict with four full-scale wars between India and Pakistan (namely those of 1947, 1965, 1971, and 1999) and continues to witness other lesser intensity wars, proxy wars, cross-border firings, artillery duels, and frequent border skirmishes. This has led to internal displacement and forced migration of the people at the border. Since 1989–90, the state of J&K has seen the rise and spread of militancy, earlier in Kashmir and then in Jammu division, with increasing militarization of the region. During this turmoil, many people were dislocated, disappeared, or killed. This has led to some estrangement and alienation of Kashmiri people and the general divide between the three regions—Jammu, Kashmir, and Ladakh. The relations between the government, the security forces, separatists, and civil society often remain at loggerheads over several issues. Consequently, the functioning of the government and the formulation of policies and laws have remained an uphill task.

The unique situation of the state of J&K under Article 370 gives it the right to make its own laws for the development of the state and the benefit of its people on the one hand and on the other prevents or delays people-centred and gender-sensitive laws to be adopted. For instance, unlike in the central Acts, the SCs and STs of the state did not enjoy the provision of reservation till 1973 and 1991, respectively; the members of Other Backward Classes do not get 27% reservation; the Panchayati Raj Act, 1992 (the Constitutional 73rd Amendment Act), is still not extended to the state of J&K; and the Domestic Violence Act that came into force in 2005 became applicable to the state after five years in 2010 with little modification. More importantly, the Hindu Succession (Amendment) Act, 2005, giving women equal property rights, is not extended to the state of J&K till date.

Besides this, the state provides its subjects a 'permanent resident certificate' (PRC) and bars the non-state subjects from several privileges that the 'citizen' of the state enjoys. Article 35A was introduced in the state through the Constitution (Application to Jammu and Kashmir) Order, 1954, which allowed the state to grant special privileges and right to permanent residents. It said,

> [N]otwithstanding anything contained in this Constitution, no existing laws in the State of J&K, and no law hereafter enacted by the Legislature of the State: (a) defining the Classes of persons who are, or shall be, permanent residents of the State of J&K; or (b) conferring on such permanent residents any special rights and privileges or imposing upon other persons any restrictions as respects—(i) employment under the state Government; (ii) acquisition of immovable property in the state; (iii) settlement in the state; or (iv) right to scholarships and such other forms of aid as the state Government may provide, shall be void on the ground that it is inconsistent with or takes away or abridges any rights conferred on the other citizens of India by any provision of this Part. (GoI 1954)

In the recent ruling, the Jammu and Kashmir High Court has stated that Article 370 has assumed a place of permanence in the Constitution and the feature is beyond amendment, repeal, or abrogation. According to this ruling, Article 35A gives 'protection' to the existing laws in force in the state and to any law enacted after 1954 by the state legislature, and saves the rights of the permanent residents of the state (*State Times* 2015).

The removal of Articles 370 and 35A was opposed by some people; some people filed cases in the Supreme Court, but such petitions were dismissed (*Daily Excelsior* 2015b).

Those who opposed the verdict of the High Court argue that Article 35A deprives the privileges of PRC to certain categories of people which are available to the residents of the state or the 'state subjects', like those who migrated from Pakistan in 1947 (popularly called West Pakistan Refugees) and women who marry outside the state of J&K to the non-state subjects. In the latter situation, the daughter of the state, on marrying a 'non-state subject' would be deprived of her right as the permanent resident of the state along with all other privileges associated with it including the right to own property and right to livelihood. The statement written on women's certificates was 'valid till marriage'.

In 2002, the State High Court, J&K, in its judgement on the Susheela Sawhney case clarified that 'the daughter of a permanent resident marrying a non-permanent resident will not lose the status of permanent resident in Jammu and Kashmir'. Hence, the sentence 'valid till marriage' was removed from the state-subject certificates of women of the state. However, to undermine the decision of the court, a bill titled 'Jammu and Kashmir Women's Permanent Resident (Disqualification) Bill' was moved in the state legislature in March 2004. The bill read: 'Notwithstanding anything contrary contained in any law... a female permanent resident on her marriage with a person who is not a permanent resident shall with effect from the date of such marriage cease to be permanent resident.' The bill was passed in the lower house with a voice vote without any discussion but could not be passed in the Upper House due to opposition by some national as well as regional parties. The bill was opposed by women's organizations and activists too.

The regional political parties, namely the Jammu & Kashmir National Conference (NC) and the Jammu and Kashmir People's Democratic Party (PDP), supported the bill in 2004 and again in 2010, which if passed would have deprived daughters of the state of J&K their right to permanent resident on marrying a non-state subject and also the right to own immovable property, including land.

The law, as it stands, is: 'A daughter of a permanent resident marrying a non-permanent resident will not lose the status of permanent resident in J&K.' It is still discriminatory as it deprives the children of such women of all the privileges that children of the state subject possess and enjoy.

Gender and Land Laws in Jammu and Kashmir

J&K has made a remarkable achievement in the area of 'land reforms'. The state has acquired a distinction for introducing revolutionary land-reform measures soon after independence by introducing a series of land laws which distinctly abolished landlords and intermediaries and provided land to the tillers.

The genesis of this change can be seen in the movement launched by Sheikh Abdullah in 1931 against Maharaja Hari Singh, the ruler of Kashmir, for the transfer of ownership rights of land from him to the oppressed peasantry that constituted more than 80% of the state's population. The peasants were united under the leadership of Sheikh Abdullah and their demands and hopes were formalized into the documents of *Naya Kashmir* (New Kashmir) in 1944. It included the land policy for the state that focused on the abolition of landlordism, land to the tiller, and cooperative association of tillers. On the eve of independence of India, absentee landlords numbering 150,000 in Kashmir possessed 11% of the total cultivable land; cultivating peasants numbering over 8 lakh possessed 32% of the cultivated land; 3 lakh tenants did not possess any land but cultivated 10% of the total cultivated land of others; and the rest of the land was vested in the hands of the state or its agents (Bhatt 2000: 140–47).

It was in the year 1948 after J&K's accession to India (26 October 1947) that the then Prime Minister (the designation now is chief minster) Sheikh Abdullah initiated a land-reform programme by abolishing the privileges of *jagirdars*, *muafidars*, and *mukarraries-khwars* (recipients of cash grants). The new state government abolished 396 *jagirs/muafis*[1] involving an annual land revenue assignment of ₹556,313. The government also abolished fixed cash grants known as *mukarraries* to the tune of ₹177,921 per annum (Prasad 2014: 130). A population of 250,000 was freed from the bondage of feudalism as a result of abolition of *jagirs* and *muafis*. About 4,000 acres of land was transferred to the tillers (Bhatt 2000: 148).

On 18 October 1950, the Jammu and Kashmir Big Landed Estates Abolition Act was passed by the J&K Assembly curtailing the jurisdiction of big landlords by fixing the land ceiling (22.75 acres or 182 kanals [8 kanals=1 acre], excluding orchards, grass farms, etc.) and granting land to tillers. At this time in all, 4.5 lakh acres of land in excess of the ceiling were expropriated from 9,000 odd landowners, of which 2.31 lakh acres of land was allotted to cultivating peasants with ownership rights and remaining land vested in the state (Aslam 1977: 62). Thus, the absentee landlords were abolished and the actual tillers were made the landowners (Bhatt 1989: 102). To overcome certain anomalies and on the recommendation of the Land Commission (1963), the Jammu and Kashmir Agrarian Reforms Act, 1972, and later on the Jammu and Kashmir Agrarian Reforms Act, 1976, were introduced, which ended the rights in land of the non-cultivators and fixed a ceiling of 12.5 standard acres including orchards with certain conditions (Prasad 2014: 135).

The record of J&K in tenancy reforms is considered to be incredible. In 1948 itself, the state government introduced an amendment of the Jammu and Kashmir Tenancy Act of 1923 by which the rights of the tenants-at-will were protected, their ejection was made illegal, and the maximum rental payable by a tenant to his or her landlord was fixed. As per this Act, a tenant who had cultivated the land of his or her landlord for seven months before the commencement of the tenancy act was entitled to the privilege of a protected tenant (ibid.: 133). The subsequent amendments and changes in the Acts of 1955, 1960, 1965, and 1970 granted more security to the tenants against their ejection. The Distressed Debtors Relief Act, 1950 abolished usury completely. These tenancy reforms benefitted nearly three-fifths of the peasantry, cultivating about 7 lakh acres of the 22 lakh acres forming the total cultivated area of the state (Bhatt 2000: 148).

The Jammu and Kashmir Agrarian Reforms Act, 1976, made comprehensive provisions to ascertain that ownership largely follows personal cultivation and tenancy is abolished except in view of certain specific requirements of the institution and people, such as displaced persons of 1947, the land held by Gumpas of Ladakh district, and a unit of land not exceeding 182 kanals held by such places of worship, $waqf^2$ or *dharamshalla*[3] as are reflected in revenue records. As a result, there was a decline in the incidence of tenancy in the state between 1971 and 1981 (Mathew 2011: 26). Besides this, the measures to provide relief to the poor debtors were taken by preventing creditors from charging excessive interest. Along with this Act, the J&K Debtors' Relief Act of 1976 and the J&K Restitution of Mortgaged Properties Act of 1976 were also passed to provide relief to the debtors. These measures had a positive impact as the total number of beneficiaries from the transfer of land to the tillers during the period 1951–85 stood at 1,122,918 (Prasad 2014: 135).

It can be said that land reforms in the state of J&K were revolutionary as they made tenants the owners of land and later on abolished tenancy and provided land to the tillers, those who were landless, or those who had limited land including mainly the poor, backward, and the marginalized sections of society (Mathew 2011: 25). Though there has been a definite improvement in the landownership base of the lower group, the improvement is more pronounced in the middle-level ownership holdings (Bhatt 2000: 165). The class differences have increased as rich farmers and orchard owners have become more dominant with emerging new technology and better facilities in agriculture (Verma 1994).

There could be many reasons for the increasing inequalities, such as defective ceiling laws, exemption of orchards from these laws, and circumventing the laws by the landed peasantry (Prasad 2014: 135). The main focus of land laws in J&K has been on the tenancy reforms and making tenants the proprietors who were in a way already cultivator-owner, and lesser emphasis was given on the landless and marginal people with virtually no focus on the allotment of land to women. Land-reform laws in the state of J&K, therefore, remained largely gender biased and inequalities persisted in agrarian reforms and Tenurial Laws.

According to the Jammu and Kashmir Tenancy Act, 1980 (1923 AD) (with exception to a right of occupancy held by any person professing the Buddhist religion, or held by a member of any tribe, or in any locality where the right shall devolve according to the customs in force regarding the devolution of rights in land in that community or tribe), the rights of landownership, tenurial or otherwise, devolve in the first instance on male descendants in the male line of descent. The widow inherits only in the absence of agnatic males and in her absence the widowed mother. After her death, the holdings go not to her heirs but to the heir of the last male landowner. She also loses her land if she remarries or fails to cultivate for a specified period. The daughters and sisters are almost totally excluded as heirs. In any capacity, a woman can hold only a limited interest in the land (Govt J&K 2006).

It was suggested and recommended that the Tenurial Laws in the state of J&K, particularly the Jammu and Kashmir Tenancy Act, 1980 (1923 AD), be amended and made gender just and equal (Agarwal et al. 1998). The Jammu and Kashmir Agrarian Reforms Act, 1976, is an important step in doing away with the gender inequality stemming from tenancy laws as according to this Act the ownership rights of land were given to the tillers and tenancy was abolished. However, as per the interviews held with the officials in the Revenue Department of J&K, it was informed that the Jammu and Kashmir Tenancy Act, 1980 (1923 AD), still exists and has not been completely done away with in practice as there are still long-pending court cases. But it was also said that there is a considerable decline in the number of tenants and since May 1973 it was notified that no tenancy is to be created or continued. In this sense, by abolishing tenants, the state of J&K has done away with the tenancy law and the gender discrepancies embedded in it to a considerable extent.

On 9 February 2007, the Roshni Bill was moved by the then Chief Minister Ghulam Nabi Azad in the J&K State Assembly. The bill that was passed aimed at providing ownership of 16.6 lakh kanals to farmers worth ₹20,000 crore and with 19 lakh cultivators as beneficiaries. The vesting of ownership was meant only for the permanent residents of the state. The farmers were to be given the right of ownership of government's land under their cultivation at a rate of 10% of the rate prevailing in the respective areas. To get the mutation in their favour, they had to pay a nominal fee of ₹100 per kanal. However, as per the Agrarian Reform Act, 1976, the total agricultural land possessed by a farmer including his or her proprietary land and the government land could not exceed the ceiling of 100 kanals (Mathew 2011: 25).

Certain limitations were imposed on the kind of land that would not be covered under the Roshni Act, such as state land allotted for cultivation to the landless agricultural labourers and petty landlords; state land on which tenancy rights were granted to the cultivators; state land which accrued to the government by virtue of Big Landed Estates Abolition Act, 1950, and Agrarian Reforms Act, 1976, and was in possession of various people to which it was allotted; land under unauthorized residential colonies regularized by the Housing and Urban Development Department up to 2005; *kahcharai* land[4] and forest land; and state land in possession for 60 years that is barred by limitation (Saxena 2007: 4–5).

There were some criticisms of the Roshni Act, for example, it was 'anti-farmer' and 'anti-people' which means that it would legalize the illegal occupants of the state land and that the state government through it wants to provide benefits to the rich and powerful land-grabbers who had already acquired vast land illegally (ibid.: 8–9). The Act is in no way anywhere closer to the concern and spirit behind the agrarian reforms. It purported to officially deprive not only various people of land such as the refugees from West Pakistan who are not 'state subjects' and the children of women who are married to non-state subjects but also indirectly most women who do not possess or even claim their land rights, in the given scenario of land-grabbing spree initiated by those acquiring forest or agricultural land for commercial purposes in connivance with the powerful people in the state of J&K today.

Some efforts are now beginning to be made by the state government to get back the land that is illegally occupied. For instance, the J&K Government retrieved 21,000 kanals (2,625 acres) of forest land from illegal possession in the first nine months of the year 2015 (PTI Jammu 2015). In a very recent instance, 437 kanals and 3 marlas (1 kanal=20 marlas) of *kahcharai* and common land (*shamlat*) measuring under various *khasra*[5] numbers in different villages of Thakrokote (district Reasi) was retrieved from 33 land-grabbers, the mafia group who had illegally occupied it in violation of the Land Revenue Act, Samvat 1996 (1939), and standing circular instructions/orders from higher authorities are issued from time to time (*Daily Excelsior* 2016).

In such a situation where government land is being encroached upon by the powerful lobby and agricultural land is converted for non-agricultural, commercial, and residential purposes, the chances of it being fairly and equitably distributed remain grim. Given the patriarchal structure of society, a nexus between the influential people, gender discriminatory land laws, and complex and cumbersome instances of land litigations and court cases, women's scope of possessing property, in particular agricultural land, is limited and indeed a daunting task in the state of J&K today.

Inheritance Laws in Jammu and Kashmir

In matters of inheritance of property, the state of J&K follows the HSA, 1956, for the Hindus and the Shariat Act, 1937, for the Muslims, and a customary law is applicable where specifically pleaded and proved by the parties alleging it. The J&K HSA, 1956, applies to any person who is a Hindu by religion in any of its form or development and to any person who is a Buddhist, a Jain, or a Sikh by religion. The Jammu and Kashmir Muslim Personal Law (Shariat) Application Act, 2007, applies to all Muslims of the state of J&K. Inheritance laws governing both Hindus and Muslims treat agricultural land as a special category. The HSA, 1956, excluded all agricultural land under tenancy from its purview and the Shariat Act, 1937, excluded all agricultural land (owned and tenanted) from its purview. Though land reforms made possible the distribution of land to a significant number of people in J&K, it remained largely in the hands of males due to the influence of patriarchal social structure and impact of customs.

For a long time in most parts of J&K, the right to inheritance of land along with other civil matters, particularly of the Hindus and Muslims, have been governed by customs that largely deprived women the right to ownership of property including agricultural land. The customary law has been all pervasive, omnipresent, and ubiquitous in the state before the personal laws were codified and enacted, and still exists in some form or the other. Sant Ram Dogra's 'Code of Tribal Customs in Kashmir' (1930) incorporated the customs of people of Kashmir, while Lala Makhan Lal's 'Rivaz-i-Am of Illaqa Poonch Kashmir' (Samvat 2000) included the customs observed by the inhabitants of Poonch. These were consolidated codes of customs observed by the people and were called *Rivaz-i-am*; the values of entries contained in these codes have been accepted with varying degrees by courts even though some of the decisions have been arbitrary and confusing (Ganai 1986: 258).

The authoritative evidence of the customs is available in Shri Partap Singh Laws, Jammu and Kashmir Consolidation Act Samvat, 1977 (Section 4), which provides that in questions regarding succession, inheritance, social property of females, marriage, divorce, dower, adoption, guardianship minority, wills, legacies, gifts, *waqf*, castes or any religious usage, institutions, etc., the rule of decision is and shall be the Mohammedan law in cases where the parties are Mohammedans and Hindu law in cases where the parties are Hindus, except in so far as such law has been, by this or any other enactment, altered or abolished and has not been declared to be void by any competent authority. On many occasions in different cases, contradictions between the customary and the personal laws have been found.

However, the HSA, 1956, specifically exempted tenancy rights in agricultural land from the scope of the Act. In J&K, the succession rules relating to land held under tenancy are devolved in a different way than specified under the personal law. The Jammu and Kashmir Tenancy Act Samvat 1980 (Act No. 2 of the 1980) shows a strong preference for succession among agnates, with a priority in favour of agnatic males (Agarwal 1994: 216) as discussed earlier. But as tenancy is abolished through the Jammu and Kashmir Agrarian Reforms Act, 1976, the gender discrepancies in it have also been done away with.

Under the J&K HSA, 1956, enacted in the state on the model of HSA, 1956, a daughter, legitimate, both natural and adopted, is a Class 1 heir inheriting equally. The distinction between unmarried, married, and widow daughters, or between indigent and rich daughters is no longer operative. A divorced daughter is also entitled to inheritance. Thus, the J&K HSA, 1956, abrogated a customary law in the state and made the position of Hindu females secure in matters relating to succession and in fact equated them with males (Govt J&K 1956). On the lines of other Acts by the centre, the legislature of the state of J&K has also enacted Acts, such as Jammu and Kashmir Hindu Marriage Act, 1955, Jammu and Kashmir Hindu Minority and Guardianship Act, 1957, and Jammu and Kashmir Adoptions and Maintenance Act, 1960, and has made the situation in the state equitable and at par with that at the Centre.

It was felt for a long time after the enactment of the 1956 Act that, though revolutionary in many aspects, by retaining the *Mitakshara* coparceners in a joint Hindu family property, the Act deprived women of complete equality in matter of inheritance of property. While the male became a coparcener at the time of birth, the women enjoyed only maintenance rights as wives, widows, and unmarried daughters. This meant that a son, unlike a daughter, inherited three-fourth share, one half by virtue of right by birth and one-fourth by succession under the Act. The daughter, however, got only one-fourth (Chowdhry 2009: xvii).

To do away with such discrepancies, the Hindu Succession (Amendment) Act, 2005, was enacted by the GoI (2005). By this Amendment Act, the daughters were included as coparceners in the Hindu joint family; Section 4(2) of the HSA, 1956, was omitted bringing agricultural land at par with all other forms of property, implying that Hindu women have equal rights in agricultural land; daughters, like sons were given equal residence rights in the parental dwelling house; and remarriage no longer remained a ground for disinheritance (the Hindu Succession [Amendment] Act 2005). However, the Hindu Succession (Amendment) Act, 2005, has not yet been extended to the state depriving women of J&K of those rights enshrined in the amended Act.

Regarding the Muslims, the Muslim Personal Law (Shariat) Application Act, 1937 (Government of India, Act No. 26 of 1937) abrogated the prevailing customs in favour of the Muslim Personal Law giving property rights to women under the Islamic law. It became applicable to all Muslims of India (except to those of the state of J&K) and to all kinds of property, with three main exceptions: agricultural land, testamentary succession in certain communities, and charities, other than *waqfs* (Fyzee 2005).

Under it, the females, namely widows, mothers, true grandmothers, daughters, son's daughters, full sisters, consanguine sisters, and uterine sisters are Class I Quranic heirs. A widow is the only heir who is made a primary heir in Quran and inherits one-eighth if there are children and one-fourth if there are none. Where the widow is the sole surviving heir, she takes the whole estate. Also, under the Muslim law of inheritance, a mother is a primary heir and she is entitled to one-third share when there are no children and one-sixth share when there are children. The mother has absolute rights over the inherited property but son's widow is not an heir under the Muslim law. A single daughter takes half and two or more daughters take two-third share. If the daughter or daughters coexist with a son or sons, she inherits as an agnatic heir, Class II, and she shares the residues with the son in the proportion of 1:2 (Diwan 2007: 221–22).

The Muslim Personal Law (Shariat) Application Act, 1937, which abolished the legal authority of customs among the Muslims of British India, did not extend to the state of J&K for a long time, and consequently, customs continued to govern the Muslims of the state in all civil matters including inheritance rights. In J&K, certain land laws have been amended from time to time to give property rights to women, though they have been very limited and confined to widows mostly. One can say that in J&K there has been a peculiar blend of custom, personal law, and piecemeal legislation that has hindered the development and growth of gender just laws.

In the Jammu and Kashmir Shri Pratap Consolidation of Laws Act, 1977 Samvat, the first rule was declared to be the personal law of the parties excepting in so far as that personal law is modified by any custom applicable to the parties concerned. In this sense, there is an initial presumption in favour of personal law in all cases whether the parties are agriculturists or non-agriculturists by occupation. However, where the parties allege and prove that their laws are guided by the customary rule they are 'regarded as valid unless they are contrary to justice, equality, and good governance or are declared to be void by a competent authority'. The civil courts, the J&K High Court and the Board of Judicial Advisors have allowed the customs to prevail. The revenue courts have clearly held that in matters of succession to agricultural property among Muslims, the customary law applies and not the Shariat (Ganai 1986: 591–93).

The general rule of succession under the customary law for the Muslims in the state of J&K has been that succession first goes to the direct male lineal descendants of the last owner to the exclusion of female descendants 'excepting in the case of daughters who have been married at home, by their fathers in their life time' called *dukhtari khana nashin* (a woman having no brother). If there are no male lineal descendants of the last male owner, subject to certain life estates in favour of some females, the inheritance devolves upon the collaterals among whom the rights of representation exists, all heirs sharing equally (ibid.: 294–95).

In Kashmir, with certain exceptions, among all agricultural communities, a 'widow' with a male lineal descendant of the deceased was ordinarily entitled to suitable maintenance. In the absence of male lineal descendants and *dukhtari khana nashin*, the widow of the deceased ordinarily succeeds to life estate till remarriage or death, whichever is earlier, among all the agricultural communities of Kashmir. After the death (or remarriage) of the widow, the heritage goes to the deceased husband's agnates. When a widow is permitted to succeed to husband's share (and if more than one, all share equally) in a joint estate, she can ordinarily claim partition of such share—the claim that has been recognized by Section 105 of the Jammu and Kashmir Land Revenue Act, 1996.

If the widow survives with *dukhtari khana nashin*, the property will devolve upon such a daughter and the widow will be entitled for only dower (*mehr*) on demand. Sections 67 and 68-A of the Jammu and Kashmir Tenancy Act, 1980 Samvat (1923 AD), recognized and legitimized these customary rules of inheritance. The objective behind this was usually to save land from fragmentation or not allow the widow to take it with her in case of remarriage. Therefore, the customary law permitted a sonless landholder to adopt a son called *pisar parvada* and entitle a daughter to inherit if she is made *dukhtari khana nashin* (ibid.: 300–09).

In all the Muslim tribes in Kashmir, 'sisters', however distant, and their issues are usually excluded by agnates according to the customary law. However, an exception to this rule is made in favour of all Muslim tribes of Khanabal and Pattan, town's people of Sopore and Baramulla, Pirs, Babas, Syeeds, Shias, and Muslims of Badgam, all of whom follow the Muslim Personal Law in these matters. Similarly, under the customary law in the state, the mother of the deceased and his son's widow (in preference to collaterals), in the absence of the widow, share the property equally. On death or remarriage, inheritance goes to collaterals of the deceased with certain exceptions. In J&K, customary rules related to property thus recognize the right of succession of the mother and son's widow in preference to that of the male collaterals or married daughters, in default of male lineal descendant, *dukhtari khana nashin*, and of a widow (ibid.: 323–28).

The Muslim 'daughters', according to the customary law in the state of J&K, as different from the Muslim Personal Law, are classified into 'three categories' in matters of inheritance, though the Sunnis of Khanabal, the Shias of Badgam and Nunar, town's people of Baramulla and Sopore, Muslim inhabitants of Srinagar, and also agriculturists of Pattam, Muslim tribes of Poonch, and the Shias follow Shariat (in case of movable property; ibid.: 349–50). First, among the agriculturalists, an 'unmarried daughter' succeeds to the agricultural land of her father and retains the inheritance till she is married out of the family. Her powers of alienation when minor are used by her guardians. The property reverts to the agnatic heirs of her deceased father on her marriage or premature death. A married daughter, however, inherits her father's property if she is a widow or barren and without male issues (ibid.: 337–41).

When an unmarried daughter succeeds to the estate of her deceased father, she cannot be forced to marry. Such a right is alienable in case she does not marry under Section 6 of the Jammu and Kashmir Transfer of Property Act, 1977 (Samvat). The second category is one in which a daughter is married outside her conjugal home in a normal procedure known as *dukhtari khana begum*. She does not succeed to her father in presence of her brothers and their male lineal descendants, widow, son's widow, and agnates. Based on the entries in the Dogra Code, the State High Court in a series of cases has held that *dukhtari khana begum* is not a customary heir in any way and, therefore, totally excluded from succeeding to her father's property. The Board of Judicial Advisors, however, observed that her right arises after the agnates. It recognized the right of a daughter to fall back upon Muslim law in case she fails to prove customary status. The State High Court has allowed in certain cases such a daughter to succeed as daughter simpliciter under the Muslim law (ibid.: 610–11).

The third category of daughters is *dukhtari khana nashin* who succeeds to all kinds of property of her deceased father whether movable or immovable, ancestral or self-acquired to the exclusion of other sisters. The custom of *dukhtari khana nashin* is not recognized in judicial decisions of the courts as such, but the mode of affecting mutations in her favour has been found in various revenue orders and Acts, such as the Jammu and Kashmir Tenancy Act, 1980 (Samvat); the Jammu and Kashmir Agrarian Reforms Act, 1976 AD; the Revenue Department Standing Order No. 23-A prepared by the revenue minister by virtue of the powers vested in him or her under Section 43 of the Jammu and Kashmir Land Revenue Act, 1980 (Samvat); and Section 32, Clauses (e) and (f) of the Jammu and Kashmir Land Revenue Act, 1996 (Samvat; ibid.: 356). She will also have an absolute right to maintenance for purposes of dissolution under the Jammu and Kashmir Dissolution of Muslim Marriages Act, 1942, that confers on her the right to ask for dissolution of marriage (ibid.: 407).

The Jammu and Kashmir Muslim Personal Law (Shariat) Application Act, 2007 (Act IV of 2007), came into force on 26 February 2007. It is applicable to all Muslims of the state of J&K from the said date. It was realized, particularly in the J&K High Court case, Yakoob Laway and Others v/s Gulla and another (2004) that the customary law prevalent in the state has resulted in chaos and confusion and has given rise to endless litigations and delay in disposing of the cases. It is alleged that more than 50% of the cases pending in various revenue courts revolve around this controversy. Many of the tribal customs have become obsolete and there is no authentic record of the same. To overcome these problems, it is believed that the 2007 Act has made provisions for the application of the Muslim Personal Law (Shariat) to Muslims of the state of J&K (Govt J&K 2007).

The Act states:

> Notwithstanding any customs or usages to the contrary, in all questions regarding intestate succession, special property of females including personal property or obtained under contract or gift or any other provision of personal law, marriage, dissolution of marriage including *talaq, ila, zihar, lain, khula* and *mubarat*, dower, guardianship, gifts, trusts and trust properties, the rule of decision, in case where the parties are Muslims, shall be the Muslim Personal Law (Shariat).

The comments mention that the Act expressly overrides and abrogates the applicability of customs in the derogation of Muslim Personal Law, in respect of matters enumerated in the section; all customs, contrary to the Muslim Personal Law, have been invalidated, and the court has no jurisdiction to administer any customary usage amongst Muslims in derogation of the Muslim Personal Law. As far as the provisions of the Shri Partap Singh Jammu and Kashmir Laws Consolidation Act, Samvat 1977 (1920 AD), are concerned, the same shall be repealed in so far as they are inconsistent with the provisions of this Act (ibid.).

It is to be noticed that though the Muslim Personal Law (Shariat) Application Act was passed as late as in 2007 in the state of J&K, 70 years after it was passed at the all-India level in 1937, the J&K Act does not make conditions regarding agricultural land and charities, charitable institutions, and charitable and religious endowments. An official in the Revenue Department of the Government of Jammu dealing with such cases informed that Muslim women in J&K have rights on all kinds of property, including agricultural land. In majority of the cases, they are now governed by the 2007 Act rather than the customary law and are entitled for their shares as designated in the Muslim Personal Law (Shariat). The application of the Shariat Act and abrogation of gender-biased customs did not make property rights of women and men completely equal, but it strengthened Muslim women's property rights. It also enforced woman's right to *mehr* as her mandatory and individual property which customarily has been a token and symbolic amount partially paid or deferred endlessly.

Like the Hindus and Muslims of J&K, the Buddhists, particularly in the region of Ladakh, till quite recently, have been governed by their customary laws. Ladakh's economy has been organized on the principle of agriculture cooperation in which women play a vital role contributing immensely to the field and hearth. The shift now is visible in the economy with men controlling trade and tourism (Norberg-Hodge 1991).

The descent, however, is largely patrilineal and the land is generally transmitted through the male line in which the eldest son customarily inherits the land and the house. In the absence of a brother, a woman can bring in a spouse (*mag-pa*) and pass on the family's land to her children. As polyandry was legally prohibited in 1941 and primogeniture in 1943, all brothers became equally entitled to the land. The daughters, especially the eldest daughter, instead of land, received kitchen vessels, livestock, and their mother's *perag* (important head ornament of Ladakhi women) over which they retain control in case of marriage failure (Aggarwal 2004: 79).

Reforms in Buddhist Civil Law come under the Hindu Civil Code in India and the Buddhists of Ladakh also follow a similar line. Likewise, the Muslims of Kargil and Leh in Ladakh are governed largely by the Shariat Act passed in 2007 in J&K. Recently, the Autonomous Hill Development Council in Ladakh is making new land allotments in Leh town jointly in the name of husband and wife (ibid.: 84).

CONCLUSION

The state of J&K is unique in many ways and the issues involving land laws here have to be understood in this context. The state, strategically located on the northwest international border of India, has 198 km of international border and 778 km of Line of Control (LoC). The area is still considered disputed by many and often results in violence and conflict, both internal and external.

The uniqueness of the state of J&K is seen clearly in its having its own constitution (the only state in India to have this), special status under Article 370, and protection of the rights of its permanent residents under Article 35A. Therefore, some of the laws, many of which are gender sensitive have been pending. The rights of women of the state on marrying non-state subjects are not certain and secured, and can be taken away any time as the experience of the past shows. Till today, children of such women do not have PRC and are deprived of their basic and fundamental rights in the state of J&K.

Gender inequalities in land rights in the state of J&K, as in other states of India, are seen in relation to (a) land-reform-related legislation and (b) inheritance laws. Several land-reform measures, as noted earlier, were undertaken in J&K which resulted in more equitable distribution of agricultural land. The analysis of land distribution in rural J&K through different indices indicates that there is a definite improvement in the landownership by the lower groups, though this improvement is more pronounced in the middle-level ownership holdings.

In the area of tenancy reforms, the state record has been much better. The incidences of tenancy have significantly declined in the state since 1973. This has happened both in terms of the number of households leasing-in/leasing-out land and also as the percentage of area owned. This achievement can be attributed to various land-reform Acts implemented in the state. The change in the Tenurial Law resulted in doing away with the gender discrimination inherent in the HSA, 1956, which had specifically exempted tenancy rights in agricultural land depriving women of complete ownership rights on land.

Besides this, the Jammu and Kashmir Agrarian Reforms Act, 1976, ensured that the land is personally cultivated and the owner of land is its tiller. As the Act extinguished tenancy, except in certain cases, there was tremendous decrease in the incidences of tenancy, thus ushering in new benefits in the matter of land distribution in the state of J&K. However, the state's record in matters of distribution of ceiling and surplus land to women is not encouraging. The court cases and illegal encroachment of government's land for personal and commercial purposes have proved detrimental in allocating land to the deserving people, including women. The need for digitization and computerization of land-related data was, therefore, felt urgently and the government of J&K has already initiated this process.

In the history of Kashmir region, the land record survey was conducted twice: The first was under the supervision of Raja Todar Mal, Emperor Akbar's Revenue Minister, who ordered land survey after Kashmir became part of Imperial Mughal Empire in 1586 AD. The second survey was conducted during the reign of Maharaja Pratap Singh around 1891 AD. Ever since, the updating of land records in the state continued on the foundation 'Lawrence's Land Settlement' laid down by British Revenue Officer W. Lawrence. The last regular settlement operations in J&K were conducted during 1920–25 (Afzal and Khan 2005: 286). As of today, data, though not gender disaggregated (except of operational landholdings), on the distribution of land in the state of J&K, are available in (a) Agricultural Censuses 1971–1972, 1976–77, 1980–81, and 1985–86 (and now also 2010–11); (b) National Sample Survey (NSS) 8th Round (1953–54), 16th Round (1961–62), 26th Round (1971–72), 37th Round (January 1982–December 1982); and (c) Land Commission Report (1968), Government of J&K (Bhatt 2000: 141).

In J&K, the ownerships of land have changed and land alienation too has taken place since Independence. In this context, in 1989, the government announced that fresh land settlement error-free record would be prepared in the state with digitization and computerization of land records (Afzal and Khan 2005: 287–89). In 1991, a task force headed by the then financial commissioner (revenue) was constituted to carry out the settlement work in a speedy and systematic manner. The work started with enthusiasm and clear instructions were issued to revenue officials in each *halqa patwar*[6] and *niabat*[7] of how the record for the settlement of land had to be prepared. Even a proper policy called 'Hayadat Bandobast' was put in place containing the guidelines for completing the settlement work (*Daily Excelsior* 2014a).

Though the measurement of land in a number of villages has been done, so far not even a single village can claim to have taken up the step towards the settlement of records. In 2013, the Chief Minister of J&K announced that the entire land record would be digitalized and its safety ensured. But again, nothing was done in this direction (*Daily Excelsior* 2015a). Now efforts are being made by the state government on digitalizing the entire land record in the state of J&K within a stipulated time period. An agency named 'Jammu & Kashmir Land Records Management' (JaKLaRMA), headed by the Financial Commissioner (Revenue) as its Chief Executive Officer in an Ex-officio capacity, has been given the charge of conducting the entire operation within a given time frame. This scheme has been sanctioned by the Union Ministry of Rural Development, Department of Land Resources, which approved an Annual Action Plan of ₹60 crore for 12 districts of J&K for Phase I (there will be two phases; *Daily Excelsior* 2014b).

The Jammu and Kashmir Muslim Personal Law (Shariat) Application Act, 2007 (Act IV of 2007), came into force on 26 February 2007. It is difficult to assess its impact as of now, but most Muslims are more confident than before that they are guided by the Personal Law. The customs under which the male lineal descendants in the agnatic line were the first order heirs in the inheritance of agricultural land were done away with, giving women their share of property under the Shariat Act 2007. It also strengthened Muslim women's legal position in terms of their share in property including land and their rights to *mehr* as their exclusive property. In practice, very few women get their share in property and even fewer claim it. In the Revenue Department of J&K, perhaps a couple of cases out of hundred odd ones a year related to property claims are those in which women are petitioners. These cases continue for a long time and are often tedious involving too many formalities and complexities for women to sustain them.

It needs to be mentioned here that the Hindu Succession (Amendment) Act, 2005, is still not applicable in the state of J&K and women continue to be deprived of the full property rights like men, particularly in matters of coparcenary rights. The land and tenancy Acts were also heavily against women's claim to property and deprived them the right to inherit agricultural land. However, this has now been done away with in J&K as the agrarian-reform legislations have made tenants the proprietors and abolished tenancy. But still, wherever they prevail in some form or the other they prevent women from claiming their share of property. They also do not get their share because daughters, unlike sons, do not have coparcenary rights in the ancestral property.

RECOMMENDATIONS

1. Woman, unmarried or married to the non-state subject, must remain a permanent resident of the state of J&K and the same must be incorporated in the law. In no way should she be deprived of her fundamental rights. Her right to own property, right to occupation and place of work, in fact right to choose a life partner should not be curtailed. Her right to own property including land must not be contingent upon her marital status.
2. The children of a woman married to a non-state subject should not be deprived of the PR status of the state of J&K and hence of all the rights that accrue to being a permanent resident. The Act should be made or amended to include those children as 'state-subjects' whose mother has married a non-state subject.
3. The Hindu Succession Act (Amendment), 2005, should be extended to the state of J&K through amendment as soon as possible so that Hindu women get complete rights in all forms of property including agricultural land and ancestral property. It is

important to make women the coparcener in ancestral property which can be done by amending the State Act in accordance with the Hindu Succession Act (Amendment), 2005.
4. There are still gender-related discrepancies in certain land and revenue laws of the J&K state which need to be removed. The gender inequalities in the land ceiling laws must be eliminated and the provision of allotment of surplus land to women must be ensured.
5. Regarding Muslims, though the changes have been brought about in the state of J&K by replacing customs with the personal law, there is a need for legal reforms to bring about gender equality in the inheritance law by emphasizing the constitutional provisions.
6. Gender-equal land laws and policies must be made and implemented by the government for fair distribution of land. Government programmes must ensure that surplus land is allotted in the name of women and the process of such transfers should be made easy and transparent. The other related facilities must also be provided to them.
7. It is seen that land records are often distorted resulting in litigation and that several cases are pending in the courts of law. The land mafia has also become active in recent times and a considerable land has been encroached upon. It is hoped that the digitization of records would solve this and many other such problems. However, the process of digitization and computerization must include gender-disaggregated data on land-related issues.

NOTES

1. Land grants/ life estate given by the rulers in lieu of the services rendered to the state.
2. An endowment made by a Muslim to a religious, educational, or charitable cause.
3. A religious sanctuary or a rest house for the pilgrims.
4. Revenue derived from levying fee, duty, tax or fine upon livestock grazing in certain territories.
5. A legal agricultural document that specifies land and crop details.
6. A basic unit of revenue administration in the state headed by a Patwari, the lowest state government functionary who keeps landownership records.
7. An administrative unit, the sub-division of a tehsil with Naib Tehsildar as in-charge.

REFERENCES

Afzal, Mohd., and Ishfaq A. Khan. 2005. 'Updation of Land Records, Computerisation and Digitisation of Cadastral Survey Maps with Reference to J&K.' In *Land Reforms in India: Computerisation of Land Records*, edited by Wajahat Habibullah and Manoj Ahuja, 286–96. New Delhi: SAGE Publications.
Agarwal, Bina. 1994. *A Field of One's Own: Gender and Land Rights in South Asia*. Cambridge: Cambridge University Press.
———. 1995. 'Women's Legal Rights in Agricultural Land in India.' *Economic and Political Weekly* 30 (12): A39–56.
———. 2003. 'Gender and Land Rights Revisited: Exploring New Prospects via the State, Family and Market.' *Journal of Agrarian Change* 3 (1 and 2): 184–224.
Agarwal, Bina, B. Sivaramayya, and L. Sarkar. 1998. *Report of the Committee on Gender Equality in Land Devolution in Tenurial Laws*. Report submitted to the Department of Rural Development, Government of India, Delhi.
Aggarwal, Ravina. 2004. 'Trails Turquoise: Feminist Enquiry and Counter-Development in Ladakh, India.' In *Feminist Post Development Thought: Rethinking Modernity, Post-colonialism and Representation*, edited by Kriemild Saunders, 69–86. New Delhi: Zubaan—An associate of Kali for Women.
Aslam, Mohamad. 1977. 'Land Reforms in Jammu and Kashmir.' *Social Scientist* 6 (4): 59–64.
Bhatt, M. S. 1989. 'A Profile of Agrarian Science in Jammu and Kashmir.' In *Land Reforms in India: Achievements, Problems and Prospects*, edited by M. L. Sharma and R. K. Punia, 99–111. Delhi: Ajanta Publications.
———. 2000. 'Land Distribution in Rural Jammu and Kashmir: An Intertemporal Analysis.' In *Land Reforms in India: An Unfinished Agenda*, edited by B. K. Sinha and Pushpendra, 139–69. New Delhi: SAGE Publications.
Census of India. 2011. 'Jammu & Kashmir Profile.' *CensusInfo India 2011: Final Population Totals*. New Delhi: Census of India.
Chowdhry, Prem. 2009. 'Introduction: Understanding Land Rights of Women.' In *Gender Discrimination in Land Ownership*, edited by Prem Chowdhary, xv–xxxv. New Delhi: SAGE Publications.
Daily Excelsior. 2014a. 'Mafia Rules the Roost as Settlement of Land Records not Completed Even in One Tehsil.' Available at: www.dailyexcelsior.com. Posted on 4 February (accessed on 19 January 2016).
———. 2014b. 'Digitizing Land Record.' Available at: www.dailyexcelsior.com. Posted on 30 December (accessed on 19 January 2016).
———. 2015a. 'Jammu Land Mafia.' Available at: www.dailyexcelsior.com. Posted on 11 May (accessed on 19 January 2016).

Daily Excelsior. 2015b. 'J&K Granted Last Chance to File Reply.' *Daily Excelsior,* Jammu.4 September.

———. 2016. '437 Kanals of Land Retrieved.' *Daily Excelsior,* Jammu. 7 February.

Diwan, Paras. 2007. *Muslim Law in Modern India.* 9th ed. Faridabad: Allahabad Law Agency.

Fyzee, A. A. A. 2005. *Outlines of Muhammadan Law.* 4th ed. 9th impression. New Delhi: Oxford University Press.

Ganai, Nisar Ahmed. 1986. 'Familial Rights of Muslim Women in the State of Jammu and Kashmir.' Unpublished PhD thesis, Department of Law, University of Jammu.

GoI (Government of India). 1937. *The Muslim Personal Law (Shariat) Application Act, 1937.* Act No. 26 of 1937, dated October 7th.

———. 1950. *Article 370 (1):* 243–44. The Constitution of India (As modified up to 1st December 2007). New Delhi: Ministry of Law and Justice.

———. 1954. *The Constitution (Application to Jammu and Kashmir) Order 1954, C.O. 48.* Appendix 1–569.

———. 2005. *The Hindu Succession (Amendment) Act, 2005.* No. 39 of 2005, dated September 5th.

———. 2006. *National Sample Survey (NSS) 2003, 59th Round.* Household Ownership Holdings in India'. New Delhi: National Sample Survey Organization. Ministry of Statistics and Programme Implementation.

———. 2012. *Statistical Profile on Women Labour: 2009–11.* Chandigarh/Shimla: Labour Bureau, Ministry of Labour and Employment.

———. 2013a, January–December. *Household Ownership and Operational Holdings in India.* NSS 70th Round. New Delhi: National Sample Survey Office, Ministry of Statistics and Programme Implementation.

———. 2013b, July 24. *Draft National Land Reforms Policy.* New Delhi: Department of Land Resources, Ministry of Rural Development.

Government of Jammu and Kashmir (Govt J&K). 1956. *Act No. (38 of 1956) 7: The Jammu and Kashmir Hindu Succession Act, 1956.* Srinagar: Government of Jammu and Kashmir

———. 2006. *Jammu and Kashmir Tenancy Act, 1980 (1923 AD).* J K Laws, Tenancy Act (Vol. 22). Jammu: Jay Kay Law Reporter.

———. 2007. *The Jammu and Kashmir Muslim Personal Law (Shariat) Application Act, 2007 (Act IV of 2007).* The Act was published in Jammu & Kashmir Government Gazette Vol. 119, Jammu, February 26, 2007.

———. Report on *Ninth Agriculture Census 2010–2011: Phase–I (Table 1).* Jammu: Financial Commissioner (Revenue) Planning & Statistical Wing.

———. *Digest of Statistics, 2012–13.* Directorate of Economics and Statistics, Planning and Development Department.

———. *Economic Survey J&K 2013–14.* Directorate of Economics and Statistics, J&K.

Mathew, George. 2011. 'Land Reforms: Jammu and Kashmir Shows the Way.' *Yojana* 55 (October): 24–26.
Norberg-Hodge, Helena. 1991. *Ancient Futures: Learning from Ladakh.* San Francisco, CA: Sierra Club Books.
Prasad, Anirudh Kumar. 2014. 'Sheikh Abdullah and Land Reforms in Jammu and Kashmir.' *Economic and Political Weekly* XLIX (31): 130–37.
Press Trust of India (PTI) Jammu. 2015. 'JK govt. Retrieves 2,625 acres of Forest Land Grabbers.' *Press Trust of India*, Jammu, December 15, 2015. Available at: wap.business-standard.com (accessed on 19 January 2016).
Samaddar, Ranabir, ed. 2004. *Peace Studies: An Introduction to the Concept, Scope and Themes.* New Delhi: SAGE Publications.
Saxena, Ashish. 2007. 'Another Leap towards Land Reforms in J&K.' *Mainstream Weekly* XLV (40). Archives (2006 on) 26 September, mainlineweekly@yahoo.com.
State Times. 2015. 'Article 370 is Permanent: JK HC.' *State Times*, Jammu, 12 October.
Verma, P. S. 1994. *Jammu and Kashmir at the Political Crossroads.* New Delhi: Vikas Publishing House.

8

Understanding Women and Land Rights in Jharkhand

M. N. KARNA

Agrarian structure and transformation forms a crucial dimension of a discourse on the socio-economic development in contemporary India. The conundrum of economic backwardness and under-development, issues of rural unrest and violence, and so also concerns of social institutions and cultural values are all involved in the basic nature of the agrarian question. This becomes conspicuous if one keeps in view the predominantly agrarian character of this country where land continues to be the mainstay of the people. Land thus constitutes not only the structural feature of the Indian countryside, but changes in land relations also act as the prime mover of social, economic, and political transformations.

Given the context and ambience, the most crucial factor in agrarian relations is patterns of landownership and possession across the locality and regions, communities and groups, and so also across castes and classes. Historically, therefore, no equity and impartiality, justice and fair play, and no uprightness and righteousness are witnessed in the distribution and sharing of land. If seen against this background, inequality between men and women is a distressful aspect of the socio-economic life today in the country. The gender-based inequality impinges upon the nature and extent of social persecution, economic deprivation, and the political marginalization existing in the community concerned. The gender demarcated injustice in the accessibility and the ownership of land is thus imbedded in the socio-economic and politico-legal structures surviving in the different regions of the country.

It is, however, commonly argued that gender-based discriminatory practices may be exterminated primarily by enabling women to gain equal access to and control over resources. This goal may be realized essentially by changing institutional settings and related statutory provisions which define and regulate the ideology and practices of subordination and servitude of women. Coming specifically to land, it is ordinarily accepted that historically land has been and continues to be the most revealing form of property in rural India. It is still a critical determinant of economic position, social status, and political power. It is commonly maintained that economic resources particularly land is in the hands of male household members and often does not benefit female members in equal degree. It is, therefore, firmly presumed that ownership and control of land may be a crucial factor in promoting the well-being and empowerment of women. It is within this conceptual framework and plan of intended objective the present micro-study takes on to examine the nature and extent of gender inequality in formal laws and customary practices governing access and control of land and its ownership in the state of Jharkhand.

The study presented here attempts to undertake and analyse the levels and intricacies of land rights for women among some selected tribal communities in the state of Jharkhand. Being a micro-study, it does not claim to highlight and focus on all the critical aspects of agrarian question in one of the poorest states in the country. It is, however, expected to augment and amplify our understanding of the gender discrimination in landownership, an issue of vital concern in the national agrarian policy and programme today.

LOCATION AND DEMOGRAPHIC ATTRIBUTES

Jharkhand was constituted as a separate state after the bifurcation of the state of Bihar in the year 2000 to fulfil the long-lasting demands of the tribals of this region. It was India's poorest state in the year 2011–12 with 37% of its population below the poverty line. The Scheduled

Tribes (STs) constitute approximately 26.3% of Jharkhand's population. According to the Census of 2001, of the state's population of 3.29 crores, 68.5% are Hindus, 13.8% Muslims, and only 4% follow Christianity. Although Sarnas (traditional tribal faith) who primarily worship their ancestors are not counted separately, they make up most of the other category, estimated at 11–13% of the population. The Sarna group claims that the actual number may be higher, given the absence of a separate category for it. The chasm between the Sarna and Christian tribals has, of late, not only widened but also emerged as an important dimension of the politico-economic domain of people's life in the region. However, a common perception has been that the Christian tribals have better access to higher education and jobs. Such a perception may be current because of strong emotions of enmities witnessed among different religious groups.

It is pertinent to call attention to the fact that although the tribals constitute approximately only one-fourth of the state's population, no study of the land-related issues in the region can escape the question of the land relations among the tribals. However, there has been considerable controversy with regard to the enumeration of tribal population in the state. It is said that enumeration was politically motivated and population was surveyed when the people migrated outside villages in search of livelihood.

The tribal population is nonetheless broadly divided into 32 STs groups including nine most vulnerable tribal groups, earlier known officially as Primitive Tribal Group (PTG). However, there were only 30 STs in the state at the time of the Census of 2001, but subsequently two more groups were added to the list in 2003. While Patar was included in the Munda community, Dhangras in the Oraon community.

Among all the tribal communities in Jharkhand, the most numerous ones are the Santhals, Oraon, Munda, Ho, Kherwar, Kharia, and Bhumij who constitute around 86% of the total tribal population of the state. Broadly, the Non-PTGs in Jharkhand can be classified as settled cultivators, artisans, folk artists, and sorcerers or medicine men according to their traditional occupation. The majority of the non PTGs are, however, settled cultivators.

The presentation of a detailed ethnographic description is beyond the scope and objective of the present study; however, even a cursory look at Figure 8.1 suggests the complex structure and heterogeneous nature of the tribal communities located in Jharkhand.

Figure 8.1
Classification of the Tribal Communities in Jharkhand

Vulnerable Tribal Groups (PTGs)	Asur, Birhors, Birija, Mal Paharias, Korwa, Suaria Paharias, Savars, Hill Kharia, Parahaiya
Non-PTGs	
Settled Cultivators	Bedia, Binjhia, Bathudi, Chero, Gond, Ho, Karmali, Kharia, Kharwar, Khond, Kisan, Munda, Oraon, Santhal, Bhumij Kora
Artisans	Mahli (basketmakers), Lohara, Karmalis (blacksmith), Chiks baraikh (weavers), Gorait (drum players, watchman, village messengers)
Sorcerers	Baiga

Source: Ramesh Sharan, 2011 PESA, PRI & Tribal Self Governance in Jharkhand, Issues, Challenges and Possibilities, Sambad, Ranchi, Chapter 2, (1) Jharkhand.

PRESENT STUDY

In the whole debate about landownership and agrarian relations in the different regions of the country, the question of women's landownership has emerged now as a crucial issue. But there are hardly any incisive and relevant studies in this field covering gender dimension in landownership in the different socio-economic regions of the country. The present micro-study in the state of Jharkhand, as indicated earlier, is expected to throw some light on this dimension of the problem under perusal.

Our attempt in the subsequent discussion will be to give an account of both the 'book view' and the 'field view' of facts with regard to the gender discrimination in the patterns of landownership. As frequently articulated in the Indian social science literature, the 'book view' is based primarily on the secondary data, whereas the 'field view' is designed with the help of empirical data collected by the researcher in course of a planned study. Accordingly, following the guidelines suggested by the sponsor, the sampling framework here includes three districts broadly representing three different sociocultural groups which are three tribes in the present case. Based on this outline, the household data have been collected from 100 families from each of the three selected districts making the sampling size of 300 in all. It, thus, includes Khunti district for the Munda, Pakur for the Santhal, and Simdega for the Kharia. The respondents selected for administering the interview schedule are in majority of the cases the Head of the household concerned who could either be male or female depending upon the structure and the composition of the family. In some cases the Head of the household was, of course, assisted by the other family members while answering certain questions. However, in no case the respondent was from the neighbouring families.

Now, we set out to talk first about the legal and customary practices prevalent in each of the three selected communities included in the study followed by an elucidation of the empirical data for relating them with the ground realities.

Any consideration of the historical journey of the land question in the region has to begin with reference to the extension of a Constitutional provision of the Fifth Schedule. When the Indian Constitution was adopted, it envisaged strong democratic institutions at the local level both in the tribal dominated region and the non-tribal areas. In view of this, the establishment of Panchayati Raj became one of the major programmes of the state policy. Thus, certain specific provisions were provided in the Constitution. It is in this background the tribal areas have been categorized broadly under two groups and they are covered under the Fifth and the Sixth Schedules of the Constitution. This specific arrangement was required to harmonize the aspirations and yearnings of the tribal people. The issue was particularly challenging in the erstwhile 'excluded' and 'partially excluded' regions primarily inhabited by the hills and plane tribals. The ethnic, linguistic, and the religious diversities among these groups further required special attention. Under the condition, separate and distinct political and administrative arrangements for the tribal areas of the central and the northeastern India were envisaged under the Constitution itself. Thus, while the Fifth Schedule of the Constitution has provisions for safeguarding the interests of the tribals located in the states other than the northeastern states, the Sixth Schedule provides the outlines for the protection and safety of the needs and requirements of the tribal people of the northeastern hills. The framers of the Indian Constitution were guided primarily by the following issues:

1. the exigency of protecting the culture and tradition of the tribal social order;
2. the necessity to provide autonomy in social, economic, and politic affairs; and
3. the obligation to prevent their economic exploitation by the rich and powerful people of the region.

As such the Fifth Schedule of the Indian Constitution as applicable to the state of Jharkhand categorically declares,

> The Governor may take regulations for the peace and good governance of any area in a state which is for the time being a Scheduled area. In

particular and without prejudice to the generality of the foregoing power such regulations may prohibit or restrict the transfer of land by or among members of the *Scheduled Tribes* in such area; regulate the allotment of land to members of the *Scheduled Tribes* in such area.

The Fifth Schedule further provides for the formation of a Tribal Advisory Council in the concerned State primarily dealing with the autonomy question for the Scheduled Areas. The Governor of the State, however, has wide ranging powers with regard to the Scheduled Areas. She or he may also make regulations for the Scheduled Areas, particularly in matters relating to land transfer from STs, land allotment to STs, and the moneylending.

Historically, lands owned by the tribal groups in Jharkhand are protected by the Chota Nagpur Tenancy Act, 1908 (CNTA) and the Santhal Pargana Tenancy Act, 1949 (SPTA) which debar buying and selling of tribal land. The provisions of these Acts have, however, been violated by design across the states. Some parts or the other of the region are in a constant state of hostilities against forcible land acquisition. Since the year 2000, the state has signed 110 memorandum of understandings (MoUs) with private companies. The tribals have also suffered from the onslaughts of powerful non-tribal neighbours causing evictions from their lands. On that account, it is frequently stressed that the struggle of tribals for land was traditionally against the *mahajans* (moneylenders) and robust non-tribal landowners, and now it is against the big private companies. Another important dimension of women's rights in land among the tribals of this region is intimately connected with the protection of customary law which has also backing of the Constitution and various regional enactments and the provisions of the tenancy Acts. The recognition of the customary law is further safeguarded under the Fifth Schedule of the Constitution even if it is not codified. In the Scheduled Areas, customary law is generally held to operate with regard to inheritance and succession.

CUSTOMARY LAWS

Historically, in Jharkhand area the recognition of customary law began much earlier when the Government of Bihar and Orissa excluded in 1931 tribal Christians residing in Bihar from the purview of the Indian

Succession Act, 1925, which overseas Christians elsewhere in India. The converts to Christianity, thus, continue to follow tribal customs in matters of succession. Likewise, the Subsection 2(2) of the Hindu Succession Act excludes STs unless otherwise directed by the Government of India. In short, neither the Hindu Succession Act (unless they are sufficiently Hinduized) nor the Indian Succession Act is fully applicable to the STs.

The main sources of the customary practices which are now recognized as customary laws in Jharkhand are some of the classical ethnographies authored by S. C. Roy (1970 [1912], 1984 [1915]) on the Oraon and the Munda, W. G. Archer (1984) on the Santhal, and Dalton's earlier ethnography of Bengal (1872).[1] These sources are considered authentic proof of the existing customs and they are routinely used by the lawyers and the courts. However, the interpretations of the customary practices assuming the form of laws by various agencies particularly by the judiciary have raised new issues in the context of women's land rights among the STs of this region. However, it is not feasible to present a comprehensive picture in the present micro-study; nonetheless, we briefly touch upon some of the emerging debates and contention in this connection to capture the complexion and essence of the problem under discussion.

A recent Supreme Court judgement held that all customary practices continue to operate till struck down by a court in view of their supposedly adverse impact on public peace or until replaced by statutory laws. The CNTA also preserves customary rights with respect to land and Section 76 protects any custom, usage or any customary right that is not inconsistent with, or modified by other provisions of the Act. It has to be highlighted at this level of our discussion that the applicability of customary law in case of a particular tribal community, more often, revolves around the question of recognition of tribal identity unlike the Hindu Succession Act. It is an intriguing fact of the socio-economic history of contemporary India that in the absence of codified customary practices, members of the tribal community had to prove and authenticate their likeness/similarity with their Hindu neighbours to be governed by the Hindu law in matter of succession or inheritance. In other words, if it can be shown that an Adivasi (tribal) is sufficiently 'Hinduized', she or he may be covered under the established Hindu Succession Act 1956. Normally, the decisions in this respect have been taken on the grounds of the practice of cremation rather than burial, the system of marriage, the religious practices in addition to some other local usages, and practices commonly found among the local Hindu communities.

It should be obvious from a brief discussion so far that the question of women's rights in land among the STs in today's Jharkhand region is apparently mixed up in the nature and extent of changes which have come about in their social, cultural and politico-legal life. Such alterations and transformations have brought far reaching changes which have made women far more insecure compared even to women of several non-tribal groups and communities. It is mainly because the struggle for gender equality in land and property rights among the latter has lately produced some positive results but such a trend does not seem to be in sight among the tribal groups. However, this issue is now being discussed and debated among the activists, opinion leaders and, some forceful tribal intellectuals.

A study on land and property rights of women of tribal communities of Jharkhand entitled 'Beyond Taben Jom' documented by Praveer Peter (2008)[2] takes into account experiences and opinions of some prominent persons who throw ample light on the question under discussion. In view of their candid and forthright judgement and vision, we attempt to paraphrase some of them to stress the focal point.

Dr Rose Kerketta, an acclaimed academic and opinion leader, shows that the tribal laws are not written one but they are customary practices and mostly translated into action by the village heads and clans in case of any dispute. Even in the SPTA and the CNTA the colonial government accepted the landownership of the tribal and protected it from sale to nontribal. Thus, tribal lands are non-transferable to others. It is not true that if inheritance right in land is given to tribal women it would promote inter-community marriage with *Diku* (outsider) for getting land transferred to the nontribal. Dr Rose strongly argues that the tribal women should have equal rights in everything like tribal men to empower them, strengthen their position in society, and stop migration and trafficking of tribal women. She does not only approve but forcefully supports tribal women's struggle for land rights (ibid.: 46).[3]

The question of land rights for women has also been advocated by Dr Ramdayal Munda, a prominent intellectual and political thinker of the community (ibid.: 49).[4] He, however, suggests that it must be done within the broader framework and redeeming features of the Jharkhand society. Women here have been traditionally left out in land, water, forest, and governance. Under the condition, the tribal traditions need to be documented and reformed. A national law (PESA) has decided that one third women's participation is required in the panchayat decisions which have also been accepted by the Jharkhand state.

When the inclusion of mother's name in records has begun for school registration, the change in laws of land records also needs to have the name of the wife added, so that the signature of just the male for land transfer will not happen. Dr Munda thus advocates that 'a retroactive law could be asked for to take back land that belonged to the tribal community'. Since all land belonged to the community all community women needed to sign off the land transfer to non-tribals. None of the land deals have women's name in them. 'So we should pass the law with 70 years retrospection where wife or women representative of the wife was not consulted, those land deals should be declared null and void.'

It has been further argued by Dr Ramdayal Munda that the growing patriarchal attitude under which the tribal widows are being driven out of their homes, the community members themselves have to think or else the law court will make them understand. Contextually, therefore, a strong 'tribal women leadership' has to emerge to take active part in decision-making of panchayat whether for rape cases or land disputes in the village. This will help in establishing gender equity, and the community needs to promote this. The actions solely from the Court will not work in the case of tribal women land rights.

Another perspective on the land rights for women in Jharkhand has come from the views of Professor Sanjoy Basu Mallick (ibid.: 52).[5] He emphasizes that the history of Jharkhand has deprived women of their land rights. Women's rights prevail in areas where the community life of collective decision-making is still alive, and it is more and more patriarchal where collective decision-making has deteriorated. Under the condition, women do not get rights where individualization process has become dominant. Professor Mallick has added a new angle to this question and shows that earlier there was little dependence on agriculture; the dependency was basically on forests and *jhum* (shifting) cultivation. But with the dwindling of forests and the restriction over access and control over these common resources increasing, the struggle has intensified. Wherever and whenever women have rights over forests, then they have rights over land. Therefore, land and forests should be seen together. It has been highlighted that the economy of forests had strengthened the position of women. Studies have shown that in forested areas the 'life interests' of women on land was also given. This was not evident in areas with no forest rights (ibid.: 53).[6]

It is conspicuous from the above that the issue of women's right in land among the tribals of Jharkhand has not only assumed a circuitous path but also no consensus has even emerged to launch concerted efforts to gender equity in land rights.

As has been indicated earlier, two major traditional tenancy Acts, the CNTA and the SPTA with scores of amendments have continued to regulate the transfer of tribal lands in the region. But they have hardly taken into account the issue of women's rights in land despite undergoing several changes even after the Independence. This question has not even acquired a central place in the politico-economic debates in the State. However, we present here a sketch of customary practices and rules which have been taken into consideration while examining this question in the context of three tribal communities which form part of our study. They are the Kharia, the Munda, and the Santhal.

Kharia

Like several other communities, in the Kharia society also father is the owner of the house. The male children are entitled to share their father's land. The eldest son, who is expected to assist and serve the parents till their last rites and if he does so, is given a little larger share in the landed property. However, the property remains in the name of the father till his death. But if partition takes place during the lifetime of the parents, they retain one equal share. The retained share is controlled and looked after by the son who keeps and looks after the parents till their last rites.

On the death of the parents prior to any division of the land and other immovable properties, the eldest son maintains the entire family and also looks after the entire landed property of the parents. If a division is demanded by other brother/s, a division is enforced and the eldest son gets a little more of the landed property, but the movable property is equally divided among all sons. On division, however, the daughters are not entitled to get any share in the immovable properties of their parents, but unmarried daughters are entitled to get maintenance out of their father's share until they are married and also the cost of marriage is met with.

A girl remains under the care of her parents till the marriage. In case the parents are not alive she remains under the care of her elder brother who has to take her full responsibility till she is married. It is further claimed that if a girl does not want to get married and wishes to stay in the house of her father for the whole life, she is entitled for it and no one can drive her out from the house. She also has the right to get maintenance from her father's landed property but has no right of possession on any portion of the land. However, if parents are not alive and if brothers wish they can also give a piece of land to her; but ordinarily such offer comes from the eldest brother.

A widow having a male child has an absolute right over the property of her husband. If she has no male child and opts to live in her husband's house for the rest of her life, she has the right to do so and to own the property of her husband provided she does not remarry, does not go to stay with her parents, and has no illegal relationship with any male.

Another issue which is usually brought into focus is the customary practice of bringing *gharjamai*. In case a Kharia couple has no son but the daughters only she has the right to suggest the parents to bring a son-in-law to stay with them who is addressed as *gharjamai*. The son-in-law living permanently with his father-in-law gets half of the landed property and all other movable properties owned by his father-in-law, and the other half of the landed property goes to the agnate kin of the deceased person. Similarly, if a widow has girls only, she can bring a *gharjamai* for one of her daughters only. If she desires to give the land to her daughter/son-in-law, she has to get the land of her husband registered in her own name first as widows have right over their husband's property provided they live in their husband's house. Another point of contention is that in case the progeny and the Kharia clans do not agree to give land to the *gharjamai*, she cannot do so. But after the death of the widow the *gharjamai* has the right to live in the house of his mother-in-law and also the right over the property.

Munda

The details of the system of succession and inheritance with regard to the Munda community are available in the classical writings of S. C. Roy and John Hoffman (n.d.).[7] These graphic accounts were compiled almost during the same time in 1912 and 1915, respectively. According to both these narratives, only sons have the right to inherit the property, and on the death of the father lands are divided among them equally by the panchayat, although the eldest son gets a larger share in most of the cases.

The *panch* (arbiter) ordinarily sets aside some portions of land for the maintenance of the widow but she has only a life-interest in this property.

If she lives separately from her sons, this land is repartitioned upon her death, but if she lives with one of her sons, he becomes entitled to that land after her death.

The property is not normally partitioned during the father's lifetime but if such a division takes place at all, an unmarried daughter generally gets some land for her daily maintenance till her marriage, but she remains under the guardianship of her father or a brother.

Likewise a widow without sons also has a life-interest in the property which she cannot sell without the consent of the agnates, to whom the property passes on her death. However, if she leaves the village or remarries, she loses her right to this land.

Thus, daughters do not have right to inherit but sons are bound by practice to support their unmarried sisters until their marriage. Ordinarily, the community *panch* may allot land for the support of an unmarried daughter living with her brother and this land is repartitioned on her marriage among the brothers.

In the absence of son, widow, and unmarried daughter, the property of a deceased man goes to the nearest male agnate or agnates. But in case there is no widow or son and only an unmarried daughter, she remains in possession of the land until her marriage.

A daughter's husband and sons are not entitled to inherit, the only exception being the case of *gharjamai* who marries into a family which has no sons in order to help his father-in-law with the cultivation and who is entitled to a share of the land as decided by the panchayat. Nonetheless, he remains in possession of this land only as long as his wife is alive. After this, the land goes to the nearest agnate. Only when there are no agnates the full possession would go to the *gharjamai*.

Santhal (Santal)

The customary practices and the laws among the Santhals are not codified but they have been recognized by the Indian state since long. Under the circumstances, the famous SPTA which is enforced since the colonial days also recognized the personal laws of the Santhal community. The activists and the researchers working in this region have appropriately suggested that the non-codification of the customary law opens it up to several interpretations in accordance with the knowledge, mood, and bias of the traditional male leaders of the community and the area. This naturally goes against women in most of the cases. It has further been argued that the various customary channels among the Santhals through which women could inherit land are such that they cannot be proved and defended in the modern courts of law.

It has been reported that most of the claims of women in the Santhal community are associated with the cases of polygyny, divorce, or widowhood. In these cases, the decisions are mostly taken by the traditional social institutions known as the Manjhi Pargana system. Most of the decisions are in favour of women, but some deviations are also seen in several recent decisions. A new debate has, of late, emerged with regard to the functioning of the traditional institutions which have acquired added importance after the introduction of PESA (The Panchayati Raj [Extension to the Scheduled Areas] Act 1996). The question of tribal identity and its related notion of community's independence has virtually revived the strength of these institutions which has given a new energy to the community leaders to take the social reins in their hands. Under the conditions, women have experienced unfavourable and cynical rulings and men-centric verdicts.

The institutional designs of *gharjamai* and *ghardijamai* are two different arrangements in marriage which have some important implications for the inheritance of land among the Santhals. Although this marital practice has also been open to several interpretations, a distinction is clearly made between these two practices. The *ghardijamai* is seen as a temporary arrangement usually for a period of five years which may be renewed. The circumstances for keeping son-in-law under this practice may be several such as the son being too young to plough, or the son-in-law unable to pay a bride-price. A *ghardijamai* as such is not entitled to anything more than his wife and is not in himself an inheritor of his father-in-laws' lands. Actually, it is the daughter who becomes inheritor but as she is not permitted to perform certain duties in the village, she has to have a representative, who is her husband. As against this, a *gharjamai* is brought as there may be a need to have an extra hand to look after the land, fill the house with children and guard against the loneliness of the old age, love for particular daughters, where the daughter is disabled, or the desire to keep the land in the family rather than letting it pass on to the kin.

It is obvious from the above that the land question, particularly the provisions regarding its transfer among the tribals (Adivasis) of Jharkhand, presents a very clumsy and complex picture as a result of sociopolitical changes experienced by the people of this region. Given such a sequence of events it is not easy to present a definitive account of the lawful and valid issues involved in the gender discrimination in land-ownership among the ST communities located in the State of Jharkhand. We have already briefly discussed the broader features of customary practices among the three tribal communities, the Kharia, the Munda, and the Santhal which form units of the present study. In view of this, it is also pertinent to report here some major provisions of land transfer contained in the two principal tenancy Acts—the CNTA and the SPTA which have been defining and regulating the land question in this region for quite some time.

CHOTA NAGPUR TENANCY ACT, 1908

Section 46 of this Act imposes a complete ban on sale of right in holding or any portion of land by a member of an ST to a non-ST. However, this section has undergone several changes since 1908. As has been reported earlier, no *raiyati* land was alienable but subsequently the land of non-ST, that is, the land of general castes was allowed to be transferred within a police station. But in 1975 even this restriction was withdrawn, although the land in possession of the Scheduled Castes was allowed to be freely sold.

A provision of this section nonetheless allows temporary alienation of the land belonging to the tribal to non-tribal in two cases, namely, mortgage or lease for a period of five years and *Bhugut Bandha* mortgage for a period not exceeding seven years. But if the mortgage happens to be to a registered society or deemed to be registered under the Bihar and Orissa Co-operative Societies Act, 1935, it may be for any period not exceeding 15 years.

However, the transfer of land under this section is also allowed for the members of the ST communities with a prior permission of the deputy commissioner (DC) within the jurisdiction of the same police station. While giving the permission the DC has to ensure that the transferor is not adversely affected by this action. Moreover, there is another provision which takes care of the interests of the tribals in this connection. Subsection 3(a) contains a provision that in case of one party being non-tribal and the other being tribal, the DC will also become a party to protect the interests of the tribals.

Furthermore, Section 49 permits the transfer of tribal land to a non-tribal mainly for the public purposes. The purposes codified then were charitable, religious, educational, industrial, irrigational, and for building grounds etc. This section, however, was amended in 1995 and the tribals' land could now only be transferred for mining and industrial purposes. It is nonetheless claimed that a number of DCs misinterpreted this provision for transferring the land of the tribals to housing cooperatives.

While granting permission a DC had to keep these issues in view, (a) the concerned person should have sufficient land left with him after transfer for subsistence of the family; (b) the price being paid to him should not be only reasonable but in no case it has to be less that the land acquisition rate; and (c) the purchaser must utilize the land only for the purpose for which the land has been allowed to be sold.

Moreover, another important check and control in this regard is that the transfer of land can be enforced only after the written consent of the DC through a registered deed. The government, however, could cancel the deed within 12 years after giving hearing to both the parties, if it is in contravention of this Act.

SANTAL PARGANA TENANCY ACT, 1949

Section 20 of the Act includes the provisions concerning the transfer of tenants' rights. According to this, no transfer of land by a *raiyat* shall be valid by sale, gift, mortgage, will, lease or any other contract or agreement, expressed or implied unless the right to transfer has been recorded in the records-of-rights. But it also provides some exceptions. They are gift to daughter or sister with a prior written permission of the DC; grant of not more than half of the area of his holding to his mother or wife for her maintenance after his death with the previous written permission of the DC; transfer in favour of *gharjamai* or *ghardijamai* and the lease for the purpose of an excise shop for not more than one year with a permission of the DC.

It is obvious from the above that the land is transferable only in limited cases but the DC has been allowed to have a further power keeping in view the prevailing customs of the community concerned. Interestingly, most of these exceptions pertain to women's rights. But it is important to point out here that the DCs have rarely used their power to enforce these customary rights primarily because of the uncodified nature of customary practices. Sometimes male members of the family also create problems which lead to difficulties in enforcing customary practices favourable to women. It is apparent that women's customary rights have no doubt social acceptance and recognition, but in the strict legal sense most of the legitimate powers and privileges accorded to women are not consistently enforced except, of course, in the case of *gharjamai* wherein the land is recorded in the daughter's name.

EVALUATING THE PREVAILING SITUATION

Our attempt so far has been to present a 'book view' of the customary practices and the statutory provisions with regard to the patterns of land-ownership prevailing in the tribal communities in Jharkhand. Given the context and the delineated objectives of the present study our attempt will now be to reflect upon the real life situation which we ordinarily confront in the area of our concern. Broadly, there are two crucial issues which have to be examined to correlate the 'book view' with that of the 'field view' to bring to the fore the crucial points in question for accommodating elements of gender equity and justice in agrarian relations. The beginning in the present study has been made by presenting first the socio-economic profile of the people followed by an assessment and evaluation of their opinion and reasoning for or against conferring land rights to women.

As indicated in the beginning, our fieldwork for collecting empirical data was confined only to the three districts of Jharkhand, namely, Khunti, Pakur, and Simdega. The details of the area of study included have been presented in Figure 8.2.

The observed facts collected in course of the field study are broadly divided not only at the levels of community but also thematically. The latter includes ethnographic outline as well as matters of opinion and belief. The communities discussed are Kharia, Munda, and Santhal. The sequence of the presentation has nothing to do with their distinctive sociopolitical position in the local tribal hierarchy, but it is just adapted alphabetically in terms of their names to avoid any short-sighted local political controversy.

Figure 8.2
Area of the Study

District	Block	Village	Community Covered
Khunti	Torpa	Japud	Munda
		Saridkel	Santhal
Pakur	Hiranpur	Bhimpur	
	Maheshpur	Bushaka	
	Pakur	Dharampur	
		Goshainpur	
		Gopalnagar	
		Pokhariya	
		Ramjitpur	
		Saharkol	
Simdega	Thethaitangar	Balsera	Kharia
		Bairtoli	
		Bhutkudar	
		Salangaposh	

Kharia

The socio-economic profile of the Kharia respondents is demonstrated in Table 8.1. All the respondents belong to the Christian religious group which obviously suggests the common pattern that is ordinarily discussed in the public domain. While the majority of the respondents come from joint family, the number of small nuclear family is also not inconsequential. However, the housing design and the size of homestead plots ostensibly reveal the levels of their poverty and privation. But the patterns of landownership provide a different and relatively contrasting picture which one notices from information and facts included in Table 8.2. It is obvious from this table that all the selected families of the Kharia community which form the sample of the present enquiry own agricultural land with, of course, different holding sizes. While 69% of them have holdings below 5 acres each, 23% of them come under the higher categories which definitely reveal a sharp inequality in the patterns of landownership in the community. But eight families nonetheless failed to provide any categorical information in this respect. It is commonly found in most of the tribal communities that some persons have no definite idea and information about the size and measurements of their lands owned because of their ignorance. The patriarchal practices are, however, clearly visible in the society when we come to the question of land

Table 8.1
Socio-economic Profile of Kharia Respondents

(N=100)
(i) Religious groups: Christian—100
(ii) Structure of Family: Joint—62; Nuclear—38
(iii) Housing Design: Kachcha—93; Pucca—05
Without own house—01; No information—01
(iv) Size of homestead plots personally owned
Below 5 decimals—82
5 to 10—08
11 to 15—03
16 to 20—02
More than 20—03

(The figures included in the tables presented here indicate both absolute numbers and percentage because the number of respondents is 100 each in all three cases.)
Source: Field Data.

Table 8.2
Patterns of Landownership Among the Kharia Respondents (N=100)

(i) Agricultural land owned—100
(ii) Size of landholding owned
(a) Below 5 acres—69
(b) 5 to 10—15
(c) More than 10 acres—08
(d) No information—08
(iii) Whether land registered jointly with women
(a) No—86
(b) Yes—08
(c) No information—06

Source: Field Data.

registration. As many as 86% families accepted that land is registered in the names of male alone. But eight of these respondents revealed that land was registered jointly in the names of female and male. In this connection, again six of them either failed to provide authentic information or they had no idea about the land registration rules and their intricacies.

It is a widely known fact of the agrarian relations in India particularly in the tribal areas that common landowners/tenants hardly know the intricacies of land laws and rules of inheritance and succession. In view of this, our attempt has been to assess the levels of awareness and understanding of our respondents in this context. The data included in Table 8.3

takes care of this dimension of our study. Majority of the respondents know that the laws and rules concerning inheritance and succession followed in their community are based on the customary practices while only four of them were aware that both the statutory rules and customary procedures are followed in this regard. However, seven respondents categorically acknowledged their ignorance in this connection.

The most striking and noticeable position taken by the respondents with regard to the land rights to women is obvious from Table 8.4. As against the common belief as many as 85 persons out of 100 do not advocate the registration of land in the names of women members of their families. Of the remaining 15 respondents only five responded positively and the rest were confused about this issue. This requires some explanation. The present day Jharkhand State formed the southern part of the State of Bihar till the year 2000, when it was carved out to constitute a separate state. This region is primarily known as a tribal area but the non-tribals also have had a substantial presence. Jharkhand is a mineral rich State; however, much of mining is regulated and a lot of it is almost loot. In addition to this, displacement of the locals has also taken place for constructing major dams/bunds on rivers such as Damodar Valley Corporation (DVC) and so also for industries like Heavy Engineering

Table 8.3

Familiarity with Inheritance and Succession Rules and Practices Followed in Land Distribution and Transfer (N=100)

S. No.	Response	No.
1.	Customary	89
2.	Both governmental rules and customary procedures	04
3.	No idea	07

Source: Field Data.

Table 8.4

Opinion and Assessment with Regard to Land Rights to Women (N=100)

Whether Land Should Be Registered in the Name of Women?		
S. No.	Response	No.
1.	Yes	05
2.	No	85
3.	Not sure	10

Source: Field Data.

Corporation (HEC), Ranchi. But no serious attempts have been made for the meaningful settlement of the local people. Consequently, in addition to displacement huge out-migration of poor people has also taken place. Thus, the backwardness of the region and the poverty and penury of the people has resulted essentially out of the unresolved contradictions between corporate and their collaborators, non-tribal businessmen and the local tribals. In addition to this, uncontrolled and illegal transfer of land from tribals to non-tribals has also taken place. Interestingly, in the whole process the non-tribals have also been marrying tribal girls to extend their control over land in this region. It is quite natural that under the condition, tribals have suffered socially, economically, and so also politically. Under the circumstances, a strong group of the so-called advanced people has emerged from within the local people which may include the *moolvasis* (indigenous non-tribal) and some outsiders. It is primarily under this predicament giving land rights to women is not preferred issue among the tribal peoples of this region.

Munda

Compared to the Kharia respondents the social composition of the Munda is substantially different. While the whole group belongs to the Christian religious fold in case of the former, only 52% respondents constituting the sample in case of the latter form part of this group (Table 8.5). The other half still follows the traditional tribal faith known locally as *Sarna*. Similarly, the most common pattern of family is 'individual' which is called sociologically *nuclear* family. However, the different size categories of homesteads reflect the overall improved condition of housing among the Mundas. Table 8.6 contains information with regard to the ownership of landholdings. It is apparent that almost 56% respondents own more than five acres each but here also the land is registered exclusively in the names of male members of the family. The exception is only one woman whose name appeared in the land registration records because it was bought in her name.

Our data amply suggest a high level of familiarity with inheritance and succession rules among the Mundas. Table 8.7 shows that most of them are aware of customary practices which are usually followed in land transfer. But here again some respondents had no idea about these practices and procedures but, of course, their number is not significant.

Table 8.5

Socio-economic Profile of Munda Respondents (N=100)

(i) Religious groups
    (a) Christian—52
    (b) Sarna—48
(ii) Structure of family
    (a) Joint—08
    (b) Nuclear—90
    (c) No information—02
(iii) Design of houses
    (a) Hut—02
    (b) Kachcha—88
    (c) Pucca—08
    (d) No answer—02
(iv) Size of homestead plots
    (a) Below 5 decimals—25
    (b) 6 to 10—38
    (c) 11 to 15—19
    (d) Above 15—18

Source: Field Data.

Table 8.6

Patterns of Landownership Among the Selected Munda Respondents (N=100)

(i) Agricultural land owned
    (a) Below 5 acres—44
    (b) 5 to 10 acres—49
    (c) Above 10 acres—07
(ii) Land registered in the name of women
    (a) Yes—01*
    (b) No—85
    (c) No answer—14

* It was bought in the name of women.
Source: Field Data.

Table 8.7

Familiarity with Inheritance and Succession Rules and Practices Followed at the Time of Land Transfer and Distribution (N=100)

S. No.	Response	No.
1.	Customary	89
2.	Both governmental rules and customary procedures	04
3.	No idea	07

Source: Field Data.

Table 8.8
Opinion and Belief with Regard to Land Rights to Women (Whether Land Should Be Registered in the Name of Women; N=100)

S. No.	Response	No.
1.	Yes	05
2.	No	85
3.	No opinion	10

Source: Field Data.

Coming to the opinion with regard to the land rights to women, our Munda respondents are not different which is obvious from Table 8.8. While seeking their views whether land should be registered in the name of women, majority of them responded negatively except 10 respondents who held no opinion in this regard.

Santhal

As against the other two communities here, the Santhals have entirely different situation with regard to the religious groupings (Table 8.9). Most of the respondents in the present case have announced *Bidin* as their religion which is a traditional tribal faith not an organized religion per se. The Christianity comes next with 36% followed by the Hinduism, *Sanatan* and *Adimjati*. The religious composition of our Santhal respondents apparently suggests that the community has been historically undergoing substantial transformation in their sociocultural life. The joint family is the most common form of family structure and the housing condition continues to be miserable, despite the fact that out of 100 households, 96 have self-owned homestead plots.

The patterns of ownership of both residential and agricultural lands are evident from Table 8.10. More than 90% respondents in both these cases have received them from their ancestors. However, seven families

Table 8.9
Socio-economic Profile of Santhal Respondents (N=100)

(i) Religious groups: Bidin—58, Christian—36, Hindu—04, *Sanatan*—01, *Adimjati*—01
(ii) Structure of family: Joint—82, Nuclear—18
(iii) Housing condition: Hut—02, Kutcha—85, Pucca—13
(iv) Ownership of homestead plots: Land self-owned—96, land not self-owned—04

Source: Field Data.

Table 8.10
Patterns of Landownership in Residential Plots and Agricultural Land (N=100)

S. No.	Response	No.
1.	Ancestral	91
2.	Purchased	07
3.	No information	02
4.	Agricultural land: Ancestral	96
5.	*Bhoodan*	01
6.	No information	03

Source: Field Data.

Table 8.11
Nature of Land Registration (N=100)

S. No.	Response	No.
1.	In the name of male members	95
2.	Jointly with male and female	03
3.	Not known	02

Source: Field Data.

have bought their own residential plots and one of them has received agricultural land under the *Bhoodan*.

The nature and patterns of land registration is evident from Table 8.11 which distinctly suggests the patriarchal system where land is ordinarily registered in the name of male members of the family. However, in this context there are other three cases in which land is registered jointly in the names of male and female. It is at the same time intriguing to observe that a substantial number of respondents are not familiar with the land laws and practices with regard to inheritance and succession (Table 8.12).

Moreover, the Santhals' appraisal and opinion with regard to the land rights to women are not different from our other respondents belonging to the Kharia and the Munda communities as we have seen earlier. Table 8.13 shows this pattern. We shall come to this issue later when its logic and explanation is proposed to be analysed.

ANATOMIZING WOMEN'S RIGHTS TO LAND

The presentation and analysis of both the 'book view' and the 'field view' of gender dimension of agrarian relations in Jharkhand apparently reflect

Table 8.12
Familiarity with Land Inheritance and Succession Laws and Practices ($N=100$)

S. No.	Response	No.
1.	Yes	34
2.	No	64
3.	No answer	02

Source: Field Data.

Table 8.13
Opinion with Regard to Land Rights to Women

S. No.	Whether land should be registered in the name of women	No.
1.	Yes	21
2.	No	79

Source: Field Data.

not only the complex nature of its history but also a lack of consensus in the peoples' opinion with regard to women's right to land. Jharkhand is known nationally as an influential tribal region even with its limited STST population. It is primarily because of its geographical location and the sociocultural contacts with the people from outside the region that it protecting their habitat and preserving their culture has been a historically arduous and formidable task for them, compared to several other tribal zones of the country. Most of these communities had to face the economic hardships, social oppression, and cultural dilution over a period of time. The forces and factors of change which impacted this region initially assumed a concrete shape during the colonial rule and became sharp and marked after the Independence.

What we wish to point out and emphasize is that the tribal communities located in different regions of the state have undergone disparate and dissimilar experiences when the well-stocked mineral rich area caught the attention of industrialists and government agencies from outside. Consequently, the inward and outward migration started which substantially affected the life of the local population. When the non-tribal people from outside the region started coming in large number, they acquired land and settled locally which brought a marked change in the demographic landscape of the tribal region. This also led to outward migration of the local tribals both male and female in search of new avenues for livelihoods. Another issue which is frequently highlighted is that the outsiders also married tribal girls to firmly establish themselves in the local social milieu. This has, however, resulted into a large number of bigamous marriages and frequent desertion of the tribal women by their non-tribal partners. Lately, the sexual exploitation is also the reason why tribal girls are prevented from interacting with the non-tribal.

Furthermore, the gender discriminatory provisions were also included in the tenancy laws which were mostly based on the ethnographic accounts of anthropologists during the early part of the 20th century. It requires to be noted that the present Jharkhand state formed the southern part of the state of Bihar till the year 2000 and also the fact that this region formed substantially the part of the Scheduled area under the provisions of the Fifth Schedule of Indian Constitution. During 2003, 112 blocks in 14 districts of Jharkhand were included in the list of Scheduled area covering 12 districts completely and 2 districts partially. Historically, this has also been one factor which has affected the agrarian scene in the region. The process of land transfer to non-tribal has undoubtedly declined, of late, due to the rising consciousness among the tribals and the struggle against land alienation which used to be the scenario till almost the 1980s. The continued and threatening alienation of the tribal land for public purposes and so also to the private industries, mining and housing has further transformed the land question.

It is distressing to note that despite a large number of amendments to both the CNTA and the SPTA no equity and justice with regard to land have been bestowed upon the common people of the tribal communities. The processes of land alienation and illegal transfer continue till date. Neither the political leadership nor the government officials forcefully raise this issue. It is because of such apathy and indifference that even the limited steps such as the joint titling of land deed has not been implemented in true spirit. For example, the National Rehabilitation and Resettlement Policy 2007 has categorically indicated that 'the land or house allotted to the affected families under this policy may be in the joint names of wife and husband of the affected family.' Although individual rights to women is preferable to joint titles with husbands but in a guarded and the middle-of-the road society even joint titling would bring change in the mindset of the people. In view of this, having joint titles with husbands would be better for women than having no land rights at all.

The empirical data collected by us and highlighted earlier abundantly suggest that the majority of respondents have not acceded to the idea of registering land in the name of women. This situation is commonly witnessed across all the three communities constituting our sample. Most of them have taken resort to their customary practices while rejecting the statutory land rights to women. The fear and apprehension of losing land if is in the name of women is ordinarily found as women may leave the family by marrying outside the community. Another interesting but unpleasant explanation given by some Kharia respondents is that when there is discord and feuds within the family only then land is usually registered in the name of women. Whatever may be the logic and explanation to reject the land rights to women, it unambiguously shows that these communities are yet to unlock the conservative shutter of their patriarchal mindset.

CONCLUSION

The debate and wrangle on the agrarian structure and land relations in any agricultural country are never ultimate and unarguable. It is particularly so if the society and economy are committed to democratic ideals based on equity and justice. It is in this context that we wish to conclude the present discussion by suggesting that no region or locality, no caste or community, and so also no rural or urban areas should be left out of the purview of land reform and reconstruction based on the fundamental principles of fairness and equity, justice and impartiality. Naturally, it will require continuous review and revision of laws and rules, practices and procedures within the broader frame of the federal democratic Constitution. It may appear utopian at the outset but no democratic polity defines and delineates its goal and objectives, ambition and destination narrowly. A national goal always transcends discrete individualistic goals.

It is against this justification and grounding, we suggest at the moment the following issues in the context of women's right to land in Jharkhand:

1. A revisional survey has to be initiated to re-examine both customary laws and distortions which have appeared in the implementation of the tenancy Acts applicable to the areas about which we have talked.
2. The land records have to be revisited with updating of records. The existing records-of-rights do not reflect the current status of landholdings and the nature of their ownership and control.
3. Women's rights to traditional land gifts and transfer, their rights to homestead plots may be recorded without much of a wrangle.
4. Those provisions of post-independent land reform measures which have not been effectively implemented till date have to be

brought into focus for the benefits of the landless, sharecroppers and the agricultural workers.

It will not be incongruous and outlandish to close this account with a cautionary note. The historical experiences concerning land issues in Jharkhand have not always been pleasant and amiable. It more often assumes the shape of intense and agonizing political debate and may also lead to communal animosity and strife. In view of this no decision should be taken unilaterally by the administration. An informed consultation and dialogue with the traditional tribal leaders and various civil society groups may be planned for smooth and frictionless decisions.

NOTES AND REFERENCES

1. Most of the classical ethnographic texts published during the early years of the 20th century have been used to give shape to the customary laws in the State. Some of these texts are:

    (i) S. C. Roy, *The Mundas and Their Country*. Bombay: Asia Publishing House, 1970 (first published in 1912) and *The Oraons*. Ranchi: Man in India Office, 1984 (first published in 1915).

    (ii) W. G. Archer, *Tribal Law and Justice, A Report on the Santhal* (in three volumes). New Delhi: Concept Publishing Company, 1984.

    (iii) Edward Tuite Dalton, *Descriptive Ethnology of Bengal*. Calcutta: Office of the Superintendent Printing, 1872.

    (iv) Edward Tuite Dalton, *Tribal History of Eastern India*, Reprinted in 1973. Delhi: Cosmo Publications.

2. *Beyond Taben Jom: A Study on Land and Property Rights of Women of Tribal Communities of Jharkhand*, documented by Praveer Peter, Ranchi, Jharkhand: *Gender, Livelihoods and Resources Forum (GLRF)*, Ranchi, December 2008 (Mimeographed).
3. Ibid., p. 46.
4. Ibid., p. 49.
5. Ibid., p. 52.
6. Ibid., p. 53.
7. S. C. Roy, *The Mundas and Their Country*, Bombay: Asia Publishing House, 1970 (first published in 1912); John Hoffman, *Encyclopedia Mundarica*, Patna, Superintendent, Government Printing, Bihar, 1950. "Principles of Succession and Inheritance among the Mundas", *Man in India* 41(4): 32, 1975 (Reprinted from the *Journal of the Bihar and Orissa Research Society*, September 1915).

9

Land, Land Rights, and Women in Maharashtra

RITU DEWAN

Among the most contested and contentious of the myriad issues impacting gender equality world-wide is that of control over resources. This struggle over the means of production generally centres on the access to, ownership of, and control over the chief means of livelihood—that of land. Consequently, attainment of gender parity especially in developing economies focuses, in the main, on issues of land rights primarily because the major proportion of those employed is dependent on the agricultural sector. This is true, particularly, in nations where the process of feminization of the rural economy is well advanced, and often, irrevocable.

In recognition of this central issue which is applicable to all women, CEDAW has given women the right to own and administer property without discrimination (CEDAW, Article 15) as well as an equal treatment in land and agrarian reform (CEDAW, Article 14[2] [g]). Also, Article 16 ensures that both spouses have equal rights in the 'ownership, acquisition, management, administration, enjoyment and disposition of property'. Additionally, Resolution 15 (paras 1 and 3) (1998) of the Sub-commission on the Promotion and Protection of Human Rights on 'Women and the Right to Land, Property and Adequate Housing' states that discrimination against women with respect to acquiring and securing land constitutes a violation of human rights law, and urges governments to amend and/or repeal discriminatory laws and policies and to encourage the transformation of discriminatory customs and traditions.[1]

India is a signatory to these and other conventions that make a commitment to gender equality, including the ensuring of land rights. While not going into details, suffice it to say that the Eighth Five-year Plan saw heartening policy support to gender equality, especially the guideline issued in 1995 by the Department of Land Resources, Ministry of Rural Development, to the states to issue *patta* (official documents stating land title and the terms on which land is held) land in the joint names of husband and wife, as well as a specific proportion to single women both unmarried and widowed. The Ninth Plan introduced, for the first time ever, individual as well as group distribution of land titles to women. The Tenth Plan recommended the distribution to women of land declared surplus under the Land Ceiling Act. This process of strengthening women's land rights continued under consecutive plans, including granting homesteads.

The Twelfth Plan has emphasized on enhancing women's land access from all three sources—direct government transfers, purchase or lease from the market, and inheritance—through a range of initiatives including joint land titles in all government land transfers, credit support to poor women to purchase or lease land from the market, increase in legal awareness and legal support for women's inheritance rights, supportive government schemes and recording of women's inheritance shares, and so on.

In this context, it would be extremely pertinent to quote from the pioneering and very seminal document written by N. C. Saxena (n.d.), former Secretary, Planning Commission, where he states categorically that

> [There is] need of taking appropriate legal and administrative steps to end the gender inequalities in providing legal rights to women on property especially on landed property, which is the most important productive asset in the rural India and, hence, access to arable land may be considered as an important instrument for economic empowerment as well as increasing the social status of rural women belonging to agricultural families including the families of landless agricultural labour.

Consequent to these policy initiatives along with the impact of the burgeoning women's movements, the share of women landholders in the country rose from 10.9% as per the Agricultural Census of 2000–01 to 11.7 in 2005–06 to 12.78% in 2010–11. Although relatively marginal, this almost 2% increase is not insignificant within a short span of a decade, reflecting the success of both policy and struggle. This study focuses on attainment levels in terms of land rights of women in a specific regional context—that of the agriculturally advanced state of Maharashtra.

However, it must be pointed out at the outset that there is no data available for landownership in India, the various data sources restricting it to 'operational' holdings, defined in the Agricultural Census as 'All land which is used wholly or partly for agricultural production and is operated as one technical unit by one person alone or with others without regard to the title, legal form, size or location.'

STRUCTURE OF STUDY

This chapter has a structural logic that extends from the macro- to the micro-level analysis. We begin by the tracing of trends in women's land rights over the last two relevant data sources spanning a decade—that of the 2000–01 and 2000–11 Agricultural Censuses. This is done at both the macro and the meso level in order to capture regional variations. After locating the issues in the context of enhancing gender equality, we present a short overview of the economy of Maharashtra, incorporating the history of land settlements in the region. Thereafter, the highlights of the several laws and several struggles relating to women's land rights are identified.

It is important to clarify at the outset that analysis is constrained by the fact of non-availability and non-accessibility of data from local sources; we had hoped very much to get at least some response to our appeal for detailed information, but are saddened that requests for such a crucial aspect of women's empowerment have been met by a deep and prolonged silence. We perceive this as yet another form of expression of the negation of women's economic rights.

The lack of relevant secondary data should, however, not be perceived as a disadvantage; rather, this very non-availability should be interpreted as an urgent and immediate recommendation for the enhancement of women's economic rights, especially in the rural context. Further, in spite of the non-collation and non-availability of 'official' data, we have been successful in mining several microanalysis of this vexed issue, including by interviewing non-governmental organizations and women's rights groups that have been working on claiming land rights for women at the ground level. Several case studies and meetings with activists and practitioners at the grass-roots levels also strengthen the quantitative and qualitative basis of this study.

Additionally and in spite of 'official' data constraints, the attempt is to capture the main aspects that form the basis of women's economic control over the chief means of livelihood, located as it is strongly in their status within society and issues of marginalization. The analysis, hence, incorporates not merely the number of titles of holdings granted to women, but also whether these trends additionally imply access to increasing their share of land. This is being especially examined as often studies tout the increasing number of women landholders in isolation from the amount of land and the size of landholdings; the perceptions have, thus, to extend beyond mere absolutism to the issues of the location of women within a strongly patriarchal society. The simplest if not simplistic illustration of this is that although the share of women with land titles has risen by the above-mentioned 2%, the proportion of land they hold has actually reduced by more than 2%.

Furthermore, we would like to reassert the now widely accepted fact that control over land forms the very basis of not only empowerment but also decision-making, as well as determining access to state support and public policy via benefitting from schemes of particularly agricultural extension, training, skill upgradation, and financial inclusion. Finally, this study concludes with going beyond the mandatory summarizing of results, to putting forward suggestions and recommendations arising from an analysis of the location of women within concrete economic and social structures.

TRENDS IN GENDERED LAND RIGHTS

Maharashtra is considered as one of the most 'advanced', in that its per capita income is ₹117,091, much higher than the national figure of ₹74,380. Also, the rural monthly per capita expenditure was ₹967 as of 2011–12, significantly higher than that of India at ₹816. It is generally perceived that the status of women is somewhat better than their counterparts in other states. While not getting into the details, it must be noted that the Bombay Presidency was the first to witness industrialization via the textile mills, women forming more than one-third of the workforce well into 1920s.

The truth, however, is rather different if judged by the single most basic indicator of the status of women, sex ratios. Maharashtra has a sex ratio of 929, much lower than the national average of an already low 943. What is worse is that the future of women in Maharashtra is extremely bleak, with the child sex ratio being a shocking 894. Also, the gender parity index for Classes I–XII is 0.98, below India's 0.99. The rural female work participation rate is 42.5%, including the 8% marginal workers.

Of the total working women, almost two-fifths are landless at 39.92%, the implication being that gender equality in land rights emerges as an urgent issue, given that Maharashtra records 29.61% as 'female cultivators'. There appears to be no information whatsoever on how many of these women are owners of the land that they cultivate. The urgency of availability and accessibility of gender disaggregated data cannot be emphasized enough, given that even details of Indira Awas Yojana do not specify gendered ownership patterns. Thus, although Maharashtra has reached a 93.3% achievement rate, we do not know if these 137,314 houses constructed under this scheme are jointly owned by women or not (Economic Survey of Maharashtra 2013–14: 166–212).

As can be seen from Figure 9.1, Maharashtra accounts for 9.9% of all landholdings in India in 2011, down from the 10.11% reported in the 2000–01 Agricultural Census. However, while the share of males rose a little during the last decade, that of women actually declined from a rather high 14.47% to 11.6%. The implication appears to be that the process of attaining land rights has been slower for women in Maharashtra than in the rest of India. However, we are rather surprised with the gendered proportion of land owned in terms of area as recorded by the Agricultural Census of both years. Apparently, the share of land held by Maharashtra women in 2010–11 is 15.66% of all land held by all women in all of India; also, that this proportion was an astounding 20.22% a decade ago. We find this quite inexplicable given that the proportion of land owned by men in Maharashtra as a share of all India continues to be a sedate 12%, and that women hold about 13% of the land in the state.

As it can be seen from Figure 9.1 with Table 9.1 showing the actual numbers, within Maharashtra, the process of marginalization appears to

Figure 9.1
Gendered Number of Holdings (Maharashtra and India) for 2000–01 and 2010–11

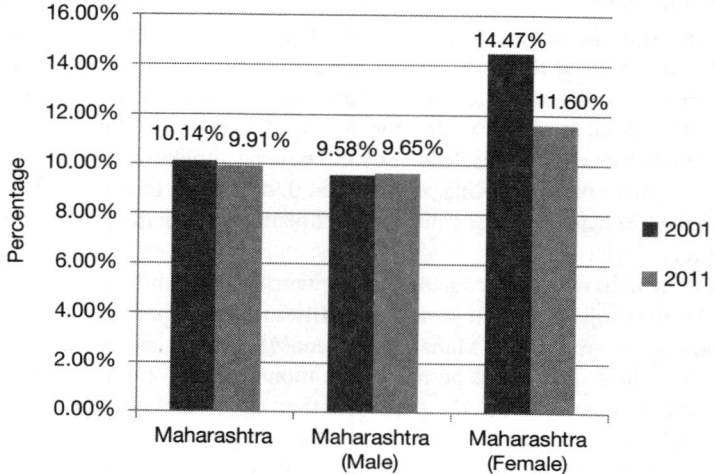

Sources: Agricultural Census 2000–01 and 2010–11.

have gathered momentum, with the number of such holdings increasing for men from 43% to 48.29 and for women almost equally from 47.57% to 52.91% over the last decade. Changes across size class of holdings within the gender categories too shows a virtually identical trend, the number of small holdings falling about a percentage point, semi-medium by a rather sharp 3% points, and medium holdings by approximately 1%

Table 9.1
Gendered Landholdings Pattern for 2000–01 and 2010–11 (in Actual Numbers)

S. No.	Size of Holdings (in ha)	Male (2001)	Male (2011)	Female (2001)	Female (2011)
1.	Marginal	4,396,671	5,612,249	894,624	1,086,108
2.	Small	3,017,979	3,431,007	582,208	616,391
3.	Semi-medium	1,963,936	1,882,923	305,056	271,935
4.	Medium	769,583	635,390	90,957	71,819
5.	Large	75,638	59,800	7,721	6,266
6.	All classes	10,223,807	5,612,249	1,880,566	2,052,519

Sources: Agricultural Census 2000–01 and 2010–11.

point. Large holdings by women are barely 0.3% that of men today, just a little higher at 0.51%.

Within the overall categories of size class of holdings for the state as a whole, the gender differentiated share does not appear to have changed much both in terms of the number and the area held. Female marginal and small farmers accounted for about 16% each of all similar holdings in 2000–01 and men obviously the remaining 84-odd percentage. The area held under these two categories, however, has declined by a percentage point each in both categories over the last decade for women holders.

Our apprehensions expressed earlier thus appear to be true—that the extent of landholdings in women's names have in all possibility declined, and, at best, have remained virtually stagnant.

Macro-level analysis camouflages the meso picture; it would therefore be extremely relevant to this study to analyse regional-level variations over the last decade. We hence examine in some detail the trends in the gendered patterns of both the number and area of holdings (Figure 9.2) held by men and women in the 33 districts that constitute the state of Maharashtra. This meso scrutiny is based on Tables 9.2 and 9.3.

Figure 9.2

Gendered Pattern of Area of Landholdings for 2000–01 and 2010–11

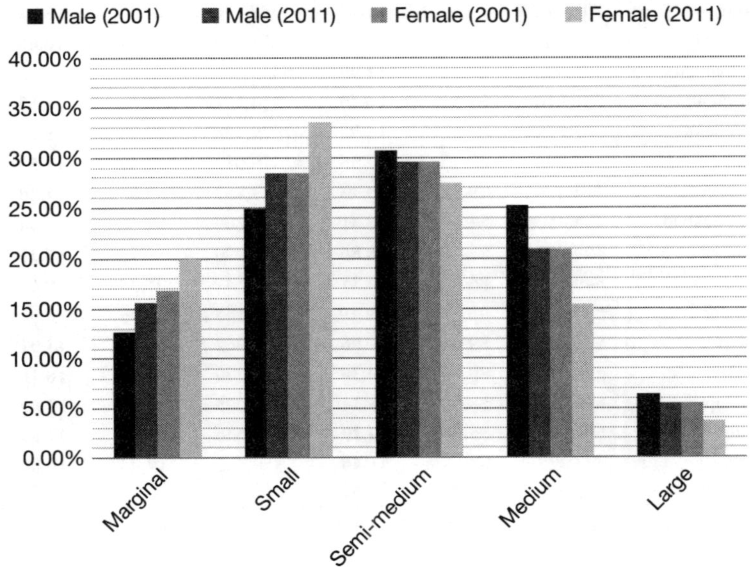

Sources: Agricultural Census 2000–01 and 2010–11.

Table 9.2
Gendered District-level Landholding Pattern for 2000–01 and 2010–11
(Numbers and %)

Region	2000–01			2010–11		
Maharashtra	12,104,373	Male %	Female %	13,673,888	Male %	Female %
Gadchiroli	115,340	86.78	**13.22**	134,807	88.19	**11.81**
Nandurbar	139,339	83.59	**16.41**	146,729	83.93	**16.07**
Vashim	156,495	84.13	**15.87**	196,063	83.56	**16.44**
Vardha	175,535	85.06	**14.94**	195,379	85.03	**14.97**
Gondiya	187,115	81.67	**18.33**	237,666	83.26	**16.74**
Bhandara	189,785	84.88	**15.12**	218,534	85.36	**14.64**
Akola	199,584	81.03	**18.97**	240,888	80.09	**19.91**
Hingoli	200,696	86.25	**13.75**	212,980	91.71	**8.29**
Dhule	229,793	80.02	**19.98**	235,915	80.80	**19.20**
Chandrapur	232,918	85.09	**14.91**	304,073	90.72	**9.28**
Nagpur	254,273	84.81	**15.19**	268,197	88.25	**11.75**
Sindhudurga	266,049	85.52	**14.48**	276,856	84.05	**15.95**
Thane	278,948	81.59	**18.41**	279,565	87.17	**12.83**
Parbhani	290,545	83.40	**16.60**	347,764	83.84	**16.16**
Usmanabad	290,857	87.81	**12.19**	356,470	85.36	**14.64**
Raygad	293,138	80.95	**19.05**	310,881	77.85	**22.15**
Latur	305,444	87.53	**12.47**	388,670	84.58	**15.42**
Yeotmal	315,765	81.58	**18.42**	378,427	83.94	**16.06**
Rathanagiri	335,506	87.01	**12.99**	453,372	82.35	**17.65**
Amravati	336,714	83.55	**16.45**	414,471	83.43	**16.57**
Buldhana	367,154	84.02	**15.98**	429,434	84.30	**15.70**
Jalna	370,992	82.15	**17.85**	410,013	82.47	**17.53**
Jalgaon	414,496	79.87	**20.13**	437,752	82.80	**17.20**
Aurangabad	434,456	81.59	**18.41**	529,809	84.56	**15.44**
Nanded	499,780	83.14	**16.86**	581,990	82.79	**17.21**
Beed	549,009	85.69	**14.31**	651,547	91.35	**8.65**
Sangali	555,345	90.81	**9.19**	537,145	91.99	**8.01**
Solapur	564,270	89.04	**10.96**	666,963	86.99	**13.01**
Nashik	590,310	80.70	**19.30**	641,279	81.89	**18.11**
Kohlapur	607,418	88.66	**11.34**	634,995	87.11	**12.89**
Pune	665,920	85.81	**14.19**	741,646	82.40	**17.60**
Satara	777,322	88.54	**11.46**	859,482	89.94	**10.06**
Ahmednagar	914,062	79.36	**20.64**	954,126	80.64	**19.36**

Sources: Agricultural Census 2000–01 and 2010–11.

Table 9.3

Maharashtra Gendered District-level Land Area Pattern for 2000–01 and 2010–11 (in Hectares and %)

Regions	2000–01			2010–11		
Maharashtra	19,915,638	Male %	Female %	19,667,796	Male %	Female %
Gondiya	202,628	85.73	14.27	206,178	85.68	14.32
Bhandara	204,474	86.82	13.18	207,289	86.63	13.37
Gadchiroli	207,602	89.24	10.76	222,624	89.93	10.07
Nandurbar	276,544	84.22	15.78	293,042	85.51	14.49
Raygad	320,137	82.39	17.61	336,606	80.88	19.12
Hingoli	367,507	88.71	11.29	358,299	93.23	6.77
Sindhudurga	371,899	87.08	12.92	275,504	84.73	15.27
Vashim	379,029	87.09	12.91	372,330	85.99	14.01
Akola	410,094	83.79	16.21	410,727	82.24	17.76
Thane	411,944	82.68	17.32	389,553	88.13	11.87
Dhule	414,165	82.73	17.27	421,704	83.12	16.88
Vardha	422,988	86.41	13.59	434,560	86.65	13.35
Kohlapur	468,505	89.98	10.02	453,568	89.32	10.68
Chandrapur	489,186	87.49	12.51	540,376	92.36	7.64
Parbhani	516,270	84.81	15.19	564,297	85.57	14.43
Nagpur	540,631	87.12	12.88	507,559	89.31	10.69
Jalna	624,412	84.70	15.30	590,525	84.77	15.23
Latur	625,433	89.53	10.47	640,212	86.47	13.53
Usmanabad	645,865	89.38	10.62	690,893	87.02	12.98
Rathanagiri	651,744	87.81	12.19	560,654	85.55	14.45
Sangali	701,731	92.72	7.28	672,480	94.27	5.73
Amravati	705,634	85.61	14.39	711,695	85.26	14.74
Buldhana	707,110	86.61	13.39	692,225	86.37	13.63
Aurangabad	724,884	84.18	15.82	691,402	86.25	13.75
Satara	759,393	90.58	9.42	640,541	91.18	8.82
Jalgaon	775,248	81.94	18.06	774,945	84.59	15.41
Nanded	776,547	84.64	15.36	824,518	84.81	15.19
Yeotmal	848,895	83.00	17.00	837,007	85.11	14.89
Beed	861,512	87.92	12.08	864,489	93.02	6.98
Nashik	977,220	83.79	16.21	978,498	84.49	15.51
Pune	1,032,559	88.37	11.63	1,003,226	85.63	14.37
Solapur	1,178,538	90.46	9.54	1,253,765	88.22	11.78
Ahmednagar	1,315,311	83.07	16.93	1,246,506	84.23	15.77

Sources: Agricultural Census 2000–01 and 2010–11.

It is indeed disheartening to note that the several laws and legislations relating to ensuring gender equality do not seem to have been an overall success in Maharashtra. The proportion of holdings as well as the area operated by women increased in 11 of the 33 districts of the state but simultaneously declined in 18 districts over the decade of 2000–01 to 2010–11. The remaining four districts of Jalna, Buldhana, Amravati, and Wardha remained un-impacted by the plethora of land laws in terms of both the number and area of holdings.

The maximum negation of women's land rights is in the four districts of Thane, Beed, Hingoli, and Chandrapur, all of them reporting a massive decline of 5%–6% in both the number and area of women's landholdings. While the fall in the district of Thane can be at least partially justified by the fact that a significant portion of its land has been transferred to non-agricultural use due to a high level of urbanization, there can be no excuse for this uncalled for negation of women's land rights in the other three regions. Other districts witnessing decrease in women's holdings are Nashik, Dhule, Nandurbar, Jalgaon, Ahmednagar, Satara, Sangli, Aurangabad, Nanded, Parbhani, Yavatmal, Nagpur, Gondiya, and Gadchiroli. The case of Bhandara is somewhat different; while the number of women holders declined by 1%, the area they operated remained virtually untouched. The implication could possibly be an increase in the size of women's landholdings.

Eleven districts witnessed a somewhat significant increase in both the number and area of women's landholdings—Raigad, Ratnagiri, Sindhudurg, Pune, Solapur, Kolhapur, Latur, Osmanabad, Nanded, Akola, and Washim. Here, we would like to point out that both the processes of increase and decrease in women's land rights are unrelated to the geographical regions they are located in and which constitute the state—whether Vidharbha or Marathwada or Konkan or Desh or Khandesh—North Maharashtra.

Changes in the pattern of gendered land rights are quite fascinating in the two districts of Ratnagiri and Raigad, both located in the Konkan region on the west coast. As of today, Raigad reports the highest proportion of female holders, at a rather remarkable 22.15% and covering the largest share of area too at over 19%. This district has overtaken that of both Jalgaon and Ahmednagar in terms of holdings and also Jalgaon in relation to area operated by women. Ratnagiri district has witnessed the largest transfer of land rights to women, up from about 13% a decade ago to almost 18% of all holdings today.

LAWS AND STRUGGLES FOR WOMEN'S LAND RIGHTS

Access to and control over resources specifically in the form of land and land rights both individual and common have to be necessarily perceived within an historical setting. This is obvious in that the granting of rights and the success achieved are additionally determined by the land laws that have defined and redefined structures and regions. In what is known as Maharashtra today, the structure of proprietary rights was altered to ensure the maximum possible advantage to British Rule. Rights came to be increasingly vested in allies and supporters of the colonial rulers in the permanently settled parts of the state, along with rich tenants in the temporarily settled regions. There is, thus, a vast array of landownership patterns that characterize the region, each one of them impacting women's access to land rights in a differing manner. This is complicated by the historical coexistence with the caste and clan system, particularly those of the Despandes, Deshmukhs, Khots, Inamdars, Kulkarnis, Patils, etc.

Thus, apart from the Ryotwari system of temporary revenue, several regions came to be permanently settled. Proprietary rights akin to the Zamindari system were given to Khots and Samants in the regions of Vidharbha, Konkan, and Nagpur; to Malguzars in Vidharbha; Jagirdars in Berar; and to Inams and Inamdars in the Deccan. Others were Deshmukhs and Deshpandes at the district level, and Patils and Kulkarnis at the village level (see Dewan 1991, Chapters 4 and 5).

It is important to note at this point that the Muslim Personal Law was enacted in 1937, and applied to all Muslims in Vidharbha and Marathwada regions. Further complexity arises from prevalence of tribals and also 'Buddhists' in the wake of the strong movement led by Babasaheb Ambedkar that originated in this state and in which a large proportion was and is of women.

The post-British era lead to the enactment and implementation of a plethora of 'secular' legislations relating to land and land rights. Maharashtra has witnessed several movements over decades relating to land rights, sometimes resulting in amending legislation in favour of the marginalized sections. While it is obviously not possible to detail all laws and movements, we identify some that are more significant in the context of our main area of concern. Suggestions of amendment to these are often integrated into each.

The Muslim Personal Law (Shariat) Application Act, 1937 (Act No. 26 of 1937 Dated 7th October)

The Shariat Act of 1937 applies to all Muslims in two major regions of Maharashtra—Vidharbha and Marathwada. It states,

> Notwithstanding any custom or usage to the contrary, in all questions (save questions relating to agricultural land) regarding intestate succession, special property of females, including personal property inherited or obtained under contract or gift or any other provision of Personal Law, marriage, dissolution of marriage, including *talaq, ila, zihar, lian, khula* and *mubaraat*, maintenance, dower guardianship, gifts, trusts and trust properties, and wakfs (other than charities and charitable institutions and charitable and religious endowments) the rule of decision in cases where the parties are Muslims shall be the Muslim Personal law (Shariat). (Emphasis added)

What is inherent is the inequality of women is that they are permitted lower shares than males; for example, daughters are allowed only half the share of sons. However, it needs to be noted that the Shariat recognized and accepted the fundamental right of women to property much earlier than other laws, even though at an unequal level. We deeply regret that no research whatsoever has been done on this aspect, nor has any movement taken up this issue seriously enough to warrant even a footnote.

Hindu Succession Act, State Amendment 1994; 2001; 2005

We are deliberately putting this Act immediately after the succession law relating to Muslims. Maharashtra is only one of the few states that have amended this Act way back in 1994 when the Government of Maharashtra declared its policy for women, by including daughters as coparceners and that too for agricultural land. 'However, an anomaly has been introduced through the amendments. By including as coparceners only daughters and not other Class I female heirs, the amendments have increased the shares of daughters but reduced those of some other Class I female heirs' (Agarwal et al. n.d.: 1; Sivaramayya 1997, quoted by Bhadbhade 2001). The policy of the Maharashtra state legislature to confer upon daughters the hitherto denied right in coparcenary property has been lauded widely, yet the amendments have been criticized for ambiguous language and interpretational difficulties. Predictably, there is no data on how many women in the rural areas of Maharashtra have benefited from this legislation.

The Bombay Prevention of Fragmentation and Consolidation of Holdings Act, 1947

This Act prohibits any fragmentation of land beyond a certain limit, which is determined by stated authorities (Section 5). The definition of a fragment is obviously perceived in dynamic terms; Section 10a states,

> [S]tandard area in respect of any class of land means the area which the State Government may from time to time determine under section 5 as the minimum area necessary for profitable cultivation in any particular focal area, and includes a standard area revised under the said section.

The implication is obvious—women are forced to write away their share in the property for the 'welfare' of their brothers, and generally receive no cash compensation. This holds true for virtually all states and regions in India, such relinquishment is generally being done in the name of 'peace in the family'. As is widely accepted, the same holds for other succession laws and legislations.

Bombay Tenancy and Agricultural Lands Act, 1948

Section 43 of this Act places restrictions on transfer of land whether through purchase or sale. The collector, who's permission is required, can do so only if the land is being leased by a landowner who is a minor, or a widow or person subject to any physical or mental disability or the member of the armed forces or one among the landowners holding the land jointly.

For instance, according to Section 32(G), the tenant can claim ownership rights from a male owner, but in case the owner is a widow or if the male owner passes away and the property holder henceforth is the widow, then both the tenant and the widow are constrained. The plot cannot be claimed by the tenant and the widow cannot dispose of or otherwise alienate her rights to this land unless a large number of pre-given conditions are fulfilled.

Government Resolution of 15th of September 1992, Revenue and Forest Department, Amendment to Maharashtra Revenue Act of 1966, Government of Maharashtra

This GR, known popularly as *'Laxmi mukti'* (emancipation of wealth for women), gives the right to women to register their names along with men on the property ownership 7/12 record. This GR, it must be noted, is based on the request made by and suggestions put forward by women's and other social groups in the state. Several organizations had struggled during the 1980s, especially in the district of Dhule, with numerous *sanghatana* (organization) members transferring land in the name of women. Villagers belonging to Shetkari Sanghatana in Vitner campaigned on the issue of land rights, took a public vow, and gave their womenfolk rights over half of the family land.

The issue here is that the inclusion of the name of the woman as co-owner is subject to two conditions—that the wife be legally wedded and that this inclusion be based on the 'request' of the owner who should be the legally wedded husband. These conditionalities become somewhat problematic in the context of the fact that, as a rather strong rural women's movement has revealed over the years, Maharashtra has probably the largest proportion of deserted wives who are not legally divorced, and also a fairly widespread practice of 'keeping a second wife' as an illustration of upward 'social' mobility.

Government Resolution of 10th of August 1994, Revenue and Forest Department, Government of Maharashtra

The GR states that all houses, forest lands, *gairan* (grazing) lands, and other such lands distributed and provided under various operative schemes by the government would be listed in the joint names of husband and wife. It also clarified that if the beneficiary was single at the time of receiving the land and/or house, his wife would automatically become a co-beneficiary or vice versa. In spite of the rather revolutionary character of this GR, the underlying patriarchal mindset is quite obvious—that the beneficiary can only be a man. There is no clarification or stipulation whatsoever for the applicability of this resolution to single women who are out of the predictable patriarchal slot.

1997 Amendment to Bombay Stamp Act of 1958, Government of Maharashtra

As a result of this amendment, land can be transferred among blood relations of specified categories by paying a nominal stamp duty and/ or fees of a mere hundred rupees. Three categories of transferees were created: A, that is, wife, husband, daughter, mother, and son; B, that is, brother, sister, and father; and C, that is, other relations. The state government has made attempts through the Department of Revenue and Forests to make this amendment more popular via its GR of 1997, but no data has been maintained nor any steps have been taken to monitor the progress of this rather interesting clause, nor has there been a gender-sensitive perspective attached to this resolution.

Government Resolution Dated 29th of May 2000, Revenue and Forest Department Based on Clause 17B of Bombay Tenancy and Agricultural Lands Act of 1948, Government of Maharashtra

The above government resolution was implemented by the Adivasi Hakk Suraksha Sanghatana in Raigad district in the Konkan region. The tribal organization utilized this GR and struggled long and hard to get it implemented. The organization finally succeeded in transferring homestead lands in the name of tribal women (SOPPECOM 2008: 5).

Government Resolution of 20th of November 2003, Rural Development and Water Conservation Department, Government of Maharashtra

Termed locally as 'Ghar doghaanche' (meaning house belongs to both), it obviously does not relate to agricultural land, but still has the potential to economically empower rural women. Under this GR, it is mandatory for the gram sevak to enlist all houses in the joint name, and that all gram panchayats should register house in the joint name on the 8A form.

We will now highlight some significant movements and struggles for land rights for women in Maharashtra; though not too numerous in number, the impact on the status of women has been quite remarkable, with several more being inspired to take up the issue so central to the foundations of women's economic empowerment in the countryside. It must also be noted that some of these struggles have often had a strong impact in the state as a whole, and that the government has sometimes responded rather sensitively at least in terms of legislation if not implementation.

Legislation particularly important for tribals is the Forest Rights Act of 2006. Section 35 of this Act allows for landownership of Adivasis on forest lands. The Act clearly recognizes the rights of women, and stipulates that all claims must be in the joint names of the husband and wife. Sakav (bridge), an NGO in Pen *taluka* of Raigad district of North Konkan region, works mainly on issues of land and forest rights of the Adivasis. The joint name clause in the Forest Act was used as a campaign point for several struggles over a period of time; *gram sabhas* were organized and people were explained why it was important for women to have ownership rights over land. Finally, Sakav was able to submit approximately 600 claims in the name of husbands and wives, of which 418 were, approved (SOPPECOM 2008: 30–31).

Women belonging to the Warli tribe in Talasari *taluka* of Thane district in Western Maharashtra have been struggling for long under the banner of All India Democratic Women's Association for their rights to both land and forests. They have been fairly successful in attaining some of these rights, although the exact numbers and locations are not available (Dhawale 2003).

However, it has been noted that often the exercise of these rights are restricted, and the Adivasi communities especially face harassment. The National Hearing organized by Community Forest Rights-Learning and Advocacy Process and Adivasi Janjati Adhikar Manch notes that in Nagzira Wildlife Sanctuary which is located in the two districts Bhandara and Gondia, "communities are being fined for exercising their grazing rights although they have received titles over community forest rights including grazing rights' (National Public Hearing 2013: 3).

A relatively strong Dalit movement in the state of Maharashtra has ensured that a significant proportion of Dalits, both men and women, have been able to extend their rights over land. For instance, 29,679 applications supported by the required proofs and documents, were forwarded to the relevant authorities by the Rural Development Centre in Beed district. This NGO, which has been working for long in seven districts located in the drought-prone region of Marathwada, mobilized a large number of Dalits in the movement for regularizing *gairan* lands, that is, common grazing grounds. As a result, 6987 claims were approved by officials, all of them in the joint names of husbands and wives (SOPPECOM 2008: 38–39).

Even if the proportion of claims approved are not even one-fourth of the total filed, the fact that the issue was popularized across an astounding 1,372 villages implies raising awareness of the most crucial of the economic rights of women. These villages extended across a total of seven districts—Beed, Nanded, Latur, Jalna, Parbhani, Hingoli, and Washim. Predictably, the success of this movement—even though partial—to regularize common grazing rights in the name of Dalits witnessed a huge backlash from the upper castes; the Dalits, however, had gained a degree of unity and self-respect that had reduced age-old submissiveness.

Disha Kendra, supported by ActionAid—Maharashtra, is quite a pioneering training and development support organization, focusing on land rights particularly among Adivasis in a remote tribal belt of Karjat Tehsil, Raigad district. Katkari's are a tribal forest community who during the days of British Rule had been given land called 'Dalli', on which depended their housing, food, and livelihood, to whatever minimal and subsistence level possible. The independent government, however, appears to have overlooked the Katkaris, and did not grant them legal entitlement to this land. This issue of legal entitlement has been taken up by the organization over a period of time, and up to last week, 111 Katkari families have got their legal registered rights.

This three-figure number may appear exceedingly miniscule given the huge range of numbers that confront the task of gendering land rights, but given that Katkaris are among the poorest of what is termed as Primitive Tribal Groups in Maharashtra with most of them being bonded labourers, this is no mean achievement. In fact, the level of poverty amongst this forest community is so high that the Supreme Court had to intervene and declare all Katkari households as Below Poverty Line (BPL).

In addition to regularization of Dalli land, the organization has assisted the primarily illiterate Katkaris to apply for land titles for homesteads for 212 men and an equal number of women, with 160 of these applications of both genders being assured implementation by the relevant authorities. In addition, the issue of forest land titles was taken up through local village committees in the three *talukas* of Karjat, Khalapur, and Panvel. Of the target of 1,100 men and 1,100 women, almost nine-tenths have been granted legal titles over the forest land.

It should be noted that most Dalits, and of course tribals, are landless and generally agricultural labourers; this transfer of land rights has given both men and women not only a renewable source of livelihood but also a strong sense of dignity. The implementation of the Government Resolutions of 1991 and 1992 is thus a huge step forward in the economic empowerment of the marginalized, especially the women. Initial discomfort and sometimes even opposition by men of the concept of joint ownership of land rights is always, of course, an issue. The point, however, is how one deals with this patriarchal attitude; as one woman put it, 'we have to convince the men that we will not leave our husbands and children just to claim a piece of land.'

Another relatively successful movement for claiming joint *pattas* has been in the erstwhile zamindari region of Vidharbha. YUVA (Youth for Voluntary Action—Rural), which is an NGO that works in about 11 districts of this rather feudal region, used primarily two land legislations in their struggle for ensuring gender equality in land rights—the Laxmi Mukti 1992 Government Resolution that allowed the inclusion of the wife's name in the land records known in Maharashtra as 7/12, and the Government Resolution of 1999 that amended the Bombay Stamp Act of 1958. About 300 women were, thus, enabled to transfer land in their names; this was across five districts—Amravati, Buldhana, Akola, Washim, and Wardha. About half the beneficiaries are OBCs, and one-fourth are Scheduled Castes.

Before moving on to another rather significant government resolution that has reportedly benefitted a relatively large number of women, we would like to highlight a few quite crucial 'case studies'.

Ahmed is a fairly well-to-do Muslim landowner in a large village in Nanded region. Being quite well read and a staunch believer in women's property rights, he attempted to transfer a part of his landholding in the name of his wife. Opposed strongly by members of his own community, he insisted on getting his marriage registered under the Special Marriages Act, and was hence able to fulfil what he calls his 'devotion to the cause gender equality contained in the Quran'.

An interesting tactic was followed by Brian, a tribal activist in Palghar *taluka* of Thane district. Emboldened by his participation in an indigenous people's movement, he convinced several of his colleagues to transfer land in their wives' names, not merely add them as joint owners. He says that 'this full and unequivocal transfer of land in women's names will ensure that no man will think of deserting her for fear of becoming landless again'.

Several instances have also been reported to us from several *talukas* of Thane, Raigad, Ratnagiri, Parbhani, and Pune, with a fairly large number of men participating in demonstrations for women's land rights. We believe that these instances where enlightened husbands have fought several odds to guarantee their wives gender equality in property rights should be highlighted and used for 'advertising' for the cause.

There have, of course, also been heartrending instances where sisters have been forced by their brothers and even in one instance by their mother to give up their rights to land.

Sangita and Medha are two sisters from a small village in Ambargaon *taluka* in Pune district who have always taken it upon themselves to look after their parents even though they were both married off in the city at a rather young age. Their brother used to telephonically 'inquire' about their health for a long time, but when the parents became aged, he started visiting the village fairly regularly. The father soon passed away, and all the property was transferred to the mother as it was in their joint names. On her husband's death, the mother, 'overwhelmed' by her son's concern, joined him in trying to convince her daughters to give up their share so that she could will everything to their brother. Finally, as in many such instances, the sisters agreed in the name of 'peace in the family', but are quite bitter about the denial of their rightful share in parental property.

Probably the most painful case is that which we witnessed in Partur *taluka* in Jalna district. We strongly believe that if any one single illustration had to be presented to argue for granting women secure and equal land rights, it is this particular instance of Sugandha tai.

The majority of single women in this area are labourers. Most widows who had held some small pieces of land after their husbands' deaths were rendered 'illegally' landless after their 'in-laws' had taken the plots away; some became non-cultivators after being deserted, illegal desertion being perceived as a 'cultural tradition' in the region. All are consequently dependent almost solely upon sale of labour-power. The bias against single and landless women workers—not unusual at all—manifests itself in several ways. We mention each one along with the 'excuse' given by the employer. Not being given wages on time—'Come again; you don't have a husband to look after, do you?' Being employed for less number of days—'Who do you want to earn and save for? Will you have any more children now?' Undefined hours of work—'Why do you want to rush back? Who is waiting for you?'

While all gender-specific agricultural tasks are, of course, performed by both single and married women, there is one utterly humiliating 'job' which only single and landless women are employed for—as scarecrows (*bujgavne*). The nature of this work as described to us by the villagers was traumatizing to hear and is even more painful to record.

The job description is simple—to stand in the fields and 'perform' the task of *bujgavne*—the act of scaring away birds. The 'skills' required are simple—the ability to shout, to flap one's hands, to throw stones (*gophan firawne*), to keep constantly moving, and, of course, the strength to stand for hours under the blazing sun. The daily hours of work average the normal eight, extendable by two hours when the sun sets late and daylight hours are longer. Wages do not depend on the number of hours but the number of days—that is, a high level of appropriation of surplus labour via the 'absolute' route through claiming time, rather than the appropriation of surplus labour power in terms of relative shares. The wages are mainly in kind—one meal for Sugandha tai and her children, the meal consisting of the inevitable '*paez*'—a thin gruel of rice and water, cooked and generally fermented both to increase the quantity and to kill hunger. The female-headed household of Sugandha is also provided housing—a place to sleep in the outhouse where cattle are kept. Additionally, two or three sets of old clothes are sometimes given for her and the children. The cash component of wages are a few 'twenties', given once in four or six weeks. Education, health, nutrition, electricity, protection from the heat and the cold, all these have no role to play in the lives of *bujgavne* families, including that of *Sugandha tai*.

The recording of such case studies are not meant to deter the implementation of women's land rights, but in fact to point out that the implementation of laws and legislations have to be viewed within the context of patriarchal mindsets and structures, including that of patri-locality that is utilized as an excuse not to transfer land to the names of women.

A rather successful legislation has been that of the Ghar Doghaanche Government Resolution. The initial weak implementation of this GR was pointed out officially by Mahila Arthik Vikas Mahamandal (MAVIM), the women's economic development corporation of the government of Maharashtra. MAVIM was established in 1975, and in 2003 it was declared as a Nodal agency by the Government of Maharashtra to implement various women empowerment programmes through self-help groups (SHGs). MAVIM took the lead by initiating the campaign which was termed as Ghar Doghaanche Abhiyan (Home of Two campaign) and started in May–June 2013 in Parbhani district.

As this campaign has been probably the most significant for women's property rights in Maharashtra, it would be useful to examine it in some detail. MAVIM has introduced a rural women's empowerment programme called Tejaswini in 33 districts of the state. This programme has four components, one being women empowerment under which the Ghar Doghaanche Abhiyan was taken up, Parbhani district being selected as the pilot area for a campaign mode and outcome-oriented approach to property rights for women.

Realizing that the translation of awareness into registration is a long struggle, detailed analysis was done of this erstwhile zamindari region, and it was decided to focus on small properties.

> There was also a clear relationship between the *size* of property involved and the difficulty in ensuring registration, with *zamindari* families having much more feudal mindsets and being much more reluctant to share property with women. Even in cases where property would be registered with women, it would be generally for the purpose of avoiding taxation and not for real empowerment. Therefore the implementation strategy adopted was to focus on families with *small* property holdings as the assumption was that these would be more receptive to the initiative. Owing to the caste system, the families with small property holdings showed a clear pattern: they invariably belonged to the SC, ST, OBC and minority communities. There was also a significant overlap between them and BPL families. Accordingly MAVIM focused its initiatives on these communities. Villages were selected where there was a strong presence of SHGs. The pilot of Ghar Doghaanche Abhiyan was conducted in 23 villages with some of them being Mooli, Sunegaon, Pimpri and Brahmangaon.[2]

Several NGO's have successfully used this 'Ghar Doghaanche' GR especially in the districts of Pune and Raigad. In Purandhar *taluka* in Pune district, 95% of households in 80 villages registered for joint property under this GR. *The Stree Mukti Sangharsh Chalwal* in western Maharashtra succeeded in transferring 1,500 sq. ft. of housing land to the single and deserted women from five villages. In Raigad *taluka* of the Konkan region, Sakav has been quite successful in implementing this GR. It got the issue discussed and resolutions passed in *gram sabhas*, after which the gram sevak was given the relevant forms to register houses in joint names. It is indeed heartening that 11,600 households spread over 14 gram panchayats in the *taluka* received the appropriate forms in joint names, along with renewed assessment forms (SOPPECOM 2008: 29). The local officials, in the main, have now become generally supportive particularly in the context of the strong women's movement; apathy and sneering has transformed into a less dismissive attitude towards women's land rights.

While we do lament the fact that there is no state-level information available on how many women have benefitted from this legislation, there are several lessons that can be learnt from the implementation of the Ghar Doghaanche by the various agencies, both governmental and non-governmental.

The rich experience of MAVIM at the ground level has led to its formulating several crucial preconditions for successful replication. We present some of them as follows:

1. Pre-existence of credible SHGs, and that too in fairly large numbers.
2. Mobilization of women on property rights via these SHGs.
3. Involvement of males as partners and not opponents.
4. Community rewarding and felicitation of good behaviour especially of men.
5. Capacity building and awareness creation.
6. Fortnightly or monthly follow-up meetings.
7. Constant involvement of local administrative machinery, and coordination between VLCs, gram sevaks, and sarpanches.

CONCLUSION

We list several recommendations and suggestions which are the result not only of the analysis in this chapter but also of numerous discussions and debates we are engaged in with gender and land academics and researchers and practitioners in almost every single state in the country, that is, India. None need an extended explanation, and are clear among and within themselves.

- Gender disaggregated database to be created within a fixed time period at all levels of macro, meso, micro, consisting of extent of public, private, and also institutional holdings across all castes and communities.
- Redefining definitions and reducing methodological and conceptual biases in all data systems, both at the central and state levels.
- Priority to be given in distribution of land to single women, female-headed households, landless households, farm suicide affected households, socially vulnerable and marginalized groups, liberated manual scavengers—the categories are several and vary across regions and production systems.
- Clear and inalienable land rights, including succession rights especially in public land distribution programmes including those related to displacement, land acquisition, resettlement, and rehabilitation.
- Leasing of all unused, potentially cultivable lands, including endowment lands, water bodies, canal embankments, inland fisheries, etc., to landless women's groups while recognizing such groups as a valid category of landowners and also leasers. Also, enumeration of all groups of landless and land-leasing women peasants. Additionally, subsidies must be given for cheap credit as well as other support systems to sustainably carry out farming activities. A similar group approach must be adopted in land purchase initiatives.
- Training courses relating to, especially, legal literacy and legal support services.
- It is suggested very strongly that the cooperative sector be given formal recognition. This would provide a formal structure and also institutionalize the many and myriad groups which are operating/functioning as of today and also have the potential to undertake joint production, maintenance, and distribution.
- The entire process of ensuring women's rights over land would be best served if linked organically with women farmer's movements and women's struggles for land. Most regions in every state of the country are brimming with the demand for gender equal property rights; to integrate and combine forces, in the private as well as public domain, would go a long way in guaranteeing land rights for women.

Several crucial issues emerge relating to the extent, pattern, quantity, and quality of the land that is transferred to women. One, often the land is of poor fertility levels, rocky, and un-irrigated. Two, the amount of land transferred is determined by the class of holders. Three, the historical land system operating in the region impacts the type of transfer itself; in an erstwhile zamindari area, as the holdings have been historically large and as the legislations relating to joint *pattas* apply to small holdings, the strategy used to ensure property rights for women may have to be initially focused on smaller holdings. Four, success of the transfer of land rights to women would depend to a large degree, additionally and sometimes even solely, on the social categories of the transferors and the transferees. Five, while it may be true that sometimes land may be transferred to women's names for tax purposes or in order to avail of government schemes, there can be no doubt whatsoever that the very act of ownership gives the woman at least some degree of independence, at least a partial say in decision-making, and certainly a certain degree of economic authority.

NOTES

1. The assistance of Radha Sehgal, Research Associate, Centre for Development Research & Action, was invaluable in completing this chapter.
2. www.mavim.org (accessed on 9 September 2015).

BIBLIOGRAPHY

Agarwal, Bina. 2002, November 21. *Are We Not Peasants Too? Land Rights and Women's Claims in India*. SEEDS Number 21, Population Council, New York.

Agarwal, B., B. Sivaramayya, and L. Sarkar. n.d. Report of the Committee for Gender Equality in Land Devolution in Tenurial Laws, LBSNAA.

Bhadbhade, Nilima. 2001. 'State Amendments to Hindu Succession Act and Conflict of Laws: Need for Law Reform.' 1 SCC (Jour) 40. Available at: www.academia.edu/1752265/State_Amendments_ to_Hindu_Succession_ Act (accessed on 22 March 2017).

Dewan, Ritu. 1991. *Political Economy of Agrarian Reforms in India*. Mumbai: Himalaya Publishing House.

Dhawale, Mariam. 2003. Adivasi Women Carry Warli Tradition Forward. Available at: www.aidwaonline.org (accessed on 22 March 2017).
Government of India. 2000–01. *Agricultural Census*. New Delhi: Government of India.
———. 2010–11. *Agricultural Census*. New Delhi: Government of India.
———. *Statistical Profile on Women Labour 2012–13*. Chandigarh/Shimla: Labour Bureau Ministry of Labour & Employment, Government of India.
Government of Maharashtra. 2013–14. *Economic Survey of Maharashtra*. Mumbai: Government of Maharashtra.
MAVIM. Ghar Doghaanche. Available at: www.mavimindia.org (accessed on 3 September 2015).
National Public Hearing. 2013, 14 December. *A Report of the National Level Public Hearing on Community Forest Rights*. Community Forest Rights-Learning and Advocacy Process and Adivasi Janjati Adhikar Manch.
Saxena, N. C. n.d. 'Theme paper on enhancement of property rights including land rights of women.' Available at: planningcommission.nic.in/reports/articles/ncsxna/index.php?repts= (accessed on 14 September 2015).
Sivaramayya, B. 1997. 'Coparcenary Rights to Daughters, Constitutional and Interpretational Issues.' 3 SCC (Jour) 25.
SOPPECOM. 2008. *Women and Land Rights in Maharashtra: A Study of Campaigns Led by SWISSAID India Partners*. Pune: Society for Promoting Participative Eco System Management. Available at: www.soppecom.org (accessed on 14 September 2015).

INTERNET SOURCES

www.dishakendra.webs.com (accessed on 3 September 2015).
www.mssrf.org (accessed on 14 September 2015).

10

Women's Access and Ownership of Land: A Case of Mizoram State in India

SAROJ ARORA

Mizoram, the land of the highlanders, is a tongue-shaped state in the northeastern region of India. Mizoram, in the local language, means the land of Mizos. *Mi means* human/people, *zo* means hill, and *ram* means land. Thus, the term *Mizo* itself means highlander. Mizoram is a hill state largely inhabited by tribal population. Majority of the population (i.e., 94.4%) of the state constituted scheduled tribes (Census 2011). The state has 14 communities notified as scheduled tribes. Each tribe has several sub-tribes and each sub-tribe has its own practices and language. Basically, it is the linguistic criterion which makes one tribal community different from the other. It is a rich state in nature and culture. It touches boundaries of three Indian states—Assam (Cachar district) and Manipur in the north and Tripura in the west. It touches international boundaries with two countries—on the east and the south by Chin and Arakan Hills of Myanmar (earlier known as Burma), and on the west by Chittagong Hill Tracts of Bangladesh. Due to a difficult geographical terrain and physical isolation, British made special provisions such as Inner Line Permit, 1873, to protect and regulate the land; prevent the entry of people, businessmen/traders, and contractors from the plains; debar the non-tribals from owning landed property in the state; and protect the tribesmen from exploitation. The regulation was also allowed to continue post-Independence. The Inner Line Permit is an offshoot of the Bengal Eastern Frontier Regulation, 1873.

The present study attempts to understand the land system in Mizoram in general, and gender and land relationship in particular. It also highlights the role of women's organizations in pressuring the state to amend gender-biased customary laws related to marriage, divorce, inheritance, and membership in the village council (VC) and bring gender parity through legislations. Before discussing the gender and land relationship, it would be important to understand the socio-demographic profile of the state of Mizoram and the factors which have led to the formation of the present-day Mizoram and land administration system.

SOCIO-DEMOGRAPHIC PROFILE OF MIZORAM

In comparison to many other states, Mizoram stands high on social indicators such as literacy rate, sex ratio, and participation in workforce. As per Census 2011, Mizoram has a population of 1,091,014 lakh, increasing from 8.89 lakh recorded in Census 2001. Out of the total population, 50.63% were males and 49.37% were females. The literacy rate in the state has shown an upward trend. It was 91.33% as per Census 2011. Of that, male literacy stood at 93.35%, while female literacy was at 86.72%. The gender ratio has also increased from 938 per 1,000 males in Census 2001 to 976 per 1,000 male in Census 2011 (Census of Mizoram 2011). This was above national average of 940.

Majority of the population in Mizoram (87.16%) has been reported to be Christians (Census 2011). The Buddhist at 8.3% constituted the second largest religious group. Chakma are the main followers of Buddhism. The remaining population (1.2%) was from other communities. The rural–urban population ratio was different from many other states in the country. The distribution of population is almost equal in urban and rural areas, that is, 52.11% people live in urban area and the remaining 47.89% live in rural areas. The percentage of population registered as workers among the scheduled tribes was 51.7% (Census 2001). This is significantly higher than the national average of 49.1% recorded for scheduled tribe population. Both males, 55.3%, and females, 48.1%, were workers, thus showing almost equitable participation in the workforce. Scheduled tribe females with 67.2% were the main workers, which is significantly higher than 53.3% recorded at the national level for scheduled tribe female workers (Census of India 2011).

MIZORAM: A HISTORICAL PERSPECTIVE

The Mizos, earlier known as Lushais, came from Burma into India during 1600–1700 AD. The British used to pronounce the term as *Lushai*, though the actual term is *Lusei*. In fact, *Mizo* is a collection of several tribes (almost 20–30 tribal communities) and *Lusei* is a common language of these tribal communities. During this period, the traditional village-level institutions were more powerful. Each village had an autocratic chief to manage the village affairs. The chief played multiple roles—the supreme administrator, a judge, and the protector and guardian of the village, running village administration with a council of elders locally known as *Upas* (Das 1990: 7).

Thus, Mizoram, formerly known as the 'Lushai Hills District', was a part of Assam. The district administration in the then Lushai Hills District began in 1891 when the territory was divided into two administrative wings—the South Lushai Hills District, a part of West Bengal, and the North Lushai Hills District, a part of Assam. Prior to 1891, there was no proper administrative set-up. The Lushais were independent tribes till the British annexed and proclaimed it as a part of their dominion on 6 September 1895. In 1898, for administrative convenience, both the hill districts (South Lushai and North Lushai) were merged by the British into one single district, that is, Lushai Hills District, and transferred to Assam under the administration of the Chief Commissioner of Assam (Lalneihzovi 2006: 7). For effective administration, the British Government further divided the district into two subdivisions, namely Aizawl and Lunglei. Thus, 1898 can be said as the beginning of settled administration in the district. In 1919, the Lushai Hills District was declared as Backward Tract under the Government of India Act, 1919. Later on, due to geographical isolation of the area, it was declared as 'excluded area' under the Government of India Act, 1935.

Soon after Independence, the process of making of nation state began in the northeastern region and boundaries were demarcated for overall stability and revenue generation (Baruah 1999). For land administration, various land laws came into force in Assam (excluding hill areas), Manipur valley, and Tripura. Agricultural land was settled on individual basis. The Bordoloi Committee recommended maintaining the autonomy of the hill regions of Northeast under the Sixth Schedule of the Constitution. The purpose of making such a constitutional provision for the hill region was to protect tribal land and their customs, and also to check social injustice and exploitation. Therefore, the land in the hill areas was allowed to be managed by traditional institutions through customary laws. The district council at the district level and VC at the village level were empowered to make decisions on land- and forest-related issues and regulation of *jhum* practice or other forms of shifting cultivation as per their customary laws.

The Lushai Hills was made an autonomous district on 26 April 1952. A simple and inexpensive administration for the tribesmen of certain hill districts including Lushai Hills District of the then state of Assam was the introduction of the autonomous district councils (ADCs) for major tribesmen and autonomous regional councils for minor tribesmen within a district. As a result, Mizo Hills ADC for the Mizos in 1952 and the Pawi–Lakher Regional Council (PLRC) for the Pawi, Lakher, and Chakma tribes were set up in 1953 under the provisions of the Sixth Schedule. The name of the Lushai Hills District was changed to the Mizo Hills District with effect from 1 September 1954 vide an Act of parliament called the Lushai Hills District (Change of Name) Act, 1954 (No. 18 of 1954).

Gradually, the leaders of the erstwhile Mizo Hills District Council built political pressure for larger autonomy for the area. With the result, the North-Eastern Areas (Reorganization) Act, 1971, came into force. As per the provisions of this Act, the Mizo Hills District was carved out of Assam and elevated to the status of the union territory of Mizoram on 21 January 1972 (Prasad 1998: 17). After attaining the status of a union territory, the then Aizawl district, the only district at that time, was trifurcated into Aizawl, Lunglei, and Chhimtuipui districts (Lalneihzovi 2006: 23). The PLRC was also trifurcated for tribesmen of each of the three tribes, namely Pawi, Lakher, and Chakma. Chhimtuipui comprised all these three ADCs. The Lai ADC was the largest council among all three ADCs. These regional councils were later elevated to the status of ADCs in 1972 under the Sixth Schedule that recognizes the customary rights of tribal communities in these areas and gives a considerable amount of protection over their lands, forest, customs, and village chiefships. The state and union legislations are not enforceable unless approved by the district council (ibid.: 52). ADCs administer revenue land as per the ADC Land Holding Act. The Land Ceiling Act has not been passed by them.

When traditional village chiefs became more powerful and exploitative, Mizo youth decided and pressurized the government to eliminate the exploitative traditional village chiefship system, and with that the Assam Lushai Hills District (Acquisition of Chiefs' Right) Act, 1954, came into force. The village-level democratic institution was introduced by enacting the Lushai Hills District (Village Council) Act, 1953, and the Pawi–Lakher Autonomous Region (Village Councils) Act, 1954. Under the Village Council Act, 1953 and 1954, the VC has functions and powers as provided for by the Sixth Schedule (ibid.: 98–99).

In 1959, due to rapid growth in the rat population, a famine *Mautam*[1] took place which destroyed paddy crops throughout the Mizo Hills. The famine became a turning point in the history of this hill area. The Mizo National Famine Front was then constituted to help the local community suffering from famine. It renamed itself the Mizo National Front in 1961. The Mizo National Front approached the union government for assistance. The apathy from the local administration and negligence to the assistance during famine led to insurgency during the 1960s which continued till mid-1980s. After much upheaval, unrest, and conflicts in the Mizo Hills District, a memorandum of settlement was signed between the Government of India and the Mizo National Front in 1986. Then, the 53rd Amendment was made in the Constitution and Article 387G was introduced which recognized customary rights of Mizos that included community land, common property resources, ownership and transfer of land, social practices, religion, and administration of civil and criminal justice. On 20 February 1987, the union territory of Mizoram attained the status of statehood and became the 23rd state of the Indian Union (Prasad 1998: 111). In comparison to the other states, Mizoram can be considered as one of the newly born state in the region.

LAND SYSTEM AND GENDERED SPACE

The land system in Mizoram is different from other states. The landholders themselves managed and looked after their land. But when British annexed Lushai Hills, they settled residential plots, shops, and wet-rice cultivation (WRC) plots in notified town areas. During the post-Independence period, a VC was competent to allot house sites within its jurisdiction for residential and other non-agricultural purposes except inside notified town areas where government (the revenue department) was given authority (House Sites Act 1953). In the state, community land and customary laws were protected under Article 387G of the Constitution. Revenue land in the notified areas is settled by the revenue department on individual basis. Community land comes under the local administration department (LAD). The administration of VCs has also been put under the LAD except in municipal council area where a VC is called as the local council which comes under the Urban Development and Poverty Alleviation Department over which the state government and the district council exercise their jurisdiction independently. Of late, in 2011, the state has enacted the Municipal Council Act which is in force only in the city area of Aizawl district.

This section deals with land system as it exists in Mizoram in general and women's relationship with land in particular. It discusses women's participation in *jhum* (shifting) cultivation, number of men or women owning land on individual basis, prevalence of land tenancy and status of land ceiling, and changes taking place in land-use pattern. The land system in Mizoram can broadly be classified into two categories, namely, community land and revenue land.

1. Community Land

In Mizoram, vast area of land belongs to the community. Community land plays a vital role in the lives of the people. The community land can be divided into three categories, namely, (a) *jhum* land, (b) community forest, and (c) grazing land. The overall administration of community land comes under the jurisdiction of LAD. A brief description on each of these categories of land is given as follows:

i. *Jhum* Land

Mizoram being a hilly area, *jhum* is the main form of agriculture system. About 80% of Mizos were engaged in this sector. *Jhum* is a shifting cultivation. Local crops such as hill paddy along with a variety of agricultural products such as maize, mustard, sugarcane, sesame, potatoes, cucumber, beans, arum, mustard, sesame, ginger, and cotton crops are cultivated on *jhum* plots.

In *jhum* cultivation, there is neither a permanent plot for cultivation nor any absolute ownership right over land by an individual household. *Jhumias* have 'usufruct rights' on *jhum* land. They do not have any right of inheritance or transfer. *Jhumias'* right over land ceases as soon as they stop cultivation on it. In other words, the land belongs to the community.

Jhum cultivation involves the clearance of forest on sloppy land, drying, and burning of dry leaves followed by the cultivation process. After harvest, land is left fallow and cultivators repeat the process on a new plot decided for the year for *jhum* cultivation. The plots of land are earmarked for *jhum* cultivation. The other plots remain fallow and vegetative regeneration takes place till the plot is reused for the same purpose in a cycle. Every year in every village a different area is selected for *jhum* cultivation.

Since the *jhum* cycle in Mizoram was 6–7 years, 6 or 7 blocks were kept for *jhum* cultivation in every village. Earlier, the principle of 'first come first serve' was practised in the allotment of *jhum* plot, but it was replaced by the lottery system. The lottery system was based on the basic principle of giving equal chance to all and avoiding favouritism.

The *jhum* plots were allotted by the VC, which is constituted for the rural areas and has full authority to control *jhum* land under the Jhum Regulation Act as amended from time to time. The VC allots *jhum* plots generally to heads of the household, usually males, but both men and women in the household work together and participate actively in the work done on the *jhum* plot. Women's involvement in *jhum* land gives them greater say in agricultural production and control on land.

ii. Community Forest

Community forests are mainly of three types.

(a) Village supply reserve forest: In these forests, the VC has full authority. Villagers, both men and women, have access to this forest and they collect fuel wood and house building materials like bamboo or cane as per their requirements form here.
(b) Village safety reserve: It ensures safety of the villagers. This is maintained as evergreen and never allowed to be cleared for cultivation.
(c) Protected forest: It is maintained with the purpose of saving the endangered species of plants.

iii. Grazing Land

In some villages, few patches have been demarcated as public grazing area. Some limited area of this land is taken care of by the VC and the remaining area by the LAD. Both men and women have access to grazing land.

This is important to mention that the above-mentioned categories of community land provide usufruct right over land and are administered through customary laws. The VC is the custodian of this land. Both men and women have access to the community lands. In fact, women are more closely linked with *jhum*, community, and forest lands for the sustenance of their households. No land records are maintained for the community land. It is said that proper records of community land are neither available nor easy to maintain. Maintaining land records for vast tract of land in hill areas is a herculean and very expensive task. It requires a different survey technology.

As mentioned, both men and women actively participate in *jhum* cultivation and take joint decisions related to agricultural crops and produces. However, recently, a debate has begun on the negative implications of *jhum* cultivation on the pretext of environmental concern. The state government is making concerted efforts in persuading people to get away from practising *jhum* and shift towards settled cultivation. Under the New Land Use Policy (NLUP), which is a flagship programme, people are being encouraged to grow commercial crops on settled land or opt for non-farm activities. Under settled cultivation, land is allotted on individual basis and revenue is being charged on such land. During a household survey, it was found that usually land has been settled in favour of a male member of the household. As a result, all the benefits of the government schemes related to bank, finance, technology, and extension education were extended to male members. Women were denied access to such benefits. Not only this, women-headed households were also not counted as heads. In the changing scenario, women are losing their access and control over land which is leading to their marginalization.

2. Revenue Land

Revenue land is allotted for two purposes, namely residential and agriculture. Agricultural land includes food and horticultural crops, WRC, cattle farm, and fish pond. The allotment of house site is regulated by the Lushai Hills District (House Sites) Act, 1953. The revenue department settles house site land in urban/notified town areas. The revenue land is administered by the revenue laws. Earlier, there were plethora of land laws, many of which were found to be overlapped, complicated, redundant, and gender biased. To overcome this, the state government has recently introduced the Mizoram Land Revenue Act, 2013, and the Mizoram (Land Revenue) Rule, 2013. Under this new Act, widows have been given a preferential treatment. This Act has repealed all previous land-related Acts. These land laws were extended to the entire state except the areas under three ADCs, namely Lai, Mara, and Chakma. The revenue department maintains land records. The revenue land is of four types, namely land allotted on temporary pass basis which extends usufruct rights, periodic *patta* basis, land with land settlement certificate (LSC), and land lease. A brief on all four types of revenue land is as follows:

A temporary pass is issued for residential purposes. House pass extends the 'temporary right of use' and 'occupancy' over a specific plot for a stipulated time frame. A pass holder has no right of transfer or inheritance beyond the period of the pass or of sub-letting (Mizo District Land & Revenue Act 1956: 8). The 'periodic *patta*' also gives 'users right over land'. Periodic *pattà* is a prescribed land document settling the agricultural land periodically under the specified rules whereby an individual or a society has entered into an engagement with the district council to pay land revenue and taxes, and legally assessed by Mizo District (Agricultural Land Rules 1971: 41). If the beneficiaries/landholders of periodic *patta* use the land satisfactorily, then they can apply for an LSC, which extends permanent ownership of land. There are lacunas in land laws. For instance, though there is a ceiling on the size of landholding of periodic *patta*, there is no ceiling on the number of periodic *pattas* a person can hold. Periodic *patta* is used either for cultivating horticultural crops or commercial crops, such as timber, spice, tea/coffee plantation, vegetables, palm, and sericulture (Singh et al. 2012). Discussion with the revenue officials revealed that mostly men have periodic *patta* in their name. Only few women have periodic *patta* in their names.

The third category is land with LSC. The LSC extends permanent ownership rights on land to an individual. This category of land gives 'heritable and transferable right of use' on or of sub-letting in the individual's land subject to the payment of all revenue and taxes from time to time. Ex-servicemen are exempted from paying tax on land with LSC for one residential plot and one agricultural plot each. But if an ex-serviceman has more than one parcel of land with LSC, he has to pay for rest of the plots. District-wise data on land settled on LSC basis show that maximum number of land plots (117,455) were allotted in Aizawl district—a state capital followed by Lunglei district (32,894); Kolasib (22,118), Champhai (15,172), and Serchhip (13,421). Mamit is one of the backward districts in the state. Relatively less number of people was allotted land with LSC, that is, 8,545 (Directorate of Land Revenue & Settlement 2009).

WRC, particularly in Kolasib and Champhai districts, was promoted in the valley areas of Lushai Hills (now Mizoram) by British and certain rights were conferred which continued even after the British period (Das 1990: 16). During 2007–08, the total area under WRC was 9,594 hectare. District-wise comparison shows that maximum area under WRC was in Kolasib district (3,515 hectare) followed by Champhai district (2,374 hectare). These two districts have ample flat land (Directorate of Economics and Statistics 2008: 24). Both men and women work on WRC plots, but most of the WRCs plots were settled in favour of men.

The revenue department does not maintain sex-segregated data; hence, it was difficult to find out the actual number of men–women owning revenue land in their names. However, sex-segregated data on landownership could be collected for four VCs, namely Rangvamual, Sairang, Sakawrtuichhun, and Tanhril, in Aizawl district. The land plots were allotted during 1976–2010. It was found that in all these four VC areas, total 1,734 persons were found owning land in their names. Out of them, 1,477 (85.18%) were men and 257 (14.82%) were women. VC-wise break-up shows that in Sairang VC, 84.53% men and 15.47% women owned land; in Sakawrtuichhun, 87.54% men and 12.46% women owned land; in Tanhril, 85.17% men and 14.83% women owned land; and similarly, in Rangvamual VC 85.71% men and 14.29% women owned land. Thus, based on the data, it can be said that majority of men in comparison to women owned land in their names in the state of Mizoram (Table 10.1).

The fourth category of land is land lease. This gives the 'right to use'. For government office establishments, the lease period is for 25 years and lease period for NGOs is 10 years. The maximum lease period in some cases was for 99 years.

NEED FOR LAND-REFORM INITIATIVES

In Mizoram, the minimum and maximum limit of landholding is regulated by the Mizoram Land and Revenue Act, 1956. A minimum ceiling for settlement of a house plot is 500 sq. ft. and maximum is one bigha (14,400 sq. ft.). Similarly, no agricultural land exceeding 30 bigha is

Table 10.1

Number of Men Women Owning Land in Their Names (1976–2010)

S. No.	Name of the Village Council	Men No. (%)	Women No. (%)	Total (row %)
1.	Sairang	956 (84.53)	175 (15.47)	1,131 (100.00)
2.	Sakawrtuichhun	267 (87.54)	38 (12.46)	305 (100.00)
3.	Tanhril	224 (85.17)	39 (14.83)	263 (100.00)
4.	Rangvamual	30 (85.71)	5 (14.29)	35 (100.00)
5.	Total	1,477 (85.18)	257 (14.82)	1,734 (100.00)

Source: Directorate of Land Revenue & Settlement, March 2015.

allotted or settled either temporarily or permanently without the prior permission of the executive committee (Mizo District Agricultural Land Act 1963: 44). This limit of landholding is applicable to the whole of Mizoram except the three ADCs. It was found that although there is a limit on the size of a residential plot and agriculture land, yet in practice, a person can have as many plots at different places locations as he/she can. It shows a serious lacuna in the Land Ceiling Act which is often being exploited by the rich people who accumulate land in their favour. The state has not yet passed the Land Ceiling Act. There is a growing demand from various associations, such as the Young Mizo Association (YMA) and the Mizoram *Kohhran Hruaitute* Committee which means a joint committee of different church leaders of Mizoram, for the enactment of land ceiling. Revenue officials were of the view that as long as land is settled on piecemeal survey, it will remain difficult to find out how much land parcels are owned by an individual.

The results of an empirical study conducted in 2014 show that of total households surveyed, a little more than one-tenth of them (11.22%) were leasing land and the remaining 88.78% were not (Singh and Arora 2012). Noticeably, the cases of tenancy could be found in areas where labour-intensive crops such as WRC or coffee plantation were cultivated. Although land was leased by male heads of the households, both men and women were found working on leased land. There is no land tenancy act in Mizoram; therefore, no tenancy records are maintained. However, in practice, the cases of concealed tenancy were found prevalent in the state in general and in Champhai and Kolasib districts in particular.

ZORAMCHHIA

Apart from revenue tax, the revenue department collects tax on land and man, locally called *zoramchhia*. It is levied on every household including landless and tenants residing in town and rural areas, unless exempted by the administrator on grounds of dire poverty. This tax is a legacy of the British which continues till date. Article 276 of the Indian Constitution has provision for this particular tax. The landless and women-headed households find it difficult to pay this tax with their meagre or no income at all.

INHERITANCE-RELATED CUSTOMARY LAWS

Mizo is a patrilineal society. Women's status in inheritance laws in Mizo society has been highlighted in the following paragraphs.

In Mizoram, the inheritance of landed property is guided by customary laws. *Mizo Hnam Dan*[2] is a book dealing with the codified customary laws of Mizos related to marriage, divorce, succession, and inheritance of immovable and movable properties such as land and house. *Hnam* is a Mizo term which means customary law and *dan* means *khel* (clan), and Mizo is a nomenclature of a tribal group. Thus, the *Mizo Hnam Dan* means customary laws of different clans of Mizo tribe. A person can inherit property only after getting an inheritance certificate that has to be brought from the court. To settle the transfer of land through inheritance, the Electoral Photo Index Card is produced as a proof. Mizoram is one of the pioneering states in the northeastern region which has codified customary laws including land-related customary laws in 1980. The codification of customary laws means that the customary practices of tribal communities are approved by the Assembly and available in a documented form. The customary laws of Lai, Mara, and Chakma ADCs are yet not codified.

A review of customary laws reveals that women did not have rights when it comes to marriage, divorce, succession, or inheritance. The customary laws have denied women the right to inherit property including landed/immovable property among others. Women were deprived of even gifts, locally known as *bungrua*, that were given to them at the time of marriage. Their husbands could have divorced them without providing financial assistance. Women were also denied participation in the decision-making process during the VC meeting and other legal entitlements.

The customary laws were guided by the patriarchal norms, and therefore, landed/immovable property has been inherited by male descendants in the family. For instance, in Mizo community, immovable property was inherited by the youngest son in the family, whereas in Paite community, the eldest son inherited it. According to the Mizo customary laws, the youngest son of the family was the natural or formal heir to his father and inherited landed property. However, the father could also leave share for other sons if he desired so. The *Mizo Hnam Dan* mentions that the reason why the youngest son inherits is because he is supposed to support the aged parents. The youngest son cannot inherit all the properties merely because he is the youngest unless he supports the aged parents till death (Das 1990: 168–69).

In case a man had no son, his property was inherited by the next kin of the male descendant. If a man dies leaving a widow and minor children, a male relation (who usually happened to be a brother of the deceased) took charge of the family and looked after the property until one of the sons came of age. If no such male relative was around, then the widow acts as a trustee of her husband's property until the time her either son becomes mature to inherit it. A divorced woman could also not claim over family properties (Phelamei 2012). Only in rare cases, one could find a daughter inheriting the property. She inherited if there was a 'will' (Directorate of Information & Public Relations (n.d.) Mizoram 27–28). A survey was conducted to study the inheritance pattern and process in Lunglei town in Mizoram. It was found that out of 40 households, 9 households had acquired property by inheritance (2 by the youngest son, 2 by the eldest son, 3 by the only son, and 2 by the widow), 7 by purchase, 17 by gifts, and 7 by fresh allotments under LSC. Out of the two cases of land inherited by the widow, in one, she was certified as the legal heir by the magistrate, and in the other, she inherited the land on behalf of the minor son (Das 1990: 168–202).

Although as per Mizo customary laws women were not entitled for land, there are certain instances of challenging the gender discriminatory customary laws in Mizo society. In this regard, one of the assistant settlement officers (ASOs) narrated his experience as follows.

A married woman put a writ petition in the district court to claim property after her parents' death. She did not have any brother. As per the customary law, property was inherited by her uncle (male descent) in the family who served her father during his old age. The daughter registered a case in the district court. The assistant settlement officer was dealing with this case in the court; he found that as per customary laws, a daughter was not entitled to inherit her father's property so a decision was taken to disinherit her from the ancestral property. But the daughter challenged the verdict of the district court and appealed in the high court where the case was still pending.

Post-1990s saw partial amendments in inheritance-related customary laws. A provision was made that a written 'will' formally executed may confer on a woman the right to inherit the family property. Women, however, were made entitled to their own property. For example, the dowry (*thuam* in Mizo) a woman gets during marriage from her parents is exclusively her own property. Though the provision was made to write a will, ironically it is practised very less and mostly communicated orally. This was observed that Mizo society is not untouched by winds of change. It was found that if a father is well-off and has large landholding, he may consider other sons and daughters for inheriting his property. The factors which influence inheritance-related decision-making leading to the execution of a 'will' by the head of the family may depend on the economic conditions or the marital status of the daughter, that is, whether the daughter was unmarried, divorcee, etc.

Generally, inheritance-related decisions were taken by the head of the family (father). In some cases, it was decided both by the head (father) of the family and the VC. The VC basically acts more as a witness and a recommending authority. It assesses the economic condition of the family and then decides accordingly.

Noticeably, not many Mizo women were found aware of inheritance-related customary laws. A study conducted by the Centre for Rural Studies, Lal Bahadur Shastri National Academy of Administration in 2015 revealed that little more than one-fourth respondents (26.24%) were aware of land inheritance laws; however, a majority of them (73.76%) were not aware of the laws. Most of the respondents who reported that they were aware of land inheritance laws (84.09%) said that as per Mizo customs the youngest son inherits the land, but, in practice, it depended on the 'will' (verbal or written) of the head of the family (father) and one-tenth of the respondents (9.09%) said that only the male members in the family inherited the land. They further explained that the main house was inherited by the youngest son and other assets were inherited by other sons. A few respondents, 4.55%, said that it depended on the economic status of the household and the quantum of assets owned; if the family owned sufficient assets in that case, they were divided among all the children. A small number of the respondents (2.27%) said that a 'widow' of the deceased is made the trustee of the land till the child becomes an adult.

FEMINIST MOVEMENT AND CHANGES IN INHERITANCE LAWS

Realizing the fact that the customary laws are gender discriminatory, the then lieutenant governor (administrator) of Mizoram constituted a committee in 1980 to examine the draft report on the Mizo Customary Laws and Practices (*Mizo Hnam Dan*), which had been prepared by the Law Research Institute, Eastern Region Gauhati High Court. The committee was to give feedback, if any, required with regard to the statement of law in the said draft report on the customary laws and practices as they were in force. They were also required to consider and suggest modifications or reforms that could be introduced in various aspects of the Mizo customary laws and to examine any other incidental or consequential issues. The Minister for Education and Social Welfare; MLA; ex-minister; ex-CEM; registrar of cooperative societies, Aizawl; president of the District Council Court; Presbyterian Church; ex-director, LAD; senior research officer of Tribal Research Institute, Aizawl; advocate; and under secretary of the Law and Judicial Department were nominated as members of the committee (Notification No. IJE 30/79/366 1980). The committee had reviewed and revised the *Mizo Hnam Dan* and submitted its report to the Government of Mizoram but no substantial changes could be made except a few amendments.

Gradually, some of the enlightened Mizo women organized themselves in a group and raised a voice that half of the population in Mizo society were discriminated in socio-economic and political arena and were kept out of the decision-making process. They argued that customary laws were repressive in nature and gender biased. These women's organizations and NGOs mobilized women at a grass-roots level and raised a movement to improve their ameliorating condition. Women's organizations such as Mizoram *Hmeichhe Insuihkhawm Pawl* (MHIP), which means Mizoram Women United Association, and other women's groups emerged as powerful pressure groups and pushed the government to review the existing customary laws from a gender perspective. Gradually, several other women organizations such as All Mizo Women's

Federation (AMWF) came forward. More than 10 women organizations got affiliated to MHIP to make the movement stronger. All these organizations emphasized the need for gender-just laws. They were of the view that woman's roles in the production and reproduction process could not be ignored. Women managed household chores and work in *jhum* fields, in formal and informal sectors, but they had no say in decision-making in public domain. Mizo women faced difficulties and constraints due to the legal biases. Women's groups also demanded for a 33% reservation in the political system. They were of the view that in such situations the only option left was to change the situation through the legislative route. They were of the view that repressive practices should be stopped by legal measures. It was argued that if a custom could not be overturned, it could definitely be made gender just and modified. The MHIP advocated for an increased induction of women candidates into local political parties. A brief write-up on MHIP is given in the annexure.

During the mobilization process, a series of consultation took place, but women organizations were not satisfied with the amendments introduced in customary laws. During 2005, a debate took place on the issue of customary laws from a gender perspective. The members of the review committee had diverse views. A group which was against amending customary laws argued that the Mizo customary ways of life should be preserved. The Mizo society should not be in a hurry to enter into the 21st century and choose the formal laws. They were in favour of documentation of the customary laws but not the amendment. The other group counter argued and emphasized the need for the codification of customary laws. They acted as a pressure group and pressed the need for amending customary laws and making them gender just. The Panchayat Mahila Shakti Abhiyan also played a crucial role to convince the lawmakers for the need of the law. Consequently, in 2008, the Mizoram Divorce Ordinance was passed. The Congress Party then in power took the case to the assembly and the assembly referred that to the Law Commission. The Law Commission's consultation with the members of the review committee including women's groups continued almost for 5 years. During this period, around 20–22 rounds of meetings took place. The committee was represented by MHIP which was one of its permanent members, Mizoram *Upa Pawl* (MUP) which means Mizoram Elder Citizens' Association, members of the Mizoram Bar Association, and prominent citizens. An MLA or a law minister was deputed the chairman of the committee. In September 2009, an open-house discussion took place. In 2012, the Law Commission completed the report and submitted that to the law department. In the meantime, somebody filed a case pointing out the loopholes in the report. Those loopholes were rectified. Thereafter, the Marriage, Divorce and Inheritance of Property Bill, 2013, was referred again to the Law Commission. Since then, the law department has conducted several rounds of meetings. It can be said that a chapter was added in the history of women's movement when the State Law Commission finally took upon to review the Mizo Marriage Bill, 2013; the Mizo Inheritance Bill, 2013; and the Mizo Divorce Bill, 2013 (Hanghal 2014). Thereafter, the state assembly passed a landmark legislation of the Mizo Marriage, Divorce and Inheritance of Property Act, 2014 (Act No. 9 of 2014), in the assembly which ended on 26 November 2014 (Dowerah 2014). The Act came into force with effect from 13 February 2015 (Mizoram Gazette Extra Ordinary 2014). This Act applies to any person who belongs to Mizo tribe. It also applies to marriages where male members of the parties belong to any Mizo tribe and connected matters therewith. The Mizo Marriage, Divorce and Inheritance of Property Act, 2014, deals with marriage, dissolution of marriage, division of property on divorce, will, inheritance of father's (head of the family) property, and inheritance of a woman's personal property. In the new law, there are specific guidelines for the dissolution of a marriage. This Act disbanded customary laws of the patriarchal Mizo society, entitled divorced women to inherit property, and also protected them from being divorced at the will of their husbands. The ex-president of the AMWF, Jane R. Ralte, said that the Act would reform the society by reducing divorce rates and reducing the number of orphans in Mizoram (DNA Agency 2014).

Thus, after many years of advocacy, struggle, consultation with lawmakers, and resending of memorandums and draft bills to the assembly and to the executive bodies, the MHIP—an apex body representing several local women's groups—ultimately could get success to push the system into considering judicial and legislative changes in the marriage, divorce, inheritance, and succession laws to safeguard the interest of Mizo women. In fact, the enactment was the result of a continuous struggle that has gone on for over a decade waged by the MHIP; therefore, women's groups have welcomed these laws as a step forward. They are hopeful that it will usher in change.

Some critics are of the view that the Mizo Marriage, Divorce and Inheritance of Property Act, 2014 (Mizoram Gazette, Extraordinary 2014), may still have some shortcomings and that they need to be addressed. They also points out that although the Act has come into force, there is a lack of awareness among most of the Mizo women about these Acts. Some have apprehension that customary laws may override this Act as people are not mentally prepared to accept such drastic changes in society. They are of the view that their customary laws should be respected.

ENACTMENT OF THE LUSHAI HILLS DISTRICT (VILLAGE COUNCIL) ACT, 2015

The Lushai Hills District (Village Council) Act, 1953, was introduced to replace the exploitative traditional village chieftainship. In 1972, when Mizo Hills District became a union territory, and attained the statehood in 1987, the Government of the Union Territory of Mizoram and Mizoram as a state adapted this Act to carry out village administration in its respective areas. The VC has elected members. The VC is a nomenclature of village court. There were 757 VCs in Mizoram having 3,339 members (Directorate of Economics and Statistics 2008, Mizoram: 24). Though women were not debarred for contesting the election of the VC, yet in practice, women have not been encouraged to join the fray. The VC which is considered as a democratic institution at the grass-roots level remained male dominated (Lalneihzovi 2006: 649–59). Women participation in the village-level democratic institution such as the VC was almost negligible. So far, only one or two women became VC members in Aizawl town area. It reveals that women were kept out of the decision-making process in the political arena. Women's participation in the political process is important for their political empowerment. Their absence in the VC has a direct bearing on their inferior position (Lalneihzovi 2014).

Realizing the absence of women members in the VC, women's groups in Mizoram raised the issue and pressurized the government to amend the existing Village Council Act, 1953, and reserved seats for women. To save the political career and the fear of losing women's votes, political parties in the state unanimously supported the demand of women's groups. Ultimately, the Mizoram Government passed the Lushai Hills District (Village Council) (Amendment) Act, 2014 (Act No. 10 of 2014), in 2015. This Act repealed and amended the Lushai Hills District (Village Council) Act of 1953. Based on the number of households in the village, women representation was determined. For instance, it was decided that villages having 200–500 households shall have five VC members, of whom one shall be a woman; those having 500–1,000 households shall have seven elected members, of whom two shall be women; and ones having 1,000 households and above shall have nine elected members, of whom three shall be women (the Lushai Hills District [VCs] [Amendment] Act 2014). At present, there are 812 VCs in Mizoram. Out of total 3,382 VC members, 858 are elected women members and 18 are VC presidents (Govt. of Mizoram, Department of Local Administration 2016).

RESISTANCE BY THE PATRIARCHAL INSTITUTIONS

Notwithstanding, the journey to achieve the goal of gender-just law was not very smooth. Women's organizations had to toil hard for several decades to achieve the goal. Since the beginning, the movement faced resistance either by male members of the society or the male-dominated institutions including churches and several NGOs. Men were apprehensive that the Act might give more leverage to women counterparts. They argued that Mizo society follows customary laws and it may not like to accept the modern laws that are based on the principle of gender equality. Religious institutions did not come forward to support women's movement. It is to point out that women in Mizo society do not have any say in a decision-making process in religious institutions including churches. Their representation in the evangelical society is almost absent. There is hardly any woman pastor in the state.

Similarly, Young Mizo Association (YMA), a youth body that is one of the powerful and the biggest non-profit organizations in the state, has a stronghold on Mizo youth with a membership of around 3 lakh youth. But it has hardly any woman representation in the decision-making unit (Dowerah 2014). Young girls are part of the forum but at a very low level. YMA maintained distance from any discourse/debate on gender issue. Contrary to men, women's perceptions for these two new Acts were entirely different. Women were very much satisfied with the socio-legal reforms brought out by the Mizo Government.

To find out women's awareness and views on the newly introduced laws, a focused group discussion was conducted in village Lungleng of Aizawl district during March 2015. Women were asked whether they knew about the two recently introduced Acts namely Mizo Marriage,

Divorce and Inheritance of Property Act, 2014, and the Lushai Hills District (Village Council) Act, 2015. Women respondents, particularly from the young age group, replied in affirmative. They were further asked from whom they have come to know about these laws. It was found that they have come to know about these Acts through newspapers and local television channels. These women further mentioned that they feel good to think that their interests were secured and find themselves empowered now as they were protected by the law. Though most women were found aware of their rights, in practice they were not able to exercise their rights. For instance, there were two divorced women in the village living in a separate house. They were engaged in tailoring or agricultural activity for their livelihood.

CUSTOMARY LAWS, LAND ACQUISITION AND ITS IMPACT ON WOMEN

Since Mizoram is situated at the international border, for defence purpose, a large amount of land had been acquired for establishment of Border Security Force. Also, from time to time, land had been acquired for various development projects such as construction/diversion/upgradation of roads, improvement of junction at national highway, playground, construction of booster pumping station, market, godown for Food Corporation of India, and school. An area of 2.7 sq. km was acquired for building an airport in Aizawl—the state capital.

As mentioned, vast land in Mizoram belongs to the community which is administered by the customary laws. The Land Acquisition Act is a formal law which recognizes only title land. This Act does not recognize community land as it extends usufruct right. For instance, only the project-affected families that own land on an individual basis in notified town or sub-town areas are compensated. But if community land is acquired, affected people are not compensated. The acquisition of community land has far-reaching consequences on the community members, particularly women, as they play a significant role in *jhum* cultivation which is the main source of livelihood.

The following example illustrates how a formal law such as Land Acquisition Act subverts customary laws and displaces a large number of households from their land which was the only source of their livelihood.

Serlui B was a Hydel Project which submerged Builung village in Kolasib district in 2001. This has displaced almost 150 households. Most of these households were dependent on community land for their livelihood. Only few households had titled land. To resettle these affected families, rehabilitation site was developed in town area in Kolasib district. Only those who had land title were given land for land. They were provided houses. Transportation facility was provided to shift from the original village to the resettled site. But families that dependent on community land and engaged in *jhum* cultivation were not compensated. With displacement, they lost their community land—the only source of their livelihood. They shifted to the town area but did not have the skill to get any job.

One of the senior revenue officials mentioned how the acquisition of community land created livelihood crisis for Mizo women:

> In Serlui B Hydel Project, rehabilitation of tribal families was a problem for the Land Revenue Department. Although households dependent on *jhum* cultivation were provided housing facility but they were not provided any alternative source for livelihood. This rendered the displaced families landless. They lost their livelihood and started facing livelihood problems at rehabilitation site. So much so that even now, women of displaced families visit Revenue Office and Directorate of Land Revenue & Settlement, Aizawl and share their grievances and plead to be provided a piece of community land so that they could start cultivation and manage their livelihood. They make complaint for taking their land which was the only source of their livelihood. (Field visit notes)

This example shows that displacement by development projects not only takes away the livelihood sources from the people but also uproots them from their native places, gardens, and cemeteries of their loved ones. So, the interruptions in sociocultural linkages and loss of property hurt them the most. Since community land laws and customary laws in Mizoram are recognized under Article 376G in the Constitution of India, the Land Acquisition Act should also consider this particular aspect.

CONCLUSION

In comparison to many other states, Mizoram stands high on social development indicators such as literacy, sex ratio, and female workforce participation. Women actively participate in the economic activity. *Jhum* cultivation and common property resources are the main sources of their livelihood. Majority of the population (80%) in the state are dependent on *jhum* cultivation. *Jhum* land provided equal opportunity to both men and women to work together and take joint decisions on crops and produces. But due to recent shift in the land policy, the state is encouraging people to get away from *jhum* and shift to settled cultivation. Commercial crops and non-farm activities are promoted over staple crops. It has been experienced that settled cultivation has negative implications on women. Women are gradually losing their access and control over land as most of the government programmes are land based and target male heads of the household.

Mizo society remained guided by the patriarchal value system. Though women play a significant role in agriculture, but until recently customary laws denied them inheritance rights and discriminated them at socio, economic, and legal spheres. Customary laws have restricted their participation in the political process. This has weakened their position. Gradually, women's groups realized the need for amendment in the customary laws. They pressurized the government to amend these laws and made them gender just. After years of struggle of women's groups, government has enacted two important laws namely the Mizo Marriage, Divorce and Inheritance of Property Act, 2014, and the Lushai Hills District (Village Council) Act, 2015. These Acts proved a landmark in the history of feminist movement in the state of Mizoram.

Besides, there are other problems also with which Mizo society is grappling; these are encroachment of community land, uneven distribution of land among individual households, and emergence of a neo-rich class within the egalitarian tribal society, land-alienation, land mortgage, and absentee landlordism. It is said that the piecemeal survey is the major cause of consolidation of land by few rich families.

RECOMMENDATIONS

- Patriarchal forces seem to be reluctant to accept the concept of women's equality in accessibility and ownership of land. There is a need to sensitize both men and women, and the patriarchal institutions towards the newly enacted laws, namely the Mizo Marriage, Divorce and Inheritance of Property Act, 2014, and the Lushai Hills District (Village Council) Act, 2015, and its positive impact.

- People in the villages are yet not aware of these two recently introduced Acts. There is a need to create awareness among men and women with special emphasis on the interiors of rural areas. This will enable women to exercise their rights at the time of need and curb their exploitation. It will strengthen their bargaining power also.
- The land reforms have yet to take-off in the state of Mizoram. There is a need for land-reform initiatives on an urgent basis—particularly the imposition of ceiling on land. The growing trend of land settlement on an individual basis has enabled few people to consolidate land in their favour. This has led to the emergence of an upper class within an egalitarian tribals society.
- Land- and agricultural-related programmes should take into account both men and women, and ensure that the benefits of development reach to them equally.
- The revenue department does not maintain sex-segregated data on land records. The scheme of National Land Records Modernization Programme is implemented in the state. The software can be revised which can include sex-segregated data on land records. It will help in devising gender-based policy in general and land-related policies in particular.
- The land allotment procedure is complicated and time consuming. There is a need to simplify the procedure so that women could also participate in the process, if they so desire.
- In Mizoram, the District Revenue Office in every district is located at the district headquarter. There is no revenue office at the block level or circle level. Besides, the process of land settlement is very difficult and cumbersome. This makes it difficult for people, particularly women, to visit these as distances are longer and transportation is a problem. A revenue office should be established at the circle level so that women could also visit conveniently.
- VC election has been held in 2015. Elected VC members both men and women need to be given proper training about their roles and responsibilities so that they can dispose of their duties in an effective manner.
- Land- and inheritance-related customary laws in the following three ADC areas, namely Lai, Mara, and Chakma, are gender discriminatory. These customary laws also need to be reviewed and amended after proper consultation.

ANNEXURE

Mizoram Hmeichhe Insuihkhawm Pawl

Mizoram *Hmeichhe Insuihkhawm Pawl* which means Mizoram Women's United Association is a voluntary organization. MHIP literally means binding women together. Its logo is *hmui*, a charkha which symbolizes Mizo women's creativity and sense of self-reliance, and *tlawmngaihna* which means philanthropy—a key characteristic of Mizo society. This was established in 1974 when Mizoram was a union territory. It was one of the largest and the strongest women's group in Mizoram. Its main aim is to ensure the welfare and upliftment of the marginalized people with special emphasis on women and children. Its headquarters is at Aizawl. Any woman from the age of 14 years or above can become the member of the MHIP with a membership fee of ₹2. The wife of a ruling chief minister is the ex-officio president of the organization.

Main activities organized by MHIP are to fight against atrocities on women, provide shelter for the destitute, arrange family counselling, impart leadership training, and provide a platform for social interaction. This organization works at the grass-roots level and mobilizes women about their rights and also raises human rights issues. One of the major challenges before the organization was how to convince people to change traditional system, customs, and mindset that suppress women, both within the family and in society (Ministry of Communication and Information Technology 2015). Mizoram since the beginning has remained a land of struggle. Women also remained a part of the struggle. Pi Sangkhumi has penned the history of the Mizo women's movement, titled 'MHPP Chanchin 1974–2009'.

NOTES

1. *Mautam* is a Mizo term. *Mautam* means death of bamboo (*mau* means bamboo and *tam* means death). It is a strange ecological phenomenon that occurs in cycles of 50 years, causing famine and immense hardship to Mizos who were earlier totally dependent on agriculture. Melocanna Baccifera, locally known as *Mautak*, comprises over 90% of the bamboo population in Mizoram. It flowers during *mautam*, triggering an increase in the rat

population, and this leads to massive destruction of crops and often results in famine.
2. *Mizo Hnam Dan* (Mizo Customary Law) is published by Law and Judicial Department, Aizawl, Government of Mizoram, 1st Edition 2006. It was first notified in the Mizoram Gazette Extra Ordinary No. Vol. XXXIV, Aizawl Wednesday 6.4.2005 Chitra 16, S.E. 1927, Issue No. 66.

REFERENCES

Baruah, S. 1999. *India against Itself: Assam and the Politics of Nationality*. New Delhi: Oxford University Press.
Census of India. 2011. New Delhi: Office of the Registrar General.
Census of Mizoram. 2011. Aizawl: Directorate of Census Operations.
Das, J. N. 1990. *A Study of the Land System of Mizoram*. Guwahati: Law Research Institute, Eastern Region, Gauhati High Court.
Directorate of Economics and Statistics. 2008. *Statistical Handbook*. Aizawl: Directorate of Economics and Statistics.
———. 2014. *Statistical Handbook*. Aizawl: Directorate of Economics and Statistics.
Directorate of Information & Public Relations. n.d. *Mizoram* 27–28.
Directorate of Land Revenue & Settlement. 2009. December, Government of Mizoram.
———. 2015, March. Aizawl, Government of Mizoram.
DNA Agency. 2014, April 29. 'Divorced Mizo Women Now Entitled to Inherit Property.' *DNA Agency*, Aizawl, PTI. Available at: http//www.dnaindia.com (accessed on 10 July 2015).
Dowerah, S. 2014, December 6. 'Mizoram's New Divorce Law Finally Gives its Women Some Hope.' Mizoram, Reuters. Available at: http//www.firstpost.com (accessed on 10 July 2015).
Govt of Mizoram. 2016. Mamit: Department of Local Administration.
Hanghal, N. 2014, June 18, 'Meet the Woman Who Has Been Leading Mizo Women's Push for Legal Reforms for 40 Years, Mizoram, Unsung Heroes.' Available at: http//www.betterindia.com (accessed on 10 July 2015).
House Sites Act. 1953. The Lushai Hills District (House Site) Act (Published in the Assam Gazette, dated 6th May, 1953).
Lalneihzovi. 2006. *District Administration in Mizoram—A Study of the Aizawl District*. Delhi: A Mittal Publication.
———. 2014. 'Political Empowerment of Women in Mizoram.' *Indian Journal of Public Administration* LX (3): 649–59.

Ministry of Communication and Information Technology. 2015. National Informatics Centre, Mizoram State Centre, Civil Secretariat, Aizawl. Available at: www.mizoram.nic.in (accessed on 6 June 2015).

'Officer Order.' Notification No. IJE 30/79/366, Aizawl.

Phelamei, S. 2012, October 17. 'Mizoram: Women's Issues, Development and Migrants'. *Z News*. Available at: http://zeenews.india.com/exclusive/mizoram-womens-issues-development-and-mig (accessed on 10 July 2015).

Prasad, R. N. 1998. *Public Administration in North–East India*. New Delhi: Vikas Publishing House.

Singh, P., S. Arora, and L. C. Singhi. 2012. *Evaluating Revenue Administration and Land Records: Their Strengthening and Updating in Mizoram*. Mussoorie: Centre for Rural Studies, Lal Bahadur Shastri National Academy of Administration.

The Mizoram Gazette, Extra Ordinary. 2014. The Mizo Marriage, Divorce and Inheritance of Property Act, 2014, Act No. 9 of 2014, XLIII, 570, Aizawl.

The *Lushai* Hills District (Village Councils) (Amendment) Act, 2014.

The Mizo District (Land & Revenue) Act, 1956.

The Mizo District (Agricultural Land) Act (1963) The Mizo District Council (received the assent of the Governor of Assam).

The Mizo District (Agricultural Land) Rules, 1971.

The Mizoram Gazette Extra Ordinary. 2014. December 17, Vol. XLIII, Aizawl.

11

Gender and Land Relations in Nagaland: Emerging Issues

C. SRIDHAR, SAROJ ARORA, AND KHUNENCHU MAGH

Nagaland is located in the extreme northeast of India. Nagaland is bordered by Assam in the north and west, Arunachal Pradesh in the east, and Manipur in the south. It shares an international boundary with Myanmar in the east. Nagaland is one of the eight states in the northeast region, the third smallest state in the country, and the first state to be carved out of Assam. It is one of the hill states having rugged mountains with only few expanses of plains in the western part of the adjoining plains of Assam. Like any other young mountain, the region has a fragile terrain and narrow valleys. It is not only a peripheral state in the context of the country but also the most remote at the regional level (Longkumer 2015). The state is predominantly inhabited by indigenous tribal communities, which constitute almost 90% of the population (Directorate of Information and Public Relations 2014). The term 'Naga' has been used to refer to the people living in the hilly region of the Indo–Burma (Myanmar) border between the valleys of Brahmaputra and Chindwin (Sreedhar 1979: 103–13). Ethnically, Nagas belong to the Indo-Mongoloid group. The state has many tribes and sub-tribes. As per the 1963 electoral list, there were 17 major tribes in Nagaland, namely, Ao, Angami, Chakhesang, Chang, Dimasa Kachari, Khiamnuingam, Konyak, Kuki, Lotha, Phom, Pochury, Rengma, Sangtam, Sema, Yimchunger, Zeliang, and Rongmies. It is to be noted that Dimasa Kachari and Rongmies, whose descendants' names have been included in the 1963 electoral role, are recognized tribes of Nagaland. Konyaks are the largest in number. Each major tribe has its own distinct features and is different in terms of its identity, culture, language, custom, traditions, and dress. Among all the Naga tribes, Aos, Angami, Lotha, and Sema, hold dominant positions in administration and education. With the advent of Christianity, missionaries first started spreading education among these communities and later on shifted to other parts of Naga Hills. Each tribe is concentrated in one or more districts, and this makes each district distinct in its sociopolitical, traditional, cultural, and linguistic characteristics. For instance, Angamis are dominant in Kohima and Dimapur. Aos are larger in number in Mokokchung district and Semas are concentrated in the Zunheboto, Dimapur, and fringes of Tuensang and Kiphire districts. Similarly, Lothas are in Wokha, Chakhesang and Pochury in Phek, Sangtam in Kiphire, Rengma in the Tseminyu subdivision of Kohima district, and Khiamniungan, Yimchunger, and Chang tribal communities are concentrated in Tuensang district. Rongmeis are located mainly in Peren. Phoms in Longleng and Zeliang are concentrated in the Peren district. Linguistically, Nagas are closer to the Tibeto-Burman family of languages. There are almost 16 major dialects spoken here. These dialects vary not only from one tribe to another but also from one hill range to another and sometimes even from one village to another village, though they are within the same tribe. Thus, each tribe has one or more dialects. Some sub-tribes also have their own dialects. In Mon district, Konyak is the main dialect. In Kohima, Angami and Rengma are the main dialects, in Wokha, Lotha dialect, and in Dimapur, almost all dialects are spoken. Ao is spoken in Mokokchung; Zeliang in Peren district; Chang, Yimchungru, and Khiamniungan in Tuensang district; Sema dialect in Zunheboto district; Chakhesang and Pochury dialects in Phek district; Phom dialect in Longleng district and Sangtam is spoken in Kiphire. Nagamese is the common lingua franca. Nagamese is an admixture of Bengali, Assamese, and Hindi languages. English is the official language of Nagaland. The state is also inhabited by a large number of non-tribal communities.

As per Census 2011, 87.93% population of the state was Christian. Among Christians, Baptists constituted more than 75% of the population. The remaining population of the state was of Hindu, Islam, Buddhism, Jainism, Sikhism and Naga folk, and other religions. In the 19th century when Christian missionaries[1] arrived, they transformed the Naga society and converted them from animism to Christianity, in particular the

Baptist faith. Individualism started to be chosen over communitarianism, monogamy was promoted over polygamy. The first Baptist Church was established in the Molungkimong village in the Mokokchung district in 1872 among the Ao tribe where missionaries started educating people. The Aos were some of the earliest converts among the Naga tribes. Today, Aos are almost 100% Christians, the majority being Baptists. It is to be noted that despite the impact of Christianity on the traditionally held religious values, even today Nagas respect and observe the customary practices in various spheres of their lives. A small group of Naga tribes continues to practise animism.

SOCIO-DEMOGRAPHIC PROFILE OF NAGALAND

The total population of Nagaland was 1,980,602 of which males constituted 1,025,707 (51.79%) and females constituted 954,895 (48.21%) (Government of India 2011). Of all the 11 districts in the state, Dimapur was the most populous with a total population of 379,769 (19.17%) and the least populated district was Longleng with 50,593 people (2.55%). Konyak Nagas were in the largest number, approximately 3.5 lakh. Ao would be around 2 lakh. The literacy rate was 79.55%, the male literacy rate was 82.75%, and the female literacy rate was 76.11%. In urban areas, the literacy rate was 89.6% and in the rural areas, it was 75.3% (Census 2011). Mokokchung had the highest literacy rate (91.62%), whereas Mon had the lowest literacy rate (56.99%) (Census 2011). The literacy rate in some of the villages in the Mon district was even lower than 20%. Districts such as Dimapur, Kohima Mokokchung, Wokha, and Zunheboto have higher literacy rates in comparison to districts like Kiphire, Longleng, Mon, Peren, Phek, and Tuensang. Thus, the literacy rate was uneven within the state. The percentage of literate females in Nagaland was considerably higher than the national average. *Nagaland is one of the most literate states in the country* (Banerjee 1996: 8). The spread of education may be attributed to the Christian missionaries. The sex ratio at 931 female to 1,000 males has been lower than the national average of 933. Zunheboto and Wokha have the highest sex ratio, that is, 976 and 968, respectively. Mon and Longleng have the lowest sex ratio, that is, 899 and 905, respectively (Directorate of Information and Public Relations 2014).

Nagaland consists of 11 administrative districts namely, Dimpapur, Kiphire, Kohima, Longleng Mokokchung, Mon, Peren, Phek, Tuensang, Wokha, and Zunheboto. With increasing urbanization, education, and work opportunities, Kohima has now become home to multiethnic groups and also to several non-residents. The second most urbanized and relatively developed district is Dimapur. 'Di' means river, 'ma' means great or big and 'pur' means city. Thus, Dimapur literally means 'the city near the great river'. Dhansiri and Chathe are the two main rivers in this district. It is the commercial hub of the state and called the gateway of Nagaland. Chumukedima, situated about 14 km from Dimapur, served as the first headquarter of the Naga Hills district of the Assam state during the British Rule. Dimapur is the ancient capital of the king of Kachari, who ruled before the 13th century AD. Garo and Kachari tribes also exist in good numbers. Trading communities such as Jains and Marwaris have been living in the town area for the last many decades. Mon district is the home of the Konyak Nagas. Konyaks are adept artisans and skilled craftsmen. Mon is rich in terms of minerals and coal deposits.

Nagas' identity in a village and traditional institutions such as *khel*, clan customary laws, and land are interrelated. The Naga ethnicity was built up through a series of events. Before discussing the land system, customary laws, and gender and land relations, it would be appropriate to snap shot the social history of the evolution of Nagaland as this will enable readers to understand the situations which paved way for the creation of the present-day Nagaland.

SOCIAL HISTORY OF NAGALAND

Nagaland has no written history; therefore, not much is known about the origin of Naga tribes. Every tribe has its own myths of origin. During the 19th century, when the British annexed Assam, of which the Naga Hills were a part, some British officials brought out an ethnographic account of Naga tribes. The following paragraphs deal with the social history of Nagaland.

In 1228, Ahoms entered Assam and ruled for almost 600 years (Sema 2011: 24–33). Except having cultural contacts with Ahoms,[2] Nagas had little or no contact with the outside world including that of greater India until British colonization. One of the reasons for the lack of contact was the geographical isolation of the region. It is said that Nagas had amicable relations with the Ahom. To maintain Nagas' identity and autonomy, the Ahom king demarcated boundaries between the Assam and Naga Hills areas. In 1816, when Burma invaded Assam including Naga Hills, instability was created in the region. In 1826, when the British annexed Assam, they found Nagas' culture different and their geographical location difficult to access. Nagas resisted British's attempt to occupy their territory. Due to continuous resistance, the British could annex only a part of Kohima with great difficulty, and failed to annex the Eastern part of the Naga Hills. Due to constant struggle, resistance, and raids by Nagas, British decided not to interfere in the Naga way of life (Longkumer 2015). To control Naga resistance, British employed some local Nagas as *Gaon Bura* to manage inter-village feuds, maintain harmony, and collect revenue. The years 1832–33 brought a jolt for Nagas when Ghambir Singh, the then king of the princely state of Manipur, joined hands with the British and tried to expand his territory by including Naga Hills in his kingdom (Alemchiba 1970: 42). During 1851, the third Battle of Khonoma created ground for the British domination over the region. In 1866, the Naga Hills District was formed as part of Assam with Chumukedima as the headquarters. The British promulgated Inner Line Regulation, 1873, to protect Nagas from exploitation from outsiders and traders, and restricted their entry (Pillai 1999). In 1878, the British established the Kohima town and made it the main administrative centre with a sub-centre at Wokha and shifted their headquarters from Chumukedima to Kohima. It is said that before British annexation, the Nagas never were under any administration. The year 1881 was considered as the beginning of an administration of the 'un-administered' Naga Hills region. However, Nagas continued their struggle to preserve their identity and autonomy of the region. Initially, they organized themselves by forming a Naga Club in 1918. Later on, the Naga Club was transformed as a political association and negotiated with the union government. Later on, the Naga Club got merged with other associations, split at different points of time, reformulated, and renamed such as NNF and Naga National Council (NNC), and ceasefire continued with the union government. In the meantime, many laws were introduced to govern the region. For instance, the Government of India Act, 1919, which first declared the hill areas as a 'backward area' and then the Government of India Act, 1935, which declared certain areas as 'excluded' and 'partially excluded' areas. The Naga Hills were declared as an 'excluded area' (Singh 2012). This Act kept the Naga Hills region outside the purview of the provincial administration and brought them directly under the governor of Assam. At the time of India's independence, the Naga Hills were a district in the state of Assam. Nagas wanted to separate the Naga Hills region from Assam. The Government of Assam, responsible to the central government, administered the North East Frontier Agency (NEFA). National People's Convention (NPC) was formed in 1957 to negotiate settlement for peace with the Government of India. In 1957, the NPC proposed the formation of a separate administrative unit by merging the Tuensang Frontier Division of NEFA (the present Arunachal Pradesh) with the Naga Hills district of Assam. The Government of India accepted the proposal; in the same year, the union government took over the administration of the Naga Hills district of Assam and the Tuensang division of NEFA, merging them in a single political entity, and made a UT called 'Naga Hills–Tuensang Area (NHTA)' (Guha and Bareh 1970). In 1961, the area was renamed as Nagaland. Later on, it was proposed that Nagas should accept statehood within the Indian Union. An important provision the union government agreed to for statehood was 'the customary laws would hold precedence in the settlement of disputes in Nagaland'. This provision was incorporated in the Constitution of India under Article 371A in 1962. Special provisions were made for Nagas to protect their religious practices, customary laws, land administration, traditional institutions, and the economic interest (Bag 2001). With the enactment of the Constitution (13th Amendment) Act, 1962, the Naga Hills District was separated from Assam and declared as 16th state of the Indian Union on 1 December 1963. However, insurgency continued even after statehood to fulfil the unfulfilled aspirations of Nagas. The negotiation process initiated by the Nagaland Baptist Church Council resulted in a ceasefire in 1964 (Gait 1926: 366) but again broke down in 1966. Although the ceasefire could restore peace for some time, sporadic encounters between the NNC and Indian Army continued. However, the church continued with its peace efforts and in 1972 formed the Nagaland Peace Council (NPC). By 11 November 1975, a faction of the NNC living within Nagaland signed a peace treaty known as the Shillong Accord with the union government (Longkumer 2015). Subsequently in 1980, the National Socialist Council of Nagaland (NSCN) was formed. Insurgency resumed in the 1980s. The negotiation process continued between the National Socialist Council of Nagaland (Isak-Muivah) and the Government of India. The NSCN group split into NSCN (IM) and NSCN (K) on 30 April 1988. On 25 July 1997, the Government of India announced a ceasefire with the NSCN (IM) with effect from 1 August 1997 which was extended further. On 1 August 1997, the NSCN split. In

April 2001, the Government of India extended the ceasefire agreement to the National Socialist Council of Nagaland–Khaplang (NSCN [K]). Under these ceasefire agreements, the Government and the civil society came closer for a dialogue aimed at socio-economic development of the region. People of Nagaland wanted to have permanent peace and stability in the region (Govt. of Nagaland State Human Development Report 2004). In 2015, the term of ceasefire extended again.

OBJECTIVES OF THE STUDY

The present study focuses on the existing land system in general and relationship of women with land in particular. An attempt has been made to review the land inheritance pattern among some of the Naga tribes. The study also reveals the extent of women's participation in village-level institutions such as village council and village development boards (VDBs).

Basically, Nagas are distributed in the four states of Northeast India, namely Assam, Arunachal Pradesh, Nagaland, and Manipur. The largest Naga population is found in Nagaland so only Nagas of Nagaland were included in the sampling framework. Three districts namely, Dimapur, Kohima (advanced districts), and Mon (backward district) were included in the sample universe. For the field study, Khonoma village in block Sechuzubza in the Kohima district, which is considered as the biggest tribal village in Asia, and Longwa village located at the international border of Myanmar in Mon district were visited. Members of the village council, various retired and in-service revenue, administration, and survey officials, and members of *Hoho* organizations were interviewed. The focus group discussion (FGD) method was used for collecting information.

NAGA VILLAGE: AN IMPORTANT UNIT OF ADMINISTRATION

Village is an important unit of administration in Nagaland. Every Naga village ranges from democratic to hereditary chieftainship. Naga village is an independent body, so often it is referred as a 'Village State'. Each

Naga village is a self-contained unit having cultivable lands, forests, water sources, and a chief along with a council to protect the residents from outsiders (Rizvi and Roy 2006). A brief on village administration before statehood and its role in land administration, structure, and functions of village council after statehood is discussed below.

Before the annexation of Naga Hills areas by the British, traditionally Naga villages functioned as independent village states which were self-governing and self-reliant, situated in contiguous geographical areas governed by a traditional village chief along with council members (ibid.: 36). Each of the Naga tribes, numbering more than 60, had their own specific territory and jurisdiction divided into independent villages loosely bound together by a set of customary laws, traditional institutions, and governance structure (Luithui 2010). Their main functions were to look after the safety of the villagers, maintain law and order, and safeguard the village boundary. The rich, the brave, the robust, and the wise used to command the village authority.

VILLAGE ADMINISTRATION BY ELECTED VILLAGE COUNCIL

After 1978, the village administration system changed. Villages were governed by village council and its members. Notably, villages in Mon district and few villages in Zunheboto continued with their traditional chieftainship along with the elected village council. Villages remained an independent socio-economic, political, and administrative unit. However, to codify and bring a uniform law for the village administration, the state passed the Nagaland Village and Area Council Act, 1978, as amended in 1990. Village as a semi-formal institution was set up under this Act. Village councils were established in every recognized village. According to this Act, 'Village Council shall consist of members, chosen by villagers in accordance with the prevailing customary practice and usages'. This provision of the Act allows the village council to practise its specified customary laws in the village administration. The village council was given administrative powers and duties at the local village level. This Act extends to the whole of the state of Nagaland (Nagaland Village and Area Council Act 1978: 61–67). In the present village council system, the village council office bearers generally consist of elected members such as the chairman, secretary, and *Gaon Buras*. While the village council chairman is to be chosen from among the members, the secretary can be a non-member with no voting rights. Members of village council are chosen by villagers in accordance with the prevailing customary practices and usages. Chairman of the village council is elected by members of the village council. Each *khel* nominates its representative unanimously for the village council. The term of village council is 5 years. The Khonoma village council was visited during field visit. This village council constitutes 21 members. The village has three *khels*: 7 members representing each *khel*. All village council members were male. Women were often not allowed to attend the council deliberations. In Nagaland, there were a total of 1,240 recognized villages. Dimapur has the largest number of villages, that is, 206, and Longleng district has the lowest, that is, 38 (Government of Nagaland 2015). There is no provision of reservation of seats for women in village council vis-à-vis municipal council. During village council meetings, the role of women was marginal. In the whole of Nagaland, only one woman, namely, Mrs Tokheli Kikon from Naharbari in Dimapur, was elected for the first time as the chairperson of the village council in the year 2005–10. She was again elected in her second and third consecutive terms, that is, 2010–15 and 2016–21.

VILLAGE ADMINISTRATION BY TRADITIONAL CHIEFTAINSHIP

Konyak Nagas continued with their traditional village chieftainship. The institution of *Anghship* was prevalent only among the Konyak Naga. *Angh* was not only the village chief but also the priest of the community. Some of the important features of *Anghship* were that it was hereditary, the *Angh* practised polygamy and only a male member inherited *Anghship*. After the introduction of the elected village council system, *Angh's* role has been reduced and restricted to only social welfare activities. He is invited to inaugurate traditional festivals and to attend religious ceremonies or some important events. However, even now *Angh* commands more respect. Longwa was among the biggest village in the district. The jurisdiction of *Angh* extends up to Myanmar and Arunachal Pradesh. Notably, one half of the *Angh's* house falls within the Indian Territory and the other half lies in Myanmar. Longwa village is administered by the *Angh* as well as the village council.

Among Sumi Nagas, villages are ruled by the hereditary chief called *Awunga* and *Akukau*. He is usually the unanimous choice of the head of the clans residing in the village (Shimray 2007: 42). In the traditional political system like the Sumis, the chief (*Akukau*) occupies a unique position in the village. He is the guardian of law and the owner of the village.

LAND SYSTEM AND CUSTOMARY LAWS

The land system in Nagaland is entirely different from other states in the country. Customary laws govern almost every aspect of the Naga life including the land system, which includes common village land, *khel* land, clan land, individual land, marriage, divorce, adoption, inheritance, succession, debt, theft, murder, etc. (Sema 2011: 24–33). A large tract of land in the state is the community land. It is very important for the Nagas to have land whether it is ancestral or acquired. In the absence of land, an individual or a family will not be considered as original inhabitants of the Naga village. Land is intrinsic not only for survival but also as the basis of their identity. Community land holds greater value than the individual land. Alienation of community land whether ancestral or individual brings down the social esteem of a community, clan/family, or the individual concerned (Longkumer and Jamir 2012). Naga values land more than lives (Jamir 2014: 121–33). Apart from the sociocultural significance, land yields economic and political power as well. It is the sociocultural significance of land which legitimizes the Nagas' traditional authority over the land (Aier 2008).

Nagas consider customary laws as intrinsic to their identity and an integral part of their tradition and culture. Nagaland is a multidialectal tribal state; therefore, customary laws are multifarious as well. There is no identical set of customs and each tribe has a distinct and different set of customary practices. Realizing the importance of customary laws, cognizance was taken of the existence of unwritten customary laws when the British brought the Naga people under their administration through the District Scheduled Act of 1874. The Bengal Eastern Frontier Regulation 3 of 1873 which gives power to prescribe and alter inner line and commonly known as 'Inner Line Permit' was made applicable in Nagaland also. This Act prohibited outsiders from entering the Naga Hills or acquiring land or the product of land without the permission of the government or authorized agency (MoDNER n.d.). Thus, the British separated the Naga

Hills areas from the rest of the Indian subcontinent. The Naga Hills areas were declared as an 'Excluded Area' in 1935 (Alemchiba 1970).

The Constitution of India was amended in 1963 and Article 371A was introduced to bring civil affairs in Nagaland under the tribal customary laws. The state has been given special status and autonomy including Nagas's customary laws and their land. The land in Nagaland belongs to the people, which means buying and selling cannot be done without the consent of the people/village authority. At the village level, land is administered by the village council. The government has no right over this land. As per estimation, almost 98% of the land in the state is under people's ownership. The remaining 2% of the land is government land (Sema 2014). Thus, Article 371A safeguards tribal laws, traditional institutions, and practices of the Nagas, and has taken away the authority of the government on land administration. The article states that notwithstanding anything in this constitution, no Act of parliament in respect of (a) religious or social practices of the Nagas; (b) Naga customary law; (c) administration of civil and criminal justice; and (d) ownership of land and its resources shall apply to the state of Nagaland unless the legislative assembly by a resolution so decides. Due to this reason, the state does not have many comprehensive land laws as its civil affairs including land are run according to unwritten customary laws.

To regulate *jhum* land, there is Nagaland Jhum Land Act, 1970. Similarly, Assam Land Revenue Act, 1886, was applicable on revenue land. This Act was enforced during the British Rule. Later on, it was amended and renamed as the Nagaland Land and Revenue Regulation (Amendment) Act 2002 (Act No. I of 2002). Section 162 of the Assam LRR 1886 was amended. In the amended Act, a provision was made that

> [N]othing contained in the rules made there under shall effect any transfer by way of a mortgage in favour of any nationalized banks, cooperative society registered under the Assam Co-operative Societies Act, 1949, or such financing institution as may be approved by the State Government provided further that such nationalized banks, cooperative societies or other financing institution shall not transfer any land to a person other than indigenous inhabitants of Nagaland except with the previous sanction of the State Government or an authority on this behalf.

This Act extends to the whole of Nagaland. Other land-related Acts are: The Nagaland (Ownership and Transfer of Land and its Resources) Act, 1990, and the Nagaland Land (Requisition and Acquisition) First Amendment Act, 1969. No revenue is charged on the cultivable agricultural land. Income through land revenue is minimal. Presently, ₹20 is charged as house tax from every household. Besides this, each household has to pay ₹208 annually as a professional tax. To maintain harmonious relations with Nagas, the British appointed local people as revenue functionaries and officially designated them as *Dubhashi* and *Gaon Bura*. The legacy of the institution of *Dubhashi* and *Gaon Bura* continues in the present-day Nagaland. *Dubhashis* and *Gaon Bura* play an important role in land management. The term *Dubhashi* means bilingual which means a person who can speak two languages. *Du* in local dialect means two and *bhasi* means language. *Dubhashi* deals with the customary laws related to land, marriage, divorce, and inheritance, solves land dispute, and demarcates village boundary. The *Dubhashi* Court has both original and appellate jurisdiction with respect to cases of customary law. *Gaon Bura* is a non-government functionary who collects tax for the Revenue Department. The members of each *khel* select one *Gaon Bura*. The *Gaon Bura* is part of village administration and works on a voluntary basis. It is important to mention that since the beginning, the *institutions* of *Dubhashis and Gaon Bura* remained male dominated. No woman has ever been nominated to these positions.

The total geographical area of the state is 16,579 sq. km out of which 8.48% is plain and the rest of the area is constituted by undulating and hilly land (Government of Nagaland 2013–14). Only in Dimapur district, 70% area is plain and 30% area is hill. The British conducted a cadastral survey in Dimapur and Kohima towns which were brought under the Assam Settlement Act, 1886, before it was declared a tribal area. Out of the total geographical area, 47.43 sq. km has been cadastral surveyed in Dimapur district (15.78 sq. km in town area and 31.65 sq. km in rural areas covering 19 revenue villages). Parts of Kohima town covering 5.71 sq. km have been cadastral surveyed. Thus, only a miniscule area, that is, 0.32% has been covered by the survey. When the British started survey, Nagas grew suspicious that the British were trying to bring them under their tax system by depriving them of their autonomy. They resisted and the British were forced to stop the survey. Later on, the survey was conducted in the administrative headquarters of the remaining districts. Vast stretches of land are still unsurveyed and no land records are maintained (Government of Nagaland Directorate of Land Records & Settlement, Dimapur 2015). However, all types of land in Naga villages are well-defined and demarcated by natural boundaries such as stream, river, trees, and plantation. In the absence of natural boundaries, demarcation is made by stones. These already established boundaries are respected by the villagers and usually not changed as Nagas strongly believe that manipulating with the boundary line for undue gain will bring miseries for them or for their family members. Since land is dealt by the customary laws, the deputy commissioner has a limited role in land administration. The deputy commissioner basically deals with issuance of affidavit, allotment of land, gifting deeds, eviction from encroached land, land registration, mutation, inheritance, land acquisition, land dispute, etc.

LANDOWNERSHIP PATTERNS AND WOMEN

In Nagaland, according to Census 2011, 71.14% population lives in the rural areas. The origin of the pattern of landholding and ownership system may be traced back to the establishment of a village. Within the Naga society, the landownership pattern varies from village to village and also from one tribal community to another. For instance, in lower Angami villages, three-fourths of the total geographical area of village land was common land, whereas in other villages, individual ownership of land was more prevalent. Among the Ao and the Lotha tribes, most of the land was owned either by clans or individuals (Ao 1999: 111). Among Chakhesangs, as per their tradition, the clan owns the land. 'Every individual in the community has his/her own property; they are basically a landowning tribe in which landlessness is not found (Singh 1994: 69)'. Agricultural land (including *jhum* field) is owned by individuals, families, or clans (Banerjee 1996: 5). As per an estimate, a majority of the Naga households (almost 99%) own land. Only 1% households may be landless. Reasons for landlessness could be (a) small parcel of land and many sons in the family and (b) as per customary law of many tribal communities, the eldest son inherits property but later on, he may turn hostile and not share with his other brothers. Usually, the landless households lease land either from the well-off families in the village or from those who have migrated to the town areas. Well-off households charge rent to ensure their stake in their land.

Notwithstanding the land system, by and large, has certain commonalities and differences across communities with the exception of Konyak and Sema communities. Broadly speaking, landownership in Nagaland can be classified into the following four categories.

1. **Community Land:** Some portion of the land is with every village as community land. Villagers absorb the land and acquire the 'right to use' the land without paying any revenue to the village authorities. Under the community landownership, the community members have the rights to use the land but they are not the sole owners of the cultivated land (Govt. of Nagaland, Human Development Report 2009). Community land is used for cultivation purposes only for a limited period of time which is around two to three years. The village elders and council keep a strict check over villagers and they fine offenders severely. Community land is further classified into four categories which are described as follows.

    a. **Common Village Land:** For the common purpose of the community, Common Village Land (CVL) is used by the villagers. Common land is available in each village. Almost 90% of the total village area, which contain thick forests, also comes under common village land. Besides this particular category of land, CVL includes the land for residential areas, educational institutes, play grounds, meeting hall for the village council, *morung*, monument, roads, church, graveyard, woodland, and other places which are used by the particular villagers for common purpose (Longkumer and Jamir 2012). Every household has the 'right to access' to this land. Permission of village council is necessary for using this land for construction purpose or extracting construction materials. Any income from this land is utilized for the welfare of the tribal community. Right to exploits the resources of the forest lies only with that particular village within which the land lies. Depending upon the availability of land and the number of households dependent on it, area covered under common village land varies from village to village and also from tribe to tribe. Since the common lands belong to the community, it can neither be mortgaged nor sold. Both men and women have access to the common village land.

    b. **Clan Land:** A clan is a group of members of families amongst whom intermarriages are not allowed. It is a single parental lineage in a village. Depending upon the size of the village, the number of clans varies. Each clan has certain land under its control within the village boundary. Clan land extends absolute ownership rights to specific clan members. The specific clan members are the custodian of the land allotted to them permanently. This land includes sites for house construction, cultivable lands (both *jhum* and terrace field), land for vegetable crops, forest land, meadows (Sema 2015), and also land for fodder and fuel wood. For construction of a house or agricultural purposes, every household of a clan is entitled to get a share of clan land. Only the eldest male member of the clan is nominated as the clan head and authorized to administer clan land. He allots clan land to the clan members as per the availability of clan land. The ownership of the land once allotted to a specific clan transfers from one generation to another. There is a restriction on selling the clan land without the consent of the clan or family. Women have access to clan land but traditionally, they neither own clan land nor are nominated as clan heads.

c. ***Khel* Land:** A Naga village is a composition of several *khels* which are also termed as *thino* locally. There are different clans within a *khel*. It is not only a residential division but it is also a collection of several exogamous kins. The number of clans in a particular *khel* varies from *khel* to *khel*. It is necessary for all the members to abide by the *khel* decisions since the *khel* is represented by several clans. Every *khel* represents one major clan, acting as the administrative and political body.

Khel land is meant for the member of a specific *khel*. Only the respective *khel* members have the right to use their *khel* land since it is a common property. It also cannot be mortgaged or sold by an individual or a group of individuals. The *khel* land is used for making assembly halls for the specific *khel m*embers, village gate, *jhum* land/terrace field, meadow, plantation, and ritual ground especially for *morungs*. Each *khel* has a *Gaon Bura*/male head of a *khel* who is the supreme authority in taking decisions on *khel* owned lands; women are never nominated as *khel* heads. To get land for cultivation, each needy household approaches the *khel* council. In a meeting, a council decides the allotment of land for each household. Over the years, there have been various changes in the structure and functions of *khel*. For instance, recently, the *khels* have been transformed into *khel* unions which are represented by clan members. One of the important responsibilities of the *khel* union is to manage the *khel* land (Khonoma Tourism Development Board 2009).

Both men and women of respective *khels* have access to *khel* land but women do not own the *khel* land nor are nominated as *khel* heads.

d. **Lineage Land:** Nagas maintain different branches of family lineage and kin group within the same clan. Residential plot, *jhum* land, or forest areas are included in the lineage land. It is the eldest male member of the family who controls and takes decision about the usage of land if the land is owned by a family. The head of the lineage, who is the senior male member, has the freedom to use the parcel of land as he finds appropriate but he is not authorized to transfer lineage land outside the village jurisdiction. Women are not allowed to become lineage heads.

2. **Individual Land:** Every Naga family has some plot of land owned individually irrespective of the tribal group (Longkumer and Jamir 2012). Through inheritance or purchase, a person can own individual land. The homestead land, the terrace paddy fields, farmlands, plantation, and granary are included in individual land. In Nagaland, rivers, quarries, and hillocks also belong to individuals. They can be either family owned or individual owned. If the land is used for purposes other than that for which it was allotted, the village authority punishes that individual/family. The ultimate and the absolute power over land whether it is owned by an individual, clan, or community lies with the village authority.

If the land is owned on individual basis, then within the village boundary it is transferable (through sale or gift) from one individual to another individual or form one clan to another but it cannot be transferred outside the village boundary. In the Naga society, individually owned land is transferable but inherited/ancestral land is not transferable. Self-acquired property can be transferred through a 'will' of the owner or it can be sold after consulting with family members and clan members only in unavoidable circumstances. They can also find out a solution whether any of them can buy land, so that the land could be retained within the agnatic and kindred group. Land cannot be sold outside one's own tribe or community in any case. These rules are followed because the village boundaries are demarcated by the ancestors and it is an offense to sell the property outside the boundary; the offender is punished by the village council (Sema 2014). Individual land is owned by the male head of the household and has absolute rights over land as per customary laws and women are not entitled to own land on an individual basis.

3. **Government Land:** The land which was transferred by the British to the state before they left or purchased from people by the state for the development projects or donated by the villagers for a common cause is known as government land (ibid.). Land records are maintained for the government land. In Nagaland, a large number of army offices have been established for security purposes, therefore, out of the total area under government land, a major chunk is with the Army cantonment. The remaining government land belongs to office buildings, government quarters, government guest houses, and government projects. The rest of the land, other than government land is owned either on an individual basis or collectively by the community and no land records are maintained for that. Unlike most states of India, the land in Nagaland belongs to the people and not the government. The government owns only about 2% of the land, the rest is held by the villagers either individually or collectively which cannot be taken away by the government without the consent of the whole village (ibid.).

4. **Land Lease:** As we know Nagaland is located on the international border and the area has remained disturbed for the last several decades. In order to safeguard the borders and to counter insurgency, the union government has established several defence units in the state. Since land belongs to the people, a large tract of land was purchased, acquired, or leased for defence purposes. Three types of land lease are practised in the state namely, (a) land lease for establishing defence units; (b) land lease for the private companies for a period of 55 years and the maximum lease period was for 99 years; and (c) leasing of cultivable land by the farmers or landless households. The third category of land lease takes place on an individual basis. During field visit, it was found that at household level, sometime, few Naga families particularly those engaged in terrace cultivation have leased their land. As per the lease agreement, one-third of the produce is taken as rent by the landowner. Usually, a basket full of paddy is given to the

landowner. In Kohima village, there would be around 500 households out of which one-third were engaged in self-cultivation and the remaining two-thirds have migrated outside the village. Many of these out-migrant families have leased their land.

Although both men and women work on leased land, dealing is done by male members of the household.

LAND SYSTEM AMONG KONYAK NAGAS

Among the Konyaks, *Angh* owned the land within the jurisdiction of their kingdom or the village. The Konyaks consider land as the most valuable property and the most important source of livelihood. Therefore, there is a restriction of selling of land without the consent of the family/clan. A brief on landownership system among Konyak is as follows:

In general the Chief *Angh* owns the land within the jurisdiction of the village. *Morung/Khel* or clan also owns a certain part of forest land called '*Wan*' within which the number of individually owned plots may also exist. Every individual owns a land in the village. Usually *Anghs* have large landholding. The *khel* and clan land are owned by the community, whereas individual landowners are the actual owners of land, which are transferable from one individual to another individual. Community land is transferable only through inheritance. All types of land are well-defined and demarcated by the natural boundaries such as streams or river or stone wherever there is no natural boundary. The Konyak custom prohibits manipulation of the ancestral boundaries of the land be it artificial or natural. Anybody who manipulates such boundaries invites punishment (Konyak 2005).

LAND USE PATTERN IN NAGALAND

Due to undulating hills area and rugged mountains, the land use pattern in Nagaland is quite different. Almost 90% of the people are engaged in agriculture. Both *jhum* and terrace cultivation depending upon the topography of the area are the most prominent forms of cultivation. The land use pattern in Nagaland is described below:

1. ***Jhum* Land:** *Jhum* (shifting) cultivation covers over 80% of the total arable area of the state (NEPED and IRRR 1999: 17). It is practised in almost all the districts although the area under *jhum* varies from one district to another. For instance, Tuensang, Kohima, and Mokokchung districts have the largest area under *jhum*, whereas Phek and Dimapur have the lowest area under *jhum* (Government of Nagaland 2001). Due to growing commercialization, urbanization, and cultivation of cash crops land under *jhum* in Dimapur district has declined to a great extent. In Mon district, *jhum* is the predominant mode of agriculture. In 2001, the total area under *jhum* cultivation in Mon was more than 75,000 hectares (Govt. of Nagaland, Human Development Report 2009).

   As per the Nagaland Jhum Land Act, 1970, *jhumland* means such land which any member or members of a village or a community has a customary right to cultivate by means of shifting cultivation or to utilize by clearing *jungle* or for grazing livestock and includes any beds of rivers provided that such village or community is in a permanent location. Some of the important features of *jhumland* are that no *jhumland* to which a community has a customary right shall be transferred by sale or mortgage to any community or to any individual except on the authority of the deputy commissioner given on the recommendation of the village and area council concerned (Government of Nagaland 1995a: 22–25). No *jhumland* can be leased by anyone having a customary right thereto unless: (a) The deputy commissioner/additional deputy commissioner has approved on the recommendation of the village and area council concerned of such lease on the ground that such lease benefits the village or the community; or (b) the lessor is by reason of age or infirmity, unable to cultivate or utilize it and the lessee is a member of the same village or community as the lessor (Government of Nagaland 1995, ibid.). The village authority based on mutual consensus decides which forest area to be cleared for *jhum* cultivation for a particular year to maintain the *jhum* cycle and productivity of the land.

   The *jhum* cultivation is a community affair even though individual plots are cultivated separately. *Jhum* cultivation is based on the principle of equality and provides opportunity to both men and women to work together. It extends access to land to women whether they are married, widow, or unmarried. Although most of the activities involved in *jhum* are carried out by the family labour including both men and women, yet certain activities are gender specific. For instance, men slash the forests, burn the *jhum* fields, clear the pathways leading to the new *jhum* fields, including construction of huts and transportation of fuel wood. Women are engaged in seed selection, sowing, weeding, transplantation, plucking, and harvesting. In case, there are no male members in the family, community members come forward to help such women in cultivation. In recent years, the *jhum* cycle has been reduced to 8 years and below due to population pressure, resulting in lower productivity (Huq 2002). Earlier Nagas used to practise *jhum* cultivation in an extensive manner. But nowadays, the government is encouraging people to go for cash crops cultivation.

2. **Terrace Cultivation:** In Nagaland, terrace cultivation is the second most practiced form of cultivation. A river or stream is the main source of irrigation. Large numbers of paddy varieties are planted in the terrace fields. Usually, one crop is cultivated in a year. Cultivation is done on the same plot every year. Terrace cultivation is done widely in Dimapur, Kohima, and Phek districts, whereas Mon and Wokha have less area under terrace cultivation. In Kohima district, mostly Angami and Chakhesang tribes are engaged in terrace (Nshoga 2009). Both *jhum* and the terrace cultivation are practised. In 2001, the area under terrace and wet rice cultivation together accounted for 1,251 hectares. Every household owns on an average 3–4 *liecha* (acre) of cultivable terrace land. *Liecha* is a local unit of measurement and one *liecha* is equal to one acre. Since terraces are on a hilly terrain, there cannot be a standard measurement for the plot size. However, most families reckon on a yield of 27–30 *tinhas* about 300 kg of unhusked paddy crop from an average sized plot (KTDB 2009: 47). Both men and women work together in terrace fields.

AREA UNDER HORTICULTURE CROPS

People are being encouraged to cultivate cash crops including horticultural crops. Dimapur, Mokokchung, and Kohima districts have maximum area under the horticultural crops. These are the districts which are relatively developed and well-connected with the market and roads. Mon and Zunheboto have minimum area under horticultural crops (Government of Nagaland 2001).

RELATIONSHIP OF WOMEN WITH AGRICULTURAL LAND AND COMMON PROPERTY RESOURCES

Naga women constitute about 48.0% of the total population (Government of India 2011). Being predominantly a rural society and having difficult geographical terrain, most of the population is heavily dependent on agriculture, farm-based activities, poultry, piggery, forestry, and natural resources for livelihood purposes. In Mon district, more than 90% population is dependent on agriculture. Both men and women participate equally in these economic activities. Both work in traditional agricultural system such as *jhum* and terrace, and cultivate crops such as paddy, maize, millets, pulse, sugarcane, oilseeds, tobacco, vegetable crops (potatoes, chillies, and tomato), and horticultural crops (cucurbits and yam) and fibres to meet everyday household needs and to generate additional income if there is surplus production. Women conserve seeds and use them for the next cropping season and do not use fertilizers (KTDB 2009: 80). It is found that women's contribution was more than 75% of the labour force in agriculture (NEPED 2006: 14). They play a crucial role in various stages of agriculture whether it is related to the selection of seeds and crops or quantity of seeds to be sown. Women's role in *jhum* cultivation is so significant that *jhum* has often been termed as 'primarily a female farming activity' (Banerjee 1996: 4). Apart from cultivation, Naga women visit forests to collect edible plants, fodder, fuel wood, manure, wood produce, medicinal herbs, fruits, and water. Women process, store and use these items for family members. Women are also involved in handicrafts for adding to the household income as well as to meet their household needs. Thus, Naga women are vital to the agricultural economy and contribute significantly to the household income. Their productive role in agriculture makes land basic to their lives. Natural resources are an integral part of Naga communities and women are the main conservers of the CPRs and in maintaining biodiversity. Naga women have the knowledge of identifying various types of plants, other biomass products, and their applications. They are the custodians of indigenous knowledge and know how to use natural resources in a sustainable manner. But despite women's significant contribution in the agriculture sector, they neither own land nor have any entitlements in ancestral property (NEPED and IRRR 1999: 166). It is men who own communal, clan, or individual land through their socio-economic and political dominance in the traditional institutions such as clan councils, *khel* unions, or village councils/municipal councils.

CHANGE IN LAND USE PATTERN AND ITS IMPACT ON WOMEN

Under the influence of the market, rapid changes are taking place in Nagaland in the land use pattern and agricultural practices. People are shifting from *jhum* to settled cultivation. The state is making concerted efforts through various agricultural schemes and encouraging farmers to cultivate commercial crops and abandon traditional agricultural practices such as *jhum*. The development programmes are emphasizing the need for registering land on individual basis. For instance, most credit schemes, bank loans, government welfare schemes, and agricultural extension schemes demand land/property, *patta* (government document of land title) as collateral. Such emerging demands are compelling Nagas to give away the communitarian land system and go for individual landownership. These changes are disrupting not only Naga community including women's traditional bond with their land but also affecting the land relations as well (Jamir 2014: 121–33). Quoting an example of Sopotimi village in Zunheboto district, Jamir says that land use policy has changed the land use and the landownership pattern which subsequently has transformed the land relations. She describes that the village had passed a resolution to cultivate only cash crops such as cardamom and passion fruits. Agencies such as the Nagaland Empowerment of People through Economic Development (NEPED), Government of Nagaland, International Research Centre, and the Indo–Canada Environment Project further strengthened the idea of the Sapotimi village resolution by providing funding support for the purpose. A large numbers of farmers have shifted to cash crops. This has brought down the land under *jhum* by almost 90% (NEPED 2006: 31). Similar changes were recorded in other villages too. In 1986, somewhat similar kind of experiment was conducted with cardamom crop in village Khonoma. Many households have invested in the cash crop, although planning production, processing, and marketing could not take off collectively at the village level. It has yet to be seen whether the cardamom contribution to the Khonoma economy was a success, partial success, or failure. There would be additional pressure on the *jhum*, on the yields, and cycles of the traditional species that have been cultivated there. If the cardamom cultivation proves to be economically viable, both terraced plots and forest lands will also come under pressure (KTDB 2009: 80). So, the success of such experiment with the commercial crop is yet to be established as marketing of products has always remained a challenge (ibid.). While criticizing the current land policy, some of the Naga scholars say that the state is creating an infrastructure which is conducive for producing commercial crops and such changes might be considered as a development from an economic point of view but moving away from *jhum* to settled cultivation would have far reaching consequences on continuance of history of the Naga communities, on the social and cultural dynamics and on gender relations with land in the Naga society. In the changing scenario, women are worst affected as men control the agricultural technology and own land. Cash crops are promoted on individual plots. Development agencies treat men as head of household and interact with them and extend all benefits to them. Men take all benefits and decisions by themselves. Women are kept out of the purview of such development programmes due to lack of formal land rights in their favour.

In recent years, cultivation of horticultural (vegetables, fruits, and flowers) is getting momentum. Studies show that the area under CPR is declining in many villages. Decline in *jhum* cultivation and CPR are posing a threat for women who are directly and greatly dependent on these resources for the sustenance of their household members. They are gradually losing control over community land.

Liberalization policy has put further pressure on land. There is a growing demand for land and, thus, land prices has increased manifold. Few rich people are accumulating large tracts of clan/lineage land in their names. This is leading to the problems of landlessness, land alienation, and deforestation (Jamir 2014: 130). Land which used to be sacred for Nagas has been reduced to a means of production. Ranghapur Pahar used to have dense forest cover but now people are cultivating rubber plantation. Change in landownership pattern has led to the fragmentation of the community, clan, and lineage land into individual landownership. This has created insecurity among women whose livelihood is under threat due to changes in the cultivation practices.

INHERITANCE PATTERN AMONG SOME OF THE NAGA TRIBES

Women in tribal societies enjoy better status in comparison to their counterparts in non-tribal societies. However, they do not have equal status with men (Elwin 1959; von Fürer Haimendorf 1939). This is evident in several spheres such as ownership of productive resources including land and participation in various sociopolitical, legal, and religious institutions. In the Naga society, women enjoy relatively greater freedom in terms of social interaction, mobility, contribution, and decision-making in traditional agricultural system in comparison to the non-tribal communities. Naga women work in the field along with their men folk. Their labour input is sometime higher than that of men but women do not enjoy ownership rights. The customary laws define and legitimize gender roles and land relations, and determine the lineage of property inheritance, succession, distribution of resources, and governance. The inheritance of property to the male line predetermines the responsibilities and duties of men and women within the household as well as in the community. Men deal with the administration and management of the community affairs. Women do not represent the kin group or the community in formal capacity. Women do not have the authority to arbitrate or pass judgements in cases of disputes or any criminal act (KTDB 2009: 80).

Naga is a patrilineal society; hence, inheritance takes place on the line of male cognate by conferring the right to ownership over land whether ancestral, community, individually owned, clan, lineage, or family land. Land is owned by male members of the household. Women do not have right to inherit ancestral property. They are excluded from governance vis-à-vis decision-making process. A famous anthropologist cum colonial administrator J. H. Hutton (1921: 137) who wrote on Naga tribes in Northeast India said, 'A man cannot leave real property to his daughter.' If the man does not have a male heir, the next of kin (male) could claim the property within the clan. In case, if head (father) dies leaving minor son(s) then wife takes the charge till son(s) get adult. When a daughter gets married, she may be provided and gifted with the moveable property only.

The land inheritance pattern in Nagaland differs from one tribe to another. Sometime within a tribe, the inheritance pattern differs from village to village. Among Konyak Nagas, the hereditary right goes from father to the eldest son of the first and legal wife. The eldest son inherits the properties of the family, be it ancestral or acquired, movable or immovable. Usually, the ancestral/joint properties of the family/clan can never be distributed or disposed of at their own will. If the head was under debt, it would be the eldest son's responsibility to pay the debt. The eldest son is entitled to distribute the properties of the family to his brothers' as per provisions of the customary laws. Movable properties are provided to younger brothers. In the event of the death of the eldest son without issue, the right of inheritance goes to the next eldest son, and so on. In case, if there is no son/heir in the family, the order of succession is confined to paternal brothers and blood-related clan members even from the different village. Women are excluded from the inheritance. As per customary laws, when daughters are married, there is a restriction even to give them domestic animals and landed properties except their belongings such as ornaments, clothes, and handicraft in order to avoid curse to her generations. Konyak (2005) says that although as per customary laws, daughters do not inherit anything yet in practice, if some family is rich enough; they can give some movable property to the daughter also (ibid.).

The Angami and Chakhesang tribal communities are also patrilineal; hence, the right to inheritance and the line of descent are considered a male prerogative (Piehyü 2015). As per the customary laws of both these communities, women have access to their ancestral land for agriculture but they do not inherit it. The right of inheritance allows the Angami men to trace their ancestors up to 14 generations but they restrict trace of their mother's lineages only up to four generation (Hutton 1969). This system was the 'complete merger of the women in their husband's exogamous division by and on marriage' (Hodson 1925: 174). In Angami tribe, the normal practice for a man is to divide his property during his lifetime. When sons marry, they get their shares. When the father dies, the youngest son inherits the father's house. The best field is given to the eldest son and the remaining properties are shared among the male members. The Angami customary law bars women from inheriting ancestral land and property but there is no restriction on a widow or a divorcee purchasing own land. However, individual owners have the right to use their self-acquired land according to their wish, to sell, mortgage, rent it to others, or bequeath it to their daughters during marriage or upon parents' death. This category of land is called as *Pozephu* land. *Pozephu* is not the ancestral land. This practice is followed in the Southern Angami villages (Das 1994: 10–75). '*Siephru*' which is the ancestral property including (land and house) can be owned only by male members. In the absence of male members, the ancestral property is handed over to the immediate male relatives. The possession of such ancestral property by the next of kin is called *Kayie*. Angami term '*Kayie*' refers to the ancestral property, that is, *Siephru* (Kelhou 1998: 55). Procedures regulating inheritance may be modified anytime by an oral agreement. The inheritance of adopted son(s) is determined at the time of adoption. The daughter can enjoy access to land during her lifetime, but it returns to male heirs after her death. Daughters cannot claim permanent ownership right on land.

In the Chakhesang societies too, all male members inherit clan land and family property. However, there are differences between *Khezha* and *Chakru* sub-tribes of Chakhesang tribe (Piehyü 2015) with regard to property distribution as per the customary laws. The eldest son owns the largest share of the property among the *Khezha* group (Das 1994: 179–86) while among the *Chakru* the youngest son receives the largest share of the family property. The ancestral property is owned by men and in the absence of the male child the ancestral property goes to the deceased brother's family or the clan or the adopted son (Lohe 2011: 168–69). Women have no natural right to share clan land nor do they have the right to own the ancestral property but women can receive a share in the family property called *Luna*. Luna lands, both moveable and immovable property, are bequeathed to the Chakhesang daughters during marriage or upon parents' death. It is the land owned by parents and not the ancestral land. There is no bar on a widow or a divorcee purchasing by themselves (Piehyü 2015).

Among Rengma tribal communities who are mostly living in Kohima district, the youngest son in a family inherits his father's house. The ancestral property especially land is shared equally among all the sons. Women are usually not given any ancestral land. However, the acquired property, that is, land purchased by father can be shared among all the sons and the daughters depending upon the size of the land and father's will. In the case of the Sema's tribal communities, the youngest son inherits the parental house. But it is the eldest son who remains overall in charge of the property especially the cultivable land. He acts as head of the family. Among the Ao Nagas, on the death of the head/father, the eldest son inherits the parental house.

An unmarried Naga woman across all tribal communities can access the land through a male relative, generally her father. She has the right to use land of her father's clan but she cannot claim proprietary right over it. Subsequently upon marriage, the right to her father's clan land gets automatically forfeited because as per the customary law, after marriage, a woman becomes a member of her husband's clan (Jamir 2014: 121–33). Although nowadays, if father is well off, daughter can be given a share in the self-acquired property through 'will', she cannot be given rights in the ancestral property. A divorced woman particularly among Angami communities gets maintenance as a temporary relief. During FGD in Khonoma village at Kohima district, villagers informed that if husband is alcoholic, lethargic, and does not earn, wife can divorce him. A divorced woman becomes entitled for one-third of paddy crop which she gets only once from her marital house. Thereafter, she goes back to her maternal house. Villagers informed that with the spread of Christianity, divorce rate in Naga society has come down and for the last 10 years, no divorce case took place in their village.

Traditionally, there is no concept of dowry in the Naga society. As per custom, daughter is given a basket locally termed as *Khasng*, one spade, different varieties of seeds, paddy, and vegetables at the time of marriage. She is also given a shawl and traditional ornaments such as bracelets but there is no compulsion to give these items. With the advent of Christianity, now ring ceremony is celebrated just before wedding. Sometime, out of courtesy, meat is provided by groom family to the girl side to manage the feast but this is not compulsory. The wedding cost varies depending on the type of marriage taking place and the status of a family. If a girl opts to elope marriage, she is disowned by her family. Bride price is not practised in the Naga society. Thus, there is limited inheritance for women at the time of marriage.

To validate the findings of a study on the gender implications of customary laws in two major tribal communities', namely, Sema and Konyak Nagas. Northeastern Social Research Centre, Guwahati had organized two workshops in Zunheboto and Mon districts on March 2014. Issues pertaining to customary laws, women's inheritance rights, women's political participation, and documentation and codification of customary laws were discussed. There was general consensus that in case there is no male descent in the family, land may be given to the daughters during their lifetime. And it can come back to the clan when the concerned person dies. The group argued that in Naga society, the self-acquired land can be shared with the daughters (Pereira, Athparia, and Borah 2014). Though not approved by custom increasingly sharing of self-acquired properties among sons and daughters through 'will' are taking place (ibid.).

STATE INITIATIVES FOR WOMEN'S DEVELOPMENT

To remove gender disparities and improve the condition of women in Nagaland, the state has taken some important initiatives. Some of these measures are mentioned below:

1. **Village Development Board:** VDB is a village-level institution introduced first time in 1976 in Ketsapomi village in Phek district on a pilot basis. It emerged out of a need to reconcile the traditional tribal institution of the village council. Subsequently, in 1978, the Nagaland Village and Area Council Act came into force which mandated that each village council should constitute a VDB for the village concerned (VDBs: The Constitutional Legal Position in Nagaland 26 April 2012). As per this Act, each village will have to constitute a VDB to undertake rural development through resource mobilization and decentralized planning with the involvement of the local community in preparation and execution of schemes using the village community or other funds. During 1980–81, VDBs were created in all the villages. A VDB is managed by a committee chosen by the village council and includes traditional leaders. All residents of the village are members of the general body of the VDB. It is important to mention that VDB was the first institution which has reserved 25% of its seats for women. Out of the total development funds, 25% of the funds the VDBs receive from the state government are kept in a separate bank account for women.
2. **Issuance of *Patta* Passbook:** The state government has notified the scheme of *patta* passbook on 30th March 2006. The scheme of '*patta*' passbook (a legal document for owning land) was implemented in 2007. The issuance of '*patta*' by the Revenue Department after due survey and verification by the Land Records and Survey Department is recognition of ownership of land on an individual basis. *Patta* is allotted to a person whose land is free from all encumbrances, title, revenue payment up to date, etc. Under this scheme, large numbers of *patta*s have been settled on individual basis. It is to be noted that the Naga customary laws do not allow women to inherit land but under the *patta* passbook scheme, provision was made both for men and women to own land.

In Dimapur town alone, 14,420 individuals were allotted *patta*s under this scheme. 10,388 (83.67%) men and 2,027 (16.33%) women were benefitted by the Scheme. However, field visits indicated that several land disputes arose on the *pattas* allotted.

The *patta* passbook scheme is criticized by several scholars. The concept of *patta* passbook which is recognition of private ownership of land is considered an alien concept and against the traditional practice of the Naga society. Critics say that '*patta*' passbook is gradually changing the communal land to private land and encouraging a shift from traditional agriculture to commercial farming and tree plantation. This has encouraged rich households to consolidate large tracts of land in their favour by depriving many households of their usufructuary right over communal land. The change in land relation is leading to the emergence of a neo-rich class and increasing the gap between rich and common people.

3. **Nagaland Women's Empowerment Act, 2006:** To empower Naga women, the Nagaland Municipal Act 2001, the 108 (Amendment) Act, 2008 (Women Reservation Bill) was passed by the state legislative assembly. The Bill granted women's 'political rights' by including them in decision-making body, that is, municipal council. But later on, the state assembly withdrew the Bill on the plea that it infringed upon Article 371A which is the basis of state autonomy from direct central rule and if implemented, it would affect the traditional landholding system of the Nagas. The Naga customary law that restricts women's ownership of land became a strong basis for not implementing the Women Reservation Bill as was evident during Mokokchug Municipal election which was objected by the landowners. The Bill was opposed by tribal bodies and even the state government in the legislative assembly to exempt Nagaland from part 1XA of the Constitution which gives reservation to women.

In 2011, the Joint Action Committee on Women's Reservation (JACWR)—a women's federation constituted by the apex women's groups of the various tribes as well as Women's NGOs including popular federations such as Naga Mothers Association (NMAs), Eastern Nagaland Women Organization, Naga Women Hoho Dimapur, Tenyimi Women Organization, and Watsu Mongdang, the apex group of Ao women—has protested against the withdrawal of the Bill and challenged government to implement the Nagaland Municipal First Amendment

Act and implement 33% reservation for women. JACWR has submitted a memorandum to the Hon'ble Governor asking to condemn the withdrawing of the Bill by state legislators and urged to intervene and ensure that their constitutional rights are protected. The JACWR has moved the apex court. The JACWR was not convinced with the argument placed by the Naga Hoho and the Eastern Naga Peoples organization which has no woman member that the law if implemented would affect the traditional landholding system of the Nagas and infringe upon Article 371A. Women groups such as the NMA and several others have decided to continue their struggle for women's right (Chozhule 2011).

CONCLUSION

Nagaland is predominantly a rural society. For Nagas, land is not only an asset and a source of livelihood but also the basis of identity and has deep-rooted cultural, historical, and political significance. Land belongs to the people. Here the total percentage of female workers engaged in agriculture was 65.2%. This exceeded the male cultivators at 44.4% of the total male workers (Census 2011). In such a scenario, it becomes necessary to incorporate the gender issue as an integral component in land policy and other development programmes. As long as the CPR was intact and traditional, agriculture remained a common practice, women had secured livelihood. Changes in landownership and land use pattern are adversely impacting Naga women, strengthening patriarchy and excluding them from the development process. Women are now losing access to and control over land and CPR.

The analysis of gender and land relationship reveals that women in Nagaland are not treated at par with men. A review of Nagas customary laws reveals that these laws are gender discriminatory. For instance, women work in agricultural field and their contribution in agriculture production is immense but as per Naga customary laws, they are not allowed to inherit ancestral land. The Naga society is patrilineal and land is inherited by male descendants in the family. In case, there is no male heir, the land reverts to the nearest male kin of the same clan such as a brother's son. A Naga woman cannot claim independent right of ownership to the land she cultivated or resided on. They have 'user right' of their father's clan/community land. Similarly, all the traditional institutions such as chiefs of clans, *khels*, tribes, village councils, and even churches are male-dominated institutions. Women are not allowed to be the members of clan or *khel* council. Women's presence in the village council, an elected body, is almost negligible. There are no reservations for women in village council/municipal council. They are kept away from participating in meetings and decision-making processes. Women's exclusion in socio-legal and religious spheres weakens their bargaining power and the existing social structure allows perpetuating gender disparity.

RECOMMENDATIONS

1. Several efforts are being made to document customary laws of different tribal communities. Various organizations such as civil society, church, resource persons, and the linguistic department in Nagaland University are engaged in the documentation process. At this juncture, it would be important to call a debate on customary laws and review it from the contemporary value of gender justice before finalizing the documentation. These laws can be documented by a representative group consisting of the village council, *Gaon Bura*, tribal men and women of different age groups in consultation with the local knowledgeable people, churches where applicable, educated youth, and women's organizations. Since many tribes, institutions, and individuals have studied customary laws and are engaged in documenting these laws, these studies and the process of documentation should become the starting point in documentation. Documentation of customary laws may help in removing ambiguities, confusion, and also ignorance by the tribal population and ensure uniformity (Jamir 2014: 121–33). Customary laws are viewed as stumbling blocks in the way of Naga women's development both socially and politically as mentioned by Rosemary Dzuvichu (Mazumdar 2013). Naga women leaders have challenged the customary laws that have denied them their constitutional right to be part of political bodies. To ensure women's participation, the state should reconsider and implement the policy of 33% reservation for women in municipal bodies.
2. Naga is an agrarian society. With increasing population growth, there is pressure on land and employment. Land is central to the Naga society. Some of the enlightened Naga people have

expressed their concern over the mindless policy formulation related to land and agriculture. They argue that agricultural land is pivotal in the lives of tribal communities including women. Nagas know only cultivation. As per the current model of development, Nagas are perceived as 'backward' but this notion is not correct. Nagas may be lacking in skills required in the present-day market but apart from being cultivators, Nagas are the best artisans and craftsmen. Some of the educated Nagas posed a question that if Någas stop cultivation, where will they go? They have yet to learn skills in different trades required in the market. They emphasized that the current development model goes against the interest of tribal communities including womenfolk. It is important first to understand Naga customs, traditions and practices, and the rationale behind them. Hence, it is necessary to re-examine the land and agricultural policies and reformulate them, keeping in view the local socio-economic and geographical conditions.
3. Indigenous knowledge is the outcome of several years of experience. Women are the custodians of indigenous knowledge. Their role in sustainable development and biodiversity conservation needs to be harnessed and embedded in development programmes. Their knowledge and skill need to be documented and should be given due recognition in policy framework.
4. Despite women being highly literate (76.11%), the scope for independent employment opportunities and access to resources continue to remain a challenge. There should be focus on enhancing employment opportunities for women. It will provide independence to women and allow them to access and ownership of land through purchase as permissible by the customary law.
5. Much of the land is unsurveyed, so efforts towards surveying all land whether it is government land or community land and developing a land record and land maps could be essential for improved land management practices. This can be done by incorporating the customary authorities in the entire process.
6. No gender segregated data related to landownership and development programmes have been maintained. The absence of land data hinders formulating a land policy including gender specific policy/programmes. Hence, a comprehensive landownership database needs to be evolved including the customary rights.
7. To ensure women's active participation in the development process, for the first time Nagaland has made a provision of 25%

seats reservation for women in the VDB. However, it was found that men were participating actively in the VDBs meetings through various traditional and modern institutions such as the *khel* unions, the *morungs*, and youth groups but women remained passive participants. Women were not aware of their roles and responsibilities as VDB members and as a women representative. Men were quite resentful of the reservation for women and were of the view that women's empowerment was bad for society as complete equality between men and women will lead to domestic tension. It was also found that VDB members including women were not experienced in implementing government schemes. Very often, there was no systematic maintenance and use of women's share of funds. To handle these problems, there is a need for training, orientation programme, exposure visit, and intensive sensitization and capacity building for the VDB members including women. This will help them to understand their roles and responsibilities and engage in income generating activities. Funds earmarked for women should be spent for their betterment.

8. There is an increasing trend of immigrants and outsiders settling in the state. It is alleged that immigrants from the neighbouring country cultivate land which comes in the jurisdiction of Nagaland but pay *Khatmani* (a kind of revenue tax) to the Assam government. Many of them allegedly indulge in illegal land transfer which is adversely affecting landownership pattern in the state. This issue needs to be addressed comprehensively.

9. Traditionally, the boundaries of land parcels in Nagaland once demarcated were inviolable and sacrosanct. However, with increasing commercialization and reducing controls of customary leaders on society, there is rise in number of land disputes which vitiate the harmonious community life. Therefore, it is essential to provide more concrete demarcation enforceable through customary authorities. Documentation of customary practices will allow commonality of decision-making in specified communities.

10. Current development programmes are often dubbed irrelevant for Nagaland. It is important to conduct feasibility survey and wide range consultation process embedding gender sensitivity in formulating policies and development programmes, and planning so that desired activities could be introduced.

NOTES

1. https://en.wikipedia.org/wiki/Christian_missionaries (accessed on 29 March 2017).
2. https://en.wikipedia.org/wiki/Ahoms (accessed on 29 March 2017).

REFERENCES

Aier, Anungla. 2008. 'Agricultural Cycle, Associated Rituals and the Role of Women.' In *Naga: A Forgotten Mountain Region Rediscovered*, edited by Richard Kunz and Vibha Joshi, 122. Basel: Museum der Kulturen.
Alemchiba, M. 1970. *A Brief Historical Account of Nagaland*. Kohima: Naga Institute of Culture.
Ao, A. L. 1999. *Practicing Naga Customary Law*. Golaghat: Modern Press.
Bag, Gunanidhi N. 2001. *Rural Transformation in Tribal Areas: A Study*. Delhi: Akansha Publishing House.
Banerjee, N. 1996. 'Exploring Integration of Gender Dimension into Nagaland Environment Protection and Economic Development.' Issue Paper in NEPED Project Coordination Unit IDRC, International Development Research Centre, Delhi.
Chozhule, Kikhi. 2011. '33% Women Reservation Bill in Nagaland: An Analysis from Women View Point.' *The Morung Express*, 23 May. Available at: http://www.nirybgexoress,com. (accessed on 19 April 2016).
Das, N. K. 1994. 'Angami Nagas in Nagaland.' In *People of India-Nagaland*, edited by N. K. Das and C. L. Imchen. Calcutta: Anthropological Survey of India.
Directorate of Information and Public Relations. 2014. *Nagaland Basic Facts*. Kohima: Directorate of Information and Public Relations.
Elwin, Verrier. 1959. *The Nagas in the Nineteenth Century*. Bombay: Oxford University Press.
Gait, E. A. 1926. *History of Assam*, 366. Available at: http://www.north-east India.com/nagaland/nagaland-history.html (accessed on 26 March 2009).
Government of India. 2011. *Census of India*. New Delhi: Office of the Registrar General and Census Commissioner, Ministry of Home Affairs.
Government of Nagaland. 1995a. 'The Nagaland Village and Area Councils Act, 1978 (Nagaland Act No. 1 of 1979). Nagaland Village, Area and Regional Councils Act, 1970'. *The Nagaland Code*. Vol. II, 2nd ed. Kohima: Department of Justice & Law.
———. 1995b. 'The Nagaland Jhumland Act, 1970 (Nagaland Act. No. 3 of 1974).' *Nagaland Code*. Vol. III, 2nd ed. Kohima: Department of Justice & Law.

Government of Nagaland. 2001. *State Department of Agriculture, Village Profile.* Kohima: Government of Nagaland.

———. 2004. *Nagaland State Human Development Report.* Kohima: Department of Planning & Coordination, 6.

———. 2009. *Human Development Report, Mon District.* Kohima: UNDP Project Department of Planning & Coordination, Government of India, 13.

———. 2015. *Directorate of Land Records and Survey.* Dimapur, Nagaland.

Guha Ray, S. N., and H. Barch, ed. 1970. *Gazetteer of India: Nagaland, Kohima District.* Calcutta: Sree Saraswati Press.

Hodson, T. C. 1925, September–December. 'Notes on the Marriage of Cousins in India.' *Man in India* 5 (34): 136–75.

Huq, Mahbub U. 2002. *Human Development in South Asia: Agriculture and Rural Development.* Karachi: Oxford University Press.

Hutton, J. H. 1921. *The Angami Nagas.* London: Macmillan. Reprinted in 1969. Bombay: Oxford University Press.

———. 1969. *The Angami Nagas with Some Notes on Neighbouring Tribes.* London: Oxford University Press.

Jamir, T. 2014, March. 'Gender Land Relations in Nagaland: Dilemma of Balancing Tradition and Modernity.' *International Journal of Gender and Women's Studies* 2 (1): 121–33.

Jamir, T., and L. Longkumer. 2012. *Nagaland—Land Alienation: Dynamics of Colonialism, Security and Development. Status of Adivasis/Indigenous Peoples Land Series 6.* Delhi: Aakar Books.

Kelhou. 1998. 'Women in Angami Society.' In *Women in Naga Society*, edited by Lucy Zehol. Delhi: Regency Publishers.

Khonoma Tourism Development Board (KTDB). 2009, October. *Environmental Impact Assessment Report.* Kohima: MKV Offset Press.

Konyak, W. Honje. 2005, September. 'Konyak Naga Customary Law.' Concept Paper submitted to Deputy Commissioner, Mon and DBs Mon.

Lohe, Kewepfuzu. 2011. *Naga Village: A Sociological Study.* Guwahati: Eastern Book House Publishers.

Longkumer, L. 2015. Core Periphery Relationship in North East India with a Focus on Nagaland. Unpublished doctoral dissertation, School of International Studies, Jawaharlal Nehru University, Delhi. Available at Shodhganga: A Reservoir of Indian Thesis @INFLIBNET.ac.in; URL: http://hal.handle.net (accessed on 5 April 2016).

Luithui, C. 2010. 'The Indian Constitution, Law and the Nagas: A Case Study of Nagaland.' In *India and the Rights of Indigenous Peoples*, edited by C. R. Bijoy, Shankar Gopala Krishnan, and Shomona Khanna. Chiang Mai: Asia Indigenous Peoples Pact.

Mazumdar, Prasanta. 2013. 'Standing her Ground in Patriarchal Naga Society.' *Agency DNA*, 8 March, Guwahati. Available at: http://www.dnaindia.com/india/report (accessed on 19 April 2016).

Ministry of Development of North Eastern Region (MoDNER). n.d. 'Inner Line Permit.' Available at: http://www.mdoner.gov.in (accessed on 13 May 2016).
NEPED. 2006. *Adding Value to Shifting Cultivation in Nagaland*. Delhi: V. N. Press. Quoted from Jamir, Toshimenla, and Lanusashi L. *Status of Adivasis/ Indigenous Peoples Land Series 6*.
NEPED and IRRR. 1999. *Building upon Traditional Agriculture in Nagaland*. Kohima, Nagaland: Environment Protection and Economic Development, and Philippines: International Institute of Rural Reconstruction.
Nshoga, A. 2009. *Traditional Naga Village System and its Transformation*. Delhi: Anshah Publishing House.
Pereira, Melvil, R. P. Athparia, R.P., and Kankana Borah.2014. Proceedings of workshop on Customary Law and Gender Equity, Nagaland. Available at: https://nagalandpost.com (accessed on 12 April 2014).
Piehyü, Medonue. 2015. A Sociological Study of Unemployment Problem. Unpublished doctoral dissertation, Nagaland University, Department of Sociology. Available online at Shodhganga: a reservoir of Indian thesis @ flibnet.ac.in (accessed on 22 March 2016).
Pillai, Sushil K. 1999, October. 'Anatomy of an Insurgency, Ethnicity and Identity in Nagaland.' *Fault lines: Vol 3. South Asia Intelligence Review*. Available at: http://www.satp.org/satporgtp/publication/ fault lines/vol3 (accessed on 5 April 2016).
Rizvi, S. H. M., and Roy S. 2006. *Naga Tribes of North East India*. Delhi: BR Publishing Corporation.
Sema, John. H. 2011. 'Naga Politics: Issues and Problems.' *South Asia Politics* 10(5): Delhi, September.
———. 2014. 'Managing Customary Laws of Land in Nagaland: Issues, Problems and Challenges.' In *Socio Economic Profile of Rural India*. Delhi: Concept Publishing House.
Shimray, U. M. 2007. *Naga Population and Integration Movement*. Delhi: Eastern Book Corporation.
Singh, K. S., ed. 1994. *Property, Succession and Inheritance, People of India: Nagaland*. Calcutta: Anthropological Survey of India.
Singh, M. Amarjeet 2012. *The Naga Conflict, Backgrounder on Conflict*. Bangalore: National Institute of Advanced Studies.
Sreedhar, M. V. 1979. 'The Functions of Bilingualism in Nagaland.' *International Journal of Sociology of Language* (22): 103–13.
VonFürer Haimendorf, Christoph. 1939. *The Naked Nagas*. London: Methuen and Spink.
'VDBs: The Constitutional Legal Position in Nagaland.' Available at: http// villagedevelopmentboardnagaland.blogspot.in/posted (accessed on 4 April 2016).

12

Persisting Inequalities: Gender and Land Rights in Rajasthan[1]

KANCHAN MATHUR

The fact that discrimination against women in their access to and control over land and property is part of the larger system of discrimination and subjugation based on caste, gender, and economic class needs no emphasis. Addressing the many aspects of this discrimination requires multi-layered and diverse strategies. In most of South Asia including India, few women own cultivable land and an even smaller numbers have effective control over it. According to Agarwal (1994a, 1994b), the contribution of women to agriculture production is well established. A disproportionate number of women are still dependent on land. Women constitute nearly 40% of the agricultural workforce in the country. Seventy-five percent of all female workforce and 85% of all rural female workforce in the country are involved in agriculture at present (GoI 2013). Indeed, the gender gap has been growing. It is increasingly becoming evident that women who make a significant contribution to and depend on agriculture do not have secure land rights. According to the Food and Agriculture Organization (FAO), women constituted about 41% of total employment in agriculture globally in 2007.

FAO's forecasts through 2010 indicate that of the total percentage of economically active women in least-developed countries, more than 70% work in agriculture. In South and Southeast Asia more than 60% of the female labour force is engaged in food production. However, in countries such as India, Nepal, and Thailand, less than 10% women farmers own land.[2] Aside from hampering women's access to land, sociocultural factors prevent them from claiming their rights to land. The ideology and practice of stringent patriarchy through which women's subordination is perpetuated is reinforced through institutional structures. Even where women do enjoy rights of ownership, they do not exercise effective control over it, being unable to lease, mortgage, or dispose of land and its products (*Hindustan Times* 2010).

The issue of land rights for women gained visibility in the development discourse with the 1980 United Nations Women's Conference in Copenhagen stating that even though women constitute 50% of the world's population, they owned only 1% of the world's resources. The exclusion of women from ownership of land has since remained on the global agenda. The United Nations Convention on the Elimination of All Forms of Discrimination Against Women (CEDAW) included specific clauses on the equal treatment of women in agrarian reforms and equal rights for both the husband and wife in the ownership, management, and disposition of property. As a result of these international treaties and laws, several national legislations across countries have specifically been targeted at women's land and property rights.

In India, the realization that agriculture land continues to be one of the most important forms of property and productive assets in rural areas and a critical contributor of economic well-being, social status, and political power has led to several policy initiatives. In 1995, under the Eighth Five-year Plan, the Ministry of Rural Development, Department of Land Resources, Government of India, sent an order/guidelines to the states to issue land *pattas* (legal landownership documents) jointly in the name of both husband and wife and a certain percentage of land *pattas* to the single women including widows and unmarried women. Subsequently, the principal secretary revenue of different states sent such directives to the district magistrate for implementation of the same. As a consequence, for the first time, the Ninth Five-year Plan (1997–2002) document included a separate section on 'gender and land rights' and stressed the need for landownership by poor women. However, despite this, the effectiveness of policies and legislation has been limited in practice. The Eleventh Five-year Plan (2007–12) agenda for women in agriculture aimed at ensuring effective and autonomous land rights for women and building women's agricultural capacities. The Plan suggested direct transfer of land to women through land reforms, anti-poverty programmes, and resettlement schemes. It included land titles to individual or groups of women in all land transfers made by the government. Besides, provisions were made for credit support to vulnerable women to purchase or lease land, incentives, and subsidies on women-owned land and legal support for women's inheritance rights. The Twelfth Five-year Plan (2012–17) emphasized enhancing women's land access from all three sources, that is, direct government transfers, inheritance, and purchase or lease from the market.

This chapter aims to critically analyse issues related to gender and land rights in the state of Rajasthan. It argues that serious gender gaps continue to exist in ownership and control over land and that land rights have remained elusive to women despite state policies and interventions to increase women's access to land. The chapter is divided into three parts. Section I presents a review of the existing studies on gender and land rights in Rajasthan. Section II provides the legal framework for gender and land rights in the state. Section III underscores the patterns of women's access to land and impact of inheritance rights. The concluding section makes recommendations for policy change.

I

WOMEN'S ACCESS TO LAND IN RAJASTHAN: A REVIEW

With a land area 10.4% of India (342.24 thousand sq. km), Rajasthan, located in the northwest of the country, is India's largest state. Rajasthan has a total population of 68.6 million inhabitants. The state is divided into 33 districts, with 297 towns and more than 44 thousand villages. It is primarily an agrarian economy, and agriculture plays a crucial role in the economic development of the state. The total cultivated area covers about 20 million hectares, of this only 20% of the land is irrigated. Groundwater level is available on an average only below 60 m. The Narmada River in the south, the rivers flowing from Punjab in the north, and the Agra Canal from Haryana and Uttar Pradesh provide water to the dry land of the state. The Indira Gandhi Canal irrigates northwestern Rajasthan. Nearly two-thirds of the total area of the state is arid or semi-arid with low and irregular rainfall characterized by extremes of climate. In Rajasthan, the farming community is dependent on various sources of irrigation including tube wells, canals, wells, and tanks. Irregular rainfall and frequent drought expose households (HHs) with a fragile livelihood base to various risks, uncertainties, and stress situations that directly impact people's access to resources.

Typically, material power—ownership of property and assets—is traditionally vested in men in the state. Women continue to lack ownership rights on land, despite the fact that majority of them work as agricultural wage labour or on farms owned by members of the family. Though the contribution of women in agricultural production is well recognized, a considerable gender disparity exists with most women having lower access and control over land, one of the most important economic resources. A lack of resource endowment coupled with low social and human capital among women leads to their further marginalization (Mathur 2004).

Very few in-depth research studies, which systematically analyse issues related to women's access to and control over land, exist in the state. Some of the earlier studies have primarily focused on more general issues relating to land reforms and economic development, implementation of tenancy, reforms in land ceiling, allotment of government and community lands, and protection of forest rights (Gupta 1994; Sagar and Ahuja 1987; Yugandhar and Dutta 1995). However, these studies have failed to look at the issue of land rights from a gender perspective.

There are only four studies which have specifically focused on the issue of women's land rights in Rajasthan. These studies highlight the gender gaps in access to land in the state. They also indicate the plight of women both who own land and those who do not own, and in particular, the dilemma of widows belonging to both these categories. The studies underscore that gender inequalities in access to land cut across intersectionalities of caste, age, religion, and ethnicity. Often women belonging to rural/urban, tribal/non-tribal, and educated/uneducated divides face similar problems in terms of their rights to property. The apathy and indifference of land revenue officials towards women claiming their rights over land is also emphasized.

One of the earliest research studies focusing on understanding the situation of women in the Indira Gandhi Nahar Project area (IDSJ 1989) reveals that women sharecroppers in the canal area of Bikaner and Sri Ganganagar (henceforth, Ganganagar) viewed their role in agriculture as a peripheral input and identified the issues of landownership not with themselves but as a right of men. Widows seldom exercised their ownership right over land. In most cases, land was transferred in the name of the son soon after the father's death. In the absence of the son, it was given out for sharecropping. A woman's inability to take up agriculture without a male member who could control the land was due to the fact that she never had a chance to participate in the market, nor did she have any say in decision-making related to agricultural produce.

The study on status of women litigants (SPRI 2007) focused on assessing the situation of cases filed by women in the revenue courts of Rajasthan. In examining women's access to justice from the lowest revenue court to the Board of Revenue, the study highlights the problems faced by women in dealing with revenue courts including attitudes of revenue officials towards women. The study was carried out in four districts of the state, namely Ajmer, Jaipur, Jodhpur, and Udaipur, and a total of 120 cases were selected in the four districts (30 in each district). It underpinned that many cases were pending for more than 20 years. Seventy percent cases had been filed for small pieces of land (land ranging from 5 to 50 bighas) and 60% litigants were from within the family. The main cause of filing the cases was denial of due share in landed property to women by family members as well as due to wrong mutation. Very few unmarried daughters were found to possess land and property. In case of married women, of the 120 cases, only two women in Girwa block, Udaipur, could specify under which act and section their cases have been filed. It revealed that the husband's brother or other family members often take control of the land even if it is in the woman's name. The study further pointed out that government functionaries showed greater bias in the distribution of land; bribing the officials in court or tampering with land records are also common. Seventy-seven percent women felt that the government system was not gender sensitive. Revenue officials, *tehsildars* (revenue officer at block/sub-district level), and sarpanches are either not aware of or indifferent to joint titles, and women are often left out of land entitlement schemes. By far, the largest resistance comes from adverse social practices, namely marriage rites, dowry, *nata pratha*,[3] death rites, etc., in Rajasthan. The study concludes that women's land rights, control, ownership, possession, and access still seem to be a far cry from reality.

In her study on women's right to land in rural Rajasthan conducted in three districts, Burns (2004) explores how the ownership of land mediates women's economic independence and social status. Data for the study was collected from 50 rural women residing in four blocks. The responses of landless women were contrasted with those of landowning women to explore differences in economic independence and social status. The study points out that only a small minority of women owns land in their own names and that this land is usually of a small size. Forty-four percent of landless women reported that they had no say at all in decisions made about selling or mortgaging HH land. Several women reported problems posed by government procedures and attitude of functionaries as obstacles to their owning land. It also makes evident that access to land without wider social changes may not radically improve women's lives and that land rights are not the only key to unlocking women's subordination.

Nandwana and Nandwana (1998) in their study on land rights of widows in Rajasthan point out the significance of land as a critical productive resource essential for subsistence. They assert that land is also crucial as a means of security against poverty and destitution. However, due to the lack of legal ownership, women are often far more vulnerable to these adverse circumstances, especially in situations of divorce and widowhood. Out of the 57 widows covered in their study of two villages of Udaipur district, 42 belonged to castes in which *nata* is permitted, while the remaining 15 belonged to castes which do not permit widow remarriage. The study points out that even if they had land rights, widows could not play an active role in the management of their land because of restricted mobility and other social customs. Hence, land was often left to the care of grown-up sons or other male relatives from the husband's family. Land records for one of the villages did not show any entries in the names of daughters. The few female tenants who featured in the land records were there as wives and not as daughters. These women had their names included in the records after their husbands had died. The widows here stated that they did not have any land in their names in their parental villages either.

Thus, even though the Hindu Succession Act (HSA) of 2005 specifies a daughter's rights as a Class I heir, this right is not being actualized in the state.

II

GENDER AND LAND RIGHTS: THE LEGAL FRAMEWORK

Historically, one of the fundamental aspects of land reforms in Rajasthan was the need to break the stranglehold of feudal landlords. Issues related to land reforms and enforcing of new land laws relating to land tenures, land revenue, land management, and rights of tenants have undergone considerable changes since the reorganization of princely states in Rajasthan. The most important enactments concerning the land tenures and land revenue administration, however, are the Rajasthan Tenancy Act (RTA), 1955, and the Rajasthan Land Revenue Act (RLRA), 1956. These enactments elevated the status of the cultivating tenants and modernized land revenue administration in the state.

The RTA (1955) came into force on 15 October 1955. Apart from consolidating and amending the law relating to tenancies of agricultural lands, it also provided for certain measures of land reforms. According to the State Land Commission (1959), the Act can safely be claimed to be one of the most progressive tenancy Acts in India. The RTA was enacted to protect the rights of tenants in Rajasthan. Under the Act, a Hindu woman has a right over the land of her deceased father, husband, and son as the primary heir belonging to Class I category as described in Section 8 of the HSA of 1956. The Act had far-reaching effects on the agrarian transition in the state. The RTA also provided for the establishment of a hierarchy of courts to settle disputes and a procedure and jurisdiction for these courts. Despite the existing legal provisions of RTA, 1955, the RLRA, 1956, and the HSA, 1956, effective rights in property and land are elusive for women as they face numerous legal, social, administrative, and ideological problems.

The RLRA came into force on 1 July 1956. It consolidates and amends the laws relating to appointment, powers, and duties of revenue courts, revenue officers, and village functionaries; preparation and maintenance of land records; survey and settlement operations; partition of estates; collection of land revenue; and other matters incidental thereto. The Act also contains provisions for the allotment of government unoccupied land to landless persons, allotment of land for non-agricultural use, trespass over government land, and procedure for ejectment of trespassers. Over two dozen sets of rules have been framed under this Act laying down a detailed procedure for the various matters provided for in the Act. All these enactments relating to land reforms, land tenures, and land administration have gone a long way in ameliorating the conditions of tenants in the state.

There is no mention, however, either in the RTA or the RLRA of the rights of widows, divorcees, or women belonging to other deprived groups. Due to tremendous pressure from women groups in Rajasthan, the Rajasthan High Court suggested the following amendments in the following rules in the year 2000:

In Rule 8 regarding regulating submission of application for allotment, one additional Sub-rule 1(a) was added, which says, 'Where applicant is a married agriculturist the application shall be submitted in the name of both husband and wife.'

Similarly, Rule 14 was also amended and a new Sub-rule 1(a) was added in this rule which says, 'In case where allotment of land is made to the married agriculturist, the allotment shall be made in the joint names of husband and wife, and the allottees, in such case, shall be deemed to be Joint allottees.'

It is important to highlight that these changes have been ineffective and remained only on paper as a huge gap exists between policy rhetoric and implementation with regard to land laws. Women have not benefitted from these changes in real terms.

The HSA, 1956, abolished the Hindu women's limited estate by removing any distinction between unmarried and married daughters. According to the Act, any property possessed by a Hindu female is to be held by her as absolute property and she is given full power to deal with it and dispose of it by will as she likes (HSA 1956). Prior to the coming of the Act, only widows could inherit. It was rare for daughters to inherit, and if at all they did inherit land, it was in the absence of four generations of related males. However, this inheritance was limited and she could enjoy property only during her lifetime and after her death it was once again inherited by her husband's heirs. A daughter could not disassociate property except in restricted conditions, namely legal necessity, religious or charitable purposes, benefit of the estate, and finally, with the consent of the reversionary.

It took five decades for gender inequalities in the 1956 HSA to be addressed. The Hindu Succession (Amendment) Act, 2005 (HSA 2005), (39 of 2005) came into force from 9 September 2005 with the Government of India issuing a notification to this effect. The path-breaking provisions in the HSA 2005 cover inequalities pertaining to agricultural land, *Mitakshara* (inherited by birth) joint family property, parental dwelling house, and certain rights of widows.

The most noteworthy aspect of the amendment in the HSA 2005, however, relates to agricultural land. The HSA 2005 made fundamental amendments to section 4 (2) of the 1956 HSA which were biased in favour of men.[4]

CUSTOMARY LAND RIGHTS IN RAJASTHAN

Section 42 of the Land Tenancy Act tried to protect the lands of tribals and Dalits from falling into the hands of non-tribals and non-Dalits (Swaminathan and Choudhary 1997). However, with the active connivance of revenue officials in Rajasthan, the section has been infringed upon even after 1955 by (a) getting false registration done on stamp paper dating before 1955 and (b) getting the land transferred to the name of another tribal who was either fictitious, dead, or acting for a non-tribal. Much of the best and most fertile lands belonging to the tribals have been lost this way. For an ordinary tribal, the ritual of getting his land recorded and his tenancy recognized officially is one of the most complicated and expensive procedures. Thousands of tribals have been unable to get their land regularized because of corruption and constant bribery that is required and which they cannot afford. Those who can afford it have been able to take paper possession of lands, though the land does not belong to them. The poor state of records and maps further increases their hardships.

Tribals in Rajasthan like elsewhere in India follow their customary laws. Tribal customary laws in the state are neither codified nor recognized in reference to the tenancy rights. Therefore, government functionaries apply provisions of HSA in certain places where these provisions are not applied and 'Shashtriya' Hindu Law is applied instead, which gives inheritance rights only to the male members. This increases the vulnerability of tribal women. Labelling of tribal women as witches is also a common practice in the state, especially in the tribal belt, to disinherit women from their land, settle family and clan disputes, punish women for resisting sexual advances, or even to discourage women from participating in local politics and elections. In the case of widows, very often the brothers-in-law try to manage her land, insist on sharecropping her land, or simply attempt to deprive her of her rightful share of the land. In Udaipur district, land/property disputes have emerged as a major cause of branding women as witches. In a majority of cases, accusations are levelled by close relatives. A case in point is cited below.

> Kanka Bai Gameti of Dauted village of Udaipur district is a widow and was declared a *dayan* by her own nephew Hagraa who wished to grab her property. Prior to being labelled a *dayan* Kanka Bai was economically well off. She had 3 bighas of land and also owned a house, a buffalo, and 35 goats. Besides, she was availing her widow pension of ₹200 per month. Kanka's nephew wanted to grab her property and hence declared her a *dayan* (witch) and assaulted her on several occasions. At first, he robbed

Kanka of a substantial amount of jewelry and stole 30 of Kanka's goats. When Hagraa saw that Kanka's land was yielding five sacks of corn, he also decided to grab the land. In a ploy to cheat Kanka, he went to her house and apologized for his past behaviour and invited her to stay in his own house for a few days. Kanka agreed to his request and Hagraa took few sacks of corn, buffaloes, and cash from her house. He kept Kanka in his house comfortably for 10–15 days but then again began alleging that she was a *dayan*, as she had caused his daughter's illness. Once he went to Kanka's house carrying an axe with the intention of killing her. Kanka got to know of his intentions and somehow managed to escape and save her life. Hagraa also bribed some of the caste panchayat members into transferring Kanka's land in his own name. As a result of the dreaded events, she shifted in with her brother's grandson. She has lost her mental balance and lives in constant fear of Hagraa. (IDSJ 2006)

GOVERNMENT OF RAJASTHAN'S INITIATIVES TO PROMOTE EQUITY IN LAND RIGHTS

In the past two decades, the Government of Rajasthan (GoR) has taken some initiatives to ensure women's access to land (GoR 2005–06):

- The Department of Registration and Stamps offers a 50% reduction (subsidy) in the stamp duty for agricultural land, in case the land is registered in the name of a woman, in order to encourage and promote ownership of agricultural land in the name of women. The stamp duty for land registered in a man's name is 8% (brought down from the previous value of 11% in July 2004); for a woman, however, the duty is lower, at 5.5% (50% of the previous value of stamp duty).
- The state government has reduced the stamp duty from 8% to 5% in the case of a gift deed of immovable property executed in favour of sister, daughter, granddaughter, mother, or wife.
- A mandatory provision of stamp duty of ₹50 for a divorce instrument has been made in the Rajasthan Stamp Act, 1998. The provision of stamp duty is primarily to ensure a legally acceptable document to safeguard the interest of the divorced woman, and not so much as a means of revenue.

Official records and reports show a sharp increase in the number of agricultural land deeds registered by women since the subsidy has been introduced. From January 2004 to December 2005, more than 2 lakh women have registered agricultural land in their names. The total benefit accrued to women under this rebate is ₹1,399 lakh, which amounts to an average of ₹6,621 per women (GoR 2005–06).

As stated in the Eighth Five-year Plan (1992–97), the state government implements a policy allocating 40% of ceiling surplus land to women alone and the rest in joint titling. Government land allocation gives priority to landless individuals and widows, yet women whose husbands own land are not considered as landless. No provisions have been made for divorced or separated women. Land acquisition requires payment of registration fee, filling of forms, and gaining a certificate of landownership from the local government body. Most often, women particularly in rural areas are unable to fulfil these requirements due to low literacy rates and lack of awareness regarding obtaining ownership titles.

Despite amendments in the RTA and the RLRA that came about due to the concerted campaigns by women's groups both within the state and nationally, and the new provisions in HSA 2005, significant gender inequalities remain in women's access to and control over land in the state.

- In the RTA wherever a person/agriculturist/landless is mentioned; it is understood to be 'male' only. Also, there are no provisions for protection of women's tenancy rights in the RTA. Though most of the rural women are engaged in agriculture and put in more hours/ arduous work in the field than their male counterparts, women are not considered worthy of landownership.
- Under the HSA 2005, in Rajasthan, the process whereby women (sisters and mothers) relinquish their share in the holding in the name of brothers and sons is very simple. Signatures can be taken on a ₹100 stamp paper to transfer the land. This lacuna needs to be addressed by having stricter laws relating to the release and transfer of land.
- The Act also leaves untouched provisions of state laws concerning the fixation of ceilings and fragmentation of agricultural holdings.
- An increase in the number of coparceners (as brought about by the amendment which includes the daughters) leads to a decline of a widow's share dependent upon that of her deceased husband. This could be rectified only if the *Mitakshara* coparcenary was abolished altogether. The latter was the demand of women's groups. In such a case, all property would go equally to Class I heirs, of which the widow is one.

- The other area left untouched by the amended law is the right granted under the provision of the will to disinherit a woman from self-acquired property, as a person has unrestricted testamentary rights over his or her property. In practice, the use of this right can and has been to disinherit women of their property.

INDIRA AWAS YOJANA

According to the information provided by the Department of Panchayati Raj and Rural Development, GoR, a large number of women have benefitted from the Indira Awas Yojana (IAY). Information regarding the allotee type-wise number of houses under various schemes of IAY reveals that during the financial year 2011–12, under Special Package Scheme[5] and out of the total registered cases in Management Information System (MIS), the percentage of women applicants was 73.4%. In the year 2012–13, under the IAY New Constructions Scheme and of the total registered applicants, the number of women applicants was 67.8% and the percentage of total sanctioned houses was the same. This demonstrates that out of the total beneficiaries, the ratio of women was two-thirds (see Table A12.2). The trend has been the same in the years 2013–14 and 2014–15. Hence, according to government records, a large percentage of women had benefitted from the IAY, and also, more women than men seem to have benefitted from it.

Land *Pattas*: Progress and Achievement Against Targets

Data provided by the Department of Panchayati Raj and Rural Development, GoR, for the years 2007–08 to 2014–15 regarding progress and achievement against targets for the allotment of free-of-cost and on-concessional-rate residential land *pattas* under the Panchayati Raj Act Rules 157 and 158 of GoR reveal:

1. *Pattas* issued under Rule 157: Data show that from the year 2007–08 to 2014–15 the achievement was 481,704 (283.3%) against a target of 170,000. Out of the targets achieved, the percentage of women *patta* holders was only 10.4%.

2. Regularization under Rule 157 (2): Data from the year 2007–08 to 2014–15 related to persons who were eligible and have occupied land up to the year 2003 show that the achievement was 127,446 (127.4%) against a target of 1 lakh. In the total period of 8 years, the percentage of women *patta* holders was only 17.3%.
3. Allotment of plots under Rule 158: This included the following points:

   a. Allotment of plots on nominal rates: Data for the target of allotted plots on nominal rates from the year 2007–08 to 2014–15 show that the achievement was 145,667 (107. 1%) against a target of 136,000. The percentage of women plot allotees was 10. 1%.
   b. Allotment of free of cost plots to BPL families: BPL families who have been allotted free of cost plots were 225,153 (216.7%) against a target of 103,900. Out of the total allotees, 23.6% allotees were women (see annexure).

The earlier section underscores that though the Constitution of India provides equal rights and opportunities to all its citizens irrespective of gender, there exists a wide gap between constitutional guarantees and ground realities. Systematic gender inequalities within HHs in the allocation of basic necessities, such as health care, education, food, and land solely in men's names. Women have been and continue to be excluded from becoming equal participants in the process of acquisition of property rights, land rights, rights to house plots/*pattas*, and homesteads, and also from being actively involved in the development process. Despite the fact that a large majority of women participate in agricultural activities, women have failed to emerge as effective landowners because of the primacy of agnate descent in the male line.

III

PATTERNS OF WOMEN'S ACCESS TO LAND AND IMPACT OF INHERITANCE RIGHTS

This section highlights some interesting insights emerging from our study into women's access to land rights in two districts of the state namely Udaipur and Ganganagar. The two districts represent contrasting social, economic, and cultural contexts. The poverty status in both the districts reveals that Ganganagar—the more developed district—has a majority of HHs falling in the non-poor category. In comparison, in the less-developed district of Udaipur, greater numbers of HHs fall in the poor category. A majority of HHs in the sample villages belong to Hindus in both Udaipur and Ganganagar districts followed by Sikhs who are 14.1%. The percentage of Muslim minority is negligible. District-wise data show that in Udaipur the majority of HHs belong to the Hindu community, while Ganganagar has a mixed population with the majority population being Hindus, that is, 59.6% followed by 39.2% Sikhs and 1.2% Muslims.

Agriculture is the main source of livelihood in both districts as in the entire state. Agarwal asserts that agricultural land continues to be one of the most important forms of property and productive assets in rural India today. It is a critical contributor to economic well-being, social status, and political power. Access to land can prove important for women, even if the plot size is not large enough to serve as the sole basis of livelihood. It can, for instance, be a critical element in a diversified livelihood system. A small plot that is insufficient for subsistence through crop cultivation can still add to other means of earnings (Agarwal 1994).

Our study demonstrates that a large majority of HHs with women having land in their name have agriculture as the main source of income in both districts. Ninety-three percent HHs with women having land in Ganganagar have agriculture as the major source of income, while in Udaipur 86% HHs with women having land in their name have agriculture as the main source of income. Seven percent HHs with women having land in Ganganagar draw income from allied agriculture, non-farm self-employment, and other sources. Some of the key industries in the area are mustard oil mills, cotton ginning and pressing factories, wheat flour mills, and the famous Rajasthan State Ganganagar Sugar Mills Ltd that is known for its Royal Heritage Liqueurs. It also has spinning and textile factories such as JCT Mills.

In Udaipur, the significant contribution of the non-farm sector is visible for augmenting HH's income for all categories of farmers in general and small and marginal farmers in particular, with 8% HHs with women having land in their name drawing income from non-farm activities and other sources. The area is known for honeybee farming and mining of zinc, copper, and stone. Hence, having some land has considerably expanded the range of non-farm options for women and has proved necessary for viable rural non-farm activities.

However, it is also a fact that though a large majority of women make a considerable contribution to agricultural production, they do not have legal rights to ownership of land; a vast gap is visible between law and practice. Hence, effective rights in property are denied to women as they confront numerous legal, social, cultural, administrative, and ideological obstacles. While significant changes have taken place in the legal sphere to provide women rights over land, the social framework within which this legal system operates has changed very little.

A key reason why women continue to find it difficult to inherit land despite existing legal provisions is the persisting patriarchal practices and gender inequalities. Several social customs and norms continue to prevent women from making claims over land. Gender inequalities in access to land cut across intersectionalities of caste, class, age, religion, and ethnicity.

As mentioned earlier, tribals in Rajasthan like elsewhere in India follow their customary laws. Tribal customary laws in the state are neither codified nor recognized in reference to tenancy rights. Tribals, especially tribal women, get easily exploited by government functionaries who apply provisions of the HSA in certain cases and the 'Shashtriya' Hindu Law in others. Since the latter gives inheritance rights only to the male members, the vulnerability of tribal women increases, thereby weakening their condition further.

Several civil society organizations (CBOs) and non-governmental organizations (NGOs) have taken up issues related to land rights of tribals/Dalits and more marginalized women including widows and single women. While these movements have gained a presence, they are yet to gain a state-wide momentum. On its part, the government has made only token changes in favour of women by reducing the stamp duty on the registration of land in women's name.

The study underscores the linkages between women's access to land and development. Areas that are more developed, have predominantly upper caste populations with non-poor HHs, and fall in the category of marginal farmers' women have greater access to land and house. However, besides development, other sociocultural factors also influence women's access to land. In Ganganagar district, Other Backward Caste (OBC) is the dominant caste primarily constituted by Jat Sikhs, Jats, Khatis, Nais, Swamis, and Kumhars. However, intracaste variations are distinct with Jat Sikhs being the predominant landed community. The district has a sizeable proportion of HHs who are Pong Dam oustees from Kangra (Himachal Pradesh). They have been allotted land by the government and identified as General castes in the district records. Many women belonging to these HHs have been allotted land in their name. However, some of the landed families do not reside in the area but in Himachal Pradesh. It is common for family members to give land in women's name among these communities.

> In this village most of the households belong to Pong Dam oustees from Kangra. It is a common practice to register land in the name of women. Earlier title deeds were largely in the name of men. Change is discernible after 2005 and now title deeds are also registered in the name of the wife and daughters. In the case of homestead land when the head of the household dies, the land is mostly registered in the name of the male heir and the wife. Daughters often relinquish their claims in favour of brothers.
>
> —Village 19 GD, Gharsana (IDSJ 2011)

Where the Hindu Succession (Amendment) Act, 2005, is concerned, there are several loopholes because of which women are deprived of their right to land. Provisions in the release deed where women (sisters and mother) release/relinquish (*haq tyagna*) their share in the holding in the name of brothers and sons are very simple. Relinquishing land is easy as it only requires signing on a ₹100 stamp paper. Many women in Ganganagar reported that they had given their land to their brothers for two reasons: First, because they feel that in case they refuse to do so they will face social stigma from the community for 'not loving' the brothers, and second, because brothers provide social security to them.

In Udaipur, the dominant castes among the ST category are Bhils, Meenas, and Garasias. Men of the community are hesitant to give land to women as they do not trust them. The reason behind this is that *nata* is customarily practised among Bhils. This system of second marriage, which confers a lower position on women and weakens their position, thereby establishes that the men can enter into multiple marriages, but a woman can only go into *nata*. The tribal community believes that if men of the community give land in a woman's name and she enters into *nata*, the children are deprived of their right to the father's land and property, whereas the woman is entitled to get a share in the second husband's property as well. The police is reluctant to intervene in such matters under the garb of its policy of non-interference in customary law. The rights of tribal women have also been taken up by women's/other collectives. One such collective is the Ekal Nari Shakti Sangathan. Becoming part of this collective has led to greater confidence and articulation among tribals to voice their issues. Many women have been enabled to access their land rights because of the backing of this collective.

Where ownership of house is concerned, majority of the women owning a house are Hindus with the highest percentage belonging to STs[6] (all STs in the state are Hindus) followed by Backward Classes (BCs). The poverty status indicates that women owning a house largely belong to the non-poor category. HHs in the name of women fall in the category of marginal farmers, majority of which are female headed. There seems to be a weak link between landholding of the HHs and women owning houses. It is therefore not necessary that big farmers give the title deed of the house to women. In rural Rajasthan, there is no practice of registering the house. Ownership of the house is determined by the name of the person, often the head of the HH (usually male), whose name appears in the ration card, electricity bill, or voting list.

The main source of obtaining house continues to be the marital family. Majority of women receiving a house from the marital family belong to ST HHs and are marginal farmers. The higher percentage of women receiving land from natal family in Ganganagar is indicative of the fact that among the Sikh community in Ganganagar, land is often given to daughters. Daughters are, however, often given in marriage to NRIs settled in Canada and very few, therefore, assert their rights over their land back home. In most cases, brothers manage the land and share the profits from agricultural produce when their sisters visit once every few years. None of the women in the sample HHs have received houses from a government source.

> 70 year old Joginder Kaur is a resident of village 37 BB in Padampur block of Ganganagar district. She belongs to the Jat Sikh community and has no formal education. Her husband died 30 years ago. She has five daughters and two sons. All her daughter are married and three of them now live in Canada. Joginder Kaur lives with her sons. They own 46 bighas of land and it is looked after by the sons. The main source of income is agriculture. Joginder Kaur of her free will gave 4 bighas of land to each of her daughters. The daughters who live in India are given a share of agriculture produce. When the daughters who live in Canada visit India, the family spends a considerable amount of money on buying them gifts including clothing and jewellery. The relationship between the brothers and sisters is cordial. Joginder Kaur asserts that she is proud of the fact that she has been fair to her daughters by giving them a share in the parental property.
>
> —Block Padampur 37 BB

Our data also show that maximum percentage of widows have received house from marital family, that is, 52%, but most of the houses are in joint ownership with other male members of the family, for example, son, nephew etc. Forty-four percent women receiving house from marital family are currently married, 3% fall in the category of unmarried women whereas a very small percentage, that is, 1% fall in the category of divorced/separated and unmarried women, denoting that this category of women are the most marginalized groups within the patriarchal set-up of the state.

It is assumed that women's access to land is closely related to the awareness of inheritance laws. The HSA, 1956, and the amendment Act, 2005, are important as HSA 2005 also gives women rights to parental dwelling house. Our study reveals that cutting across religion, social category, poverty status, and size of landholding, awareness levels regarding HSA 1956, 2005, or any other Acts are low. Of the two variants, that is, land and dwelling house, Hindu women in the study area are more aware of land rights followed by awareness regarding dwelling house. Among these, majority belong to OBC communities. They belong to non-poor HHs and fall in the category of marginal farmers.

In both the developed and less-developed districts, overall women who have control over land participate more in agricultural activities. However, there is a distinct difference between the two districts, Ganganagar and Udaipur, in this regard. In the former, a direct correlation is found between control over land and participation in agriculture. Since there is greater dependence on canal irrigation, the percentage of women owning agricultural tools and participating in agriculture is again higher. Women having good and irrigated land also have greater participation in agriculture. In Udaipur, by contrast, women's participation in agriculture is low; nonetheless, women who own pump sets were more likely to participate in agriculture.

The lesser number of workers per HH has increased women's participation in agriculture in both the developed and less-developed districts. Women belonging to marginal farmer HHs in the less-developed districts and those belonging to small and medium farmer HHs in the developed districts have greater probability of participating in agriculture. However, it is evident that in both the developed and less-developed districts, the participation of women belonging to poorer HHs is greater where agricultural activities are concerned. The role of government programmes has not made a significant contribution in increasing women's participation in agriculture.

Data indicate that women owning land and participating in agriculture activity have higher chances of participating in decision-making regarding land-use, agricultural inputs, agricultural credit, marketing agricultural produce, and negotiating with the concerned public institutions. They also participate in procuring production inputs, gaining information on new technologies, obtaining agricultural credit, marketing agricultural produce, and interacting with public institutions concerned in comparison to women who owned land and had not participated in agriculture. It is also interesting to note that women who did not have land but had participated in agriculture had no role in these two spheres of participation.

In attempting to analyse whether women approach various institutions at the local level for demanding their entitlement to land and resolution of disputes related to land rights, the study highlights that caste organizations play an important role in the study area, especially in the resolution of disputes related to land, followed by gram panchayat. Women are hesitant to approach the police for help. In Udaipur district, 40% women were found to be approaching caste organizations for the resolution of land disputes and 33.3% had approached the gram panchayat. The percentage of women approaching the police or other organizations like NGOs was 13.3%. In contrast, in Ganganagar district, there was an absence of cases related to land taken up by individual women. Women who own land can be divided into two categories: (a) women who own land but are not residing in the village, and mostly live out of Rajasthan or abroad and (b) women who belong to rehabilitated families and their cases are mostly taken up collectively by members of HHs who have been rehabilitated, and hence, the chances of litigation are minimal.

In exploring the linkages between women's participation in agriculture and women's empowerment, this chapter underscores that access to land is the initial step in ensuring control over land. Women's access to land may increase their participation in agriculture, which in turn may lead to decision-making in utilization of productive resources and ultimately to ownership of land. Ownership of land rights is seen as a definite step in women's empowerment as it enables them to expand their space at the HH level, especially in organizing agriculture. However, it has not significantly impacted the expansion of spaces to other domains of participation at the HH and community levels as cutting across castes and class divides increased educational levels have not necessarily led to greater participation or voice in decision-making.

Owning of land and participating in agriculture has had some positive, though not significant, impact on women's mobility and autonomy.

Despite district-wise variations, a large majority of women who owned land reported that their self-esteem had gone up and they were more confident as a result of owning land. They also said that the respect they received in their families had gone up. District-wise variations revealed that the tribal women reported lower self-esteem and confidence compared to women in Ganganagar district. A small percentage of women reported that their husbands felt disempowered due to their (wives) owning land. Women who owned land also stated that that their standard of living had improved with increased access to land. Some also asserted that they were treating their daughters at par with their sons and their husbands were helping in HH work. This percentage was lower in the less-developed districts.

Land rights can serve manifold functions in rural women's lives and empower them to challenge socio-economic and political inequalities prevalent in a patriarchal feudal state like Rajasthan. Women's access to land can lead to alleviating poverty, employment creation, improving agricultural productivity, and promoting gender equality. However, women's access to land has to necessarily be backed by effective control over productive resources in a state like Rajasthan ridden with discrimination based on class, caste, and patriarchy. Alongside the value systems, the culture and the nature of institutions, including the family, need to change. The existing social and political movements in the state need to expand and be intensified to include issues related to women and land rights.

IV

RECOMMENDATIONS

Some recommendations emerging from this chapter emphasize that notwithstanding legal enactments put in place for enabling women to access their land rights, effective rights are contingent on two factors both the existing socio-economic conditions and the role of implementing agencies. Policy implications regarding women's access to land essentially need to touch upon both these aspects. At a broader level, the state policy needs to focus on more inclusive development strategies across geographical regions resulting in better indicators of gender and development.

Most women are not aware of the steps involved in obtaining operational rights to avail benefits of owning land from the government. State interventions also require a more focused attention to raise awareness among women regarding their rights to land. There is a need for legal awareness camps and providing legal aid to women cultivators and landowners to prevent them from situations that hinder them from gaining access and control over their land. At another level, the state has to take an initiative to raise the awareness levels of the implementing agencies regarding HSA 2005, by issuing relevant rules and directives.

In order to facilitate obtaining operational rights over land by women, a 'single window approach' to land records with close coordination between survey, revenue, and registration departments has recently been introduced. However, it needs to be strengthened.

At present, the HSA 2005 is not applicable to Bhil and Meenas in the state. Hence, daughters do not have the right to ancestral property since customary laws are applicable. There is a need to amend the central legislation to include tribal groups under HSA 2005 in order to make it more inclusive.

The institutions of Panchayati Raj or/and the revenue department dealing with the implementation of issues related to women's access to land can be linked to the women's self-help groups (SHGs) at various levels (village, block, and district) for better implementation of both inheritance rights and government land distribution programmes. Linkages with CBOs and NGOs can also be established for effective dissemination of knowledge on women's land rights and implementation strategies for better access of land to women.

It is evident that women's participation in agriculture has been high especially in the case of marginalized sections—the SC and ST. But state interventions are not adequate to make their participation more productive and effective. Secure rights to land for women are one aspect for ensuring productive use of land. Another important realm is the government intervention in making appropriate programme design and implementation for their productive participation in agriculture. To make institutions sensitive to women's needs, women's 'voices' need to be integrated into both the design and implementation of different programmes. Women in tribal areas need to be prioritized and strategies that are suitable to their needs and conditions need to be developed. It is also important to enhance the overall infrastructure in agriculture by enhancing financial allocations which facilitate supply-induced conditions through which women can also effectively participate in agriculture.

One of the biggest challenges encountered in analysing gender issues pertaining to land rights in the state has been the lack of sex-disaggregated data. It is strongly recommended that sex-disaggregated data be generated at the state level. The Board of Revenue, GoR, in particular could evolve a system to generate sex-disaggregated data on land records. This will enable better planning and policy analysis.

For any land transaction in the state, three documents are required, namely the *jamabandi* (registry), *khasra girdawari* (record of land use), and the site map. The computerization of land records in the state has so far been limited to only registered land. There is need to computerize the information of the other two related documents. This will facilitate the availability of all information related to any piece of land at one place. The computerization of all three documents will have a positive impact on women's right to land as it will lead to direct transfer of the land to all legal heirs at the time of mutation. The role of revenue officials will be limited to the post-land-transfer phase. This step will ensure that the percentage of release deeds signed in favour of brothers will reduce because the land would already be in women's/girls' name. At present, brothers get the release deed signed before the land is transferred in the name of the sister. Recently, the GoR has made an attempt to digitize land records and an investor can extract a copy of land records along with details of mutation from Apnakhata.[7] Women, especially non-literate women, need to be made aware of these developments.

Relinquishing of land owned by women in favour of their brothers is a relatively simple procedure in Rajasthan. It requires merely her signature on a ₹100 stamp paper in the presence of the *tehsildar*. It should be ensured that if women relinquish their claims, the relinquishment is done through a formal deed of law rather than informally. To deter this practice, the value of the formal deed should be increased to one-third of the women's share of land.

All landowners in rural areas are entitled to loans from cooperative banks. A policy decision should be taken to increase the number of women who can avail loans by increasing the loan amount and reducing the rate of interest. This will lead to greater number of land deeds being registered in women's name.

Inheritance laws in the state should be made more stringent and care should be taken while implementing laws to ensure that daughters are not deprived of their right to inheritance. Fathers should not be allowed to deprive their daughters of their share in inheritance and partition of property by resorting to the provision of making a will in favour of sons. The violation of the law of succession should be made a cognizable offence.

Revenue and other officials of the state also need to be sensitized to the needs of women cultivators. They should make sure that women's rights to land are not encroached upon by collaterals and others in mutations, *jamabandis*, and *girdawari* records. Their approach to women landowners and cultivators needs to be more sensitive. Towards this end, special trainings need to be organized by the government. A women-friendly environment could be created by appointing a greater number of women revenue officials.

Village-based NGOs/CSOs, women's organizations, and other groups should be encouraged to take up individual cases of discrimination in matters of inheritance and usurpation of women's rights to land and property and act as watchdogs for women's interests. NGOs can also help to create strong public opinion against the infringement of laws in general and on the positive aspects of women inheriting and owning land.

The state officials need to generate awareness among women farmers on new agricultural technologies and practices through the provision of agricultural knowledge and experience. Special training should be provided to women farmers to raise their management and risk-bearing capacity, and to help them access easy capital, facilitating marketing and procuring remunerative prices for their produce. The training programmes should be designed keeping in mind the special characteristics and requirements of women cultivators who are in large majority in the state.

CONCLUSION

Land is the major means of productive activity in rural Rajasthan. Ownership and effective control of land is crucial for women's empowerment. This can be made possible through a sociocultural environment that is supportive of the implementation of legal measures and Acts. However, land rights in the state are embedded in a strong cultural bias against female inheritance in the implementation of laws. This has prevented women from having effective ownership of land rights. Alongside, several sociocultural practices continue to exist, which hinder women's access to land and restrict the expansion of spaces in both agriculture and their participation in other domains at the HH and community levels. Women's empowerment through land rights requires removing the persisting gender inequalities and barriers at multiple levels. One of the main challenges in this regard relates to the social acceptance of women's right to land cutting across caste, class, and religious groups.

ANNEXURE

Table A12.1

Panchayati Raj Department Information for Land *Pattas* for the Year 2007–08 to 2014–15 (Progress and Achievement Against Targets)

Year	Allotment of Land Pattas Under Rule 157			Regularization of Land to People up to 2003 Under Rule 157 (2)			Allotment of Plots Under Rule 158					
							Allotment of Plots at Nominal Rates			Allotment of Free of Cost Plots to BPL Families		
	Target	Achievement	Female	Target	Achievement	Female	Target	Achievement	Female	Female	Achievement	Female
2007 to 2008	30,000	48,380	2,978	30,000	22,889	1,303	17,000	23,564	2,175	13,000	15,016	2,718
2008 to 2009	20,000	28,538	2,067	10,000	20,245	665	17,000	16,815	1,173	13,000	20,017	3,727
2009 to 2010	20,000	24,153	2,336	10,000	14,662	2,504	17,000	13,436	1,305	13,000	14,336	4,205
2010 to 2011	20,000	255,801	9,798	10,000	20,632	1,573	17,000	51,892	1,226	13,000	106,697	7,825
2011 to 2012	20,000	27,112	4,048	10,000	13,087	4,219	17,000	10,700	2,550	13,000	24,710	13,917

(Table A12.1 Continued)

(Table A12.1 Continued)

Year	Allotment of Land Pattas Under Rule 157			Regularization of Land to People up to 2003 Under Rule 157 (2)			Allotment of Plots at Nominal Rates			Allotment of Plots Under Rule 158			Allotment of Free of Cost Plots to BPL Families	
	Target	Achievement	Female	Target	Achievement	Female	Target	Achievement	Female		Female	Achievement		Achievement	Female
2012 to 2013	20,000	49,170	17,766	10,000	21,856	7,773	17,000	14,846	3,691		12,900	26,839			12,798
2013 to 2014	20,000	33,459	6,151	10,000	8,688	2,461	17,000	9,198	1,938		13,000	11,701			4,362
2014 to 2015	20,000	15,096	5,122	10,000	5,387	1,594	17,000	720	720		13,000	5,837			3,518
Total	170,000	481,704	50,266	100,000	127,146	22,092	136,000	14,778	14,778		103,900	225,163			53,070

Table A12.2

Allotee Type-wise Number of Houses Sanctioned Under IAY for Financial Years 2011–15

Financial Year	Select Scheme	Registered in MIS				IAY Incentives—Homestead Scheme House Sanctioned			
		Male	Female	M+F	Total	Male	Female	M+F	Total
2011–12	Special Package	7,608 (13.5)	41,117 (73.4)	7,323 (13.1)	56,048 (100)	7,517 (13.6)	40,443 (73.2)	7,295 (13.2)	55,255 (100)
2012–13	IAY New construction (Target-68,578)	14,713 (20.9)	47,592 (67.8)	7,931 (11.3)	70,236 (100)	14,599 (21.0)	47,113 (67.7)	7834 (11.3)	69,546 (100)
2012–13	Special Package	3,236 (21.7)	9,822 (66.0)	1,821 (12.2)	14,879 (100)	3,222 (21.8)	9,706 (65.8)	1,823 (12.4)	14,751 (100.0)
2013–14	IAY New construction (Target-85,460)	26,051 (29.7)	51,410 (58.5)	10,361 (11.8)	87,822 (100)	25,757 (29.8)	50,397 (58.4)	10,236 (11.8)	86,390 (100)
2013–14	Special Package	6 (6.7)	84 (93.3)		90 (100)	0	10 (100)	0	10 (100)
2014–15	IAY New construction (Target-76,068)	22,281 (28.7)	30,900 (39.8)	24,519 (31.5)	77,700 (100)	21,959 (28.9)	29,788 (39.2)	24,201 (31.9)	75,948 (100)

Source: Department of Rural Development and Panchayati Raj, Government of Rajasthan.

NOTES

1. This chapter has relied on an earlier study conducted by the author and a team of researchers from IDSJ in the year 2011. Data were collected from 240 households in two districts, 12 villages of 4 blocks of Rajasthan. Jhadol and Salumbar blocks in Udaipur district and Gharsana and Padampur blocks in Ganganagar district.
2. http://www.fao.org/worldfoodsummit/english/fsheets/women.pdf/ (accessed on 5 September 2014).
3. The custom of *nata* initially took place when one of the partners in a marriage died or simply walked out on the other or when they separated due to disagreement. This system of second or subsequent marriage took place within the caste and predominantly with the desire and consent of the ex-husband and the girl's father and generally with the girl's approval. The man who accepted the woman in *nata* had to pay a mutually agreed upon sum of money (*jhagra*) usually to the former husband.
4. HSA, 2005, gives the following rights to daughters under Section 6:

    > The daughter of a coparcener shall by birth become a coparcener in her own right in the same manner as the son;

    > She has the same rights in the coparcenary property as she would have had if she had been a son; She shall be subject to the same liability in the said coparcenary property as that of a son; and any reference to a Hindu Mitakshara coparceners shall be deemed to include a reference to a daughter of a coparcener; She is allotted the same share as is allotted to a son; The share of the pre-deceased son or a pre-deceased daughter shall be allotted to the surviving child of such pre-deceased son or of such pre-deceased daughter; The share of the pre-deceased child of a pre-deceased son or of a pre-deceased daughter shall be allotted to the child of such pre-deceased.

5. There is no provision for sanctioning special packages under the IAY except for the release of a small amount out of 5% IAY funds meant for natural calamity to meet the exigencies of certain natural calamities such as heavy rains, floods, cyclones, earthquakes, and fire (see http://iay.nic.in user _ manual_iay.pdf).
6. Few families have converted to Christianity, but none of them belonged to our sample.
7. Apnakhata is a Rajasthan Government's project which works under the Revenue Department of Rajasthan, Ajmer. This project was started to provide Online Records of Rights (NAKAL) of Land Records of Rajasthan State. An authorized copy of records of rights (NAKAL) can be obtained

from selected kiosks. The landholders' entire record can now be viewed by selecting the *tehsil*, name, *khata* (account), and *khasra* (serial) numbers on Apnakhata's website (see apnakhata.raj.nic.in).

REFERENCES

Agarwal, B. 1994a. *A Field of One's Own: Gender and Land Rights in South Asia*. Cambridge, MA: Cambridge University Press.
———. 1994b. *Gender and Command over Property: An Economic Analysis of South Asia*. New Delhi: Kali for Women.
Burns, Katherine. 2004. 'Women's Land Rights and Social Empowerment in Rural Rajasthan.' Paper prepared for CECOEDECON, Jaipur.
Government of India (GoI). 2013, July. *Draft National Land Reforms Policy*. Ministry of Rural Development. Available at: http://rural.nic.in/sites/downloads/latest/Draft_National_Land_Reforms_Policy_July_2013.pdf (accessed on 12 August 2014).
Government of Rajasthan (GoR). 2005–06. *Gender Responsive Budgeting for the Department of Registration and Stamps*. Vol. 5/2005–06. Jaipur: Government of Rajasthan.
Gupta, L. C. 1994. *Land Ceiling and After*. Jaipur: IDSJ and Rawat Publications.
Hindustan Times. 2010. 'Sexist land Ownership Causing Gender Inequality in India: UN.' *Hindustan Times*, February 18. E-paper at http://www.hindustantimes.com/world/sexist-land-ownership-causing-gender-inequality-in-india-un/story-yo3Nr6LhhOcv32yrxNOkGJ.html (accessed on 15 March 2010).
HSA Amendment. 2005. *The Hindu Succession (Amendment) Act, 2005*. Available at: http://www.hrln.org/admin/issue/subpdf/HSA_Amendment_2005.pdf (accessed on February 22, 2016).
IDSJ (Institute of Development Studies Jaipur). 1989. 'Development of Women in Indira Gandhi Nahar Project: Situational Analysis and Action Plan.' IDSJ Research Report No 77, Jaipur.
———. 2006. 'Local Customs and Practices in Rajasthan and Their Impact on Women: An In-depth sStudy of Dakan/Dayan.', IDSJ Research Report No 184, Jaipur.
———. 2011. 'Existing State Policies: Women's Access to land and Women's Empowerment.' IDSJ Research Report, Jaipur.
Mathur, K. 2004. *Countering Gender Violence: Initiatives towards Collective Action in Rajasthan*. New Delhi: SAGE Publications.
Nandwana, Shobha, and Ramesh Nandwana. 1998. 'Land Rights of Widows in Rajasthan.' In *Widows in India: Social Neglect and Public Action*, edited by Martha Alter Chen, 228–40. New Delhi: SAGE Publications.

Nandwana, R., and S. Nandwana. 1994. Land Rights of Widows Paper 7 in Conference on Widows in India Organised by Harvard Institute for International Development, Bangalore, March 23–25.

Sagar, V., and K. Ahuja. 1987. *Rural Transformation in a Developing Economy*. Jaipur: Kumar and Company.

SPRI. 2007. A Report on the 'An Assessment of the Situation of Cases of Women Litigants in the Revenue Courts in Rajasthan and the Need for Gender Sensitisation of Revenue Officers to Expedite their Disposal.' Supported by IFES and USAID. Jaipur: State Policy Research Institute.

Swaminathan, Srilata, and Mahendra Choudhary. 1997. In *People, Law and Justice: Casebook on Public Interest Litigation,* Vol. 2, edited by Sangeeta Ahuja, 520. New Delhi: Orient Longman Publishers.

Yugandhar, B. N., and P. S. Dutta. 1995. *Land Reforms in India: Vol. 2. Rajasthan—Feudalism and Change*. New Delhi: SAGE Publications.

13

Locating Gender in Land Rights Discourse of Sikkim

SOHEL FIRDOS

Sikkim was declared as the 22nd state of the Union of India on 16th May 1975. It is the smallest state in India based on the population count and also the youngest member of the Northeast Council. At the beginning of the 20th century, Sikkim had a small population of 59,014 in 1901 that has increased sharply to 610,577 in 2011, constituting 0.05% of the total population of the country (Census 2011). It indicates that the state has registering a ten-fold increase over a period of 110 years. The female population in the state is 287,507 (47.09%) against 323,070 males (52.91%). Population is unevenly distributed across the four districts of the state owing to physiographic constraints and economic opportunities. Among the four districts of the state, the East district is having more than one-third of the population, the largest population, concentrated in the district. On the other hand, the North district, having a relatively larger geographical area, provides habitation to a population of 43,909 only. Sikkim is a multilingual, multi-religious and multiethnic state. Historic events have played their part in creating such a mosaic. The Lepchas are considered the original inhabitants of Sikkim and Darjeeling Hills (Darjeeling Hills were part of Sikkim and annexed by British India in 1835). In the 17th century (1641), they came in contact with the Tibetan Bhutias, resulting in the Tibetization of the Lepchas. British contact

(1884–85) encouraged Nepali (a generic term that includes many castes and tribes) immigration as labour was required for construction of roads and extension of agriculture in the 19th and early 20th centuries (Sinha 1975). The ethnic scene of Sikkim changed rapidly with the multiplication of the number of Nepalese (Sinha 2003). According to the 1891 gazetteer of Sikkim, the Nepalis constituted 56%, the Lepchas constituted 19%, and the Bhutias constituted 16% of the population (Bhasin 2011). However, the proportionate distribution of such population groups has witnessed significant changes over a period of 120 years. In 2011, the percentages of Lepchas and Bhutias have declined to 7.06% and 11.45%, respectively, while the share of the non-tribal population, which may be taken as a proxy for the Nepalis, has grown to about 67%. In terms of spatial spread, the Dzongo area in North Sikkim has been declared as a reserved area for Lepchas, where a large majority lives. However, their population is found in other three districts also. The Bhutia and Nepali groups practising different religions and speaking various languages are distributed all across the length and breadth of the state (ibid.). Table 13.1 reveals a skewed spatial distribution of population across the four districts of the state. The East district has the largest population where 46.45% of the total population of the state is concentrated. Though the North district has the largest geographical area, it provides habitation to a relatively small population of 43,709 owing to physical constraints. The sex ratio of the state is lower than the national average. Moreover, it is depressingly low in the North and East districts. Surprisingly, the phenomenon of low sex ratio has not drawn the attention of researchers as of now and hence further research is required to provide an explanation for it. The literacy rate in the state is impressive but the gender disparities are quite glaring (Table 13.1). The female literacy rate in Sikkim is

Table 13.1

Demographic Characteristics of Sikkim for 2011

District/State	No. of Households	Population	Sex Ratio	Literacy Rate		
				Total	Male	Female
North District	8,873	43,709	767	78.01	83.30	70.97
West District	28,023	136,435	942	77.39	83.53	70.86
South District	30,543	146,850	915	81.42	86.52	75.82
East District	61,567	283,583	873	83.85	88.47	78.50
Sikkim	129,006	610,577	890	81.42	86.55	75.61

Source: Census of India, 2011.

75.61 as compared to the male literacy rate which is 86.55. The highest female literacy rate is reported from the east district as 78.50% followed by the south district for which it is 75.82%, while in the north and west districts, it hovers around 70%. Subsequent to the discussion on demographic characteristics, we will turn to the distribution of population of different tribal groups in the state.

DISTRIBUTION OF SCHEDULED TRIBES

According to the 2011 Census, the Scheduled Tribes (STs) with a population of 206,360 constitute 33.80% of the total population of the state. The ST population is in majority in the north district as they constitute 65.70% of the total population of the district, while in the west district, the percentage is 42.38% (Table 13.2). The four major tribal groups in the state are Bhutias, Lepchas, Limboos, and Tamangs. Bhutias with a population of 69,598 are the largest tribal group in the state, and constitute about one-third of the total ST population. About one-half of Bhutia population is concentrated in the economically prosperous and well-connected district of East Sikkim. Limboos, the second largest tribal group with a population of 53,703, constitute about one-fourth of the

Table 13.2

Distribution of ST Population and Individual Tribes for 2011

District/ State	Total ST Population	% of ST Population	Population of Individual Tribes			
			Bhutia	Lepcha	Limboo	Tamang
North District	28,715	65.70	7,971 (27.76)	13,748 (47.88)	4,543 (15.82)	2,118 (7.38)
West District	57,817	42.38	13,779 (23.83)	9,775 (16.91)	27,622 (47.77)	6,072 (10.50)
South District	41,392	28.19	13,805 (33.35)	6,959 (16.81)	9,625 (23.25)	10,230 (24.71)
East District	78,436	27.66	34,043 (43.40)	12,427 (15.84)	11,913 (15.19)	19,276 (24.58)
Sikkim	206,360	33.80	69,598 (33.73)	42,909 (20.79)	53,703 (26.02)	37,696 (18.27)

Source: Census of India, 2011.
Note: Figures in parentheses indicate the percentage of each tribe to the total ST population in the district/state and have been computed by the author.

total tribal population and they are mainly concentrated in the west district. Lepchas with a population of 42,909 form the third largest tribal group in the state and constitute about one-fifth of the total tribal population. A large majority of their population (about one-third) is concentrated in the north district while about 29% is concentrated in the east district. The Tamangs have a relatively smaller population of 37,696, and they constitute about 18% of tribal population which is mainly concentrated in the east and south districts.

MAJOR COMMUNITIES IN SIKKIM AND THEIR LANDOWNERSHIP PATTERN

'The settlement report of 1958 mentioned that the 'highest percentage of the total cultivated land is owned by the Nepalis (66%) who are migrants to Sikkim. Bhutias and Lepchas, who are the sons of the soil, own 20% and 14%, respectively' (Bhasin 2002). However, a perusal of landownership by holding sizes reveals that the Bhutias own a majority of larger landholdings. Datta's (1992) study of 48 revenue blocks under Namchi Police Station of Sikkim corroborates the above statement that 77.28% cultivable land is under the possession of Nepalis, and 11.30% and 11.42% cultivable land is owned by Bhutias and Lepchas, respectively. However, it was found that Bhutias possess the highest amount of per capita cultivable landholding (10.73 acres) followed by Lepchas (10.61 acres) and Nepalis (4.81 acres). It can be seen that even in South Sikkim where Nepalis are in majority, the Bhutias and Lepchas have more cultivable land. It is due to the fact that, though less in number, Bhutias and Lepchas own large plots of land and there are many Nepalis who are landless and work as share croppers, agricultural labourers, and skilled and non-skilled daily wage earners.

DISTRIBUTION OF LANDHOLDINGS

The distribution of operational landholdings in Sikkim is skewed (Firdos 2014). The marginal landholdings constituted more than one-half of the landholdings in 2010–11, but only 13.88% of the total operational land area. The concentration of marginal landholdings is the highest in the east district (56%) occupying only 12.8% of the land area. As opposed to this, the percentage share of large holdings (more than 10 hectares) is very small (1.04%), but covers 11.53% of the land area. The landownership scenario is relatively different in the north district. In this district, 30% of the land is occupied by a mere 5% of the operational holdings. Interestingly, there is parity in the proportionate distribution of landholdings and area under the small and semi-medium categories in all the districts except in the east district.

DISTRIBUTION OF LANDHOLDINGS AMONG SCHEDULED TRIBES

About one-half of the total operational holdings in Sikkim belong to ST farmers. The marginal operational holdings constitute more than one-half of the total holdings among the STs with about 12% of the total area. On the other hand, landholdings belonging to the semi-medium and medium categories constitute more than one-fourth of the holdings but occupy about 57% of the land. Importantly, the inequality in landownership is pervasive among the STs also as 28% of the land is owned by just 5% of the large landholders.

DECLINING PER CAPITA AVAILABILITY OF LAND

Per capita availability of net cultivated area has also recorded a continuous decline over the last four decades owing to significant population growth. In 2010–11, the per capita availability of net cultivated area declined from 0.31 hectare in 1971 to 0.27 hectare in 1981, 0.17 hectare in 1991 and 0.13 hectare. However, wide variations continue to exist across the districts.

SIKKIMESE IDENTITY AND STATUS OF WOMEN WITH REFERENCE TO LAND

The question of Sikkimese identity versus women's identity in Sikkim is entangled in the political and social web that so far has remained unexplained. On the surface of it, the issue of identity, owing to its strong political anchoring, has been so overarching that gender implications have eluded any discussion. What or who is Sikkimese in itself is a problematic question that we have never got around to answering. But who is a Sikkimese woman is a question that is asked every six months as the state asks a woman to prove that she is unmarried every six months (unmarried certificates have a 6-month validity) or marry a Sikkimese man to earn a living or get state benefits. It has its antecedents in a proclamation made by Sikkim Durbar on 15th March 1969, stripping Sikkimese women of their citizenship if they married someone not belonging to Sikkim which was then a separate kingdom. More than half a century later, this law continues to be in practice. The state uses 'residential certificate' and 'Certificate of Identification (CoI)' as instruments of differentiation between the two genders in terms of providing public goods and services as is evident from the following decisions taken by the government. In this context, it is important to mention that CoI is essential for just about everything in Sikkim, from being able to conduct business to applying for government employment to receiving state benefits. For old settlers, this role is played by the residential certificates issued to those who were residents of the state as on the cut-off date of 26th April 1975.

On 27th January 2015, the Government of Sikkim decided to make it mandatory for all married daughters of the old settlers of the state to furnish their own, their father's, and their husband's residential certificates when applying for trade licenses, contract works, driving licenses, and other benefits and services. On 23rd February 2015, less than a month later, the government took a decision to withdraw the provision of issuing CoI to non-local women married to Sikkimese by bringing in a partial modification to Notification No. 66/Home/95, dated 22nd November 1995 as amended pertaining to the issue of CoI. Those women not having residential certificate/CoI but married to Sikkimese men holding such certificates were included into the Sikkimese fold with the 1995 amendment of Notification No. 66/Home, but now have been denied again as the protection of local status gets further reinforced. Unfortunately, Sikkimese women who found spouses outside were cast away much earlier.

While the problems with rules such as those mentioned above run deep and wide, even on the surface it sounds obnoxious for a woman's identity to be based on the identity of not one, but two men—her father's and her husband's—at all times! A Sikkimese woman will be considered

Sikkimese only if both her father and husband are also Sikkimese. In the case of non-local women marrying Sikkimese men, it is again the woman who is made to bear the brunt, being refused acceptance as a local and thereby denied economic or professional prospects in the state. Whether women are willing to bear this burden or not is a question that is not asked often and even if it is, the answers come in a coagulated mix made mostly of the local–non-local positions and peppered lightly with that of gender equality and hence end-up making no sense at all.

A woman advocate Ms Doma Bhutia, one of the few vocal about the issue, says that the recent decisions passed by the cabinet go against Article 15(1) of the Constitution which observes that 'The State shall not discriminate against any citizen on grounds only of religion, race, caste, sex, place of birth or any of them.' It can hence be challenged in the court of law, she believes. 'It is a form of violence against women. Violence need not be only physical but it can also be mental or psychological,' says Doma. She argues,

> Through such decisions, the state is perpetuating violence against women in the state. It can also be called sex selection in a way where a woman in Sikkim may not be killed in the womb but she is cast out if she chooses to marry a non-local.

A senior officer with the state government who is married to a man who is a non-local says, 'I am very happy with the government's decision but if the law is applicable to Sikkimese women married to non-locals then it should also apply to Sikkimese men married to non-locals.' This is another common view that is probably expressed by many in the state.

However, she also says that women's empowerment in Sikkim is a vague term that is expressed very often but does not exist in reality. She contends that actual empowerment is still a far cry. 'Women are very good decision makers but sadly we are not allowed to make any decisions,' she says. Her Sikkimese status being taken away because of her marriage to a non-local, she cannot pass on her inheritance to her children. This forced cutting-off from her roots rankles her, but is not enough to obsess her. On a more practical level, she has, therefore, not developed property in Sikkim. 'I will sell off the property I have here and probably moved out of the state later. It is sad that I will not be able to leave anything for my children here in Sikkim,' she adds.

The rules are also incomplete because they remain silent on whether a woman reclaims her Sikkimese status if she divorces her non-local husband or what identity status extends to children born out of wedlock to

Sikkimese women. No thought has clearly been spared to wonder what would happen to Sikkimese women married into equally 'protective' regimes like, say, J&K or for that matter daughters from such societies married into Sikkim—they will end up belonging to neither place and would have no career or livelihood prospects at either address.

Social and political discourse on identity in Sikkim is mostly dominated by the 'local' and 'non-local' issue where the woman finds little or no space at all. The identity issue is undeniably a complex one and with much at stake, governments have forever struggled to keep everyone happy.

WOMEN AND AGRICULTURE

In Sikkim, as is the case elsewhere, women are more dependent on agriculture than men. The share of cultivators among the female main workers in rural Sikkim is 58.33% as compared to 42.20% among the males. The share of agricultural labourers is also higher among the female than the male. It indicates that the responsibility of carrying out agricultural activities has been left to women while men have moved to the non-farm activities. The gender differentials in the agriculture sector become sharper when we analyse the data at the district level. In the west district, about 70% of women main workers are cultivators while the corresponding figure for men is about only 58%. Even in the east district with a relatively high level of urbanization and a strong service sector, almost one-half of the women main workers are cultivators.

LAND ADMINISTRATION SYSTEM

Historical Context

Traditionally, the land in Sikkim belonged to the king. All the farmers' land in Sikkim was held from the King. Edgar wrote,

> [T]he cultivators have soil and man may settle down and cultivate any land he may find unoccupied without going through any formality whatever,

and when once he has occupied the land no one but the Rajah can turn him out. But the Rajah can exclude him at any time and if he should cease to occupy the land, he would not retain any lien upon it. There is a kind of tenant-right, however, under which cultivators are enabled to dispose of unexhausted improvements. Thus, a man who has terraced a piece of hill side could not sell the land but is allowed to sell the right of using the terraces. This custom is acknowledged not to be absolutely a right, but more of the nature of an indulgence on the part of the Rajah, by whom it was allowed to grow up for the sake of convenience.

Also there were Kazis and headmen and various other officials who exercised jurisdiction over specific tracts of lands. The Kazis and officials enjoyed some authority but the final authority was the king in all important matters. For example, major legal disputes that might arise on the territory held by an official would be referred to the king. Aside from exercising some authority, judiciating minor disputes, and referring to the ruler thing of moment, the officials also assessed the revenue payable by all the people settled on the lands within the king's jurisdiction; they paid over the ruler a certain fixed contribution and kept the greater portion for themselves. The Kazis had no proprietary right in the lands, although they did have a kind of hereditary title to their office.

The area of the land allotted to the subjects of the king was not measured and the subjects did not pay any revenue to the king. The assessment was on the payer of revenue personally, and in theory he was permitted the use of king's land so that he could prosper and be able to give to the king services which he was bound to do as the kings 'live chattel'. If the system had been extended to the theoretical perfection, he would have been obliged to have given over to the King all the produce of the land. Actually, the subject was only obliged to give a small share of his labour or the result of his labour to the state. When he had no actual service, the amount of his property was roughly assessed, and his contribution to the state was fixed accordingly. But such assessment was made without reference to the amount of land occupied by the subject. The value of his wives, children, cattle, furniture, etc., was all accounted for but not the extent of his fields. The land under a person in Sikkim could be transferred by the king to another party.

During the period of monarchy, most parts of the state were controlled by the landlords (the Kazis) who 'acted as barons' (Basnet 1974) in order to collect taxes for king and rule with an iron grip. This period is marked by the absence of women as landlords or as those holding any position in the kings' ministry. People had to suffer the atrocities in the form of forced labour (Sinha 2008). The peasant women were utilized for pleasure by the landlords with the aid of henchmen. Socially, they were exploited and legally they did not have any right (Subba 2014). The laws of Sikkim enacted during the monarchy did not give any property inheritance right to the women. The customary law 'permits women to get divorce from their men only after paying certain amount of money (zho) and if there was dispute over a child then women are allowed to take the girl child only whereas father takes the son' (White 1971). The law clearly shows the gender biasness which separated the child in form of a son from his mother and a daughter from his father. One of the discriminatory laws were enacted when Sikkim Durbar on 15th March 1969 initiated the proclamation of scrapping Sikkimese citizenship from women who marries an outsider (non-Sikkimese; Basnet 1974). From the day of proclamation of this law, women had no legal rights over the inherited property leading to discrimination in the ownership of land.

LEGISLATIONS RELATING TO LAND AND THEIR GENDER IMPLICATIONS

The process of framing legislation relating to control, regulation, and transfer of land in Sikkim began towards the beginning of the 20th century. The major driving force for enacting the first legislation was to check the land alienation of Bhutia and Lepcha tribes. The Durbar, at that point of time, took a serious note of the fact that a large area of land belonging to Bhutias and Lepchas are being sold/transferred to the Nepalis, and if it continues, these two tribal communities will lose land under their possession. In the following paragraphs, legislative measures have been explained.

1. **Revenue Order (R.O.) No. 1 of 1917:** One of the important orders passed by the Chogyals[1] during the pre-merger period is 'Revenue Order No. 1 of 1917'. It prohibits transfer of land from Bhutias and Lepchas to other communities. As per this order,

    No Bhutia and Lepchas are to be allowed to sell, mortgage or sublease of their land to any person other than a Bhutia or a Lepcha without the express sanction of the Darbar or Officers empowered by the

Darbar in their behalf, whose order will be obtained by the landlord concerned.

2. **Revenue Order (R.O.) No. 105 Dated the 25th February 1961:**
This order was issued by the Darbar because it came to their notice that Nepalese were 'marrying Bhutia–Lepcha girls or non-Sikkimese marrying Sikkimese women and such men were acquiring immovable properties of Bhutia–Lepcha'.[2] In order to prevent the alienation of the immovable property of Bhutia–Lepcha, the above mentioned R.O. was issued that asked the Registration Officers to strictly follow and observe the procedures given as follows 'in cases of transaction relating to transfer of immovable properties'.

   a. 'that Nepalese who are marrying Bhutia–Lepcha girls or non-Sikkimese marrying–Sikkimese women are acquiring immovable properties of Bhutia–Lepcha cannot be alienated in favour of a non-Bhutia–Lepcha and that non-Sikkimese are not entitled to acquire any immovable properties in Sikkim'.
   b. 'this order further asked the Officers that whenever a transfer of a landed property in Sikkim happens to involve women, the registering officer before allowing the registration of the document relating to such transfer, should make an enquiry as to from "what is the source of the money for the purchase of the property" to where the transfer is by sale.' It is also to be ascertained whether the money used to purchase the land comes from her actual property, or it is to be provided by her husband if she is married, in which case such other particulars of her husband including the community to which he belongs, his home address, what landed property he holds already in Sikkim, etc., should be enquired at the first stage. In the case of transfer otherwise than by sale also such as gift, similar particulars of the husband of the woman if she is married are to be furnished. The registering officer is to undertake and complete all the preliminary enquiries as intended above, and should then refer to the case to the *Dewan* of Sikkim with his forwarding report for a decision. Pending specific decision forthcoming from the authority concerned, the registration of such transfer documents should on no account be finalized.'[3]

DEFINING THE RIGHTS OF WOMEN TO PURCHASE AND SELL BY ISSUING OF NOTIFICATION NO. 28 IN 1969

Since this R.O. No. 1 of 1917 was silent 'about the right of a woman to purchase or sell land after her marriage to a person of other community, the Land Revenue Department issued a notification (No. 28) on the 21st April 1969 in order to clarify the position in this regard'.[4] This notification is reproduced verbatim and reads as follows:

1. 'Woman follows the nationality and community of her husband.'
2. 'Bhutia/Lepcha woman marrying a person of community other than her own may sell land to her own community only if such land was acquired by her prior to her marriage.'
3. 'Land acquired by her after her marriage to non-Bhutia, Lepcha may be sold to any Community.'
4. 'Sikkimese of Tibetan and Bhutanese origin enjoy all rights and privileges of Bhutia Lepcha except that they may not buy land from the latter community.'

MARRIED WOMEN'S PROPERTY REGULATION, 1962

This regulation

> provides for the rights of Sikkimese women married to persons other than Sikkim Subjects to acquire, hold and dispose of immoveable property in Sikkim and to provide for rules of succession to property held by such Sikkimese women. In this Regulation, the term 'Sikkimese' means a person who is a Sikkim Subject at the time of her marriage.[5]

The relevant Sections 4–8 of this regulation are reproduced as follows:

Section 4: 'A Sikkimese woman who holds immoveable property in Sikkim at the time of her marriage shall continue to hold such property notwithstanding her marriage with a person who is not a Sikkim Subject and shall have the power to dispose of such property either by sale, mortgage or otherwise to a Sikkim Subject during her life-time.'

Section 5: 'A Sikkimese woman married to a person who is not a Sikkim Subject shall have no right to acquire any immoveable property or any interest in such property in the territory of Sikkim subsequent to her marriage.'

Section 6: 'If a Sikkimese women marries a person who is not a Sikkim Subject, the husband and any offspring born of that marriage shall acquire no interest in any immoveable property which she may hold in Sikkim by virtue of Section 4 of this Regulation.'

Section 7: 'Notwithstanding the provisions of any other law to the contrary any immoveable property in Sikkim which may be held by a Sikkimese woman at the time of her marriage shall not on her death devolve on her husband if she had been married to a non-Sikkim Subject nor shall it be inherited by any offspring of such marriage.'

Section 8: 'Any immoveable property held by a Sikkimese woman married to a person who is not a Sikkim Subject is contemplated in Section 4 of this Regulation shall devolve on her death and be inherited by such person or persons who would have been regarded but for her marriage as her next of kin under the rules for intestate succession, provided always that such next of kin in order to succeed to such property is a Sikkim Subject.'[6]

In this context, it is pertinent to mention here that neither the Hindu Succession Act, 1956, nor the Indian Succession Act, 1925, was extended or enforced in Sikkim and, hence, it was considered expedient to enact a legislation for succession pertaining to movable and immovable properties of Sikkimese people in the form of Sikkim Succession Act (SSA), 2008, which is explained further in relation to property rights of women.

SIKKIM SUCCESSION ACT (SSA), 2008, AND PROPERTY RIGHTS OF WOMEN

The State Assembly of Sikkim passed a bill in 2008 that entitles equal property rights for Sikkimese women. The Sikkim Succession Bill, 2008, which became an act in the same year, provides legislation for equal property rights to daughters, wives, and divorced and abandoned wives having Sikkim subject holders. After the Act was notified, property (movable and immovable) of a male Sikkimese, if he dies, went to the surviving members of his family: wife, sons, and daughters in equal proportion. However, a Sikkimese woman who has married a non-Sikkimese or has acquired foreign citizenship is not entitled to enjoy the benefits under this Act.

However, the inheritance right of property is not enjoyed by women at the same level as the males do, owing to association of such rights with their marital status. According to the SSA 2008,

> [T]he immovable property inherited, gifted or purchased by women cannot be transferred and registered in the names of local Sikkimese women after marriage. The immovable assets are also not registered or transferred to the legal heirs and children of Sikkimese women if their husbands happen to be non-locals.[7]

Although this piece of legislation was hailed as a major milestone in women's empowerment in the state, it is ironical that it provided equal property rights only to women who remain 'pure' Sikkimese. The written fine print was the words stating that rights under the new Act did not extend to women married to non-locals. According to 'Daughters of the soil of Sikkim', an organization consisting of 58 local women,

> [T]his is very demoralizing to us. Many of us have developed the assets gifted to us by our family by investing all our life's earnings and savings. It is but natural that as mothers we would like to see our children enjoy the fruits of our labour. However, under the existing laws, this is not possible. Such gender blind policies are discriminator

The memorandum states,

> The problem has been further compounded by the mandatory requirement for a Sikkimese woman to submit an 'unmarried certificate' in all government procedures. Even for matters like issue of employment card, a Sikkimese woman has to prove her identity every six months which is highly unjust and biased.

This group has made a representation to Chief Minister Shri Pawan Chamling drawing his attention to the problem of gender inequality faced by the married women of Sikkim and requested him to provide equitable inheritance right of property at par with their male counterparts irrespective of their marital status. This petition has also requested him to look into this matter in the light of Hon'ble High Court of Sikkim's judgement in the case of Padma Ganeshan. The court observed that despite the proclamation of a Regulation in 1962 concerning the married woman, the Maharaja of Sikkim never enforced it. It is ironical that the present-day registration authorities of Sikkim are enforcing this regulation in a democratic state whose basic principles are ingrained in gender equality.

In their petition, this women's organization has also urged the Chief Minister to formulate non-discriminatory, gender-friendly policies as laid down in Articles 14, 15, 15(3), 16, 19, and 21 in the Constitution of India so that they may be cited as examples in the entire country.

In this context, it would be relevant to point out that

[A]ccess to land can prove important for women, even if the plot is not large enough to serve as the sole basis of livelihood. It can, for instance, be a critical element in a diversified livelihood system. A small plot, which is insufficient for subsistence through crop cultivation, can still add to other means of earnings.' (Agarwal, Sivaramayya, and Sarkar n.d.)

DISTRIBUTION OF AGRICULTURAL LAND *PATTA*

An analysis of Table 13.3 reveals that a large majority of beneficiaries of allotted agricultural land *patta* (official documents stating land title and the terms on which land is held) are women in the east, south, and west districts. The share of women beneficiaries in all these three districts is more than 70%. On the other hand, the share of women beneficiaries in the north district is relatively much lower, only 23%. Though the reason behind such a low share of women beneficiaries in the north district as compared to the other districts is a matter of further investigation, it may perhaps be accounted for by lower involvement of women in agriculture and/or by large landholdings owned by Lepchas and Bhutias, the two principal communities inhabiting the district. However, the high share of women beneficiaries in the remaining other three districts indicates that the state government gives preference to women while distributing the *patta* which is a positive step in the direction of economic empowerment of women (Dheeraja, Sivaram, and Rao 2010). However, it is pertinent to mention here that the area of *patta* land is very small as a number of beneficiaries have got land under Sukumbasis (landless) scheme, implemented in the rural areas by Government of

Table 13.3

District-wise Beneficiaries Allotted Agricultural Land *Patta* in Sikkim (Since Inception till Date; Area in Ha)

S. No.	District	Year	Allotment of Agricultural Plot on Joint Ownership Basis to Husband and Wife	Area Allotted Under Agricultural Land on Joint Ownership Basis (ha)	No. of Women Beneficiaries Allotted Agriculture Land	No. of Men Beneficiaries Allotted Agriculture Land	Total No. of Beneficiaries Allotted Agriculture Land (5+6)	Total Allotted Area Under Agricultural Plot (in ha)
1	2		3	4	5	6	7	8
1.	East District	2014	15600	90.85	1,096	406	1,502	154.85
2.	North District	2014	249	295.64	177	593	770	383.64
3.	South District	2014	12100	549.42	1,648	521	2,169	560.42
4.	West District	2014	10050	346.67	2,004	859	2,863	401.67

Source: Compiled from unpublished and unverified data of Land Revenue and Disaster Management, Government of Sikkim 2014.
Note: The figures in the above table should be read as indicative only, as the data has not been published by any government agency.

Sikkim. Under this scheme, '0.25 acre of land is allotted to each of the Sukumbasis for construction of dwelling house, cultivation and other allied activities with a view to raise the income of such Sukumbasis and bring them above poverty line.'[8] So far as the allotment of agricultural plot on joint ownership basis to husband and wife is concerned, out of the total 37,999 such *pattas* distributed, about 40% are concentrated in the east district, followed by 32% in the south district and about 25% in the west district. However, only 249 such *pattas* have been allotted in the north district which is comparatively much lower than the other three districts.

CONCLUSIONS AND POLICY RECOMMENDATIONS

The rest of the country and the world are questioning and deconstructing gender to build a progressive society with equal rights but unfortunately Sikkim asks a woman who is a 'Sikkimese Subject' to prove that she is unmarried every six months or marry a Sikkimese man to earn a living or even drive a car. This rule is discriminatory and should be corrected. A woman should have freedom to choose her own partner without affecting her right to inherit or transfer or acquire both movable and immoveable property, and hence the relevant sections under 'Married Women's Property Regulation, 1962' should be suitably amended.

This is also apparent from the discussions on identity that the women's identity gets lost within the overarching celebration of the protection of the Sikkimese identity. The Sikkimese society should be more sensitive towards the legal rights of women, particularly those relating to property rights. Importantly, suitable amendments have been made in the Hindu Succession Act 1956 in different states ensuring equal rights for both women and men over the ancestral property. In such states, women have full freedom and can exercise their rights to handle their property as they deem fit and can transfer and buy property irrespective of their marital status. Given this context, the SSA, 2008, in its present form appears to be biased and discriminatory against women. The state should take appropriate measures so that the law may be amended to suit the interests of women.

NOTES

1. Chogyals were monarchs of the former Kingdom of Sikkim that ruled from 1642 to 1975.
2. www.districtcourtsnamchi.nic.in (accessed on 29 March 2017).
3. www.districtcourtsnamchi.nic.in (accessed on 29 March 2017).
4. www.sikkim.gov.in (accessed on 29 March 2017).
5. www.districtcourtsnamchi.nic.in (accessed on 29 March 2017).
6. www.districtcourtsnamchi.nic.in (accessed on 29 March 2017).
7. www.sikkimexpress.in
8. www.sikkimlrdm.gov.in (accessed on 29 March 2017).

REFERENCES

Agarwal, B., B. Sivaramayya, and L. Sarkar. n.d. *Report of the Committee for Gender Equality in Land Devolution in Tenurial Laws*. Report submitted to the Department of Rural Development, Government of India.

Basnet, L. B. 1974. *Sikkim: A Political History*. New Delhi: S Chand & Sons.

Bhasin, V. 2002. 'Ethnic Relations Among the People of Sikkim.' *Journal of Social Sciences* 6 (1): 1–20.

———. 2011. 'Settlements and Land-use Patterns in the Lepcha Reserve—Dzongu Zone in the Sikkim Himalaya, India.' *Journal of Biodiversity* 2 (1): 41–66.

Datta, A. 1992. 'Land and Ethnicity in Sikkim.' *Man in India* 72 (2): 165–78.

Dheeraja, C., P. Sivaram, and K. H. Rao. 2010. 'Changing Gender Relations through MGNREGS.' Sikkim State Report, Centre for Wage Employment and Poverty Alleviation National institute of Rural Development, Hyderabad.

Firdos, S. 2014. 'Changing Land Ownership Patterns and its Impact on Social Relations in Sikkim.' In *Land Records Management in India: A Plea for Reforms*, edited by A. A. A. Faizi and H. C. Behera, 205–13. New Delhi: Concept Publishing Company.

Sinha, A. C. 1975. *Politics of Sikkim: A Sociological Study*. Faridabad: Thomson Press.

———. 2003. *The Nepalis in Northeast India: A Community in Search of Identity*. New Delhi: Indus Publishing Company.

———. 2008. *Sikkim: Feudal and Democratic*. New Delhi: Indus Publishing Company

Subba, B. 2014. 'Women "Quest" for Empowerment in Sikkim's Society.' *International Journal of Scientific and Research Publications* 4 (9): 1–5.

White, J. C. 1971. *Sikkim and Bhutan: Twenty-one Years on the North East Frontier 1887–1907*. Delhi: Vivek Publishing House (First Indian Print).

INTERNET SOURCES

www.districtcourtsnamchi.nic.in (accessed on 20 May 2015).
www.sikkim.gov.in (accessed on 27 May 2015).
www.sikkimexpress.com (accessed on 5 July 2015).
www.sikkimlrdm.gov.in (accessed on 10 July 2015).
www.nerlp.gov.in (accessed on 15 July 2015).

14

Women's Land Rights in the Context of Neo-liberal Tamil Nadu

RANJANI K. MURTHY

Agricultural land is an important resource, ownership and control of which expands women's agency within the household and vis-à-vis community institutions, markets, and the state. It also leads to the well-being of women and girls and protects them from domestic violence. Ownership and control over land facilitates women's political participation.

Nationally, the Hindu Succession (Amendment) Act, 2005, gave equal rights to daughters to ancestral property. Yet according to a 2014 study by UN Women and Landesa of some agrarian districts in the states of Andhra Pradesh, Bihar, and Madhya Pradesh in India, covering 360 men and 1,400 women, only 12.5% (1:8) of women inherited agricultural land from their parents (Sircar and Fletchner 2014). Women working on farms they don't own are not much better than labourers tilling for wages (ibid.). Barriers to women's inheritance traditionally include parental attitudes, their own attitudes in not wanting to claim their rights, and the attitudes of local officials. Interestingly, 34% of women interviewed in the southern state of Andhra Pradesh anticipated inheriting property from their parents, or had already done so (ibid.).

This study examines gender issues in landownership in Tamil Nadu (TN), including a review of the existing laws around women's rights to land. In addition to the general questions for all state-level research on women's land rights listed in the Introduction to this book, it examines if TN reflects the Bihar and Madhya Pradesh trends, the trend in Andhra Pradesh, or an altogether different model. It must be remembered that rural landlessness is high in TN and has been increasing. As per National Family Health Survey (NFHS) 3, 64.3% of rural TN households were landless as of 2005–06[1] (International Institute for Population Sciences [IIPS] and Macro International 2008). Micro-studies suggest that the proportion of rural Muslim households who are landless is higher than their Hindu counterparts in TN (Jeejeebhoy and Zathar 2001).

The chapter is structured as follows. The first section examines different legislation and customary laws related to inheritance of land in TN and the variations across religions and communities from the lens of gender. The second section examines TN government's programmes for women's development and rural livelihoods from the lens of whether they promote women's rights to land. It also examines the policies and government orders of the Revenue, Agriculture and Social Welfare and Justice Departments for the period 2013–14 from the perspective of whether they promote women's rights to land. The third section presents data and information from studies (covering TN) and interviews[2] (Chennai and Kancheepuram districts) on attitudes towards women's land rights, and the actual landownership by women. Feedback on whether the system of dowry is being affected/has been affected by women claiming land rights is also discussed. Finally, the fourth section provides suggestions on directions for strengthening women's rights to land in TN, several of which may be relevant to India as a whole. There is a paucity of studies on women's land rights in TN, with studies being more focused on issues facing women agricultural labourers, violence of development process, interlocking of masculinity and caste (Anandhi, Jeyaranjan, and Krishnan 2002; Mencher 1998; Swaminathan 2002).

Before delving into the findings, a brief statistical profile of the state follows. TN is urbanizing rapidly, with only 52% of its population in rural areas in 2011 (Department of Economics and Statistics 2014). Of the population, 20% comprise of Scheduled Castes (SCs) and 1.1% of Scheduled Tribes (STs) as of 2011; while the proportion of SCs is higher than the national average, that of STs is lower. The literacy rate is 80% as of 2011, with literacy rates being lower amongst rural, female, and SC/ST populations (ibid.). Of the population, 46% were workers as of 2011 (ibid.). In rural areas, a high percentage, 64.3%, of households were landless in 2005–06, and this trend may continue with the agricultural land being used for industries, tourism, and real estate (IIPS and Macro International 2008; Joshi Adhikari Institute of Social Studies 2011). The proportion of marginal farmers was more than that of small and medium farmers. A higher proportion of SCs, STs, and Muslims were landless than the households from other communities (Harris et al. 2010; Joshi Adhikari Institute of Social Studies 2011). The percentage of the total area cultivated was 39% in 2012–13 and the net area sown per capita was only 0.06 hectare in 2011, with 58% of the net area sown being irrigated (Department of Economics and Statistics 2014). Of the total population of TN, 11% is estimated by the government to be living below the poverty line as of 2011–12, lower than the all-India estimate of 22% (ibid.). Non-government studies place the figure higher. A study covering nine districts[3] of TN observes that 50% of households are nuclear, and dowry was given in 60% of marriages (Centre for Women's Studies, n.d.).

LEGISLATION AND CUSTOMARY LAWS RELATED TO INHERITANCE OF LAND IN TAMIL NADU

Historical Rules and Customs

Mukund (1999) observes that in ancient times,[4] property could be acquired by women by way of gifts or inheritance, and through self-generated income. Assets and gifts a girl received from her natal family, and others at her marriage and prior to her departure to her husband's family were considered her property (*stridhan*). *Saudayika* (also known as *pritidana* and *pritidatta*), comprising gifts from her husband and in-laws at her marriage, was considered part of *stridhan* (ibid.). However, the issue was more complicated when it came to immovable property. The *Mitakshara* system, which governed much of South India (including TN), acknowledged that while women could inherit immovable family property, at best women received usufruct rights (ibid.). Widows were entitled to maintenance from their late husbands' heirs, but not to a share in the family property, unless the husband had split from the rest of his family. With regard to rights to the woman's self-earned income, the old legal documents state, without exception, that they rest not with the woman, but with her in-laws (ibid.). This restriction also applied to gifts she received while residing with her husband (ibid.).

While the above rules did not uphold women's inheritance, the customary practice during ancient times in TN was more liberal (ibid.). Two inscriptions from the 10th century in Brahmini refer to women's property (money or land) ownership and transfer rights. Interestingly, the majority of women property owners had royal or similar elite backgrounds; however, women of lesser stature, such as temple dancers and maids also find mention as property owners (ibid.). Further, the author observes that it was a usual custom with landowners of all TN castes to transfer small land areas, called *manjal kani* or turmeric land, as *stridhan* to daughters set for marriage. *Manjal kani* passed on from mothers to daughters, with the women controlling the earnings from the land. However, women had only usufruct rights. Non-landowning castes like the Chettiars gave jewels and gifts to their daughters during their weddings, which remained their property until death. However, the *stridhan* was controlled by the fathers. The scriptures indicate that around 1,270 widows without sons struggled to hold on to the property of their late husbands. They were not given any help in cultivation of their lands but were helped by their fathers or brothers in sale negotiations. Mukund observes that temple dancers exercised more freedom in owning and disposing of property than widows. They were referred to as *devaraidyal* or servants of god, and received several kinds of gifts that came to the temples, including property (Mukund 1992). Royal families, local chiefs, the elite, and military families were the main donors to temples. *Devaraidyals* were married, single, or concubines, and were considered to be employees of the state assigned to the temples. Anandhi (1991) observes that the status of *devaraidyal* varied from case to case, and the varying agency and voice of the women themselves need to be taken into account while analysing their status. It is not clear whether they were from SC families. It is also not clear as to what percentage of households owned land in ancient times, how much of the land was in women's names, and how much was inherited.

Mukund (1992) notes the presence of matrilineal communities amongst Muslims in Kilakarai, southern TN (period unspecified). Muslim women in this small town were divers who caught chank shells (heavy shells found in the Indian Ocean, as well as the Caribbean). They earned their own income and property passed on from mothers to daughters. At the time of marriage, each daughter received a house, necessities, and jewels. If there were several daughters, the property was divided. If there was money left after all the daughters were provided for, the cash was divided as per the Shariat laws (ibid.). However, to what extent the daughters controlled this property is not clear.

Legislation During Recent Times

Recent legislation on women's rights to land through inheritance, tenancy, and land allotment is discussed as follows:

The Inheritance Route

The Hindu Law of Inheritance Act of 1929 follows the *Mitakshara* system of inheritance—the Madras school of which recognizes the following females as heirs: daughters of sons or daughters and sisters. In Madras and Bombay, daughters of sons and daughters received recognition as *bandhus*[5] (cited in Centre for Women's Studies, n.d.). In 1937, the Hindu Women's Right to Property Act (XVIII) recognized widows as successors, with rights to shares equalling those of sons. However, while widows exercised rights resembling coparcenary interests and were members of their joint families, they were not actually considered coparceners (ibid.). The Hindu Succession Act, 1956, which followed next, excluded daughters from coparcenary ownership purely on the basis of their sex. In 1989, the Hindu Succession (Tamil Nadu Amendment) Act, 1989, noted that the exclusion of women from coparcenary rights in the Hindu Succession Act, 1956, was contradictory to the principles of equality enshrined in the Indian Constitution, and led to the dowry system (Law Commission of India 2000). Hence, this amendment gives daughters coparcenary rights similar to sons. They can dispose of their properties as per their own will or testamentary disposition. If a daughter is deceased at the time of partition, her property goes to the surviving children. The Act, however, does not apply to daughters married before the Amendment of 1989 (ibid.). The state government has established 568 registrar/joint registrar offices in TN, in deference to the number of registrations (Centre for Women's Studies, n.d.).

Inheritance by Christian women in TN, like in the rest of India, is governed by Sections 31 to 49 of the Indian Succession Act, 1925 (ISA), which deal with succession for Christians. The Act gives equal succession rights to daughters and sons. However, TN Christian widows' rights to property are not absolute. They are subject to the rights of any other heirs that may turn up. The widow enjoys exclusivity to the entirety of the property only when no other kindred to the intestate remain (ibid.). The widow is entitled to a third of the marital property, while lineal descendants receive the other two-thirds. If there are no such descendants, one half of the property devolves to the widow and the other half goes to the surviving kindred of the deceased (ibid.). The widow of a pre-deceased son of the person who died has no entitlements; however, her children have title to equal shares, whether they are already born or in her womb when the death occurs (ibid.).

TN Muslim women, like elsewhere in India, are governed by the (Shariat) Application Act, 1937, which has not been codified (Agarwal, Shivarammaya, and Sarkar 1998). Succession opens when the ancestor dies, after which heirs to the property are recognized. A daughter has one half the inheritance right of a son. Initially, the (Shariat) Application Act, 1937, did not cover agricultural land. In 1949, the provisions of the 1937 Act were extended in TN to agricultural land (ibid.). Women's rights in tribal communities of TN vary from tribe to tribe.

Tenancy Route

As per the Tamil Nadu Agricultural Lands (Record of Tenancy Rights) Act, 1969, also known as the Tamil Nadu Act 10 of 1969, people engaged with cultivation of agricultural land belonging to landowners or state public trusts can register themselves as such, and this supposedly protects them from eviction (PRS 1969). Under this Act, record officers for this purpose are the *tehsildars* of each taluk; they must maintain a tenancy rights record to secure tenant interests. Under Section 4 of this Act, record officers are empowered to take suo moto action to register tenants (ibid.).

The Tamil Nadu Cultivating Tenants (Protection from Eviction) Act, 1997, prohibits eviction of tenants on the ground that the cultivating tenant is in arrears with respect to the rent payable to the landowner (PRS 1997). Any cultivating tenant who had already been evicted from any land on such grounds has a right to reclaim access to the land (ibid.). Tenants can, nevertheless, be evicted on grounds such as damage to land and crops, use of agricultural land for other purposes, or denial of ownership of land by the owner (Revenue Department 2013b). This legislation is indeed laudable, though poorly implemented. Registration of tenants under this Act has been limited (Mearns 1999). Further, the Act refers to the tenant as 'he', signifying the underpinning assumption that the tenant is a man. Data on proportion of tenants who are women is not available. There is no amendment of the Act so as to protect collectives of women farmers who have taken land on lease from eviction (PRS 1997). In areas where land value is escalating due to industrialization, real estate development, or infrastructure development, the Act is routinely violated.[6]

Under the provisions of the Tamil Nadu Cultivating Tenants (Payment of Fair Rent) Act 1956 (Tamil Nadu Act 24/1956), the fair rent landowners/public trusts can collect from cultivating tenants is fixed at 25% of the gross produce. The onus of paying land revenue and other land-related dues lies on the landowner; the tenant is responsible for bearing cultivation-related expenses. Fair rent is payable in kind, as an alternative to cash. Revenue courts settle any disputes that landowners may have with the tenants. As on 31 December 2014, 93 cases had been received by the revenue court of which only one had been disposed of; 92 were pending (Commissionerate of Land Reforms n.d.). What is not clear is the percentage of these cases that pertained to charging of rent beyond 25% of the gross produce, and as to the percentage of them that were won. Data is not available on the proportion of cases where the tenants were women, and on the verdicts in these cases (Commissionerate of Land Reforms n.d.; Revenue Department 2013b). Scaling rents is a reason why women are not able to lease land individually or collectively in TN.[7]

Land Allotment Route

A SC-specific route for accessing and owning land is the Depressed Classes Land Act. Under the Depressed Classes Land Act passed by the British Parliament in 1892, 1,200,000 acres of land was distributed to the SCs—considered as Depressed Classes (DC) in TN (Gandhimathi 2014). Official data as of 2012 reveals that only 115,841.24 acres of DC land (10% of the 1892 amount) exists in government records, of which 19,743.67 acres (17%) are occupied by other communities. This is a violation of the purpose for which the land was originally allotted. Data on whose names the DC land—also referred to as *panchami* land—was originally allotted is not available. The Special Commissioner and Commissioner of Land Administration issued a letter in 1996 that instructed government officials to restore *panchami* lands in occupation by non-SCs to the original assignees or their legal heirs (cited in ibid.).[8] However, in a majority of the places, the *panchami* lands continue be in the hands of non-SCs. As shall be analysed in a later section, SC women's rights groups have launched a movement for access to and control of DC land by SC women.

The Tamil Nadu Land Reform (Fixation of Ceiling) Act 1961 fixes a ceiling of 15 standard[9] acres per family of not more than five members, and 5 standard acres for every additional member up to a maximum of 30 standard acres per family (PRS 1961a). The Act further stipulates that in families where the total landholdings exceed 15 standard acres, and where one or more female family members hold *stridhan* land, such female members can possess a maximum of 10 standard acres (ibid.). However, there is no specific mention of whether land that is redistributed should be in women's names or joint names (ibid.). Land reforms have been poorly implemented in TN (Harris et al. 2010; Mearns 1999). The Tamil Nadu Public Trust (Regulation and Administration of Agricultural Land) Act, 1961 (Tamil Nadu Act 57/61), permits public trusts to personally cultivate a maximum of 20 standard acres; any excess land must be let out on lease (PRS 1961b). There is no policy on to whom religious trusts' surplus land should be leased (proportion of women and SCs/STs or collectives of these groups). Interestingly, religious trusts of a public nature that have been in existence from before 1 March 1972 are not subject to the provisions of any land ceiling act (Revenue Department 2013b).

Bhoodan (voluntary donation of land by landlords) is another route for the landless to gain access to and own land. The Tamil Nadu Bhoodan Yagna Act, 1958, governs donation and distribution of lands to the landless poor, and the Bhoodan Board manages the same. There is no mention in the Act that the land should be distributed in the names of women or jointly (PRS 1958). There were two amendments made to the Act in 1964 and 2000, which again do not address gender issues.

The Central Act 1/1894 is invoked in TN for acquisition of land for public purposes in general. The time limit for acquisition under this Act varies from 180 days (if need for land is urgent) to three years. The TN government has enacted three special Acts related to land acquisition (Revenue Department 2013b):

1. Tamil Nadu Acquisition of land for Harijan Welfare Schemes Act 1978 (Act 31/1978)—covering both SCs and STs.
2. Tamil Nadu Acquisition of land for Industrial Purposes Act 1997 (Act 10/1999).
3. Tamil Nadu Highways Act 2001 (Act 34/2002; Revenue Department 2013b).

It is not clear as to how much land has been allotted to SCs and STs under these Acts and in whose names. Groups like *Munn Urumiya* (mud rights) have pointed that more land has been acquired for industrial purposes and highways than for SCs/STs (Gandhimathi 2014). There is no provision in the Act to safeguard the land owned by women, women's collectives, SCs, and STs from being acquired for industrial purposes or highways[10] (Government of TN 2002; PRS 2007).

STATE SCHEMES, POLICIES, ORDERS, AND ATTITUDES

State Schemes

Mahalir Thittam

In 1983, the Government of TN set up the TN Corporation for Development of Women (TNCDW) to concentrate on women's empowerment (TNCDW n.d.a). Two major schemes are implemented through the TNCDW, namely, the *Mahalir Thittam* (Women's Scheme) and the Tamil Nadu State Rural Livelihoods Mission (TNSRLM; ibid.). The *Mahalir Thittam* is a self-help group (SHG)-based programme with the objective of reducing poverty among women by empowering them on the socio-economic front. This scheme focuses on forming women into SHGs and training them on social, technical, and managerial issues. Women are also provided with links to bank credit to enable them to take up activities for income generation (ibid.). Village and panchayat-level federations (PLFs) of SHGs enable strengthening of the 'SHG movement', capitalization on economies of scale, and facilitation of loan routing to SHGs (TNCDW n.d.b). With the launch of the TNSRLM, *Mahalir Thittam* will concentrate on consolidating SHG achievements with respect to convergence with other departments, marketing, literacy, raising awareness on gender issues, environment conservation, and health (Rural Development and Panchayati Raj Department 2013). Training has been imparted to the women members of SHGs on gender and women's legal rights. However, the TNCDW officials we met reported that women's land rights are not integrated into training at present.[11] There is scope for including legal provisions on women's legal rights to land in the training given by the TNCDW. Further, a cluster of federations themselves could provide members access to gender-sensitive lawyers once a week or fortnightly, as is done by NGOs like MYRADA in TN, Karnataka, and Andhra Pradesh (Murthy with Priya 2010).

Pudhu Vaazhvu Thittam

The *Pudhu Vaazhvu Thittam* was launched in 2005 with the support of the World Bank. The objective of the *Pudhu Vaazhvu Thittam* (literally 'new life initiative or scheme') is to alleviate poverty and empower poor by improving their livelihoods (Rural Development and Panchayati Raj Department 2013).

The scheme, ending in September 2014, is operational in 26 districts, 120 blocks, and 4,174 village panchayats (Rural Development and Panchayati Raj Department 2013). It is implemented through an independently registered society, which comes under the Rural Development and Panchayat Raj Department (Rural Development and Panchayati Raj Department 2013). The scheme focuses on the extremely vulnerable, including women-headed households. The strategy is to form groups, build skills, and help vulnerable groups access credit, markets, and benefits through convergence. The project, however, does not have a focus on strengthening women's land rights (see posters,[12] booklets[13]), but nevertheless, women in a few areas[14] have come together on their own to collectively purchase or lease land for agriculture[15] (ibid.).

Tamil Nadu State Rural Livelihood Mission

The TNSRLM commenced in TN in 2012–13. The objective of the TNSRLM is to 'build strong and vibrant institutional platforms of the rural poor that enable them to increase household incomes through livelihood enhancements and improved access to financial and other services' (ibid.). The TNSRLM is implemented through the TNCDW. It is envisaged that TNSRLM will be put into effect in all 32 districts of TN, barring Chennai (ibid.). TNSRLM will work intensely in those blocks not covered by the *Pudhu Vaazhvu Thittam*. TNSRLM's three primary components are group formation, skills development and placement, and the Women Farmers' Empowerment Programme (ibid.). Of concern here is the Women Farmer's Empowerment Programme which seeks to promote sustainable agriculture practices amongst women to reduce women's drudgery. The activity is intended to benefit 42,359 women (ibid.). While there is no explicit focus on helping rural women from landless families to lease or acquire land, this has happened on its own in around 10 locations, with a majority being successful. Some women's SHGs have also leased trees and ponds.[16] The exact data on the number of trees or ponds leased was not readily available.

Where the TNSRLM is being implemented, a baseline has been created on households, which however does not include gender-disaggregated landownership data.[17] This is a missed opportunity. TNSRLM seeks to make sure that at the minimum, one woman from every poor and rural household enters the SHG network within the given time frames (ibid.). It also has a focus on single women. The TNSRLM builds upon the experience of previous schemes by promoting federations at block and district levels (ibid.).

Policies of Revenue and Other Relevant Departments

Revenue Department

The Policy Note of Revenue Department, 2013–14, observes that every Monday, petitions are to be received by the district collector, including on granting of *pattas*, *patta* transfer, granting of house sites, etc. As per the Policy Note of the Revenue Department, a mass contact programme must be held in one village of the district each month to receive and, if possible, address petitions (Revenue Department 2013b).

As on 31 March 2013, 150,112 petitions have been received and orders have been passed on 55,672 petitions, since the introduction of the scheme[18] in 2013. In addition, a *jamabhandi*—mass meeting—is to be conducted every year to close revenue accounts, where unaddressed petitions are again to be brought out and, where possible, addressed (ibid.). However, there is no data on how many of these cases pertained to women's land rights and how many resolved in favour of women.

The Policy Note provides for *patta* transfer, but does not mention that while transferring *patta*, land or house titles could be registered in joint names. However, it mentions that house *pattas* for homeless will be issued by the government in the names of women on the basis of 3 cents in villages and half a cent in urban areas. Against a target of one lakh house site *pattas* during 2012–13, 131,299 *pattas* were issued. Information on how many of the house *pattas* were issued in women's or joint names is not clear (ibid.).

The Policy Note of Revenue Department 2013–14 mentions that the TN government permits land acquisition and, recently, permits land acquisition through private negotiation[19] (ibid.). A district-level committee under the headship of a collector has been constituted, and there is no mention of representation of women farmers' groups or federation leaders in these forums.

The Policy Note points out that land or buildings belonging to the government can be leased for non-agricultural use to individuals, associations, private institutions, companies, local bodies, and trusts for not less than three years and not more than 20 years (ibid.). There is no specification on the proportion of lessees that should be women or women's associations or trusts. In a similar manner, there is no specification that salt pans could be given on lease to women or women's cooperatives (ibid.).

The Policy Note points that in the interests of communities, the TN government is compelled to set out an action plan to identify and evict encroachments on *poramboku* or other lands vested with local bodies and village panchayats (ibid.). There is no data on how much of encroachment is by upper castes and how much by marginalized groups. A discussion on whether encroachments by marginalized groups could be regularized by issuing *pattas* in the names of women of the household is missing (ibid.).

Moving on to land reforms, the Policy Note provides data as of 2013 on how many people have benefitted how much from land reforms. While caste-wise data is provided, sex-wise data is not made available. Cumulatively, 190,713 acres of land have been distributed to 150,920 people as of 31 March 2013, with more beneficiaries belonging to Other Castes, followed by SCs (Revenue Department 2013a).

Moving on to land tenancy, the Policy Note observes that 2,273 cases of tenancy disputes have come to the revenue court, of which 1,254 have been disposed, leaving 1,019 cases pending as on 31 March 2013. Records are not available on what proportion of tenants and landowners are women, in whose favour (tenants or owners) the verdicts have been made, and the sex- and caste-wise breakdown of the verdicts (ibid.).

The Bhoodan Board received the total land donation of 28,050 acres. Of this, beneficiaries received 20,494 acres, while the remaining 7,556 acres are held up by litigation or are under procedures like registration and confirmation. Again, it is not clear as to whether the land has been allotted in women's names, men's names, or joint names, and whether the land has gone to SCs, STs, and marginalized groups (ibid.).

Finally, the policy note refers to training VAOs on survey and administration (ibid.). However, there is no reference to training them on women's land rights (including under the Hindu Succession (Amendment) Act, 2005).

Policies of Other Departments

There is a gap between the national commitment[20] to promote women's land rights under the Twelfth Five-year Plan (in particular, through collective lease or purchase of land) and what is outlined in the Policy Note of Department of Social Welfare (also cover's women's development) and Nutritious Meal Programme and the Agriculture Department—neither of which makes any reference to women's land rights (Agriculture Department 2014; Social Welfare and Nutritious Meal Programme Department 2013).

It is only the Policy Note of the Adi-Dravidar and Tribal Welfare Department which mentions allotment of funds for purchase of land by SC women. On stamp duty, 100% exemption is given; landholding can be 2.5 acres of wet land or 5 acres of dry land. Financial assistance for land development and irrigation is also made available. The seller can only be a non-SC. Yet another scheme under the same department promotes free house site *pattas* for poor SC and ST families. The land for this purpose is acquired through private negotiation or under the Tamil Nadu Acquisition of Land for Harijan Welfare Schemes Act, 1978 (Tamil Nadu Act 31/1978), to distribute free house site *pattas* to the eligible persons. Details on whose names the housing will be provided are not mentioned (Adi-Dravidar and Tribal Welfare Department 2013).

Government Orders of Revenue Department

Between 1968 and 2013, 80 government orders issued by the Revenue Department were uploaded on the Internet as of 8 June 2014. Of these, 23 government orders directly or indirectly pertain to issues related to land.

None of the 23 government orders of the Revenue Department address gender issues, but show some possible strategies for the future. The 23 government orders pertain to issue of *patta* passbook, computerization of land records, online mutations[21] and *patta* transfers, use of vacant land acquired by industries, leasing salt pans, whom *poramboku* land can be leased to, regularization of encroachments, payment of compensation in terms of land acquisition, and petition sorting (Revenue Department 1993a, 1997, 1999, 2001a, 2001b, 2003, 2008a, 2008b, 2011a, 2011b). Some of the government orders of the Revenue Department pertain to structures and staff. There is no mention of representation of Department of Social Welfare in structures for resolution or proportion of women staff from marginalized communities.[22]

Commissionerate of Land Reforms

Spanning the period 21 June 1982 to 28 April 2014, 47 government orders have been uploaded on the website of Commissionerate of Land Reforms. They pertain to land reforms, revenue courts, Chief Minister's Farmer's Security Scheme, and administration of *bhoodan* land. There is no mention of women's land rights within the government orders. Like in the case of the Revenue Department, government orders on recruitment staff do not mention recruitment of women staff to the new posts created.[23]

Attitudes of Government Officials

The attitudes of government officials varied towards women's rights to land, with some being favourable and others being adverse to the same. Lower-level officials expressed a more positive attitude towards women's land rights than those in higher positions. A senior woman official[24] from the TNCDW expressed that the TNCDW does not include land rights of women in their training. She observed that it can 'rock the boat' too much. However, she observed that women occasionally came together to lease or buy land and engage in collective agriculture (mainly vegetable cultivation or floriculture). The TNCDW supports them in accessing bank loans. According to her, this 'bottom up' approach is less controversial.

A young revenue development officer of Kancheepuram district was met to discuss the issue of women's land rights. He was a strong supporter of women's land rights, as he perceived that land rights enhanced women's status. Further, he observed that women do not sell agricultural land easily (unlike men).[25] In the event of the husband dying before the wife, it gives the wife security. He also shared that elderly women with land are respected and looked after by their children. A Muslim woman *tehsildar* from the same district supported these views, and expressed that in the case of Muslim women, getting their share of land (half of a son) enhanced their bargaining power in marriage (including bargaining against triple *talaq*). A dynamic SC woman VAO, on the board of a small women's NGO, echoed similar benefits to women's ownership of land. She also noted high rates of male migration in the district, and that any way women were left to manage the land. Having land titles helps women managing farms gain access to institutional credit. She observed that for SC women, ownership of land enhances their status vis-à-vis caste Hindu women and men.

Interestingly, the lawyer coordinating the Free Legal Aid Board of Kancheepuram district had a benevolent view than rights-based attitude. In the room allocated for mediation between people in dispute, there was a message stuck on the wall 'A bad compromise is better than a good case'. He opined that women should 'lovingly' and 'peacefully' take what is given by their brothers (even if not equal), and not lose their relationships with their brothers. However, this lawyer may not be a typical case. Centre for Women's Studies interviews of 69 lawyers from nine districts[26] of TN suggest that 91% had handled property dispute and 93% (of 91%) had used legal methods in an attempt to gain women rights to land.

RURAL WOMEN'S ACCESS TO AND OWNERSHIP OF LAND

For rural women from Other Backward Classes and the 'general' community, inheritance is a good route, as the majority are landed. For women from SCs and STs in TN, women's ownership of land has to be located within the struggle for SCs and STs to gain rights to land. The case of rural women from MBCs falls in-between (Centre for Women's Studies n.d.; Gandhimathi 2014; Joshi Adhikari Institute of Social Studies 2011).

Do Women Stake Their Claim to Property?

According to the RDO, women in Kancheepuram district are increasingly aware of their equal right to inherit land as a coparcener, and they come forward to claim their rights to property. This awareness, according to him, is due to information disseminated through television, SHGs, and federations by NGOs, and due to women's improved access to credit. Further, their husbands are also aware of their wives' rights to ancestral property, and put pressure on them to claim their rights from their natal families. However, women require awareness of the rules pertaining to the Hindu Succession (Tamil Nadu Amendment) Act, 1989, and the Hindu Succession (Amendment) Act 2005. In Kancheepuram district, the value of land is going up as it is near to Chennai and land is in demand by industrial houses and real estate developers. As a result, the value of dowry given during marriage is much lower than that of land and cannot be compared. However, the RDO observed that upper caste and Muslim women do not come in proportion to their representation in population with land to claim their rights to land, while SC women who are most organized do. He observed that unlike most of TN (where SCs were landless), SCs in Kancheepuram district had small amount of land. Sometimes, 3–4 persons have *patta* (only one legal) to the same land and such problems have to be sorted out before inheritance can be discussed.

The *tehsildar* met by the author (again from the same district) concurred with most of the views of the RDO. In contrast to the RDO, she noted that Muslim women, too, are well aware of their inheritance rights and roughly two out of 10 Muslim women come to her seeking help to claim their inheritance rights. Whether her personal identity as a Muslim *tehsildar* had a role to play is a moot question. She observed that across communities, women married into landless families come to claim their rights to land upon death of parents, as they struggle to eke out a living. In her opinion, women prefer share in land to cash, as the former appreciates. She reiterated the views of the RDO that married women were under pressure from husbands to stake a claim; with the land value going up, dowry and property cannot be compared. Speaking on a related issue, she observed that 30% of men wanted to register newly purchased property in women's names as they migrate for work, and want to protect their families.

A VAO also observed that SC women were coming more than women from other communities to claim their right to ancestral land.[27] Most of the SC women were poor and were members of SHGs. Poverty and awareness made them stake a claim, even though their parents may have just been marginal farmers. An interesting observation from the VAO was that women in love marriages were more open to staking claim to property. She observed that love marriages were on the rise; in such cases, the couple got married with very little or no dowry or support from parents. She reiterated the views expressed earlier that few upper caste women, Muslim women, and women heading households staked their right to land.

A lawyer from Kancheepuram met by the author observed that women and their husbands came in larger numbers to officials of the legal aid centre in 1989, when the Hindu Succession (Tamil Nadu Amendment) Act was passed, to stake a claim to their property rights. At that time, 50% of the total cases pertained to property disputes. According to him, now there was greater societal acceptance of women's right to inherit. Now, 15% of cases coming to the legal aid centre pertain to women's property claims. The lawyer working with the free legal aid board also held the view that SC and MBC women came to stake their claim to ancestral land more than women from other communities and Muslim women.

Women's Actual Ownership of Agricultural Land[28]

Individual Ownership and Individual Cultivation

Gough (1981 cited in Rao 2005) analysed the landownership records of two villages in TN's Thanjavur district. She noted that the records for 1,827 showed no women owners, but 1,897 records showed 11 women among 90 registered owners (12.2%), which went up to 27 of 139 (19.4%) in 1952 (ibid.). Gough asserts that disintegration of extended families resulted in personal ownership of land, which included land given as dowry to daughters (ibid.). On the deaths of married male landowners, their widows received life interests in their lands; many of them personally took up management of their properties. This trend indicates that declining kin-group control benefits women by granting them greater access to property (ibid.).

A seven-state study carried out by Marty Chen in 1991 notes that only 3% of TN women inherited as daughters, but 49% of widows inherited as widows (from marital family). She observed that widows tend to be older and exercise little control over land (cited in Agarwal 2002). The question is, have things changed with regard to inheritance by daughters since then?

A more recent study (around 2010[29]), covering 1,298 women from 9 districts of TN revealed that 20.4% of women had inherited property, of whom 15% reported getting shares equal to their male siblings. Building was the most common form of property inherited (66%) followed by land (30%). A majority of the women who inherited property had accessed it from their fathers or grandfathers. In 83% of the instances, women's property was controlled by the men. Sub-data for 207 women from ST communities (Todas, Kotas, Irulas, Kattunayakkans, Panaiyans, and Kurumbas) reveals that 33% of women reported that their households possessed assets, of which 96% was land. Of the women whose households owned land, 87% reported that it was in women's names (Centre for Women's Studies n.d.). While ST women seem to have greater property rights, practices vary from tribe to tribe. According to this study, 67% of the 207 women came from matrilineal tribes (ibid.).

A study by Dasthagir (2012) of gender composition of members of Water Users Associations (WUAs) involved in Sathanur irrigation systems in Villupuram district found that out of 21,058 members of 24 WUAs only 12% were women. As only those who own land can become members, the author concludes that 'ownership of land is very limited among women' (ibid.: 2). However, the focus of the study has not been on inheritance of land by women and it is possible that women with land were not members of the WUAs.

The strategies adopted by women to claim their rights to land are many. Members of the TN Women's Collective (TNWC) observed that a few women have succeeded in claiming rights to natal property. This has resulted in, at times, in brothers and sisters residing in the same village but not speaking to each other. In contrast to the perception of government officials, TNWC members expressed that women were mainly claiming rights on their own, and not due to pressure from husbands. It is possible that women associated with rights-based women's groups assert their rights on their own, as compared to microfinance SHGs or NGOs. Similarly, two sisters who are members associated with women's groups formed by a women's rights NGO Guide in Kancheepuram district fought for their rights to natal property. Being together helped them. However, they got only two lakhs rupees each when their brothers sold ancestral land of five acres.

An SC woman from Idarpur village, Tiruvallur district approached the SC women's *sangam* (attached to another collective, TN Dalit Women's Federation) in her village to help her and her three sisters gain access to land belonging to their ancestors. When her father died (her mother had already passed away), her brother wanted to own the entire three and a half acres of land. The four sisters demanded that they be given one acre (all together), which the brother did not agree to. With the help of the Dalit *sangam* in the village, they managed to gain legal ownership to one acre of land. Cases of women fighting for rights to marital property are also not uncommon. In Kadanganallur village, Vellore district, an SC woman was residing with her husband and in-laws, when he suddenly passed away. The in-laws asked her to leave the house though she had a right to inherit her husband's land as per the Hindu Succession (Amendment) Act, 2005. The Dalit women's *sangam* in the village intervened and prevented the same. The experiences of women in the districts covered by the TNWC are similar.

Individual Ownership of Land by Women When There Is No Natal Property

Nagappan (2012) observes that where SCs and SC women have been organized at village and gram panchayat levels (as federations), they have been slowly able to claim land demarcated for DCs. Drawing upon the case of the Integrated Rural Development Society in Villupuram district, he notes that SCs were organized into village action committees (with 50% of members and leaders being women) and federated as Dalit Land Rights Federations (DLRF) in the northern districts of TN (ibid.). By using the Right to Information and other means, information was sourced on where the *panchami* land, *bhoodan*, temple land, and surplus land were located. SCs were sensitized through group meetings, theatre programmes, and similar activities, with the support of VACs. Lawyers who were in favour of the SCs' cause were identified and their services were used. They have started using SC/ST Atrocities Act as well to take up cases of encroachment (ibid.). Further, SC groups in TN are demanding 2–5 acres of land per landless SC family in women's names (Ramdas 2013). At the time of the study, they were yet to secure rights to land.

Individual Ownership and Collective Cultivation

The Tamil Nadu Dalit Women's Movement adopted a unique approach to help SC women access land in 19 villages near Thiruvallur district on the border between TN and Andhra Pradesh. In these villages, 5–10 SC women from landless households formed themselves into *sangams* and carried out an informal survey of any *poramboku* land available for cultivation (other than grazing land and land related to water bodies/ channels). Once they identified such land, the women headed to the village accounts officer and PRIs and located the land in the village map. The women then went collectively to the revenue inspector for facilitating survey of the land. Some revenue inspectors were cooperative (in particular SC women), while others were not, and repeated pressure had to be exerted. Once the survey was completed, the women went to the taluk office and met the *tehsildar*, asking him or her to allot land and give title deeds in the names of the women. In instances when the revenue inspectors or *tehsildars* were not cooperative, the women submitted petition to the collector on the grievance day held every week, as well as in public hearings.[30] In this manner, an impressive 850 SC women from 19 villages in TN and Andhra Pradesh have managed to claim and own dry land of 1–2 acres each. More land has been claimed by women on the Andhra side than in TN as there is little common land in TN with scale of conversion of common land being higher. The Dalit women's farmer's association in several villages engage in collective farming. In some instances, the SC women farmers have linked with the Mahatma Gandhi National Rural Employment Guarantee Scheme (MGNREGS), which has a provision of paying labourers to develop land of Dalits. Right to land, the women claim, has given them economic security, enhanced their social status and reduced domestic violence.[31]

CONCLUSION AND RECOMMENDATIONS

Historically, it appears that Hindu women in landowning castes in TN had the right to inherit land from their mothers as part of *stridhan*. This land was referred to as 'turmeric land'. While the daughter could enjoy the income, she had only usufruct rights. She was expected to pass it on to her daughter(s). Devaraidyal and other working women also owned land, but it was often acquired through their own earnings and gifts. Their control over the land was, however, limited. Widows' right to inherit land was also restricted in the past. Historically, Muslim women's property rights vary with whether they were from matrilineal or patrilineal community, with a majority being patrilineal. The *Mitakshara* system of inheritance was followed in the state by the Hindus. The Hindu Succession (Tamil Nadu Amendment) Act, 1989, gives daughters coparcenary rights similar to sons (provided they were not married at 1989). If the daughter is deceased at the time of partition, her property would go to the surviving child. The Act does not apply to daughters married before the Amendment of 1989. Nationally, the Hindu Succession (Amendment) Act, 2005, gave equal rights to daughters in ancestral property irrespective of when the women got married, and now this applies to TN.

While there is no historical data on what proportion of households owned agriculture land, the NFHS 2005–06 states that 64.3% of rural households are landless in TN (varying from district to district). Other studies have noted that landlessness is higher amongst SCs, STs, and MBCs. Thus, any debate on women's access to and control over land in TN has to look at not just the inheritance route, but also government allotment and lease of land, as well as changing the development path wherein conversion of agriculture land is happening on a rapid scale in TN. Sex disaggregated data gathered by the Centre for Women's Studies from 9 districts of TN suggests that 20.4% of women from households had inherited property (of which 30% land) and only 15% had received an equal amount as sons. It found that amongst the STs inheritance by women was more common (Centre for Women's Studies n.d.). However, a more systematic study is required to come to firm conclusions. What is clearly emerging is that rural women, revenue officials, women's rights organizations do not consider dowry as equivalent to inheritance rights. Unlike *stridhan*, dowry was seen as a negotiated settlement with the bridegroom's family, and was far less than value of property, especially in areas near cities and towns where land value has gone up. Women members of rights-based women's organizations who staked claim on land rights, seem to largely do so of their own accord, while women members of government-formed or welfare NGO-formed groups are also under pressure from their husbands to asset their rights. The faster the area around the land is developing, the more the pressure!

Revenue officials who were met held positive attitudes on women's rights to land, naming 'equality', 'welfare', and 'agricultural productivity' as reasons due to which women should have rights to land. The attitude of lawyers and higher level officials needs to be explored more. Women heading households, officials observed, do not come forward in equal proportion (to their numeric representation) as married women to claim their right to land, as they feel they need their brothers' support. There are no state-level policies on land rights of women heading households. Government programmes for SCs/STs have a component on land and housing rights for SC women, but such a focus is not seen in policies of revenue, agriculture, and social welfare and justice departments. While land has been allocated for DCs, several acres have been encroached on, creating possible opportunities for land rights of SC women when the problem is addressed.

It is in this context that the recommendations listed as follows are made to strengthen women's land rights in TN.

Stop Conversion of Agriculture Land and Expand Land Pool

Given that 64.3% of rural TN households were landless, as per the NFHS 2005–06, it is suggested that there be no more conversion of agricultural land for non-public purposes. In fact, in keeping with legal provisions, the government should take back vacant land with industries, trusts, and religious institutions for distribution. Land allocated to SCs under the *bhoodan* movement as well as classified as *panchami* land that has been encroached upon by caste Hindus may be reclaimed by the government.

Expand Women's Access to Ownership of Land and Resources

Common land not used for grazing-could be allocated to registered women farmers' groups either through a group title deed or on long term lease of 20 years. The members of the group should ideally come from landless households (with the majority being SCs/STs/WHHs). A government directive that the gram panchayat or town panchayat lease trees, ponds, tanks, and salt pans to women's groups could also be considered, but to women's groups that have not benefitted from the suggested land allotment scheme.[32] The lease amount could be lower in the case of women's groups that include mainly SCs, STs, or women heading households. A government order may be passed exempting registered women farmers' groups from income tax along the lines of what has been attempted with respect to registered PLFs under the *Mahalir Thittam* of the TNCDW (n.d.b).

In geographical areas where women's preference is for individual land titles/leases, this may be promoted by the government, provided women are part of an association or group to support each other. An added recommendation is that when there is *patta* transfer or when new *pattas* are issued, this is done in women's names or in joint names. All encroachments by SCs, STs, and poor women heading households on *poramboku* land may be regularized, and title deeds be issued in women's names or joint names where applicable. Further, when private land is acquired by the government for education or health services run by the state, half the compensation may be paid into the account of the women, irrespective of whether the title deed is in her name, so that she could purchase land elsewhere if she wishes. Every *patta* passbook issued by the government may compulsorily mention the woman spouse's names as well, irrespective of whether she is the legal co-owner.

Ensure Not Only Access, but Also Ownership and Control

As discussed earlier, access to land does not mean ownership or control. Women have fought for their inheritance rights, only to find their husbands registering part in their names. It is suggested that when land is inherited or purchased by women using their income, they are trained on their legal rights and responsibilities (relating to issues such as taxes) by the Department of Land Registration. Alternatively, a flyer may be evolved, which is compulsorily given to women at the time of land transaction, outlining their legal rights under the Hindu Succession (Amendment) Act, 2005, and personal laws of other faiths. Further, sensitization of male relatives is a must on women's legal rights. Television and radio could be used as well to broadcast knowledge on women's land rights. Further, a policy like that of the Maldives could be considered, wherein the husband cannot sell/mortgage land without the consent of his wife, expanding control of women over land even if they do not own it (Government of Maldives 2009). With respect to both collectively leased and purchased land, keeping the spouses and sons out of land management is important, especially after a collective investment has been made in land development or sustainable irrigation. An investment needs to be made in sensitizing men on women's empowerment and to the fact that this promotion of women's land rights is an effort to empower women and improve the well-being of family members.

Promote Inter-generational Collective Land Rights

Given that some of the women themselves hold patriarchal values, it becomes important to ensure that lands purchased by women collectively go to the next generation of women. Specifically, a policy to the effect that lands should pass on to daughters or daughters-in-law or other female relatives of members could be considered. Such a measure would also strengthen the extent to which elderly women are looked after.

Convergence of Government Schemes to Promote Women's Land Rights

As discussed, there are various national- and state-specific schemes in TN wherein women play a central role. There is a need for integrating these efforts to strengthen women's land rights. Firstly, under the *Mahalir Thittam*, there are habitat-level forums and PLFs of women's SHGs. It is suggested that one person from each habitat-level forum be trained on land rights of women and another on rights issues pertaining to women. One of the different sub-committees of the PLFs could be on women's land rights and sustainable agriculture. A budget could be created to invite gender-sensitive lawyers to PLFs once a week for addressing cases of violation of women's rights, including those that are property related. This lawyer may provide advice to habitat-level paralegal workers. Women's land rights may be incorporated into training given to leaders of habitat-level forums and executive committee/sub-committee members of PLFs (TNCDW n.d.a). Further, a national or state-level government order could be considered for development of all marginalized women's individual land (after completing development of land of SC/STs), collectively owned land, and collectively leased land (for long term) under MGNREGS.[33] Yet another recommendation is provision of meso-credit[34] to women farmers' collectives through banks, the

Mahalir Thittam, the Tamil Nadu State Rural Livelihood Mission or the World Bank supported Tamil Nadu Pudhu Vaazhvu Project, irrespective of whether the groups are promoted under government schemes or independently by NGOs. Women run farmer's service centres[35] and marketing centres at village and higher levels could be supported independently by banks or under these schemes. Other supportive policies for dry land collective farming by women which could be considered are supply of millet under the public distribution system and transfer of seed and fertilizer subsidies to women's farming groups[36] in lieu of organic farming and using indigenous seeds.

Creating Voice

The women farmers' groups at village level formed by both non-government and government actors could meet once in six months at panchayat, block, district, and state levels for exchange of ideas and strategies on negotiating land rights and sustainable agriculture, as well as for lobbying with government, politicians, and media on protecting agricultural land and common property resources, women's rights to land, and agricultural policies. They could also be trained to become members and leaders of agricultural cooperatives and PRIs.

Institutional Structures and Systems

All petitions received by district collectors may be categorized subject wise, with one subject being claims by collectives or individual women related to land, so that it is possible to monitor progress in addressing the same. Of the post of Personal Assistant-Legal to district collectors (Government Order 45), 50% may be reserved for women lawyers, in particular from marginalized communities. Similar reservation may be made with respect to the posts of VAO and *tehsildar*. The TNCDW and the Department of Women and Child Development may be represented in the PMU of the National Land Record Management Programme.

To sum up, TN is a special case that does not adopt either the Andhra or Bihar models. Rural women's land rights in TN have to be positioned within the context of right to land of the landless poor. The development model adopted by the state government has to change so that agriculture is prioritized and land under agriculture increased. In addition, policy, customary practices, and institutional rules and structures have to be altered in support of rural women's rights to land. However, much depends on the voice and agency of marginalized rural women and support available from women's rights groups working on this issue.

NOTES

1. According to Mearns (1999), between 1961–62 and 1982 the proportion of households neither owning nor cultivating land grew at a faster rate in TN than in India as whole.
2. Interviews were held with the village administrative officer (VAO), the *tehsildar*, the rural development officer (RDO), the Legal Aid Board, and the NGO GUIDE in Kancheepuram district of TN. In Chennai, the author met officials from the TNCDW, Tamil Nadu Dalit Women's Movement members, and TNWC members. Discussions were held over phone with the Law Trust for Women. She is grateful to all the individuals/organizations for their valuable inputs and to the NGO GUIDE for coordinating visits in Kancheepuram district, TN.
3. Nine districts include Chennai, Dharmapuri, Kanyakumari, Theni, Trichirapalli, Ariyalur, Coimbatore, Salem, and Nilgiris (Center for Women's Studies n.d.).
4. Period not specified, but inscriptions that are referred to are from the 10 century (Mukund 1999).
5. The term *bandhus* refers to persons related to deceased through one more female link.
6. Discussion with TNWC on 27 June 2014.
7. Discussion with Tamil Nadu Dalit Women's Movement and TNWC on 18 June 2014 and 27 June 2014.
8. It also mentioned that the officers who effected the transfer of *patta* registry of DC lands to non-SC people are liable for disciplinary action (Gandhimathi 2014).
9. Standard acre takes into account whether the land is wet land or dry land and the land's market value (PRS 1961a).
10. There is no reference in the Act as to whether compensation for land acquired would be paid to the joint account of women and men or in equal measure to women and men.
11. Discussion with the Managing Director, TNCDW, 8 June 2014.
12. See http://www.pudhuvaazhvu.org/posters.html (accessed on 30 June 2014).

13. http://www.pudhuvaazhvu.org/booklets.html (accessed 30 June 2014).
14. Exact details of how many groups were involved and how much land has been purchased or leased could not be gathered.
15. Discussion with the Managing Director, TNCDW, 8 June 2014.
16. Discussion with the Managing Director, TNCDW, 8 June 2014.
17. Discussion with the Managing Director, TNCDW, 8 June 2014.
18. Vide G.O. (Ms) No.70, Revenue [RA.3(2)] Department, dated 4-3-2013.
19. The TN government is working on a Rehabilitation and Resettlement policy to uplift livelihoods and improve living standards of people displaced.
20. As reflected in the Twelfth Five-year Plan of the National Planning Commission.
21. Mutation means transfer or change of title in the records for the concerned property (*Economic Times* 2017).
22. Government Order (Ms) 45 dated 24-02-2012, on appointment of data entry operators for computerization of land records, (Ms) 82 dated 9-3-2012 on appointment of 'Personal Assistant-Legal' attached to the district collector for monitoring progress on land-related disputes, and (Ms) 439 dated 15-7-2008 on appointment of VAO do not make any reference to one-third appointment of women (Revenue Department, 2008c, 2012a, 2012b). The order on recruitment of 'Personal Assistant Legal', however, mentions that preference would be given to SC, ST, and backward class candidates. Government Order (Ms) 181 dated 30-05-2012 on Constitution of (registered) Project Management Unit (PMU) as part of National Land Records Modernisation Programme mentions that the governing body of the PMU is to consist of representatives from revenue administration, survey and settlement, land administration, information and technology development, finance, and planning and development (Revenue Department 2012c). There is no mention of including Social Welfare and Nutritious Meal Programme Department in the PMU (which covers women's 'welfare').
23. For example, the Government Order Ms 2535 dated 21-11-1979 states that the assistant commissioner in the Office of Director of Land Reforms shall be recruited from the superintendents with five years of experience from the Board of Revenue or the deputy collectors (from the Tamil Nadu Civil Service; Office of the Director of Land Reforms 1979). There is no mention of quota for women, SCs, and STs to this crucial appointment, and in fact the term 'he' is used when referring to potential candidates. Such omissions are also reflected in more recent government orders, like Ms (66) dated 4-3-2013 pertaining to retention of 258 new positions of enforcement revenue inspector, sub-inspector of survey, deputy *tehsildar*, joint commissioner (Land Reforms), district revenue officer, etc. (Revenue Department 2013a).
24. Discussion with the Managing Director of TNCDW, 8 June 2014.
25. In Ullavur village, Kancheepuram district, 60 Dalit households were cultivating 220 acres of *odai porombokku* land (common land near stream)

for 30 years. A real estate company people gave the Dalit men an advance with the intention of purchasing the land for real estate. The Dalit Women in Resource Protection Committee formed by the NGO GUIDE raised an objection. With the encouragement of GUIDE they held a meeting with the men to convince them about retaining the land for agriculture production. Most of the men got convinced, and the next time officials from the real estate company came, they communicated their decision to not sell the land. The women want de-silting of water bodies so that they can better irrigate the land (Discussion with the NGO GUIDE, 19ᵗ February 2015).

26. See note 3.
27. She observed that the scope of collective lease of *poramboku* land was limited in her area as *poramboku* land was itself limited.
28. Women have also accessed title deeds with regard to housing. This, however, is not the focus of this report
29. Exact date not specified, but articles published in 2012 have been referred to (Centre for Women's Studies n.d.).
30. Discussion with TN Dalit Women's Movement in 18 June 2014.
31. Discussion with TN Dalit Women's Movement in 18 June 2014.
32. Discussion with Trustee, Guide, 21 June 2014.
33. Suggestion from TNWC during a meeting with the core team on 27 June 2014.
34. Meso-credit is credit of larger amounts than micro-credit to individuals/ groups which can create employment and strengthen livelihoods for several people (Akosile 2010).
35. For example, run by women farmer's groups under Gorakhpur Environment Action Group.
36. Many women collective farming groups manage their own seed banks and engage in organic farming (interview with TNWC on 27 June 2014 and Tamil Nadu Women's Forum on 18 June 2014).

REFERENCES

Adi Dravidar and Tribal Welfare Department. 2013. *Adi Dravidar And Tribal Welfare Department Policy Note 20142015*. Chennai: Adi Dravidar and Tribal Welfare Department, Government of Tamil Nadu.

Agarwal, B. 2002. *Are We Not Peasants Too: Land Rights and Women's Claims in India*. SEEDS, Number 21. New York: The Population Council.

Agarwal, B., B. Sivaramayya, and L. Sarkar. 1998, February. Report of the Committee for Gender Equality in land Devolution in Tenurial Laws. Submitted to the Department of Rural Development, Government of India, New Delhi.

Agriculture Department. 2014. *Policy Note Demand No. 5—Agriculture 2013–2014.* Chennai: Agricultural Department, Government of Tamil Nadu

Akosile, A. 2010. 'MESO Credit: Novel Poverty Alleviation Tool.' *This Day Live,* July 7, 2010. Available at: http://www.thisdaylive.com/articles/mesocredit-novel-poverty-alleviation-tool/83863/ (accessed on 16 June 2015).

Anandhi, S. 1991, March. 'Representing Devadasis: Dasigal Mosa Valai' as a Radical Text.' *Economic and Political Weekly* 26 (11/12, Annual Number): 739–41, 743, 745–46.

Anandhi, S., J. Jeyaranjan, and R. Krishnan. 2002, October 26–November 1. 'Work, Caste and Competing Masculinities: Notes from a Tamil Village.' *Economic and Political Weekly* 37 (43): 4397–406.

Centre for Women's Studies. n.d. *Property Rights of Women in Tamil Nadu.* Chennai: Centre for Women's Studies, SIET College. Available at: http://ncw.nic.in/pdfReports/PROPERTY_RIGHTS_OF_WOMEN_IN_TAMIL%20NADU.pdf (accessed on 16 June 2015).

Commissionerate of Land Reforms. n.d. 'Revenue Courts.' Available at: http://www.landreforms.tn.gov.in/RevenueCourt.html#f)_Kudiyiruppu (accessed on 16 June 2015).

Dasthagir, G. K. 2012. 'Fencing Women in Water User Associations: An Appraisal of Gender Strategy for Participatory Irrigation Management in Tamil Nadu.' *Water Policy Research Highlight.* Available at: http://www.iwmi.cgiar.org/iwmi-tata/PDFs/2012_Highlight-24.pdf (accessed on 16 June 2015).

Department of Economics and Statistics. 2014. *Statistical Hand Book of Tamil Nadu 2014.* Department of Economics and Statistics, Government of Tamil Nadu. Available at: http://www.tn.gov.in/deptst/index.htm (accessed on 16 June 2015).

Economic Times. 2017. 'Definition of Mutation.' Bennett, Coleman and Co limited, Mumbai. Available at: http://economictimes.indiatimes.com/definition/mutation (accessed on 1 May 2017).

Gandhimathi, A. 2014. *Draft—State-specific Recommendations on Improving Access to Land by the Poor.* Chennai: ActionAid.

———. 2002. No. 34 of 2002—Tamil Nadu Highways Act, 2001. Available at: www.tnrsp.com/Highways%20Act.doc (accessed on 16 June 2015).

Government of Maldives. 2009. *'Aneh Dhivehiraajje'—The Strategic Action Plan, National Development Framework for 2009–2013.* Male: The President's Office, Government of Maldives. Available at: http://planning.gov.mv/en/images/stories/publications/strategic_action_plan/SAP-EN.pdf (accessed on 16 June 2015).

Harris, J., J. Jeyanranjan, and K. Nagaraj. 2010, July 31. 'Land, Labour and Caste Politics in Rural Tamil Nadu in the 20th Century: Iruvelpattu (1916–2008).' *Economic and Political Weekly* xlv (31): 47–61.

International Institute for Population Sciences (IIPS) and Macro International. 2008. *Tamil Nadu National Family Health Survey (NFHS-3), India, 2005–06: Gujarat.* Mumbai: IIPS.

Jeejhebhoy, S., and Z. Zathar. 2001, December. Women's Autonomy in India and Pakistan: The Influence of Religion and Region.' *Population and Development Review* 27 (4): 687–712.
Joshi Adhikari Institute of Social Studies. 2011. *Agrarian Crisis Life at State in Rural India*. Pune: Joshi Adhikari Institute of Social Studies.
Law Commission of India. 2000. 174th Report on Property Rights of Hindu Women, May 5th 2000. Available at: http://www.lawcommissionofindia.nic. in/kerala.htm#tamilnadu (accessed on 1 April 2017).
Mangubhai, J. 2014. *Human Rights as Practice: Dalit Women Securing Livelihood Entitlements in South India*. New Delhi: Oxford University Press.
Mearns, R. 1999. *Access to Land in Rural India: Policy Issues and Options*. Rural Development Sector Unit, South Asia. Washington, DC: The World Bank.
Mencher, Joan P. 1998. 'Women's Work and Poverty: Women's Contribution to Household Maintenance in South India.' In *A Home Divided: Women and Income in the Third World*, edited by D. Dwyer and J. Bruce. Palo Alto, CA: Stanford University Press. Available at: https://books.google. co.in/books?hl=en&lr=&id=LBe_brmRMtwC&oi=fnd&pg=PA99&d-q=Tamil+Nadu+women%27s+land+rights&ots=w7Q_w65Elz&sig=9wx-KNs7aBjyOBKLEIlYTWYvOqzY#v=onepage&q&f=false (accessed on 29 March 2017).
Mukund, K. 1999. 'Women's Property Rights in South India: A Review.' *Economic and political Weekly* 34 (May 29–June 4): 1352–58.
Mukund, K. 1992, April 25. 'Turmeric Land: Women's Property Rights in Tamil Society Since Early Medieval Times.' *Economic and Political Weekly* 27 (17): WS2–WS6
Murthy, R. K., with L. Priya. 2010. *A Study of CMRCs: Services and Leadership*. Bangalore: MYRADA.
Nagappan, S. B. 2012. Assertion for Resources and Dignity: Dalit Civil Society Activism in Tamil Nadu. Available at: https://casteout.files.wordpress. com/2013/06/babu.pdf (accessed on 1 April 2017).
PRS Legislative Research (PRS). 1958. 'The Tamil Nadu Bhoodan Yagna Act, 1958 Act 15 of 1958.'Available at: http://www.lawsofindia.org/pdf/tamil_ nadu/1958/1958TN15.pdf (accessed on 16 June 2015).
———. 1961a. 'The Tamil Nadu Land Reforms (Fixation of Ceiling on Land) Act, 1961 Act 58 of 1961.' Available at: http://www.lawsofindia.org/pdf/ tamil_nadu/1961/1961TN58.pdf (accessed 16 June 2015).
———. 1961b. 'The Tamil Nadu Public Trust (Regulation and Administration of Agricultural Land) Act, 1961 [Tamil Nadu Act 57/61].' Available at: http:// www.lawsofindia.org/pdf/tamil_nadu/1961/1961TN57.pdf (accessed on 16 June 2015).
———. 1969. 'The Tamil Nadu Agricultural Lands Record of Tenancy Rights Act, 1969 Act 10 of 1969.' Available at: http://www.lawsofindia.org/pdf/ tamil_nadu/1969/1969TN10.pdf (accessed on 16 June 2015).

PRS Legislative Research (PRS). 1997. 'The Tamil Nadu Cultivating Tenants (Protection from Eviction) Act, 1997 Act 20 of 1997.' Available at: http://www.lawsofindia.org/pdf/tamil_nadu/1997/1997TN20.pdf (accessed on 16 June 2015).

———. 2007. 'The Tamil Nadu Acquisition of Land for Industrial Purpose Act, 1997. Act 10 of 1999.' Available at: http://www.lawsofindia.org/pdf/tamil_nadu/1999/1999TN10.pdf (accessed on on 1 May 2017).

Rao, N. 2005. 'Kinship Matters: Women's Land Claims in the Santal Parganas, Jharkhand.' *Journal of the Royal Anthropological Institute* (N.S.) 11: 725–46.

Ramdas, A. 2013. 'Land Is Not Ancestral Property, It Has to Change Hands: Sivakami.' ADMIN on May 1, 2013. Available at: http://www.dalitweb.org/?p=1740 (accessed on 16 June 2015).

Revenue Department. 1993. *Government Order (Ms) No. 249 dated 23-3-1993*. Chennai: Revenue Department, Government of Tamil Nadu.

———. 1997. *Government Order (Ms) No 318 dated 21-3-1997*. Chennai: Revenue Department, Government of Tamil Nadu.

———. 1999. *Government Order (Ms) No. 242 dated 14-5-1999*. Chennai: Revenue Department, Government of Tamil Nadu.

———. 2001a. *Government Order (Ms) No. 324 dated 10-9-2001*. Chennai: Revenue Department, Government of Tamil Nadu.

———. 2001b. *Government Order (Ms.) 336 dated 14-9-2001*. Chennai: Revenue Department, Government of Tamil Nadu.

———. 2003. *Government Order (Ms.) 382 dated 3-9-2003*. Chennai: Revenue Department, Government of Tamil Nadu.

———. 2008a. *Government Order Ms (34) dated 23-1-2008*. Chennai: Revenue Department, Government of Tamil Nadu.

———. 2008b. *Government Order (Ms) 409 dated 2-7-2008*. Chennai: Revenue Department, Government of Tamil Nadu.

———. 2008c. *Government Order (Ms) 439 dated 15-7-2008*. Chennai: Revenue Department, Government of Tamil Nadu.

———. 2011a. *Government Order (Ms) 12 dated 7-1-2011*. Chennai: Revenue Department, Government of Tamil Nadu.

———. 2011b. *Government Order (Ms) 364 dated 28-11-2011*. Chennai: Revenue Department, Government of Tamil Nadu.

———. 2012a. *Government Order (Ms) 45 dated 24-02-2012*. Chennai: Revenue Department, Government of Tamil Nadu.

———. 2012b. *Government Order (Ms) 82 dated 9-3-2012*. Chennai: Revenue Department, Government of Tamil Nadu.

———. 2012c. *Government Order (Ms) 181 dated 30-05-2012*. Chennai: Revenue Department, Government of Tamil Nadu.

———. 2013a. *Government Order Ms (66), dated 4-3-2013*. Chennai: Revenue (Ser 5) Department, Government of Tamil Nadu.

Revenue Department. 2013b. *Revenue Department Policy Note: 2013–2014.* Chennai: Revenue Department, Government of Tamil Nadu.

Rural Development and Panchayati Raj Department. 2013. Rural Development and Panchayat Raj Department Policy Note 2013–2014. Chennai: Rural Development and Panchayati Raj Department, Government of Tamil Nadu.

Sircar, A., and D. Fletschner. 2014. 'The Right to Inherit Isn't Working for Indian Women, Says U.N. Study.' *The Wall Street Journal* (March 2). Available at: https://blogs.wsj.com/indiarealtime/2014/03/02/the-right-to-inherit-isnt-working-for-indian-women-says-u-n-study/ (accessed on 1 May 2017).

Social Welfare and Nutritious Meal Programme Department. 2013. *Demand No. 45, Social Welfare And Nutritious Meal Programme Department Policy Note 2013–2014.* Chennai: Social Welfare and Nutritious Meal Programme Department, Government of Tamil Nadu.

Swaminathan, Padmini. 2002. 'Violence of Gender-biased Development, Going Beyond Social and Demographic Indicators.' In *The Violence of Development: The Political Economy of Gender*, edited by Karin Kapadia. London: Palgrave Macmillan.

Tamil Nadu Corporation for Development of Women (TNCDW). n.d.a. 'Training.' Available at: http://www.tamilnadumahalir.org/sample-sites/mahalir/federation.html?id=82 (accessed on 30 June 2014).

TNCDW. n.d.b. 'Block Level Federation.' Available at: http://www.tamilnadumahalir.org/sample-sites/mahalir/federation.html (accessed on 30 June 2014).

15

Gender Justice and Law: A Gender-specific Study of Landownership in Uttarakhand

INDU PATHAK

INTRODUCTION AND CONTEXT

Women constitute half of the world population but they are constantly deprived of the ownership and inheritance rights of property. Gender discrimination in the ownership of productive assets and immovable property like land can be seen all over the world (Agarwal 1994). Gender unequal laws/policies and the existing sociocultural values are the significant reasons for this discrimination. The gender-based discrimination in society can be removed by empowering women and transforming those institutions which are responsible for reinforcing the ideology and practice of subordination.

While analysing the property rights of women, it will be important to highlight the class differentiation among women as majority of them do not belong to the working class and sharp differences have been seen across women from different socio-economic backgrounds. Agarwal (ibid.) argued that in a patriarchal system, the class of a woman is usually decided through the status of men particularly in marriage. A husband's prosperous status would enhance her status, while widowhood or divorce would lower it. Due to marital breakdown, even women of prosperous families can be left destitute and forced to seek wage work. This is a reflection of their property-less status and economic vulnerability as women. Thus, strengthening women's position as landowners supports a gender responsive inclusive growth and creates a culture of equality (Kelkar and Nathan 2001).

Land has always been considered as the most important form of property in rural areas. For a significant majority of rural household, it is the single most important source of security against poverty (Agarwal 2002). It is recognized as a significant determinant of economic well-being, social status, and political power. But rural women in India have only marginal rights to agricultural land and to other productive assets. It is an irony that in India, while 83% of rural women provide agricultural labours, only 10% (approximately) of rural land is actually titled to them (Ministry of Rural Development 2011).

The problem of gender inequality in inheritance of landed property is due to deep cultural bias against women. The cultural and customary practices play a dominant role in depriving women of their legal rights. The law of the land that is the customary law dictates that the land can only be inherited by the descendants, who can trace their origin from a common ancestor in the male line. Daughters and sisters who are made to observe clan and territorial exogamy in marriage stand excluded under the customary law. Observance of clan exogamy makes a daughter/sister an outsider, belonging to another clan, and territorial exogamy makes it difficult, if not impossible, for her to take over the effective possession of her land, in case she inherits it.

PROPERTY RIGHTS OF INDIAN WOMEN

In the Indian Constitution, both the central and state governments are competent to enact laws on matters of succession. In post-colonial India, legislative jurisdiction was put under three different lists: a union list, a state list, and a concurrent list. Agriculture- and land-related legislations were put under the state list, while laws relating to property and succession were put on the concurrent list. All states have taken important measures in relation to agricultural labours, tenants, and other farmers, land ceilings, allocation of surplus lands, distribution of *pattas* (official documents stating land title and the term on which land is held), and other land reforms. Some states have their own variations regarding property laws within each personal law. Hence, there is no single law which can govern and protect the property rights of Indian women. Different religious communities are governed by their own personal laws. In India inheritance was traditionally patrilineal with some limited matrilineal pockets as in northern and central Kerala and Meghalaya in the Northeast (Agarwal 1995).

Looking at the gender discrimination in the implementation of landed property rights, several policy initiatives have been taken by Government of India through the Five-year Plans. At the initial stage of planning, 'welfare' approach has been accepted for the weaker section including women. There was a shift in the Sixth Plan (1980–85) from 'welfare' to 'development' by placing more emphasis on health, education, and employment. Then the Ninth Plan (1997–2002) made a significant shift from 'development' to 'empowerment' with a focus on creating an enabling environment, especially for women. The Ninth Five-year Plan document included a section on 'gender and land rights' and emphasized the need for landownership by poor women. The Eleventh and Twelfth Five-year Plans (2007–12 and 2012–17) also encourage more ownership rights for women. However, despite this the effectiveness of policies and legislations has been limited in practice.

REVIEW OF LITERATURE

Women's inheritance rights are influenced by several factors. The very purpose of the laws, providing equal rights in inheritance for women, is negated due to social factors. Either women are hardly aware of those laws or they give up their rights for the sake of safeguarding the support of their maternal family. Every married woman has to face the issue of her marriage expenditure, when she intends to claim her inheritance right. Agarwal (1994) pointed out that for Indian women, land is the most important resource, and the issues of ownership and control over property are crucial to understand the unequal relationship between men and women.

Sen (1990) observed that in the Indian inheritance system, property, especially landed property, has always been preserved for male heirs. The role of women and men in economic and non-economic spheres is normally defined by the culture of patriarchy; intra-household allocations are also located in this culture which is rooted in patrilineal and patrilocal practices.

Chowdhry (1997) pointed out that in many Indian families, dowry is considered as a share of women in family property, and women themselves give validity to dowry by accepting this as their share of patrimony. Women's independent right over productive assets is essential for their welfare, efficiency and equality, and empowerment (Agarwal 1996). Women's independent command over productive assets and property is necessary for the improvement of their capabilities and overall gender development. Besides the rights, the power to use ownership and effective control over it can be beneficial for their poverty alleviation (Moser 1998; World Bank 2001a).

Sherraden (1991) argued in favour of a policy shift from income to assets. According to him, income sustains only consumption but assets can change thinking of people and their interaction pattern with the world. A World Bank report on poverty (World Bank 2001b) highlighted the linkage between empowerment and expansion of assets. According to Moser (1998), a negative correlation has been found between assets ownership and vulnerability of people. More ownership of assets makes people less vulnerable, while reduction in ownership right increases their vulnerability.

In fact, women's ownership right and effective control over assets is not just a legal or policy matter, but a serious issue of transformation of those social institutions which are the determining factor of gender relations in society. The challenge is not only to create a positive condition for women's property rights at the legal level but also to develop such mechanisms that can fundamentally change the mental framework and social practices at different levels of a society, which is more challenging.

METHODOLOGY

The study is focused on the inheritance and landed property rights of women of Uttarakhand, a northern hilly region of India. It is primarily based on secondary data and information which included print and online publications, reports, journals, and official statistical data of Uttarakhand government. The laws related to inheritance and landed property are also examined. To assess the awareness level and attitude of general women regarding women's property rights, an empirical micro field study has been conducted with the help of a small structured interview schedule.

A voluntary response sampling technique was used to select respondents. The interview schedules were administered to the women of Nainital and Udham Singh Nagar districts, and within the study period, 58 respondents were contacted. To collect secondary information, interaction has also been done with lawyers, journalists, activists, government officials, and some members of the grass-roots level organizations, namely Mahila Samakhya and Sainion Ka Sangathan. Chairperson, vice-chairperson, member secretary, and some other members of Uttarakhand State Women Commission were also interviewed to achieve the grass-roots level realities in this regard.

PROFILE OF UTTARAKHAND

Uttarakhand, 27th state of the Indian Union, was carved out of Uttar Pradesh on 9th November 2000. The state is divided into two divisions, Garhwal and Kumaon, and 13 districts. Among these 13 districts, Uttarkashi, Chamoli, Pauri, Tehri, Dehradun, Haridwar, and Rudraprayag are in the Garhwal region of the state while Nainital, Almora, Pithoragarh, Udham Singh Nagar, Champawat, and Bageshwar fall in the Kumaon region. Out of these 13 districts, four districts (Nainital, Haridwar, Dehradun, and Udham Singh Nagar) have large area of the plains, whereas the other nine districts comprise the hilly region of the state (Mittal, Tripathi, and Sethi 2008).

The economy of Uttarakhand is predominantly an agricultural economy and approximately three-fourths population of Uttarakhand depends on agriculture for their livelihood. The landholdings especially in hilly regions are small and fragmented and irrigation facilities are limited. The geographical area of the state is 53,483 sq. km which is only 1.63% of the total area of India. About 4.53% of India's forest area and about 3.1% of India's agricultural area is in this state. Table 15.1 shows a brief demographic profile of Uttarakhand.

According to Census 2011, about three-fourths population of Uttarakhand lives in rural area. Uttarakhand has achieved commendable success in attaining a relatively high level of literacy in comparison to many regions of the country. More than 78% of population of the state is literate but there is a gender gap in education.

Gender Justice and Law • 381

Table 15.1
Demographic Profile of Uttarakhand for 2011

Population (in millions)	Male	Female	Total
Total Population	5.138	4.948	10.086
Rural Population	3.519	3.517	7.036
Urban Population	1.619	1.431	3.050
Sex Ratio	963 Female per 1000 Male		
Child Sex Ratio (Population 0–6 Age Group)	890 Female per 1,000 Male		
Density of Population	189 per sq. km		
Literacy Rate	87.40%	70.0%	78.00%

Source: Statistical data of Director of Economics and Statistics Planning Department, Government of Uttarakhand.

LAND AND GENDER RELATIONS IN UTTARAKHAND: HISTORICAL PERSPECTIVE

At the time of colonial occupation in the early 19th century, Uttarakhand had an exuberant economy (Guha 1989; Nanda 1999), but today the situation is totally adverse. A high percentage of productive workforce of this area is employed outside the region due to lack of local employment and insufficient agricultural productivity. Of the geographical area of Uttarakhand, representing most of the uncultivated commons, 67% stands legally notified as 'forests' (Ghildyal and Banerjee 1998). It is a distinctive feature that all the forest land is not under the jurisdiction of the forest department in Uttarakhand. The reserve forest (about 69%) is under the forest department; the protected forest (16.8%), known as civil land in Kumaon and 'soyam' land in the erstwhile state of Tehri Garhwal, is under the jurisdiction of the revenue department that manages it in collaboration with elected village panchayats; and 13.6% legally notified village forests are managed by elected van panchayats (Sarin 2001).

The history of state appropriation of the uncultivated commons had an intensive influence on reshaping traditional gender relations in this area. Prior to the colonial regime, the community institutions of this area were powerful enough to control the use and management of both cultivated land and the uncultivated commons within customary village boundaries, and they had to face little interference from earlier rulers (Agarwal 1996; Guha 1989; Nanda 1999; Somnathan 1991).

During the colonial regime, a number of interferences had been faced by local people that permanently changed this landscape of entire local land resource use and management, initially in both the regions, that is, Kumaon and British Garhwal, and subsequently even in the adjoining state of Tehri Garhwal. In 1823, first revenue settlement had been undertaken by the British regime in the Kumaon region. Under this settlement, the land within the customary village boundaries has been classified in two categories—cultivated *'naap'* (measured) and uncultivated *'benaap'* (unmeasured) land. In 1893, all unmeasured 'waste' (*benaap*) lands in Kumaon were declared 'districts protected forests' under the control of the district commissioners. During 1910–17, colonial government had notified 7,500 sq. km uncultivated commons as reserve forests and tried to take possession of forest resources. This decision severely prevented user's rights of local people and played havoc with the customary patterns of resource use, dislocating existing agrarian practices (Sarin 2001).

It is a well-known fact that women have played a significant role in community forest management as well as in the protection of forests in this area. In this regard, the Chipko movement is an excellent example of women's contributions. Apart from these economic activities, forests have also been a source of emotional support for rural women. During the tough daily routine, women share their happiness as well as problems with each other in that place while working. In this area, it has been a tradition that women work collectively. Due to the deep involvement with their forest, colonial intervention created an intense resentment among women against administration. Hence, consequently, British regime constituted the Kumaon Grievance Committee.

In 1921, the Kumaon Grievance Committee was established by the administration to find the reasons of unrest among local people. The report of this committee (GoUP 1922) gave an insight about gender relation and gendered nature of resource use. Under the customs in Kumaon, tasks such as lopping, collection of minor forest produce, and grazing are performed by women and children. The intervention of forest guards in these activities was identified as a major grievance by this committee (ibid.). To observe the sentiments against forest guards' daily interference with the use of forest produce by women, the committee recommended for the removal of forest guards so as to do away with the real grievance in all classes of the affected parts of forests. Hence, to restore the forest rights of local people, 4460 sq. km of commercially less valuable forests were taken away from the forest department and transferred to the revenue department. Though the bona fide residents of Kumaon got their right over the commercially less valuable class-I reserve forest but, thereby, customary common property resources were converted into open access areas.

LAWS RELATED TO LAND/PROPERTY RIGHTS APPLICABLE IN UTTARAKHAND

In Uttarakhand, particularly in the hilly region, a large percentage of rural households are de facto female-headed from widowhood or male outmigration. The census data of 2011 reveals that the decadal population growth rate has been exceptionally high in four districts of the state. It is more than 30% in Dehradun, Haridwar, and Udham Singh Nagar, over 25% in Nainital, and moderately high in Champawat (14.5%) and Uttarkashi (11.75%). In the remaining seven districts, population growth has been rather low, being about 5% or less. In two of these districts, Pauri Garhwal and Almora, it is negative (Census of India 2011). All mountain districts exhibit substantial decline in decadal population growth. In this condition, an increasing number of household have to depend on women, managing agricultural activities and bearing the major burden of family subsistence. Without the land title, these women face a serious livelihood disadvantage and poverty risk.

Uttarakhand has no specific act on landed property right and it has been governed by Uttar Pradesh Zamindari Abolition and Land Reform Act 1950 and other property rights by Hindu Succession Act (HSA) 1956 and Hindu Succession (Amendment) Act (HSAA) 2005. But after the enactment of HSAA 2005, issues related to the right on agricultural land are decided according to this Act.

Gender-wise analysis of land-related laws is also important, especially from women's point of view. Nowadays, legally and with due respect to some initiatives, like reduction in stamp duty, taken by state government, women enjoy greater rights on property than they did at the turn of the century. But substantial inequalities remain in the inheritance laws of both Hindus and Muslims. To understand inheritance and landed property rights, an in-depth analysis and review of the above-mentioned Acts/laws are necessary. After independence, inheritance of Hindus is governed by HSA 1956 and inheritance of Muslims is governed by the Muslim Personal Law (Shariat) Application Act 1937. Agricultural land is treated differently from other forms of property. Tenancy rights in agricultural land were specifically exempted from the HSA 1956, and the 1937 Shariat Act excluded all agricultural land (owned or tenanted) from its purview. The fact is that agricultural land has been under the jurisdiction of state legislatures since the passing of the Government of India Act of 1935. As a result, in a number of states, the succession rules relating to land held under tenancy have a different order of devolution than the personal laws affecting the devolution of all other property.

Hindu Succession Act (HSA) 1956

Indian women have been facing gender discrimination in inheritance right for a long time. In the mid of 1950s, the Hindu personal law was revised due to which polygamy was banned and Hindu women got the right to inheritance, adoption, and divorce. Under Hindu law, son has birthright over ancestral property, but daughter's share was based on that share which was received by her father as his birthright. Hence, there was a possibility that a daughter could effectively be disinherited from property if her father gave up his right over ancestral property. In this situation, a daughter will get nothing whereas son's right will be safe as he has birthright over the ancestral property.

HSA enacted in 1956 was the first law to provide a comprehensive and uniform system of inheritance among Hindus and to address gender inequalities in the area of inheritance. It was a process of codification as well as a reform at the same time. The Act is applicable to all the Hindus, Buddisht, Jains and Sikhs by religion. The Act was made to codify the law relating to intestate succession. At that time, the Act was possibly considered as revolutionary, but retention of the *Mitakshara* coparcenary without including female in it meant that females could not inherit ancestral property as the males do (HSA 1956).

Under the *Mitakshara* law, the son acquires a right and interest in the family property by birth. According to this school, a son, a grandson, and a great grandson constitute a class of coparceners, based on birth in the family. No female member of the family was included in coparcenary under the *Mitakshara* law. In this system, joint family property devolves by survivorship within the coparcenary. According to this law, females have no right in ancestral family property by birth.

The *Mitakshara* law also recognizes inheritance right by succession but only to the property separately owned by an individual male or female. Females are included as heirs to this kind of property. If a joint family gets divided, each male coparcener takes his share and female gets nothing. Only when one of the coparceners dies, a female gets a share as an heir to the deceased. Thus, the law, by excluding the daughters from participating in coparcenary ownership, not only promotes gender bias but also leads to negations of their right to equality and erodes their fundamental rights guaranteed by the constitution. In spite of all these flaws, the Act marked a beginning for the property rights of Hindu women.

Hindu Succession (Amendment) Act (HSAA), 2005

This Act is an amended version of the HSA 1956, which removes gender discriminatory provisions of the previous Act. The HSAA 2005 came into force on 9 September 2005. This Act was enacted to enlarge the rights of a daughter, both married and unmarried, and to bring her at par with a son or any male member of a joint Hindu family governed by the *Mitakshara* law. It also sought to bring the female line of descent at an equal level with the male line of descent, including children of a predeceased daughter of predeceased daughters (Lawyers Collective Women's Rights Initiative 1956). At present, HSAA 2005 is applicable to govern women's property rights as well as their right on agricultural land. This Act gives the following rights to daughters under Section 6:

1. Sons, daughters, and their mothers can get an equal share in the land.
2. A daughter has the same right over the property as a son.
3. This Act includes daughters as joint owners in the joint family property with the same birthright as sons to share, to claim partition, and to share the liabilities.
4. Daughters (married or not) shall have the same rights as sons to reside in or seek partition to the family house.
5. Widows can claim and inherit the deceased's property even if they have remarried.

Section 6 of the amended Act has an overriding effect, so far as the partition of a coparcenary property and succession of interest of a deceased member (male or female) is concerned. It also supersedes all customs and usages or Shastric Law in this regard. The deletion of Section 4(2) of

HSA 1956 is definitely a right step towards removal of gender inequalities in the inheritance of agricultural land. In this section of HSA 1956, it is stated that

> For the removal of doubts it is hereby declared that nothing contained in this act shall be deemed to affect the provisions of any law for the time being in force providing for the prevention of the fragmentation of agricultural holdings or for the fixation of ceiling or for the devolution of tenancy rights in respect of such holdings. (HSAA 2005)

Uttar Pradesh Zamindari Abolition and Land Reform Act, 1950

The inheritance laws governing both Hindus and Muslims treat agricultural land as a special category of property. Women's inheritance rights in land under tenancy, thus, depend on the state-level tenurial laws. In Uttarakhand, the tenancy rights related to agricultural land are governed by Uttar Pradesh Zamindari and Land Reform Act 1950. In the tenurial laws of Uttar Pradesh, the specified rules of devolution show strong preference for agnatic succession with a priority for agnatic males, and the tenancy develops in the first instance on male lineal descendants in the male line of descent. The widow inherits only in the absence of these male heirs. Here, daughters and sisters are recognized but appear very low in the order of heirs. A woman can hold only a limited interest in the land and after her death the holding goes not to her heirs but to the heirs of the last male landowner. She also loses the land if she remarries or fails to cultivate it for a specified period, usually a year or two.

The tenurial laws of Uttar Pradesh (Uttarakhand) are applicable to all religious groups. Section 171 of this Act holds,

> [G]eneral order of succession-subject to the provision of Section 169, when a bhumidhar or asami, being a male dies, his interest in his holding shall devolve in accordance with the order of succession given below:
> 1. The male lineal descendants in the male line of descent in equal share per stripes.
> 2. Widow and widowed mother (step mother not included) and widow of a predeceased male lineal descendant in the male line descent etc.

The above-described order of succession proves that this provision has strong gender bias, as a daughter has no right of inheritance in agricultural land when sons are alive. No doubt these gender discriminatory provisions cannot be applied after the enactment of HSAA 2005 as it brought all the agricultural land at par with other property and it is also applicable in Uttarakhand. UPZA & LR Act has a special provision for the succession to a man's holding. Under this provision, the male lineal descendants in the male line of descent inherit in equal shares. The widow comes only after them along with the widowed mother and widow of the predeceased male lineal descendant in the male line of descent.

Married and unmarried daughters come even after the father. Unmarried daughters are preference between married and unmarried. In addition, the widow mother or a daughter inheriting the holding in that capacity does not get an absolute right as on her death; the devolution of the property will not be in favour of her heirs, but to the heirs of the last *bhumidhar* (tenure holder). General order of succession, given under Sections 171 and 174, shows a clear gender bias and the conditions applicable as follows:

1. Widows should not have remarried if they want to inherit the holding.
2. In the preferential order of succession, the daughter gets a lower place.
3. Woman as a widowed mother or as a daughter inheriting the holding does not get an absolute right on it.

Apart from the UPZA & LR Act 1950, some sections of the Uttar Pradesh Imposition of Ceiling and Land Holding Act, 1960, are also gender biased. Provisions of this Act did not define women as tenure holders as Section 17 of this Act does not include a woman as a tenure holder whose husband himself is a tenure holder.

Kumaon and Uttarakhand Zamindari Abolition and Land Reform Act (KUZALR) was enacted in 1960. This Act is expedient to provide for the acquisition of rights, title, and interest of people between state and the tiller of the soil in certain areas of Kumaon and Garhwal divisions and for the introduction of land reform therein. But no section is given regarding devolution of landed property rights in relation to gender perspective.

It is a fact that our constitution guarantees equality on the bases of gender and government is gradually aiming to move towards the constitutional provisions guaranteeing gender egalitarian land and property rights. In this context, HSAA 2005, which grants rights to women that are equal to those of men, is laudable but there is a vast gap between legal rights/ownership and effective control over it. Though women have a legal right on property, but the question is how far she can effectively control it. Unless our sociocultural values based on patriarchal mindset would be changed, it is difficult to achieve gender equality in property rights.

LAND/PROPERTY RIGHTS OF WOMEN IN UTTARAKHAND: GRASS-ROOTS LEVEL EXPERIENCE

The practice of inheritance in our society has been patriarchal and gender discriminatory in nature. Feminists have perceived disinheritance of women as a problem of culture. Laws of inheritance, governing different religious communities, have been framed in such a way that gives more privileges to men. To experience grass-roots level realities regarding land/property rights of women of Uttarakhand, the following measures have been adopted:

1. Gender-wise analysis of operational landholdings and allotment of houses under government-funded schemes.
2. Analysis of micro field study.
3. Consultation with members of the Uttarakhand State Women Commission.
4. Discussion with members of women organizations, activists and lawyers.
5. Impact of stamp duty concession.

GENDER-WISE ANALYSIS OF OPERATIONAL HOLDINGS

Gender-wise categorization of operational agricultural landholdings can highlight the position of women in agricultural economy. The latest agriculture census in Uttarakhand has been carried out with 2010–11 as the reference year at the instance of Government of India. This is a large-scale statistical operation for the collection and derivation of quantitative information about the structure of agriculture in the country. An agricultural operational holding is an ultimate unit for taking decision to develop agriculture at micro level. In this census, gender is taken as an important variable. On the basis of these data, three types of tables have been prepared:

1. Gender-wise categorization of operational landholdings.
2. Gender- and division-wise (Kumaon and Garhwal) categorization of operational landholdings.
3. Gender- and area-wise (hill and plain region) categorization of operational landholdings.

Here, operational holding means all land which is used wholly or partly for agricultural production and is operated as one technical unit by one person alone or with others without regard to title, legal form, and size of location. A technical unit has been defined as that unit which is under the same management and has the same means of production such as labour force, machinery, and animals (Agricultural Census of Uttarakhand 2010–11).

An operational holder is a person who has the responsibility for the operation of agricultural holding and who exercises and is responsible for the operation of the technical initiative. He may have full economic responsibility or may start it with others. The operational holder may be individual/joint/institutional. The holding of the actual cultivator and not the owner is the unit for data collection. In the following tables, only individual and joint holdings are displayed because institutional holdings are not categorized gender-wise (ibid.).

The data shown in Tables 15.2–15.4 are a reflection of the size of holdings, male–female holding size and gender category of the holdings of Kumaon and Garhwal division and hill and plain areas of the state. The holdings are divided in five size categories—marginal to large-size holdings. As expected maximum holdings (73.65%) are marginal and below one hectare. Only 0.12% holdings are large holdings (more than 10 hectare). As shown in Table 15.2, large-size holdings in Uttarakhand are nominal. Maximum holdings are either marginal or small in size. Gender-wise distribution of operational landholdings highlights the nominal representation of female in relation to landholdings. It is to be noted that more than 90% holdings are male holdings while women's representation is less than 10%. The vast gap between male and female holdings is same in both the divisions and hill and plain areas

Table 15.2
Gender-wise Distribution of Number of Operational Landholdings in Different Categories in Uttarakhand for 2010–11

Categories	No. of Holdings			% Distribution		
	Male	Female	Total	Male	Female	Total
Marginal holdings (below 1.0 ha)	600,063	70,762	670,825	89.45	10.55	100.00
Small holdings (1.0–2.0 ha)	143,087	13,970	157,057	91.11	8.89	100.00
Semi medium holdings (2.0–4.0 ha)	60,496	4,097	64,593	93.66	6.34	100.00
Medium holdings (4.0–10.0 ha)	16,389	806	17,195	95.31	4.69	100.00
Large holdings (10.0 ha–above)	950	28	928	97.14	2.86	100.00
Total	820,985	89,663	910,648	90.15	9.85	100.00

Source: Computed from the data available in Agriculture Census of Uttarakhand 2010–11.

Table 15.3
Division- and Gender-wise Distribution of Number of Operational Landholdings in Different Categories in Uttarakhand for 2010–11

Categories	Kumaon Division			Garhwal Division		
	Male	Female	Total	Male	Female	Total
Marginal holdings (below 1.0 ha)	293,177 (89.58)	34,118 (10.42)	327,295 (100.00)	306,886 (89.33)	36,644 (10.67)	343,530 (100.00)
Small holdings (1.0–2.0 ha)	65,215 (91.74)	5,868 (8.26)	(71,083) 100.00	77,872 (90.58)	8,102 (9.42)	85,974 (100.00)
Semi medium holdings (2.0–4.0 ha)	26,470 (93.45)	1,856 (6.55)	28,326 (100.00)	34,026 (93.82)	2,241 (6.18)	36,267 (100.00)
Medium holdings (4.0–10.0 ha)	8,324 (94.24)	509 (5.76)	8,833 (100.00)	8,065 (96.45)	297 (3.55)	8,362 (100.00)
Large holdings (10.0 ha–above)	611 (96.52)	22 (3.48)	633 (100.00)	339 (98.26)	06 (1.74)	345 (100.00)
Total	393,797 (90.29)	42,373 (9.71)	436,170 (100.00)	427,188 (90.03)	47,290 (9.97)	474,478 (100.00)

Source: Computed from the data available in Agriculture Census of Uttarakhand.
Note: Percentage is shown within parentheses.

Table 15.4
Hill and Plain Areas and Gender-wise Distribution of Number of Operational Landholdings in Different Categories in Uttarakhand for 2010–11

Categories	Hill Areas			Plain Areas		
	Male	Female	Total	Male	Female	Total
Marginal holdings (below 1.0 ha)	403,342 (88.97)	50,000 (11.03)	453,342 (100.00)	196,721 (90.45)	20,762 (9.55)	217,483 (100.00)
Small holdings (1.0–2.0 ha)	97,746 (90.44)	10,332 (9.56)	108,078 (100.00)	45,341 (92.57)	3,638 (7.43)	48,979 (100.00)
Semi- medium holdings (2.0–4.0 ha)	31,584 (93.24)	2,291 (6.76)	33,875 (100.00)	28,912 (94.12)	18.06 (5.88)	30,718 (100.00)
Medium holdings (4.0–10.0 ha)	5,343 (95.67)	242 (4.33)	5,585 (100.00)	11,046 (95.14)	564 (4.86)	11,610 (100.00)
Large holdings (10.0 ha–above)	192 (96.97)	06 (3.03)	198 (100.00)	758 (97.18)	22 (2.82)	780 (100.00)
Total	538,207 (89.54)	62,871 (10.46)	601,078 (100.00)	282,778 (91.35)	26,792 (8.65)	309,570 (100.00)

Source: Computed from the data available in Agriculture Census of Uttarakhand.
Note: Percentage is shown in parentheses.

of Uttarakhand. There seems a positive correlation between the size of holding and the number of male holdings. As size of holdings increases from marginal to large, percentage of male holdings also increases gradually, but at the same time a negative relation is seen between the size of holding and the number of female holdings. With the increasing size of a holding, female holdings decrease. In this regard, no specific difference is seen in the Kumaon and Garhwal division, as well as in hill and plain areas of Uttarakhand. These statistical data of agriculture census prove gender discrimination at grass-roots level.

HOUSING SCHEMES IN UTTARAKHAND

Indira Awas Yojana

Indira Awas Yojana (IAY), a programme of Ministry of Rural Development, is the most comprehensive housing scheme for rural people in India. The basic objective of this programme is to eradicate rural poverty and enable rural households to access the rural development programmes.

Since its inception, the scheme has been providing aid to those BPL families who are either houseless or having inadequate housing facilities for constructing a safe and durable shelter. The target groups of this scheme are Scheduled Caste (SC)/Scheduled Tribe (ST) families, women-headed households, people with disabilities, and non-SC/ST rural poor living below poverty line. The beneficiaries are identified and selected from the BPL list approved by *gram sabha* (village assembly).

The information provided by the Department of Rural Development, Uttarakhand, reveals that a large numbers of women have benefitted from the scheme. Information regarding the year-wise status of IAY beneficiaries highlights that the ratio of women is higher in comparison to men. Year-wise data regarding IAY (from 2002–03 to 2014–15) demonstrates that out of the total beneficiaries, the ratio of women has been more than three-fourths (Table 15.5).

Table 15.5

Year-wise Status of IAY and Deendayal Uttarakhand Awas Yojana from Financial Year 2001–02 to 2014–15

Name of Scheme	Year	SC	ST	Gen.	Minority	Total	Women
Indira Awas Yojana	2001–02	6,523	253	4,489	0	11,265	6,566
	2002–03	4,307	526	4,178	0	9,011	7,204
	2003–04	9,531	1,549	8,152	0	19,232	14,428
	2004–05	8,826	1,932	6,588	0	17,346	14,073
	2005–06	3,432	968	2,990	0	7,390	6,627
	2006–07	3,368	898	2,815	0	7,081	6,106
	2007–08	5,274	1,522	4,146	594	11,536	9,688
	2008–09	5,535	1,101	3,280	1,258	11,174	8,986
	2009–10	8,216	561	8,456	3,140	20,373	15,862
	2010–11	4,340	997	7,503	3,084	15,924	12,266
	2011–12	4,349	1,408	7,703	2,048	15,508	12,448
	2012–13	3,354	727	7,373	2,348	13,802	11,314
	Total	**67,055**	**12,442**	**67,673**	**12,472**	**159,642**	**125,568**
Deen Dayal Uttarakhand Gramin Awas Yojana	2007–08	862	126	2,390	641	4,019	3,180
	2008–09	1,486	249	5,571	117	7,423	5,342
	2009–10	761	156	2,455	151	3,523	2,577
	2010–11	448	120	1,324	182	2,074	1,310
	2011–12	188	40	631	65	924	564
	2012–13	57	18	171	7	253	76
	Total	**3,802**	**709**	**12,542**	**1,163**	**18,216**	**13,049**

Source: Computed from the data provided by Rural Development Department, Uttarakhand.

Deen Dayal Uttarakhand Gramin Awas Yojana

A state-funded scheme 'Deen Dayal Uttarakhand Gramin Awas Yojana' has also been initiated by the state government since 25 September 2007 for the families living below poverty line, unsheltered, and residing in *kuccha* (houses made up of wood, mud, straw, and dry leaves) houses. The basic objective of this scheme is to provide financial assistance for the construction of houses. Records of Uttarakhand government reveal that under this scheme, the number of women beneficiaries is higher and a total of 18,216 people were benefited till 2012–13, out of which women beneficiaries were 13,049 (71.63%). Hence, according to the government records, a large percentage of women had benefitted from both the schemes (Table 15.5).

MICRO FIELD STUDY

To evaluate and analyse the position, awareness level, and attitude of women regarding their property rights, a micro field study has also been done for which a structured small interview schedule was used. Voluntary response sampling technique was used to select the respondents. The tool was applied to the women of Nainital and Udham Singh Nagar districts and within the study period, 58 responses were received. Though with such a small sample, the results cannot be generalized, but can give a tentative glimpse of women's concern about their property rights.

Majority of women who participated in this survey were from the age group of 20–40 (91.11%) and belonged to all caste categories, that is. general, SC, and ST. Three Muslim OBC category women also participated in this survey. As far as the marital status of the respondents was concerned, more than 50% respondents were married and one was separated. Educational level of respondents revealed that most of them were graduates and postgraduates.

Some important findings of this micro study are as follows:

1. The respondents did not hold any immovable asset in their name.
2. Majority of women (82%) reported that they had not inherited any property and the remaining got their share in the form of jewellery and gifts.

3. 95% respondents accepted that women are aware about their property rights but 53% were of opinion that generally women are not willing to use this right.
4. Majority of the respondents (65%) strongly recommended that women should have equal or at least partial rights on property, but 35% suggested that women should give up their property rights if it affects their family relationship negatively.
5. Respondents accepted that rights of women in landed property could be a cause of sociocultural controversy. They strongly felt that the traditional mindset of men is responsible to deprive women of their property rights.
6. It is highlighted that women were aware of their property rights. They accepted that the sociocultural norms are against these rights and they should fight to achieve their property rights. But at the same time, they themselves did not agree to fight for their property rights against the will of their family.

This micro study was carried out in the month of August 2015 for the purpose of this report. Fieldwork was conducted with the help of the research scholars of Kumaun University and the fieldworkers of Mahila Samakhya from the Okhalkanda and Ramnagar block of Nainital district. The study revealed that the awareness level of women regarding property rights is increasing. Respondents had a strong feeling about women's property rights, and they wanted women to fight for their rights. But it was also noticed that on the one hand, they think that the traditional mindset of men is to deprive women of their rights, but on the other hand, their own mindset, socialized by traditional sociocultural norms, motivates them to let go of their property rights.

OPINION OF MEMBERS OF THE UTTARAKHAND STATE WOMEN COMMISSION

For this study, members of Uttarakhand State Women Commission were approached and they responded positively. All of them accepted that women are not getting proper share in property. Some women have approached the women commission and the commission is trying to solve their cases. Data provided by the commission are given in Table 15.6.

Table 15.6

Total Cases Pursued by Women for Their Land Rights

Year	Total Cases	Districts from Where Maximum Cases Pursued	Districts from Where No Case Pursued
2013–2014	49	Udham Singh Nagar, Dehradun	Uttarkashi
2014–2015	39	Udham Singh Nagar, Dehradun	Chamoli, Uttarkashi, Bageshwar
2015–2016 (Up to 31 August 2015)	32	Dehradun	–

Source: Data collected by telephonic talk to member secretary of the Uttarakhand State Women Commission.

Data shown in Table 15.6 reveal that now women are pursuing their property rights, though their number is nominal. The number of women who have approached the women commission is high from plain areas rather than hilly areas of the state. The member secretary of the Uttarakhand State Women Commission, Ms Sujata, states, 'Now women are talking about their inheritance and landed property rights which were not possible 5 to 10 years ago. They are specially talking for their rights in house.' She is of the opinion that by providing property rights to women, customs like dowry can be eradicated.

Ms Sujata shared the problems of some women whose brother/brothers emotionally manipulated them in a manner that they had agreed to furnish 'no objection certificates (NOCs)' for giving up their share in the family property. After some time, they came to know that their brothers had divided the whole property among themselves and they had been deprived of their right. By referring to the plight of these women, she suggested that NOCs should not be given by women in any case. In her opinion, women should be strong enough to face these types of compulsions from the family side. They should not give up their property rights, whether they are enjoying it or not.

MAHILA SAMAKHYA AND SAINION KA SANGATHAN

Mahila Samakhya is an innovative programme funded by the Ministry of Human Resource Development, Government of India. This organization is working in Uttarakhand for educational and legal rights of women. Sainion Ka Sangathan is an NGO working for the cause of women. Both the organizations are active in rural areas of Uttarakhand. In order to assess the position and awareness level of rural women regarding property rights, some members of these organizations were contacted personally and telephonically. The interviewed project officers and fieldworkers were from both the divisions of Uttarakhand. The information provided by them revealed that some landholding and houses are in the name of daughters in that area but they can get property in the absence of male sibling/siblings in that family. The same is the case with widows. A widow can be the owner of property only if there are no adult son/sons in the family. They stated that due to concession on stamp duty, now land is being purchased in women's name but in practice it is totally controlled by the male members of the family. They pointed out that local administration in rural areas is not sensitive towards women and limited mobility of rural women goes against them.

OPINION OF LAWYERS

Some lawyers were also consulted in this regard. In fact, property disputes come to notice when they are registered in the court of law. Input from lawyers can shed more light on the prevailing situation of women regarding inheritance rights. Lawyers interviewed for this study think that the legal provisions are sufficient and the existing laws guarantee equality to women regarding property rights. Especially, HSAA 2005 saves women's inheritance rights. They accepted that now women are approaching to get legal assistance for their property rights, but their number is nominal.

They agreed that women are basically discriminated by their parents and male siblings and they themselves are not fully aware of their property rights. Lawyers suggested that awareness should be created among women by public awareness programmes. Apart from this, educating the women, effective implementation of policies, effective judiciary, and public cooperation is also necessary. They gave an important suggestion that the sensitization of male towards women's property rights may reduce gender discrimination in this context.

STAMP DUTY CONCESSION

To empower women economically, some of Indian states have initiated a scheme of providing concession on stamp duty, if property is purchased in the name of women. The programme is based on this basic idea that ownership of productive resources would make women socially and economically secured (Singh and Arora 2013). Uttarakhand is one of the states which took initiative to amend the Stamp Duty Act. From 18 August 2006, the stamp duty was reduced up to 25% in respect of transfer of immovable property for a value of 10 lakh in favour of one or more woman, and from 6 October 2009, the reduced stamp duty is applicable up to the property for value of 20 lakh. This can be considered as an important step taken by the Government of Uttarakhand in favour of women. Table 15.7 shows the number of women beneficiaries from this scheme.

The data revealed that the number of women beneficiaries was highest in Dehradun district in both financial years and the lowest number was in Champawat district during the financial year 2009–10

Table 15.7

Details of Land Deeds Done in Favour of Women in Uttarakhand

		No. of Women Beneficiaries	
S. No.	Districts	Financial Year 2009–10	Financial Year 2010–11
1.	Dehradun	14,896	14,796
2.	Haridwar	8,894	12,091
3.	Udham Singh Nagar	8,298	10,789
4.	Nainital	6,856	7,814
5.	Pauri	2,156	2,270
6.	Tehri	336	241
7.	Chamoli	249	240
8.	Uttarkashi	24	12
9.	Rudraprayag	115	116
10.	Pithoragarh	731	622
11.	Almora	354	290
12.	Bageshwar	224	182
13.	Champawat	19	18
Total		43,152	49,489

Source: Information received from the office of Mahanireekshak Nibandhan Uttarakhand, Dehradun.

and in Uttarkashi district during 2010–11. The data closely pointed out that maximum woman beneficiaries were from plain districts and minimum from hilly regions. Whatever the number is, but due to the concession on stamp duty, immovable property is being purchased in the names of female members of the family. Registrars and sub-registrars, contacted telephonically, informed that now-a-days approximately 60%–70% housing plots and even agricultural land in urban and rural areas are being purchased in women's name. Though it is an initial stage, but its long-term consequences will definitely be in favour of women.

CONCLUSION AND RECOMMENDATIONS

Women constitute nearly half of the population of our country. In Uttarakhand, due to outmigration of young population, they constitute more than half of the population in some hilly areas of the state. Hence, inclusion of women in the formation of any development policy should be considered necessary for the development of the state. Their right over immovable property can be a significant component for their economic empowerment. Today a number of Indian women have legal right over property. The HSAA 2005 granted women equal rights as men in all property including agricultural land. This amendment abolished the highly gender-unequal inheritance of land which was earlier subject to state-level tenurial laws. But legal amendment on papers alone would not make the law a success. Women must be made more aware about their rights and should have access to better legal aid.

On the basis of grass-roots level realities, it can be suggested that the impediments regarding entitlement of property among women need to be considered from a practical point of view. Women have to face many social and psychological barriers while approaching for their legal rights. Steps must be taken to overcome these problems, and social and cultural legitimacy for women's property rights should be established. It is necessary to break the patriarchal mindset that does not appreciate women's property rights. Unless the mindset of both men and women is not changed, the laws and amendments would have a negligible impact on the property rights of women.

It is appreciable that the Government of Uttarakhand had initiated the digitalization of land records in the year 2006, and computerization of record of rights (*Khata Khatoni*) has been completed. But gender-wise segregated data about ownership on agricultural land, distributed *pattas* by state government to women, and distribution of land to forest dwellers under the Forest Rights Act 2006 are not available properly in the government records. A systematic documentation of all government records is needful not only for the formation of development programmes and policies but also for the inclusion and empowerment of weaker sections of society including women. Beside all these measures, it will be important to have empirical qualitative and quantitative research both at the state as well as at the regional levels to prepare a detailed database in this regard.

Several measures are required to address gender inequalities and to change the existing sociocultural norms. Universalization of education and to increase the awareness regarding individual rights and legal provisions through the promotion of legal literacy can be important measures. Besides these measures, women's organizations can help in making and pursuing land claims as well as in developing mechanism to record women's share of land, assets, and property. Only legal reforms cannot be beneficial without the additional support of improved education and awareness level of women.

In Uttarakhand, some grass-roots level organizations are significantly working for the cause of women. They are trying their best to improve women's educational and awareness level. Uttarakhand State Women Commission is also supportive and providing free legal aid to those women who are pursuing their property rights. But the most important step would be to sensitize the government officials who are responsible for the implementation of land laws. Specific instructions should be sent to all the concerned officials, including at the village level, such as patwari/*lekhpal*, to safeguard women's rights. Appointment of women functionaries at the grass-roots level in revenue and agricultural department may be significant in this regard.

REFERENCES

Agarwal, B. 1994. *A Field of One's Own: Gender and Land Rights in South Asia.* Cambridge: Cambridge University Press.

———. 1995, March. 'Gender and Legal Rights in Agricultural Land.' *Economic and Political Weakly* 30 (12): 39–56.

Agarwal, B. 2002. *Are We Not Peasants Too? Land Rights and Women's Claims in India*. SEEDS Pamphlet Series No. 21. New York: Population Council.
———. 1996. 'Gender and Land Rights Revisited: Exploring New Prospects via the State, Family and Market.' *Journal of Agrarian Change* 3(1–2): 184–224.
Agriculture Census in Uttarakhand. 2010–11. *Report on Operational Holdings in Uttarakhand (Agricultural and Census Division)*. Part I. Dehradun: Board of Revenue Uttarakhand.
Arora, S. and Singh, P. 2016. Concession in Stamp Duty: A Tool for Women Empowerment—An Empirical Assessment. In *Women Empowerment and Development*, edited by Sameera Maiti. Jaipur: Rawat Publications.
Census of India. 2011. 'Uttarakhand Urban/Rural Population.' Available at: census2011.co.in (accessed on 28 August 2015).
Chowdhry, Prem. 1994. *The Veiled Women: Shifting Gender Equations in Rural Haryana 1880–1990*. New Delhi: Oxford University Press.
———. 1997. 'A Matter of Two Shares: A Daughter's Claim to Patrilineal Property in Rural North India.' *Indian Economic and Social History Review* 3 (July–September): 321–54.
Ghildyal, M. C., and A. Banerjee. 1998. 'Status of Participatory Management in Uttarakhand Himalaya.' Paper Presented at the regional Work shop on Participatory Forest Management Implications for Policy and Human Resource Development, Kunming, People's Republic of China, May. (Quoted by Sarin [2001]).
Government of India. 1956. 'Hindu Succession Act (HSA) 1956.' Available at: www.lawyercollective.org (accessed on 2 September 2015).
———. 2005. 'Hindu Succession (Amendment) Act (HSAA) 2005.' Available at: www.hrln.org (accessed on 10 March 2017).
Government of the United Provinces (GoUP). 1922. Kumaun Forest Grievances Committee Report. Government of the United Provinces, Lucknow. (Quoted by Sarin [2001]).
Guha, Ramchardra. 1989. *The Unquiet Woods: Ecological Change and Peasant Resistance in the Himalaya*. New Delhi: Oxford University Press.
Kelkar, G., and D. Nathan. 2001. 'Gender Relations in Forest Societies in Asia.' *Gender Technology and Development* 5(1): 1–31
Lawyers Collective Women's Rights Initiative. 1956. 'Mapping Women's Gains in Inheritance and Property Rights under the HAS.' Available at: lawyerscollective.org (accessed on 10 March 2017).
Ministry of Rural Development. 2011. *Mahila Kisan Sashaktikaran Programme*, Government of India (mimeo.).
Mittal, Surabhi, Gaurav Tripathi, and Deepti Sethi. 2008. 'Development Strategies for the Hill districts of Uttarakhand.' Working Paper No. 217, Indian Council for Research on International Economic Relations, Delhi.

Moser, Caroline. 1998. 'The Assets Vulnerability Framework: Re-assessing Urban Poverty Reduction Strategies.' *World Development* 26 (1): 1–19.

Nanda, N. 1999. *Forest for Whom? Destruction and Restoration in the UP Himalaya*. New Delhi: Har Anand Publications.

Sarin, Madhu 2001. 'Empowerment and Disempowerment of Forest Women in Uttarakhand, India.' *Gender Technology and Development* 5(3): 341–64.

Sen, Amartya 1990. 'Gender and Cooperative Conflicts.' In *Persistence Inequalities*, edited by Irene Tinker, 123–49. New Delhi: Oxford University Press.

Sherraden, M. 1991. *Assets and the Poor: A New American Welfare Policy*. New York: Armonk M. E. Sharp.

Somnathan, E. 1991. 'Deforestation, Property Rights and Incentives in Central Himalaya.' *Economic and Political Weekly* 26(4): 37–46.

World Bank. 2001a. *World Development Report 2000–2001: Attacking Poverty*. Washington, DC: Oxford University Press. Available at: siteresources. worldbank.org (accessed on 5 January 2015).

———. 2001b. *Engendering Development Through Gender Equality in Rights, Resources and Voice*. New York: Oxford University Press. Available at: siteresources.worldbank.org (accessed on 5 January 2015).

About the Editor and Contributors

EDITOR

Prem Chowdhry, an eminent Social Scientist, is a former Professorial Fellow of the Nehru Memorial Museum and Library, Teen Murti, New Delhi, and also a former Senior Fellow of the Council of Historical Research, New Delhi. Currently an independent researcher, she is the author of *Political Economy of Production and Reproduction: Caste, Custom, and Community in North India*, 2011; *Contentious Marriages, Eloping Couples: Gender Caste and Patriarchy in Northern India*, 2007; *Colonial India and the Making of Empire Cinema: Image, Ideology and Identity*, 2000 (Indian edition by SAGE, 2001); *The Veiled Women: Shifting Gender Equations in Rural Haryana, 1880–1990*, 1994; and *Punjab Politics: The Role of Sir Chhotu Ram*, 1984. She has also edited *Understanding Politics and Society, 1910–97*, 2010 and *Gender Discrimination in Land Ownership*, SAGE, Delhi, 2009. Other publications include research articles on politics, society, land and inheritance, popular culture and cultural practices, and gender both in colonial and contemporary India, in edited works and reputed national and international journals. She is currently engaged in exploring different aspects of masculinities both in its historical and present-day manifestations in northern India. Prem Chowdhry is also a well-known, nationally recognized artist who has exhibited her paintings in India and abroad.

CONTRIBUTORS

Saroj Arora is Senior Research Officer, Centre for Rural Studies, Lal Bahadur Shastri National Academy of Administration, Mussoorie.

Abha Chauhan is Professor and Head of Department of Sociology, University of Jammu, Jammu. She is Secretary, Indian Sociological Society.

Ritu Dewan is former Director and Professor of Economics, University of Mumbai; President, Indian Association for Women's Studies, India; Director, Centre for Development Research and Action, Mumbai; Executive Director, Centre for Study of Society and Secularism, Mumbai.

Sohel Firdos is Associate Professor, Department of Geography, Sikkim University, Gangtok.

M. N. Karna is former Professor, Department of Sociology, North Eastern Hill University, Shillong, Meghalaya.

Khunenchu Magh is Deputy Director, Directorate of Land Records and Survey, Dimapur, Nagaland.

Kanchan Mathur is Professor and (acting) Director, Institute of Development Studies, Jaipur.

Ranjani K. Murthy is Researcher and Consultant, Gender and Development Chennai, Tamil Nadu.

Indu Pathak is Head, Department of Sociology, Kumaun University, Nainital, Uttarakhand.

Itishree Pattnaik is Assistant Professor, Gujarat Institute of Development Research, Ahmedabad.

E. Revathi is Professor at the Centre for Economic and Social Studies, Begumpet, Hyderabad, Telangana.

Ramesh Sharma is associated with Ekta Parishad (a Bhopal-based NGO), Bhopal, Madhya Pradesh.

C. Sridhar is IAS, Deputy Director (Senior) and Centre Director, Centre for Rural Studies, Lal Bahadur Shastri National Academy of Administration, Mussoorie.

Rimi Tadu is Fellow, Council for Social Development, Hyderabad, Telangana.

Index

1997 Amendment to Bombay Stamp Act of 1958, Government of Maharashtra, 223
adverse possession, 29
agriculture landownership, 97
anatomizing women's rights to land Jharkhand, 204
Andhra Pradesh Land Reforms, 31
Andhra Pradesh, 8
    AP Ceiling on Agricultural Holding Act, 29
    engendering tribal land rights for gendering land, 59
    Hindu Succession Act, 26
    land legality and women, 27
    land policies, 25
    LPP, 26
    policy implications for, 48
AP Ceiling on Agricultural Holdings Act, 29
AP Occupants of Homesteads Act, 40
Arunachal Pradesh Public Premises Act, 2003, 63
Arunachal Pradesh
    feminizing tribal agricultural economy and re-looking at women's status, 71
    jhum cultivation vs development-induced displacement, 64
    men own property, 73
    sex ratio, in, 72
    status of land rights, in, 62
    women and landownership, 76

Beyond Taben Jom, 189
Bhoodan, 351
Bhumiswamis, 92
Bombay Tenancy and Agricultural Lands Act 1948, 221

Central Act 1/1894, 351
Chhattisgarh Land Revenue Code 2000
    components, 91
Chhattisgarh
    gender
        issues in landownership in, 88
    landholdings among women in, 95
    operational landholdings status in, 95
    tribal women in, 95
    women's land rights, 89
Chota Nagpur Tenancy Act (CNTA) 1908, 187–189, 191
clan land, 274
common property resources, 100
common village land (CVL), 273
communitarian society
    re-visiting women's status, 78
community land

clan land, 274
CVL, 273
khel land, 275
constitutional recognition, 82
Convention on the Elimination of All Forms of Discrimination against Women (CEDAW), 2
customary laws and inheritance rights, 141
customary laws in Jharkhand CNTA, 188, 189

Deen Dayal Uttarakhand Gramin Awas Yojana, 393
deputy commissioner (DC), 63
Disha Kendra, 225
dowry and land rights, 102

empowerment, 133
engendering tribal land rights for gendering land
case study, 59

feminist movement and resistance by the patriarchal institutions, 252
Forest Conservation Act 1980, 63
Forest Rights Act of 2006, 224

Gender Discrimination in Land Ownership, 3
gender-wise
participation in agriculture in Gujarat, 137
Ghar doghaanche, 224
gharjamai, 192
Goa, 15, 16
Common Civil Code, 114
gendered economic overview, 108
gendered rural labour force participation rate 2011–12, 110

structural logic, 107
women and land rights in, 106
Goa Agricultural Tenancy Act 1964, 116
government resolution of 10th of August 1994, government of Maharashtra, 222
government resolution of 20th of November 2003, 224
Dalit movement, 225
Ghar doghaanche, 224
government
land, 276
MAVIM, 230
wastelands distribution of, 40

Hindu Succession (Amendment) Act (HSAA) 2005, 383
Hindu Succession Act (HSA), 303
1956, 5, 385
1986, 26, 32
horticulture crops in Nagaland, 280
housing schemes in Uttarakhand, 391
Deen Dayal Uttarakhand Gramin Awas Yojana, 393
IAY, 392

Indian women
property rights of, 378
Indira Awas Yojana (IAY), 307, 392
individual land, 275
individual ownership of land by women
collective cultivation, 363
no natal property, 362
inheritance laws
effects of, 33
inheritance of landed property, 101
initiatives for women's development
issuance of *patta* passbook, 287

Jammu and Kashmir, 15, 174
issues in landownership, 16

land laws, 167
landownership question in, 154
history of, 175
special status and location affecting land laws, 160
tenancy, 175
uniqueness of, 174
Jammu and Kashmir Agrarian Reforms Act 1976, 175
Jammu and Kashmir Muslim Personal Law (Shariat) Application Act 2007, 176
Jharkhand, 14
anatomizing women's rights to land, 204
Chota Nagpur Tenancy Act (CNTA) 1908, 187
customary laws, 188
evaluation of prevailing situation in, 197
Kharia, 192
location and demographic attributes, 183
Munda, 192
Santal Pargana Tenancy Act (SPTA) 1949, 187
Santhal, 195
tribal communities in, 184
understanding women and land rights in, 182
jhum cultivation vs development-induced displacement, 64

Kharia, 192
evaluation of prevailing situation in, 197
familiarity with inheritance and succession rules and, 200
khel land, 274
Konyaks
land system among, 277
Koya women in forest geography

economic deprivation and disempowerment, 39
Kumaun Grievance Committee, 382

Land Purchase Programme (LPP), 42, 48
land rights
rural women in Goa, 115
women, 3
women in Chhattisgarh
agriculture landownership, 97
common property resources and land, 100
dowry and land rights, 102
homestead landownership, 97
inheritance of landed property, 101
key findings, 103
limitations of the study, 93
methodology, 93
recommendations, 104
women in Maharashtra, 209
structure of study, 211
trends in gendered land rights, 212
land
access programme, 43–45
IKP, 44
major land issues, 44
administration system in Sikkim
history, 332
holdings among women in Chhattisgarh, 96
lease, 277
legality and women, 27
AP Ceiling on Agricultural Holding Act, 29
AP Inams Act in 1956, 27
report of the Land Committee, 30
tenancy, 27
ownership
government land, 276
individual land, 275

land system and gendered space in
  Mizoram, 238
  community land, 241
  revenue land, 243
pattern in Nagaland, use, 277
  jhum land, 278
Laxmi mukti, 222
legislation and customary law in
  Tamil Nadu
  during recent times, 348
  historical rules and customs,
    346
  land allotment route, 350
  tenancy route, 349
legislation and customary law related
  to inheritance of land in
  Tamil Nadu, 346
legislations relating to land in Sikkim
  Land Revenue Order (R.O.)
  No. 105, 335
lineage land, 275
Lushai Hills, 237
Lushai Hills District
  (Village Council) Act 2015,
  251

Mahalir Thittam, 352
Maharashtra, 9
  Amendment to Maharashtra
    Revenue Act of 1966,
    222
  Bombay Tenancy and Agricultural
    Lands Act 1948, 221
  gendered district level land-
    holding pattern, 216
  laws and struggles for women's
    land rights, 219
  Muslim Personal Law (Shariat)
    Application Act 1937, 220
  The Bombay Prevention of
    Fragmentation and
    Consolidation of Holdings
    Act 1947, 221

Mahila Samakhya and Sainion Ka
  Sangathan, 380, 395
Married Women's Property
  Regulation 1962, 336, 341
Mizo society, 255
Mizoram, 234
  customary laws, land acquisition
    and its impact on women,
    253
  feminist movement and changes in
    inheritance laws, 248
  historical perspective, 236
  inheritance and customary laws,
    248
  land system and gendered space,
    238
  land-reform initiatives, 243
  socio-demographic
    profile of, 235
  women's access and ownership of
    land, 234
Mizoram *Kohhran Hruaitute*
  Committee, 244
Mizoram Land and Revenue Act
  1956, 243
modernization, 80
Munda, 192
  evaluation of prevailing situation
    in, 197
  familiarity with inheritance and
    succession rules and, 200
Muslim Personal Law (Shariat)
  Application Act 1937, 220
Muslim Personal Law, 143

Naga tribes
  inheritance pattern among some
    of, 283
Naga village, 266
  administration by elected village
    council, 267
  functions of, 267
Naga women, 280

agricultural land and common
  property resources, 280
  change in land use pattern and its
    impact on, 281
  exclusion from, 290
Nagaland, 15, 260, 289
  dialects, 261
  horticulture crops, 279
  land system and customary laws,
    269
  population, 262
  social history of, 263
  socio-demographic profile of, 262
  tribes, 261
National Forest Policy 1952, 63
Ninth Five-year Plan
  (1997–2002), 2
Notification no. 28 in 1969, 336
Nyishi community, 69

opinion of members of Uttarakhand
  State Women Commission,
  394
ownership of homestead land, 97

pattern of land access
  dry land geography, 37
patterns of women's access to land
  and impact of inheritance
  rights, 308
PESA, 189
Policy Note of Revenue Department,
  354
PoP strategy in CMSA (2005–08)
  number of women leased in land
    under, 46
possessing, 2
Pudhu Vaazhvu Thittam, 353

Rajasthan, 9
  customary land rights in, 304
  gender and land rights, 301
  Indira Awas Yojana, 307

land *pattas*, 307
tribals in, 304
reading land, 61
Revenue and Forest Department
  Based on Clause 17B of
    Bombay Tenancy and
    Agricultural Lands Act of
    1948, 223
rural women's ownership of land
  claim to property, 358

Santal Pargana Tenancy Act (SPTA)
  1949, 187, 189
Santhal, 193
  familiarity with land inheritance
    and succession laws and
    practices, 205
  opinion with regard to land rights
    to women, 205
sarnas, 184
scheduled tribes (STs) in
  Sikkim, 327
Sikkim, distribution of
  landholdings among, 328
Sikkim, 15
  declining per capita availability
    of, 329
  demographic characteristics of,
    326
  distribution of
    agricultural land *patta*, 339
    landholdings, 328
  identity and status of women, 329
  locating gender in land rights
    discourse of, 325
  major communities and their
    landownership pattern, 328
Sikkim Succession Act (SSA), 2008
  and property rights of
    women, 337
state initiatives for women's
  development, 287
State Land Acquisition Act 1990, 63

state schemes in Tamil Nadu, 352
  Mahalir Thittam, 352
  state rural livelihood mission, 353

Tamil Nadu, 9
  attitudes of government officials, 357
  institutional structures and systems, 368
  inter-generational collective land rights, promotion of, 367
  policies of other departments, 356
  revenue officials, 364
  rural women's ownership of land, 358
  stop conversion of agriculture land and expand land pool, 365
  turmeric land, 363
  women's land rights, 344
  women's access to ownership of land and resources, expand, 365
Tamil Nadu Agricultural Lands Act 1969, 349
Tamil Nadu Land Reform (Fixation of Ceiling) Act 1961, 351
Tamil Nadu State Rural Livelihood Mission (TNSRLM), 353
terrace cultivation, 279
The AP Ceiling on Agricultural Holdings Act, 29
the Community Managed Sustainable Agriculture (CMSA), 46
tribal areas, 14
tribal women, 82
tribal women in Chhattisgarh overview of study, 94

Uttar Pradesh Zamindari Abolition and Land Reform Act 1950, 383
Uttarakhand
  demographic profile of, 381

gender justice and law, 376
gender-wise analysis of operational holdings, 388
Kumaon Grievance Committee, 382
land and gender relations in, 381
land/property rights of women in, 388
laws related to land/property rights applicable in, 383

village development board (VDB), 287

women accessed land from natal family
  characteristics of, 51
women and land rights
  legal framework, 30
women as tenants
  agricultural land of, 46
women empowerment, 1
women land inheritance and societal impediments, 144
women landownership, 133
  status in Gujarat, 135
  background, 135
women's access to land from family, determination of
  under different situations, 33
women, land rights and common civil code, 114
women's access to land in Rajasthan review, 298
women's actual ownership of agricultural land
  cultivation and, 360
women's economy
  interface with state and market-driven modernization, 80
women's land rights
  Chhattisgarh, 89

importance given to, 90
convergence of government scheme, 367
women's right to land in Jharkhand issues, 207

Working Group for Women and Land Ownership (WGWLO), 134

Young Mizo Association (YMA), 244

zoramchhia, 245

Land Reforms in India

Vol. 1 *Bihar–Institutional Constraints*. 1993. B.N. Yugandhar and K. Gopal Iyer (eds).

Vol. 2 *Rajasthan–Feudalism and Change*. 1995. B.N. Yugandhar and P.S. Datta (eds).

Vol. 3 *Andhra Pradesh–People's Pressure and Administrative Innovations*. 1996. B.N. Yugandhar (ed.).

Vol. 4 *Karnataka–Promises Kept and Missed*. 1997. Abdul Aziz and Sudhir Krishna (eds).

Vol. 5 *An Unfinished Agenda*. 2000. B.K. Sinha and Pushpendra (eds).

Vol. 6 *Intervention for Agrarian Capitalist Transformation in Punjab and Haryana*. 2001. Sucha Singh Gill (ed.).

Vol. 7 *Issues of Equity in Rural Madhya Pradesh*. 2002. Praveen K. Jha (ed.).

Vol. 8 *Performance and Challenges in Gujarat and Maharashtra*. 2002. Ghanshyam Shah and D.C. Sah (eds).

Vol. 9 *Tamil Nadu: An Unfinished Task*. 2003. M. Thangaraj (ed.).

Vol. 10 *Computerisation of Land Records*. 2005. Wajahat Habibullah and Manoj Ahuja (eds).

Vol. 11 *Gender Discrimination in Land Ownership*. 2009. Prem Chowdhry (ed.).

Vol. 12 *Agrarian Crisis and Farmer Suicides*. 2010. R. S. Deshpande and Saroj Arora (eds).